AMERICAN ODYSSEY, 1607-1789

AMERICAN ODYSSEY, 1607-1789

Paul Robert Lucas
Indiana University, Bloomington

Prentice-Hall, Inc., Englewood Cliffs, New Jersey 07632

Library of Congress Cataloging in Publication Data

LUCAS, PAUL ROBERT.
American odyssey, 1607–1789.

Bibliography: p.
Includes index.
1. United States—Civilization—To 1783. 2. America—Discovery and exploration. I. Title.
E162.L82 1984 973 83-11040
ISBN 0-13-028233-2

Editorial/production supervision
and interior design: Dee Amir Josephson
Cover design: Ben Santora
Cover photo: New York Public Library Picture Collection
Manufacturing buyer: Ron Chapman

Printed in the United States of America
10 9 8 7 6 5 4 3 2 1

ISBN 0-13-028233-2

Prentice-Hall International, Inc., *London*
Prentice-Hall of Australia Pty. Limited, *Sydney*
Editora Prentice-Hall do Brasil, Ltda., *Rio de Janeiro*
Prentice-Hall Canada Inc., *Toronto*
Prentice-Hall of India Private Limited, *New Delhi*
Prentice-Hall of Japan, Inc., *Tokyo*
Prentice-Hall of Southeast Asia Pte. Ltd., *Singapore*
Whitehall Books Limited, *Wellington, New Zealand*

Contents

For Rebecca and Robert

Prologue

Most books about the development of the United States argue that our experience has been unique in human history. They contend that our society and its ideals have evolved along lines not duplicated elsewhere. Such thinking reflects several popular and apparently enduring theories about the process of "Americanization"—that is, the method whereby Europeans, Africans, and Asians mixed together to become "Americans." One notion—appropriately labeled the *melting-pot* theory—likens American society to a great bowl of soup. Its texture and composition have resulted from the immigration and settlement of generations of people with different racial, ethnic, and national backgrounds. Each group contributed something to the whole; and in the end, a new social type—the American—emerged.[1]

Another popular view suggests that immigrants engaged the American environment and were transformed by it. That theory is usually associated with Frederick Jackson Turner, a historian of the nineteenth and early twentieth centuries who argued that immigrants were changed through contact with the American frontier. Life in the wilderness made demands upon the settlers that old cultures could not meet. Immigrants were forced to innovate and adapt, and in the process they lost their original identities and assumed new ones. More than geographical determinism, Turner's *frontier thesis* suggested that the frontier represented a spiritual force as well as physical space. In the wilderness, Turner maintained, men and women encountered Nature and Nature's God. They had to conform to Nature's (i.e., God's) demands or be lost. Those who survived the wilderness experience emerged transformed into Nature's image. They were the Americans.[2]

The frontier thesis, the melting-pot theory, and the derivatives of each contend that Americanization involved the rejection of the authoritarianism, class rigidity, and communal orientation of the "Old World" and the creation of an egalitarian, individualistic, materialistic, and democratic modern America. Of late, though, many American minorities have questioned this conventional wisdom about Americanization. They reject theories espousing a common American character or a single American type. Such ideas, they argue, are the myths of a White, Anglo-Saxon, Protestant (WASP) elite insensitive to or ignorant of the cultural, racial, and ethnic diversity of America. The United States, they maintain, has a dominant WASP culture and a multitude of subcultures that have resisted absorption and now seek a kind of separate but equal status. Yet, even these critics of traditional views of Americanization do not reject the possibility of a truly democratic and egalitarian society in the future. They argue with their opponents over means, not ends. They conceive of America as a society in progress, not a finished product. Hence, though they deny the validity of a single American type—now or in the future—they want to build a society that will be more democratic, more egalitarian, more open, and more sensitive to the aspirations and talents of diverse groups and individuals.[3]

Although the democratic ideal was invented in the nineteenth century, the notion of a distinctly "American" character is as old as settlement itself. The New England Puritans portrayed America as a "new Eden" and tried to construct "godly commonwealths" free from the sin and corruption of the Old World. They never considered themselves to be anything but transplanted English citizens; yet their rhetoric often hinted that they were morally superior to those who had stayed behind. A century and a quarter later, the leaders of the American Revolution stated the case in a bolder, more secular vein. America was distinct from Europe or England. Lacking the vices of the Old World, it served as the cradle of liberty and the torchbearer for a new order in human affairs. The patriots argued that a century in the wilderness had purged them of their ancestors' sins and prepared them for the challenge of liberty and republican government. Theirs was an arrogant position, to be sure; but it reflected the beliefs of many eighteenth-century Americans—like Benjamin Franklin, who built a legend around the entrepreneurial, practical virtues of the self-made American, or Franco-American J. Hector St. John de Crevecoeur, who asked, "What, then, is the American, this new man?" He answered:

> He is an American, who, leaving behind him all his ancient prejudices and manners, receives new ones from the new mode of life he has embraced, the new government he obeys, and the new rank he holds. He becomes an American by being received in the broad lap of our great Alma Mater. Here individuals of all nations are melted into a new race of men, whose labours and posterity will one day cause great changes in the world.[4]

To what extent did Anglo-America depart from its English and European heritage? There will probably never be a single answer, for the question is too much entwined in national myths about our origins and destiny. Not so many years ago the preponderance of evidence favored America's uniqueness, and historical literature emphasized America's rejection of European habits, ideals, and institutions. In two highly influential works, Perry Miller charted the rise, reign, and ruin of American Puritanism. Puritanism, Miller argued, was an intellectual edifice based on some of the oldest and newest ideas of medieval Europe. The Puritans in America tried to construct a society conforming to preconceived theories, but it foundered—partly from its own weight and partly from the demands of an alien environment. Daniel Boorstin echoed Miller's conclusions. Anglo-American institutions and habits of mind owed more to the experience of living in America than anything else. Success in America demanded the ability to adapt to changing circumstance; and much of the cultural baggage the Europeans and the English brought with them proved to be too rigid and inflexible to last. Anglo-American success, Boorstin argued, emerged from the residue of Europe's failures. Finally, Louis Hartz portrayed the differences between Europe and America in graphic terms. Europe's burden, both in the seventeenth century and later, was feudalism: the system of laws, contracts, and traditions which formed the basis for medieval society. Its hierarchical structure restricted individual freedom and tied individuals to society in an intricate and inescapable web. Modern Europe, Hartz contended, constantly warred with its feudal past. Anglo-America, however, had no such problem, for feudalism did not take root. Thus, from its conception American society was more open and more democratic than England or Europe.[5]

Recently, many studies have emphasized the enormous debt colonial ideas and institutions owed to European and English antecedents. For example, Kenneth Lockridge's study of Dedham, Massachusetts, characterized the Puritan town as a utopian commune rooted in an English and European peasant tradition. Lockridge also stressed the continuing importance of communal thinking and behavior in American history. In their book on Salem, Massachusetts, Paul Boyer and Stephen Nissenbaum argued that the witchcraft "hysteria" in late seventeenth-century Salem was a byproduct of two distinctly European phenomena fighting for supremacy in America: merchant capitalism and the "traditional" world view of the peasant. Moving into the eighteenth century, Bernard Bailyn's essay on the pamphlet literature of the American Revolution showed how Anglo-America's revolutionary ideology of the 1770s grew directly from the preceding century and a half of political and constitutional debates among the English.[6]

On the surface, then, it would appear that interpreters of early American history divide neatly into two camps: those arguing for America's uniqueness, and those insisting that Anglo-America was an extension of European and English culture. Unfortunately, the divisions are not so neat. Many of the historians who cite America's debt to Europe argue that at some point America moved away from England and Europe toward something new and different. Moreover, they share with the proponents of American uniqueness a sense that the movement away from Europe was swift and dramatic. Together, scholars in both camps endorse a special view of historical change—we call it the *cataclysm*—in which the old order or ideology passes away quickly and decisively and something new rises from its ashes. Why the cataclysm? In *Community and Social Change in America*[7] Thomas Bender maintains that the best of modern historiography has been influenced by a particular strain of social theory borrowed from sociology—one which emphasizes the decay of social systems and ideologies. American history, Bender notes, seems to be dotted with communities and ideals which have their day and then collapse from forces beyond the control of the historical actors. Taken individually, books describing such cataclysms make fascinating and often provocative reading; but collectively they deny continuity in American history (except persistent rot and decay). They render our total history unexplainable and unintelligible.

While social theory continues to influence historians, sociology is not the only source for the "history-as-collapse" school of analysis. Our historical thinking has been conditioned to think of historical change as "rise, reign, and fall" for a very long time. Much of this thinking began with the Protestant Reformation, when apocalyptic history became fashionable among reformers. The theory of the decay of European civilization and an approaching millennial kingdom found many exponents among early English and Continental Protestants and many persons in early America well. The Renaissance fostered a cyclical theory of historical development in which people—not God—could create an earthly kingdom of bliss if only they learned to manipulate and overcome the whims of fortune. From English political and constitutional history, Americans inherited the "whig" interpretation of English historical development. That emphasized a cyclical approach to history with liberty and tyranny constantly at odds. Stated another way, the whig interpretation chronicled the rise and fall of absolutism (tyranny) in England's past and the ultimate triumph of Parliament (liberty). From the Enlightenment of the seventeenth, eighteenth, and nineteenth centuries, Americans learned from Europeans the distinction we still hold between medieval and modern. The Enlightenment introduced the notion of human progress toward an earthly utopia through science and reason. It molded our historical consciousness with the theory that after the medieval world or "dark ages" decayed and collapsed, the modern world emerged from its remains. In that transformation America represented an example of the "modern" and a flat denial of the medieval. Although we no longer uncritically accept the inevitability of progress through science and reason or the theory that the medieval world represented a dark period of human history, the historian's preoccupation with America's uniqueness is evidence of a continuing intellectual debt to the eighteenth-century mind.

This book presents a more linear view of Anglo-America's evolution. My thesis is that Anglo-America developed along lines envisioned by its founders—that is, parallel to Europe and England and not as the antithesis of either. My belief is that eighteenth-century America reflected the successes of the colonial founders, not their failures; that it signified goals achieved, not goals frustrated. Moreover, it is evident to me that those goals were English and European in origin, not American. Nevertheless, it must be admitted that, by 1783, when England's North American Odyssey concluded, profound differences separated English and American society. Therefore, one may reasonably ask how Anglo-America developed in a manner consistent with English and European goals when colonial society differed in fundamental ways from the Old World. Or, put another way, how were Anglo-American society and culture both derivative and unique?

Many interpreters of Americanization have based their theories on a false dichotomy: European class rigidity, authoritarianism, and communalism versus American egalitarianism, democracy, individualism, and materialism. Actually, these interpreters have distorted England's and Europe's history after 1650 very badly. Within a span of about five and a half centuries (1350 to 1900), England and the nations of Europe moved at varying speeds from the medieval to the modern, from feudalism to industrialization. A byproduct of that transformation was a decided shift toward materialism and the emergence of more egalitarian, individualistic, and democratic social and political orders. Thus, against the real English and European background, the presumed "uniqueness" of Anglo-America fades somewhat. We find that Americanization did not produce a "new" society so much as it created a spectacular and not altogether laudable refinement of the old.

Moreover, the differences that did arise between English and Anglo-American society grew from perhaps the most obvious source: the fundamental purpose behind England's expansion into North America. Like all of England's colonies, British North America existed to create wealth. While the English found no precious metals or profitable trade with natives, England fostered the growth of societies that ultimately produced even greater wealth than the colonies of Spain or France. In a very short time, Anglo-Americans became remarkable producers. They exported great amounts of agricultural products and raw materials such as timber and tar. But the essential, producing character of the colonies exaggerated certain institutional features and retarded others. In areas such as agricultural production and commerce—where activity stimulated England's development—the colonies experienced rapid, extensive growth. But in areas such as capital formation and manufacturing—where activity hurt England's economic development—colonial status retarded the colonial economy. Instead of progressing steadily toward modernization, Anglo-America grew as a kind of economic mutation. It expanded and even prospered, but it did not fully mature. Rather it became a highly successful fulfillment of its creators' dreams: It became a dependent, if productive, society that created wealth for England and allowed it to approach self-sufficiency.

Anglo-America's economic success resulted from several factors. First, the North American continent possessed certain obvious, abundant resources. Of these, the most important was land. Second, by 1600, England had progressed into a more modern stage than its European neighbors. As Louis Hartz concluded, England's advanced development allowed Anglo-America to avoid any massive introduction of feudal beliefs or practices. Finally, the people who settled America's shores came from the middle level of English society and were often dissatisfied with life in England. Though many settled America to avoid religious persecution, most came because they were upwardly mobile, ambitious men and women who saw little hope of achieving their goals in the Old World. Above all, they were land hungry; and that, more than anything else, provided the key to England's imperial success. To create wealth, England made colonization attractive to those who wanted economic opportunity. That resulted in a colonial system rooted in acquisitiveness. Both England and Anglo-America prospered because colonists instinctively pursued those activities which aided England's drive toward wealth and self-sufficiency and which offered individual colonists themselves the opportunity to fulfill their private dreams.

In this book, then, we posit no dichotomy between Anglo-American "uniqueness" and any presumed English or European social models. Rather, we emphasize that Anglo-Americans embraced all useful ideological, cultural, and institutional tools of the Old World to accomplish England's great imperial goal: the creation of wealth, power, and self-sufficiency. The "colonial" purpose of Anglo-America made it by definition unique—that is, it was a society that functioned for a specific aim: to enhance England's world position. That same purpose, in turn, fashioned both Anglo-America's best and worst features. In order to create wealth, the colonies encouraged social mobility, wide distribution of land, egalitarianism, and a democratic political order. But the productive character of Anglo-America also resulted in white servitude, black slavery, and the exploitation of native peoples.

The American Odyssey that follows describes the successful fulfillment of the original aims of America's founders. But success also meant that Anglo-America became a society in equilibrium—a society held in place by its dependent, subservient status. Certain aspects appeared modern, but many others remained backward. Only after the establishment of an enduring federal government under the Constitution would the United States shed its dependent, mutant character and move toward a modern social, political, and economic order.

This book grew from a suggestion made by H. Trevor Colbourn, my former colleague who is now President of the University of Central Florida. The contours of the book developed slowly. Timothy L. Smith of The Johns Hopkins University helped me immensely with a question he raised half in jest. Knowing my interest in Puritanism in old and New England he asked me how it was that so many American historians who were not of English descent placed so much emphasis on the supposedly pivotal role played by American Puritanism in the shaping of modern America. The question reminded me of my own boyhood in a small Iowa community composed almost entirely of immigrants who arrived in the United States in the late nineteenth and early twentieth centuries. The first arrivals—the Scandinavians—farmed. Then came peoples from southern and eastern Europe. They dug coal. Interspersed among those two large blocs of immigrants were people representing just about every group that had ever immigrated to America from either Europe or the British Isles. In addition, as I grew up I was very aware that a few miles from my home lay the scattered remains of a once sizable—and entirely separate—enclave of southern blacks who had worked in the mines, then left when coal mining ended. What did the inhabitants of my town and its immediate vicinity owe to the society of early America? The distinctive interpretive framework of *American Odyssey* reflects my personal attempt to connect the United States of the twentieth century with the colonial world of the seventeenth and eighteenth centuries.

The character of this book began to emerge in 1977 when I started a research project on anti-Catholicism in early American history with the aid of a fellowship from the American Council of Learned Societies. Since 1977 *American Odyssey* has evolved through several stages. I have accumulated many intellectual debts along the way. I have built upon the research and conclusions of many fine historians whose works appear either in my footnotes or my bibliography. Although I have tried to list the books and articles that have influenced my thinking, I know I've missed some and I apologize to any scholar to whom I've failed to give proper credit.

My colleagues Walter Nugent and Bernard Sheehan read an early draft of the book and made valuable suggestions. More recently I have been helped by insights and support offered by Maurice Baxter, Charles Boxer, Jon Butler, William Cohen, James Diehl, Otto Pflanze, and Anita and Darrett Rutman. The students and faculty who attend the weekly History Seminar sponsored by the Indiana University History Department heard a synopsis of my arguments and contributed suggestions and criticisms. My perception of the role of religion in early America has been sharpened by listening to the comments of the participants in the biannual Cushwa Seminar on American Religion at the University of Notre Dame the past several years. John Lombardi introduced me to the history and historiography of Latin America. At the same time I deepened my understanding of the French experience in North American while using a course development grant from the History Department, Indiana University, to create an undergraduate course on the History of Canada. Finally, I offer very special thanks to John Rusk who read the entire manuscript of *American Odyssey* and gave me a useful critique.

The staff of Prentice-Hall, Inc. has helped immensely in bringing this project to fruition. I appreciate the work of Brian Walker, John Busch, and especially, Steve Dalphin, editors; Dee A. Josephson, production editor; and Louisa Hellegers, copy editor. Numerous anonymous referees read the book at various stages and contributed to its development. I could not utilize all the suggestions they made but *American Odyssey* is a much better book because of their efforts.

I used the facilties of many research libraries but I want to thank, especially, the staff of the Indiana University Library and William Cagle and the staff of the Lilly library for their aid as I coped with the inevitable problems of historical research.

The Department of History, Indiana University, provided funds to partially offset the cost of typing the manuscript. The typing was done by an unusually competent person, Ethel Richardson. Cathryn L. Lombardi created the outstanding maps that grace these pages. John Erwin gave me considerable help with the footnotes and the bibliography. My wife, Judy, took time from her own teaching responsibilities to serve as a critic and to construct an index.

Bloomington, Indiana — Paul Robert Lucas

AMERICAN ODYSSEY, 1607-1789

Part I
EUROPE, ENGLAND, AND AMERICA

As the Prologue suggested, one of the central aims of this book is to show how Anglo-America evolved both parallel to England and yet in some respects unique from it. Part I, which examines the environment of North America prior to colonization and then traces European exploration and settlement, approaches those topics with that central theme in mind. In part, the "unique" qualities of Anglo-American society reflected the New World environment. Hence, we explore just what land and conditions greeted colonials upon their arrival in North America. Likewise, Anglo-American values, institutions, and ideas owed a tremendous debt to England. For that reason, it is important to learn about the world which immigrants left behind.

The first chapter examines what one could call the preconditions of colonization. That is, it looks at the dominant characteristics of both precolonial North America and preexpansionist Europe. Although sparsely populated by European standards, North America on the eve of colonization was the home of numerous groups of native Americans. Europeans came to call them collectively and indistinguishably "Indians," but in fact native American tribes often differed culturally as much from each other as they did from Europeans. Some Indian tribes, such as the Pueblo, were agricultural and sedentary, and actually built great permanent communities in the cliffs of the Southwest. Other tribes, such as the Iroquois, roamed throughout the Northeast hunting and fishing, their migratory life dictated by the demands for food and clothing. Despite these differences, however, the communal orientation, political disunity, and primitive technology of native Americans put them at some disadvantage in the confrontation with the European intruders.

In contrast, by the sixteenth century European society had begun to undergo a complex series of interconnected changes which provided the impetus for expansion. The major factors that propelled European nations to explore the New World were political unification and the advent of the central state, technological development especially in nagivation, the rise of trade coupled with the transformation of the traditional medieval economy, the decline of the power of the Roman Catholic church along with the Protestant Reformation, and a change in intellectual outlook epitomized by the Renaissance. Political centralization signaled an end to much domestic conflict in Europe, an increase in royal power, and the consequent ability of the state to finance exploration. The development of better ships and more sophisticated navigational equipment made long-distance sea travel a possibility for the first time. The rise of trade and its potential wealth offered strong inducement to expand. Finally, the erosion of the power of the Catholic Church, the evangelical fervor and individualism of the Protestant Reformation, and the unleashing by the Renaissance of ideas that asserted people's ability to accomplish great things all indirectly or directly created a climate conducive to expansion.

With the stage set, Spain, France, Portugal, and the Netherlands all sent out numerous explorations to the New World after its discovery in the late fifteenth century. Spain found vast wealth in gold and silver and subsequently built a huge colonial empire that exploited the riches of the New World for Spain. Although neither France nor any other European power discovered gold and silver, France's forays into North America reaped a highly profitable trade in furs and fish. Portugal's imperial activities centered more in Africa than in the New World, yet it too built a significant trade with its possessions in South America. The Netherlands, which sponsored several explorations into North America, was unable or unwilling to become much of an imperial power in the New World.

Chapter Two, which focuses upon England prior to colonization and then British colonizing efforts in North America, attempts to demonstrate why English colonial ventures proved ultimately the most successful in North America. Although the tiny island was the last European nation to explore the New World, Britain's very political, cultural, and economic differences with nations on the European continent help explain the reason for its ultimate success. After some initial failures, and then much trial and error, England carved out an empire. Britain never found gold, but discovered instead a greater, more lasting source of wealth in colonial trade. By exploiting the vast agricultural resources of North America and by creating settlements that consumed British manufactured goods, England, not Spain, became the greatest imperial power in the world by the middle of the eighteenth century.

1

Two Worlds

When Christopher Columbus sailed west in 1492 he hoped to find a shorter route to the Orient. For many years Europe had traded with portions of Asia, and Europeans envied the wealth and the apparent power of the great moguls of the Orient. By comparison, much of Europe was poor and backward, and some areas were more poor and more backward than others. European kings and nobles languished while money flowed into the coffers of great merchants in a handful of cities. Some of those cities lay on the river systems of central and northern Europe where they controlled the intra-European trade. Still others were in Italy, where they sat astride the great land-based trade routes to the East and the water routes of the Mediterranean. Countries bordering on the Atlantic, like Spain, Portugal, France, and England, derived little benefit from Europe's trade with Asia. Thus, the Italian sea captain from Genoa—Columbus—convinced Ferdinand and Isabella of Spain to back his scheme of sailing west to reach the East (Portugal had already turned him down) because he offered the possibility of a new trading system with Spain as its hub.

Columbus thought he might encounter a few islands before he reached either Japan or India. He had no inkling that he would find new continents (he died years later still convinced he had reached islands close to Japan and the mainland of Asia). Upon his return from his first voyage he sent a letter to Lord Raphael Sanchez, one of his patrons, to announce the discovery of the "Indies." "Thirty-three days after my departure from Cadiz," he wrote, "I reached the Indian Sea, where I discovered many islands, thickly peopled, of which I took possession without resistance in the name of our most illustrious Monarch." He named the islands San Salvador, Santa Maria de la Concepcion, Fernandina, Isabella, and Juana

(Cuba). "As soon as we arrived at that, which as I have said was named Juana," he continued:

> I proceeded along its coast a short distance westward, and found it to be so large and apparently without termination, that I could not suppose it to be an island, but the continental province of Cathay [China]. Seeing, however, no towns or populous places on the sea coast, but only a few detached houses and cottages with whose inhabitants I was unable to communicate, because they fled as soon as they saw us, I went further on, thinking that in my progress I should certainly find some city or village.[1]

Columbus was typical of his age. Fifteenth-century Europe possessed no evidence of "America's" existence. Although religious and secular legends and prophesies describing great civilizations to the west existed in abundance, they were questioned by practical men like Columbus and aggressive, power-hungry rulers like Ferdinand and Isabella.

Long before Columbus, some Europeans had already colonized America. Around 1000 A.D. the Vikings (Norwegians) crossed the North Atlantic to Ireland. Then, men such as Bjarni Herjolfsson and Leif Erikson sailed to Greenland (where they established a colony), went west to Labrador and the Baffin Islands, and then followed the coast down to the tip of Newfoundland. They erected a colony they called *Vineland* because of the apparent fertility of the region. For an unknown reason, however, the Vikings abandoned their colonial venture after three or four years and never again returned to settle the continent. Although the Norse voyages were recorded in stories that filtered down into the rest of Europe, the society of the eleventh century was too tied to local or Mediterranean concerns to look beyond its shores to the North American continent. The significance of the Vikings' achievement was lost.[2]

THE AMERICAN ENVIRONMENT

The First Americans

When Columbus landed on San Salvador, an island in what would come to be known as the West Indies, he encountered dark-skinned peoples whom he immediately assumed were Asians. Thus, he labeled them *Indians.* As it turned out, his and Europe's ignorance of America and Americans was matched by America's ignorance of Europe. The Indians Columbus found were representatives of peoples throughout the Americas who had lived for centuries with no knowledge of lands beyond the seas. We know now that those first Americans, or Amerinds, were not themselves an indigenous race, but were the descendants of migrants who had settled in America thousands of years earlier.

They came from Asia—Siberia to be exact—migrating to North America perhaps as early as 40,000 years before Christ. Like the Europeans who would begin to settle North America's shores in the seventeenth century, these Amerinds also came in search of a better life. Anthropologists believe that they originated in Mongolia and moved north only after persistent drought and increasingly scarce food supplies forced them to leave. The Amerinds either crossed the Bering Strait or migrated to North America via a since-submerged isthmus that joined Alaska and Asia. Once in North America they probably followed game south to warmer, lusher climes. For thousands of years they roamed two continents until, between 7000 and 12,000 B.C., agriculture and husbandry appeared among the Indians clustered in Mexico and Central America.

Gradually, great Indian civilizations developed. The most spectacular and awesome were the Mayas in Guatemala, the Aztecs in northern Mexico, and the Incas in Peru. Those civilizations rivaled, and in some ways eclipsed, contemporary cultures in Europe and Asia Minor. The Mayas built cities, erected strong, sophisticated governments, and devised an elaborate division of labor. Around the time of Christ the Mayas moved northeast into Yucatan, the far southeastern tip of present-day Mexico, and developed a mighty culture which dominated the region until the thirteenth century. Then, the Mayas were overrun by the fierce, aggressive Toltec tribe under the leadership of King Quetzalcoatl. The Toltec empire that Quetzalcoatl and subsequent rulers built, however, was short-lived; it was quickly conquered by the highly developed tribe that would meet Cortez—the Aztecs. Farther south, in the Andean Mountains of Peru, the Incas forged an equally impressive empire that would control and influence northern South America until that civilization, too, fell to the Spanish.

The Aztecs and Incas developed the most elaborate and technically sophisticated civilizations of all the Amerindian peoples. It was their gold and silver that whetted the appetities of the Spanish conquerors and filled the coffers of Europe. At their peak, the great civilizations of Mexico and Peru probably contained more people than the population of Europe in the fifteenth century, and their principal cities were larger than either medieval London or Paris. In some ways, the Incas and Aztecs built societies which resembled those of Europe at the same time. Both the Aztecs and the Incas developed empires with elaborate agricultural systems that sustained large populations and created ample surpluses for trade. As in Europe, agriculture supported a ruling class or aristocracy augmented by an elaborate ecclesiastical structure or priesthood. Both Indian civilizations conducted extensive and frequent military operations against recalcitrant neighbors.

Often, the Aztecs and Incas are equated in the modern mind with the "barbarian" tribes which once menaced the Roman Empire. Grade "B" Hollywood thrillers emphasize the Amerinds' martial qualities and some of their peculiar religious proclivities (such as human sacrifice among the Aztecs) while overlooking their technological achievements and their intellectual abilities. Simply stated, the Aztecs and Incas were the Romans—not the barbarians—of their time. Like the ancients of western civilization, they developed complex theoretical premises to explain the past, present, and future. For example, they believed that the world had evolved in stages and that humanity had made its appearance after a specific act of creation by the Gods. In the Aztec and Toltec traditions humans evolved in stages. The highest stage involved the death of the warrior-king Quetzalcoatl, his struggle with the "Dead Land Lord," his transformation into the planet Venus, and his creation of modern humanity using materials collected in the Dead Land. *The History of the Kingdoms of Colhuacan and Mexico,* a sixteenth-century manuscript, contained the following description of the defeated King Quetzalcoatl burning himself in preparation for his transformation into a "great star":

> And it is said that when he burned, his ashes rose up and every kind of precious bird appeared and could be seen rising up to the sky: roseate spoonbill, cotinga, trogon, blue heron, yellow-headed parrot, macaw, white-fronted parrot, and all other precious birds. And after he had become ash the quetzal bird's heart rose up; it could be seen and was known to enter the sky. The old men would say he had become Venus; and it is told that when the star appeared Quetzalcoatl died. From now on he was called the Lord of the Dawn.
>
> Only four days he did not appear, so it is told, and dwelt in Dead Land. And for another four days he sharpened himself. After eight days the great star appeared called Quetzalcoatl on his ruler's throne. And they knew, on his rising, which people, according to Sign, he penetrates, shoots into and loathes.[3]

Technologically, the Aztecs and Incas had no peers on the American continent. They utilized mathematics and astronomy and they were masters of organization. Like the Egyptians, Greeks, and Romans, they gave form and direction to their societies through magnificent public-works projects. Their public buildings, temples, roadways, and irrigation systems testified to the extraordinary level of their organizational skills.

However, important differences separated both pre- and post-Columbian Europe from the civilizations of Incas and Aztecs. Amerindian religion, for example, was polytheistic rather than monotheistic. In many ways, the religious beliefs and practices of the Aztecs and Incas were typical of all Amerinds. As agriculturalists, the Incas and Aztecs sought to understand the cycles of nature which governed their lives and determined their fates. Consequently, their religious systems tried to decipher and explain those cycles and to force human compliance. The Amerinds envisioned no greater sin than to violate the cycles of nature or the deities symbolizing those cycles. Also Amerindian religion lacked the pietistic or inner spiritual life which played such an important role in Christianity's history and impact.

The civilizations of the Aztecs and Incas differed from those of Europe in many other respects. The Amerinds lacked the draft animals common to daily life in Europe. Also, the strongest metal available to the Amerinds was bronze; iron and steel were nonexistent. One of the most striking differences was the absence of nationalism and the sense of destiny which molded the early modern and modern state in Europe; another was the lack of an evangelistic strain which pervaded Christian belief. Amerinds conducted no holy wars and possessed neither the unity nor the perception of national mission which so strongly influenced the unfolding imperalistic designs of Spain, France, and England.

No Indian civilization in North America ever rivaled those to the south. During the first centuries A.D., in what is now New Mexico and Arizona, several Amerind groups, including the Hopi and Zuñi tribes, turned from hunting to primitive agriculture. Gradually, they established permanent villages securely enclosed by adobe walls and comprised of multiple-family dwellings similar to apartment-house complexes. The Pueblos (The Spanish word for town)—as the Spanish called them—became accomplished farmers and weavers, and later, skilled artisans as well. Their greatest accomplishments were their cliff dwellings: enormous communal adobe buildings that were virtually impervious to attack. Because of the cliff fortresses, the Pueblos maintained their independence for centuries (though both the Apache and Navajo encroached upon them periodically) until the Spanish conquered them in the sixteenth century.

North and east of the Pueblos another civilization, also based on agriculture, developed in what is now southern Illinois and southern Missouri. Known as the Mississippian culture, its influence spread as far west as Oklahoma, as far south as Louisiana, and as far north as Wisconsin. The Mississippian tribes probably borrowed many of their ideas and customs from the Mexican civilizations. Expert carvers, pottery makers, and weavers, they left fragments which suggest that they shared crafting techniques and artistic styles with their southern Indian neighbors. They erected great earthen pyramids for burial of their dead as well as for various other religious and ceremonial purposes. The largest of the mounds uncovered—the one at Cahokia in southern Illinois—was nearly fifteen acres in size and flanked a great fortified Indian city of perhaps 30,000. Although the Mississippian culture declined long before the arrival of the Europeans, its influence was felt among the eastern woodland tribes in their forms of social organization and agriculture.

The ancient Indian tribes most noted for their earthen burial mounds, however, were the Mound Builders—forbearers of the Natchez, Creek, and Choctaw—who lived in the Ohio and Mississippi valleys. Archaeologists have determined that by the first century A.D. the Mound Builders had developed fortresslike cities and were operating an extensive commercial network that spread over much of eastern North America. Besides hunting and trading, the Mound Builders also engaged in agriculture and became skilled artisans. The great mounds they built to bury their dead can be found throughout the Midwest.

As this brief survey of American Indian cultures reveals, when Europeans invaded North America, the Indians they encountered were not quite the "primitives" the Europeans labeled them. They practiced agricultural methods nearly as modern as those of the English. They lived sedentary lives in villages and took advantage of the resources their area afforded them. Most of these Indian tribes raised corn and vegetables and supplemented their diet with fish, wild game, nuts, and berries. Still, in two important respects, Indian life differed from European life. First, the Indians of the East were communally oriented, usually holding land in common and exalting the good of the whole over that of the individual. To be sure, the English arrived with some communal values, but those eroded somewhat as the desire to exploit the resources of the new land encouraged the growth of individualism. Second, the tribes of eastern North America were divided both culturally and linguistically from each other. These differences put the Indians at a serious disadvantage when confronting the culturally homogeneous and politically centralized English or French.[4]

Nevertheless, before 1600 the Indians of eastern North America provided formidable opponents for potential enemies. Out of the three main language groups—Algonquian, Iroquoian, and Siouan—the tribes comprising the Iroquois Confederation were the most powerful. Organized sometime in the fifteenth century to end intramural squabbling and to present a united front against the Algonquins, the Iroquois Confederation included five tribes: the Mohawk, Seneca, Oneida, Cayuga, and Onnondaga. Numbering about 10,000 the tribes populated most of the northeastern states. By the early seventeenth century, when Europeans arrived, the Iroquois were nearly impervious to attack.

The English viewed the Iroquois with a mixture of awe and disdain. They marveled at the strength and apparent fearlessness of the Iroquois but saw little in their culture worthy of emulation. Like the English, the Iroquois were hunters and farmers, but they had no real concept of private property. Both hunting and farming were considered communal enterprises. Consequently, as European observers quickly noted, the Iroquois avoided some of the problems which plagued European communities. They had fewer poor, less crime, and less vice; further, Europeans remarked how humanely the Iroquois treated the less fortunate in their midst.

Given such laudable traits, one might wonder why the Europeans were not eager to learn from the Iroquois. The answer lay in the fact that the Iroquois achieved their "peaceable kingdoms" at the expense of traits essential to the European personality. The Iroquois did not covet worldly goods, and they had little sense of individual competitiveness—two characteristics which were very important in bringing Europeans to America. The Iroquois competed in hunting and in battle, to be sure, but the personal glory achieved was mostly an extension of the tribe's or the village's glory, and only partly that of the individual. Had the Europeans imitated the Iroquois way of life, they would have undergone a transformation more profound than a religious conversion.

Of all the tribes the English and other Europeans confronted in North America, the Iroquois proved the greatest stumbling block to European hopes of expanding inland. The tribes along the coast, mostly Algonquin, fell fairly quickly to the diseases, incursions, and intrigues of the English. But the Iroquois, whom the English faced as soon as they began to move inland more than 100 miles, refused to budge. Using a combination of violence and sophisticated diplomacy (playing off the French and English against each other), the Iroquois kept the Europeans bottled up along the coast for about a century and a half. Only when the French empire on the continent fell in 1763, and the English moved west by the thousands, did Iroquois defenses collapse.

The saga of the Iroquois reveals much about the character of contact between the Europeans and the Indians, just as it dispels some long-cherished myths about Indian-white relations. First, Europeans possessed technological superiority (guns and gunpowder, for example), but technology only partially explained their success. They came as invaders and conquerors, and they demonstrated a unity that their Indian antagonists could not match. Some tribes proved too weak to resist and became slaves. Others were vanquished through violence and intrigue. Some, like the Plains Indians, fell because their food supplies were extinguished. Still others were ravaged by diseases brought to America by Europeans. In nearly every case, however, it was the traditional insularity and parochialism of the tribes which proved their undoing. Often their feuding with other tribes—some of it centuries old—took precedence over the threat of the whites, and Indians sought not to overcome the whites but to use them as allies in their own struggles. This tactic worked for the Iroquois, but it destroyed lesser tribes.

Too often the centuries-long struggle between Amerinds and whites has been viewed as a great morality play in which good resided with one side and evil with the other. In fact, neither side was all that virtuous. The whites were the invaders, but they attacked peoples who were themselves territorially expansive and aggressive. The struggles between Indians and whites differed little from the power politics each group knew so well. The whites were not the inherently superior peoples they believed themselves to be, nor were the Indians the primitive savages whites often imagined. Conversely, the real Indians did not fit the bucolic, peace-loving, virtuous, innocent image of some later legends. The fact that, culturally, neither whites nor Indians ever showed much interest in emulation or assimilation provides ample evidence that from the beginning, each side viewed the other as an enemy to be either manipulated or exterminated.[5]

THE EUROPEAN ENVIRONMENT

The Land and People

Late-medieval European society, which spawned New World colonization, was preindustrial, static, and predominantly agricultural. Europe's population was relatively small: perhaps 55 to 60 million people lived on the Continent in Western Europe, and perhaps another 3.5 to 4 million lived in the British Isles, with two-thirds of that number concentrated in England and Wales. Not surprisingly, Europeans settled most heavily in coastal and river-accessible areas—such as eastern France, the Netherlands, the Rhine Valley, northern Italy, and land along the Mediterranean shore—where water transportation was available. Although a few cities such as London, Paris, Genoa, or Venice were beginning to expand (London, for example, grew from around 80,000 to almost a quarter of a million by the seventeenth century), the countryside rather than the cities dominated European life.

For the ordinary tenant or small landholder, life in medieval Europe was very harsh. The uncertainty of the food supply and the unavailability of fresh fruits and vegetables for much of the year meant that even if people did not face starvation, they were still prone to suffer from vitamin deficiencies, frequent constipation or diarrhea, or infections. The entire spectrum of society, from the king to the lowest peasant alike, fell victim to poor hygiene and lack of sanitation. Periodically, the medieval world experienced waves of smallpox, typhus, influenza, and the most feared of all diseases—the bubonic plague. In 1348 to 1349 perhaps as much as a fourth of the population of Europe died from the Black Death, and through the fifteenth and sixteenth centuries Europe suffered epidemics of plague, dysentery, and other diseases. In addition, the primitive state of medicine made recovery from accidents or injuries of war highly improbable. The early surgeons (members of the barber's guild) had only one real treatment for serious wounds: amputation. If gangrene did not kill the patient first, shock following amputation or sepsis during recovery often would.

In addition to widespread disease and primitive medicine, the medieval Europeans faced other dangers in daily life. Floods, fires, and periodic famines were common occurrences. As a result, Europeans were very likely to experience sickness and premature death. Even among the upper classes, where presumably diet and hygiene were better, the life expectancy for a newborn child was short. Although estimates vary considerably, perhaps only two-thirds of the children born between the fourteenth and seventeenth centuries were expected to survive their fifth birthdays. Equally common, women died in childbirth. The innumerable hardships of life made the medieval Europeans continually aware of the great uncertainty and precariousness of their existence.

The Medieval Church and State

In light of this uncertainty, it is not surprising that religion played a large role in the lives of ordinary people. Lacking knowledge about the physical laws governing the universe, medieval people relied on supernatural explanations for natural disasters such as famine, flood, or disease. Men and women attributed human-made calamities such as war to humanity's sinful nature. In a world full of misfortune, uncertainty, and evil, the common person turned to the institutional church for help, reassurance, forgiveness, and comfort. The Roman Catholic Church, which was the dominant and virtually the sole religious force in medieval Europe, served as the bridge connecting people with God. It provided the means for salvation and gave spiritual guidance in temporal matters. Equally important, it reassured men and women that whatever disasters befell them were transitory, and they would reap joys in the next world. Finally, the unchanging, seemingly indestructible character of the Catholic Church offered medieval people stability and permanence against the chaos and turmoil they faced in their daily lives.

Politically, the map of Europe revealed a group of small states who continually warred against each other for territory and political power. The authority within each state usually rested in the hands of a prince or king; but since power was tied to ownership of land, the ruler represented only one of several major political forces in the medieval state. For example, the prince had to give due regard to the feudal nobility. Without its loyalty and good will, he could not exercise power effectively or for very long. The nobles supplied soldiers and material for the royal army and money to run the government. In addition to the aristocracy, rulers also had to contend with the largest single landowner: the Catholic Church. The Church controlled much of the wealth of the medieval world and claimed secular as well as religious authority over the state. The Church considered all temporal rulers to be under the authority of the pope, who united the states together into one Christian empire. For most of the Middle Ages temporal rulers at least tacitly acknowledged the authority of the pope and paid various duties and annates in order to obtain his approval. The "temporal" powers of the pope, however, depended heavily upon the acquiescence of the prince. Still, in the largely local and provincial society of medieval Europe, the institutional church maintained a continental network of bishops, priests, and abbots that alone united Europe. Through this institutional fabric the Catholic Church exerted considerable political as well as spiritual influence over the lives of great and small and provided a measure of stability against the divisive tendencies of the states.

THE EMERGENCE OF WESTERN EUROPE

The Rise of the Early Modern State

By the end of the Middle Ages in western Europe, the positions of the feudal nobility and the Catholic Church had deteriorated. A series of extended wars in England, France, and Spain during the fifteenth century killed off a large section of the aristocracy and weakened the power of those remaining. In addition, the power and wealth of the Church also declined. During the fourteenth century the Church endured the French king Philip the Fair's sack of the Vatican, the transfer of the papal court to Avignon for years of "Babylonian captivity," and then the "Great Schism"—a protracted internal split of the church hierarchy into pro-French and anti-French factions that lasted from 1378 to 1417. Taking advantage of the Church's internal difficulties, secular powers began taxing church property or in other ways siphoning off its revenues. The fragmentation of the church hierarchy had other adverse effects as well. Internal trouble fueled long-standing grievances against the corruption, ignorance, and greed of the clergy. In reality, though, the medieval church was probably no more corrupt than it had been in earlier periods. Such abuses as the buying and selling of church offices, or the immoral behavior of the parish clergy, had always existed to some degree, but the church's persistent internal stresses both increased its vulnerability and made it less capable of imposing discipline on the clergy. Further, the Catholic Church faced new, rapid, economic, political, and social changes it neither understood nor liked. It failed to respond effectively to new conditions, and saw its prestige and power decline as a consequence.

The weakened conditions of the nobility and the church, accompanied by the increased power of a few ambitious rulers, produced a fundamental change in the political order of Europe. Gradually, the multitude of independent principalities on the Continent were unified into a few national states. Portugal was one of the first to centralize authority, and by the end of the fourteenth century Portugal had become the supreme commercial power in Europe. The end of the Hussite Wars in Germany by the middle of the fifteenth century allowed political centralization to proceed there. In the same period Spain successfully expelled the Moors and was unified by Ferdinand and Isabella. Although civil wars in England and France hindered the erection of national states there until the end of the fifteenth century, by the time of the "discovery" of America, a few families dominated the political landscape of Europe. The Hapsburgs in Austria, Spain, and the Netherlands; the Tudors in England; the Valois and then the Bourbons in France—all of those families had built up legal dynastic claims to rule and had laid the foundations for modern national states.

The Transformation of the Medieval Economy

When feudal provinces were slowly developing into national states, a profound economic transformation took place which helped to solidify and strengthen the early modern state. Basically, the economy of the medieval world was a rigid system that maintained a standard of living barely above subsistence level. Regulated by the manor, town, or other political unit, economic transactions usually involved only a local exchange of goods and services. Even before the Crusades (1095 to 1270), of course, the medieval world, principally the Italian city-states on the Mediterranean, had maintained some distant trade with the East; but this existed only on a very small scale. Most of the population was engaged in agricultural pursuits. Typically, peasants lived on manors. There they were required to devote a certain part of their time cultivating the lord's fields and to give him a portion of their harvested crops for the right to use his land. Although customs varied from manor to manor, most of the medieval peasants' daily activities were regulated. For example, the peasants usually needed the lord's permission (granted by a fee) to grind wheat at the mill, bake bread, cut wood in the forest, marry, or even leave the boundaries of the manor. Those few who owned a freehold, pursued a trade, or ran a store exercised more personal freedom, but even their lives were highly controlled by the state, town, or guild. The prices of goods as well as the wages of laborers were fixed by custom, guild regulation, or law.

By the fourteenth century, however, medieval economic life underwent certain fundamental changes. As trade increased with the East, the economic isolation and independence of localities diminished, and a new economic and social type emerged: the great merchant. Appearing first in the Italian city-states of Venice, Naples, or Genoa, the great merchant not only became one of the wealthiest, most powerful elements in society, but also one of the prime engineers of its transformation. Increased commercial activities began to create new bonds between areas of Europe, bonds which in turn made the economy more fluid and expansive. Trade began drawing people off the land and into cities. In addition, the growth of trade put a premium on gold and silver rather than on land, and in so doing it undermined the old feudal values that were rooted in the land. Lacking the established position in society that the landowner traditionally possessed, merchants began to carve out their own domains. To win both social position and guarantee order and stability essential for trade, the commercial classes generally extended their financial backing and power to ambitious princes who in turn used this support to unify their territories and expand their authority.

Taken together, such economic and political changes produced a realignment in social arrangements. Increased trade eroded the traditional feudal relationships that had united the noble and the ruler and tied together the lord and the peasant. As gold and silver became a source of power equal to land, the aristocracy abandoned some old feudal arrangements based on an exchange of duties and obligations and demanded instead that these duties be commuted to cash payments. In addition, although the Black Death of the fourteenth century decimated the peasantry, population recovery was steady and by the middle of the sixteenth century there was actually an oversupply of labor in most areas of Europe and England. This condition combined with the great influx of Spanish New World gold and silver to produce inflation and a "price revolution" in the late sixteenth century. Between 1500 and 1650 spiraling costs for goods—especially foodstuffs—and services far outstripped wage increases. The fixed rents from land which had supported the aristocracy for so long proved woefully inadequate in the face of rising prices. In the long run the price revolution emancipated the peasantry, but immediately it caused them and portions of the nobility great hardships. Some of the landed aristocracy prospered from rising food prices and cheap labor but many landlords were forced to sell their lands or engage in new practices of land management, such as draining swamps or "enclosing" common lands (traditionally reserved for the peasantry) to increase wool production. The end result of such practices was the expulsion of a large group of landless, unemployed, or underemployed peasants from their homes. Some became agricultural laborers. Others moved to the commercial centers and towns which had arisen under the impetus of growing trade.[6]

The Renaissance

The evolution of medieval society was in part aided by a new intellectual outlook which began to characterize many members of the ruling and merchant classes during the fourteenth and fifteenth centuries. As some feudal relationships disintegrated, Europeans became more open to new ideas and began to look at themselves—as well as at the world and God—in a different light. The set of cultural and intellectual achievements associated with this new outlook has been labeled the *Renaissance,* meaning a rebirth. Beginning in Italy's trading cities, the movement eventually spread into France, Germany, the Netherlands, and Switzerland. Not surprisingly, the Renaissance drew most of its support from those less wedded to the old order, such as members of the merchant class like the Medicis in Florence. The movement revived interest in the literature and culture of ancient Greece and Rome. One of the central themes of the Renaissance was a great confidence in individuals' ability to govern and direct their own lives. Renaissance painters and sculptors such as Leonardo Da Vinci, Michaelangelo, Raphael, Giovanni Bellini, and Hans Holbein emphasized the traits of self-sufficiency, independence, self-will, and individualism in the subjects they portrayed. The preoccupation of Renaissance artists with people's powers, rather than God's, led inevitably to a more secular view of the world. Art moved away from symbolic lines and abstract themes and toward greater realism. Portraits, for example, used more familiar backgrounds and conveyed more facial expressions and personal characteristics. Likewise, political thinkers, such as Machiavelli, departed from the medieval concern for God's will in government and questioned the actual operation and nature of politics. In his *Discourses,* but more particularly in *The Prince,* Machiavelli rooted political decisions in self-interest—that is, he argued that the ruler made war and peace, or entered into treaties and alliances, according to the way in which the prince assessed his best interests. Machiavelli assumed that the successful prince possessed superior human talents or *virtu* (coming from *vir,* Latin for man). Equally important, the prince was an opportunist who made use of "fortune" or chance. "I conclude then," wrote Machiavelli:

> inasmuch as Fortune is changeable, that men who persist obstinately in their own ways will be successful only so long as those ways coincide with those of Fortune; and whenever these differ, they fail. But, on the whole I judge impetuosity to be better than caution; for Fortune is a woman, and if you wish to master her you must strike and beat her, and you will see that she allows herself to be more easily vanquished by the rash and violent than by those who proceed more slowly and coldly.[7]

Developments such as Gutenberg's printing press helped spark a literary outpouring during the fifteenth century. Called *humanism* because of its preoccupation with human traits and concerns, the literary movement of the Renaissance strongly reflected the secular, rather than clerical, background of its leading thinkers. Often writing in the vernacular instead of the traditional Latin, such men as Paracelsus in Basel, Muller in Germany, Sir Thomas More in England, and the most renowned of the humanist thinkers, Erasmus of Rotterdam, advanced new ideas in all areas of human endeavor: medicine, astronomy, mathematics, politics, philosophy. Particularly sensitive to what they felt were moral and spiritual failings in their own society, humanists glorified the ancient past and searched for truth and guidance among the writings of antiquity. Throughout Europe but especially in Germany, new universities sprang up under the growing interest in learning. Although the Renaissance made some tears in the fabric of the medieval world, it did not "overturn" an old way of life. Nevertheless, the Renaissance did encourage Europeans to reach out beyond the limits of old ideas and it strengthened people's faith in their ability to control their own destinies.[8]

The Protestant Reformation

Although the Renaissance helped prepare Europeans for changes in the medieval way of life, it was fundamentally a movement sponsored by and directed toward the elite. Upon the heels of the Renaissance, however, followed another significant development that would ultimately influence all classes of society. This was the Protestant Reformation. The very size and diversity of the Catholic Church made it difficult for it to meet changing political, economic, and social conditions to everyone's satisfaction. This made the Church vulnerable to criticism and encouraged divisiveness and factional squabbling. Charges of "corruption" became commonplace. In the fifteenth century Erasmus and other humanists had recognized the existence of some real abuses in the Church and had urged reforms. The rise of universities as well as growing interest in early church practices and doctrines had prompted scholars to examine old Greek and Hebrew biblical texts and translate them into the vernacular. As laity and clergy read the original biblical texts, some came to the conclusion that current church practices deviated from those of the early Christian Church. Hence, by the sixteenth century, many within the Church viewed the sale of church offices (simony) or the issuance of indulgences (a papal dispensation or certificate that nullified particular punishments for sin an individual otherwise expected to suffer in purgatory) as scripturally unsound. Inside the Church considerable opposition to such practices developed, and clerics in many corners called for a restoration of the pure state of the Christian Church they believed had existed during the early Middle Ages.

Luther's Protest

Before the sixteenth century a few individuals such as John Wycliff (c. 1320-1384) and John Hus (c. 1369-1415) had denounced some corrupt practices they saw in the Catholic Church and had demanded reform. In England Wycliff and his followers (called the Lollards) were suppressed, as was the teaching of Hus in Bohemia (Hus was eventually burned at the stake for heresy). By the early sixteenth century, however, conditions made Europe more receptive than ever to religious reform. Martin Luther, the father of the Reformation, initially followed in the footsteps of the Christian humanists in attempting to work within the Roman church to correct abuses. Unlike his reforming predecessors, however, Luther eventually broke away from the Catholic Church. A volatile, sensitive, introspective man, Luther had entered the monastic orders in 1505, when he was 22. He hoped to obtain relief from the gnawing spiritual uncertainty he felt. Luther did not attain the inner peace he sought in the fasts, prayers, and vigils that filled his solitary, austere life. Despite his efforts to satisfy the Almighty, Luther continued to fear that he had not received God's forgiveness.

In 1511 Luther received an appointment as Professor of the Bible at the newly established University of Wittenberg. In pursuing his scholarly responsibilities there, he began studying the Bible intently. Sometime in 1512 or 1513, while preparing lectures on the Bible, Luther read St. Paul's letter to the Romans with a new understanding. As he pondered *Romans* 1:17, "the just shall live by faith," Luther came to the conclusion that St. Paul was declaring salvation as a free gift of God, not the result of one's own efforts. Christ's death and resurrection—wholly an act of God for mankind—fully absolved people from their sins if they believed; individuals, then, became righteous by "faith alone," not by any works they performed.

In coming to that conclusion, Luther adopted a position opposed to the theological teachings popular in the Church at that time. Those teachings maintained that man through "good works" could help determine his own salvation. Nevertheless, Luther did not immediately see that his belief had monumental implications—that is, if faith alone were necessary for salvation, then the entire structure of the Catholic Church, along with the priesthood, papacy, and ceremonies, were extraneous.

For several years, Luther quietly taught, studied, and preached in Wittenberg. In 1517, however, when a Dominican friar named John Tetzel began selling certificates of the Maintz Indulgence to Luther's students and parishioners, Luther became outraged. Still, the public challenge to the sacrament of penance and the doctrine of indulgences that Luther posed in his ninety-five "theses" was originally intended to provoke a scholarly debate within the Church, not a revolution. Between 1517 and 1521 he petitioned successively the pope and then church councils to reform the Church's position on indulgences. On June 15, 1520, the Church responded formally with the Bull *Exsurge Domine,* ordering Luther to recant on forty-one propositions or face excommunication. Luther refused and his excommunication took effect in January, 1521. About a month later, Emperor of Germany and King of Spain, Charles V, opened his Diet (Parliament) at Worms and ordered Luther to appear. When he did he was asked to disavow his heresies. Luther replied that he could not take back his attacks against papal authority: "Unless I am proved wrong by Scriptures or by evident reason," he announced, "then I am a prisoner in conscience to the Word of God. I cannot retract and I will not retract. To go against the conscience is neither safe nor right. God help me. Amen."[9] A month later the Diet declared him an outlaw in the Holy Roman Empire.

When Luther first attacked the sale of indulgences in 1517, he found many sympathetic to his views. Much of the sympathy he won, however, resulted from discontent over nondoctrinal issues. Germans everywhere had long opposed ecclesiastical abuses and resented papal control over the Church. By the time Luther was excommunicated, therefore, he drew widespread support from nationalists, from German princes who disliked paying taxes to Rome, among the professional and commercial classes who found Catholic doctrines restrictive to trade, and among the lower strata of peasantry who keenly felt the stresses and hardships that accompanied economic, social, and political change.

The new church that Luther formed appealed to those groups for several reasons. Although retaining a strong Catholic character, the "Lutheran Church" ended subordination of the German church to Rome. It also abolished many of the old ceremonies and practices such as saint worship and the adulation of relics. It disbanded the monastic orders (freeing the lands and wealth of the monasteries as well) and drew the clergy closer to the people by encouraging them to marry and to use the vernacular in church services. By the 1530s Lutheranism had become the state religion in many German principalities and quickly spread north into Scandinavia. The Protestant Reformation in Germany was accompanied by a national revolution. Under the League of Schmalkald, a group of German princes allied against Charles V, head of the Holy Roman Empire, and waged a political and religious war that lasted for more than twenty years.

The Radical Reformation

Luther was only the first of many "Protestant" thinkers to attack the Catholic Church during the 1520s and 1530s. Ulrich Zwingli in Zurich and Martin Bucer in Strasbourg turned their cities into centers of Protestantism and helped fan the fires of reform throughout Europe. Such reformers, however, were essentially conservative in their political and social outlook. In spite of the Protestant emphasis upon the authority of the Bible alone, the reformed churches maintained a learned, ordained clergy and viewed the institutional church as performing an essential role in the Christian's religious life. In the fever and excitement of the 1530s, however, a number of religious radicals took a different view of the institutional church. Collectively called *Anabaptists,* because of their rejection of infant baptism and their call for rebaptism, these radicals maintained that the Christian Church was a group of regenerate adults voluntarily joined together in Christian fellowship and independent from the authority of the state. In addition, a number of these radical sects held strong *millenarian* views—that is, they interpreted the economic and social changes they were experiencing as signs that the world was coming to an end and that Christ would soon establish his millennium, or thousand-year rule, with his saints.

The Anabaptist movement was almost immediately held in disrepute and fear. In 1524 to 1525 the Peasants' War erupted, gaining strength in the same areas in which Anabaptist views were prevalent—sure proof to political and religious leaders that these ideas led to revolution. Although the revolt was inspired by social and economic grievances and was soon suppressed, it made most Germans fearful of radical religious ideas. Then, about ten years later, a second event occurred which horrified religious and political leaders even more. In 1534 a Dutch tailor by the name of John of Leyden took over the city of Münster and established a military, communistic regime that lasted for over a year. Leyden and his supporters were eventually suppressed by the joint efforts of Catholic and Lutheran princes, but by that time Anabaptism had become a universal term for religious and social excess. Luther vehemently denounced such social revolution and began calling for submission to civil authority.

Calvin

The spread of Protestant ideas throughout Europe produced a second generation of reformers. The most significant of those, John Calvin (1509-1564), was a French attorney who converted to Protestantism during the 1530s. Out of all other reformers, Calvin became the central organizer and theologian of Protestantism. In his *Institutes of the Christian Religion* (1536), Calvin carried Luther's doctrine of free grace to its ultimate conclusion. Drawing as Luther had upon the theology of St. Augustine, Calvin emphasized the total sovereignty and power of God and argued that the Almighty had predetermined or predestined all people either to salvation or damnation. This doctrine of *predestination* drew a sharp distinction between the elect and nonelect, and conceived of the church primarily as a body of saints whose principal functions were to worship God and curb the sinfulness of the unregenerate masses. In Geneva Calvin created a church-dominated state that ruled over the social and political, as well as the religious, conduct of its citizens. Calvin's church design in Geneva provided the model for other Protestants in Europe, and his *Institutes,* reprinted into virtually every European language, influenced religious thinkers on the Continent, in England and Scotland, and finally in America.[10]

The Counter-Reformation

Thanks mainly to Calvin and Calvinists, Protestant militancy and evangelicalism played an important role in Europe's expansion into North America. The same may be said of Catholicism's influence in the exploration and colonization of South America. Histories of the period sometimes leave the impression that the Roman Catholic Church was so corrupt and so obsessed with the threat of Protestantism that it hindered New World expansionism as much as it helped. Such a view, of course, ignores the whole history of Spain, Portugal, and France in the New World. Actually, a revitalized Church was a potent force in expansionism. The same impetus for reform which had spawned Luther continued to spread in the Catholic world even as the Protestants gained strength and converts. The *Counter-Reformation,* as the reform movement came to be known, proceeded in three stages and left the Church stronger than ever. Stage one involved a revitalization of the devotional life of the Catholics and proceeded through the work of new orders like the Jesuits (Society of Jesus), the Ursulines, and the Capuchins. Stage two focused on the doctrine and discipline of the Church and revolved around the Council of Trent (1545 to 1563). Among other things, the Council reformed many alleged abuses of the clergy and reaffirmed or clarified elements of Catholic doctrine under attack by Protestants.

Stage three revived the church militant and led to political and military activities against Protestants and missionary work in Protestant areas. The Catholic cause in Europe was greatly aided by the machinations of Charles V and Phillip II of Spain and, later, by Louis XIV of France. Catholic missionary work in Protestant regions was carried forth by evangelical orders like the Jesuits. The results were striking. In the fifteenth and sixteenth centuries Catholicism reclaimed most of the territory lost to Protestants on the European continent. At the same time, predominantly Catholic areas were held in line by the Inquisition (begun in 1542).

Spain was the leader in Catholicism's counterattack against Protestantism and it is to Spain that we look for Catholicism's role in European expansion. To begin with, the unification of Spain in the fifteenth century took place through a religious crusade against the "Moorish infidels." Thus, from the beginning Spanish nationalism and Catholic militancy were inextricably linked. Moreover, the Church showed no lack of interest in the possibilities of the "New World," for Columbus' discoveries were followed quickly by the Pope's division of the New World between Spain and Portugal (Treaty of Tordesillas, 1494).

The sixteenth century was the "Spanish century" and Spain's rise to power owed much to the Church. While the Inquisition nipped heresy (and a budding Protestantism) among Spaniards, and spurred reform of the Church, Spanish military and diplomatic influence spread across Europe as Charles V (the Holy Roman Emperor) gave meaning to his role as "defender of the faith." In America, Spanish conquest was blanketed with the same moral sanction as earlier activities against the Moors. It was Spain's duty—and religious mission—to subdue the American "infidels." The Church played an even greater role in the construction and evolution of Spanish colonial society in America. While the Spanish Crown gained nearly total control over the ecclesiastical apparatus in the New World, Catholic priests and missionaries worked to convert the Indians (the Jesuits performed brilliantly in frontier regions) and tried to teach them to accept their new status as slaves. At the same time, much of the responsibility for guaranteeing the well-being of Spanish colonial society fell upon the Church and church personnel responded with considerable enthusiasm and zeal. The eventual success of both Spain and Portugal in South America bore eloquent testimony to the power and the vitality of reformed Catholicism.[11]

DISCOVERY AND EXPLORATION

The Idea of America

Our analysis of the preconditions for European expansion would not be complete without consideration of the role played by the European imagination. Centuries before the voyages of Columbus, Europeans had developed preconceptions about a "New World." Many folk legends and myths—such as the story of Atlantis, accounts of the Vikings, or the heroic tales in the classical writings of Virgil and Homer—had told of the existence of a distant, exotic land separated from Europe by the ocean. Although descriptions of this strange, remote world varied from tale to tale, they shared many common characteristics. Most legends depicted a blissful, harmonious, peaceful civilization thriving in a tropical climate and surrounded by great forests, rivers and lakes, and lush vegetation. Because of the fertility of the soil, the inhabitants of this New Eden had only to pick fruit from the heavily laden trees or drop seeds into the rich soil in order to obtain the necessities of life. Resembling Europeans in some ways, these distant people differed from their Old World counterparts in manners, customs, and often physical appearance (such as skin color). In general, tales of this utopian civilization pictured a society possessing enormous wealth and power, one that greatly surpassed Europe in economic, social, and political organization, in technology, in intellectual activity, and in morality. Having conquered disease, famine, poverty, and even war, these simple, virtuous, peace-loving people remained aloof from their less civilized, war-mongering, morally inferior neighbors on the European continent.

The paradisical, utopian image of a distant civilization advanced by such secular legends, was also reinforced by certain deep-seated religious notions. From the Jews and early Christians medieval Europe had inherited a powerful tradition of prophecy. Apocalyptic texts of the Bible—especially those in Daniel, Isaiah, and the Revelation—put forth an eschatology, or doctrine of the last times, that grew increasingly popular toward the end of the Middle Ages. These texts predicted that as the final days approached, the world would become controlled by a demonic, tyrannical, destructive power: "Antichrist" or Satan himself. After inflicting plagues, wars, droughts and famines, turmoil, and great suffering upon God's people, Satan would be bound. This event would then be followed by an age of spiritual revival, the rise of new learning, a reformation of society, Christ's second coming, and the *millennium,* or Christ's reign on earth for a thousand years.

Following the writings of Origen and particularly St. Augustine, the medieval church had sanctioned a spiritualized interpretation of such prophecies. Nevertheless, periodically through the Middle Ages various individuals and groups—Tanchelm, Joachim of Fiore, Peter Waldo, the Taborites, to name a few—interpreted apocalyptic texts literally. To many people, millennial ideas possessed great appeal, and apocalyptic doctrines occasionally led political and social malcontents actively to pursue the millennium through revolution. Still, such movements were repeatedly denounced by the medieval church.

Increasing social, religious, and economic changes during the fifteenth, sixteenth, and early seventeenth centuries, however, lent a new attraction to biblical prophecies. Under the impetus of societal changes, not only unorthodox lay thinkers, but many clerics as well began seriously to examine apocalyptic texts. John Henry Alsted in Germany, John Napier in Scotland, John Foxe, Thomas Brightman, and Joseph Mede in England all began interpreting biblical prophecies in light of recent events and developing an apocalyptic view of history. The Crusades, the Black Death, and particularly the Reformation, Counter-Reformation, and religious wars all persuaded Protestant scholars that they had reached the prelude to the end of the world.

Hence, by the age of discovery, Europeans had formulated strong preconceptions about "America," even though they knew nothing of its physical existence. Engrained secular and religious notions influenced the views of early explorers about the civilizations they encountered. Spaniards surveying the tropical areas of South and Central America were confronted by proud peoples of a different color living in a warm, rich climate. Both the Incas in Peru and the Aztecs in Mexico demonstrated technological sophistication prophesied in old legends. But perhaps more than any other factor, the wealth of these civilizations reinforced the idea that America was a New Eden. Only after the seventeenth century, when European settlers had given up hope of finding precious metals in North America and had experienced hostile Indians and a harsh, cruel climate, did Old World myths concerning America begin to be dispelled.

Nevertheless, even as secular legends of America faded against raw experience, the religious dreams about the New World grew stronger. Upheavals in England and on the European continent led people to view America as a religious haven that God had kept pure and holy for his chosen remnant. The New World became a refuge from religious persecution as Pilgrims, Catholics, Quakers, Huguenots, and many others flocked to its shores. But even more significantly, America became the site for building the perfect, godly, well-ordered Christian society that people expected to see created in the last days. During the early seventeenth century, for example, many English people physically separated themselves from the corruption and decay they saw in the Old World in order to erect holy commonwealths that would sustain the elect during the coming times of trouble.[12]

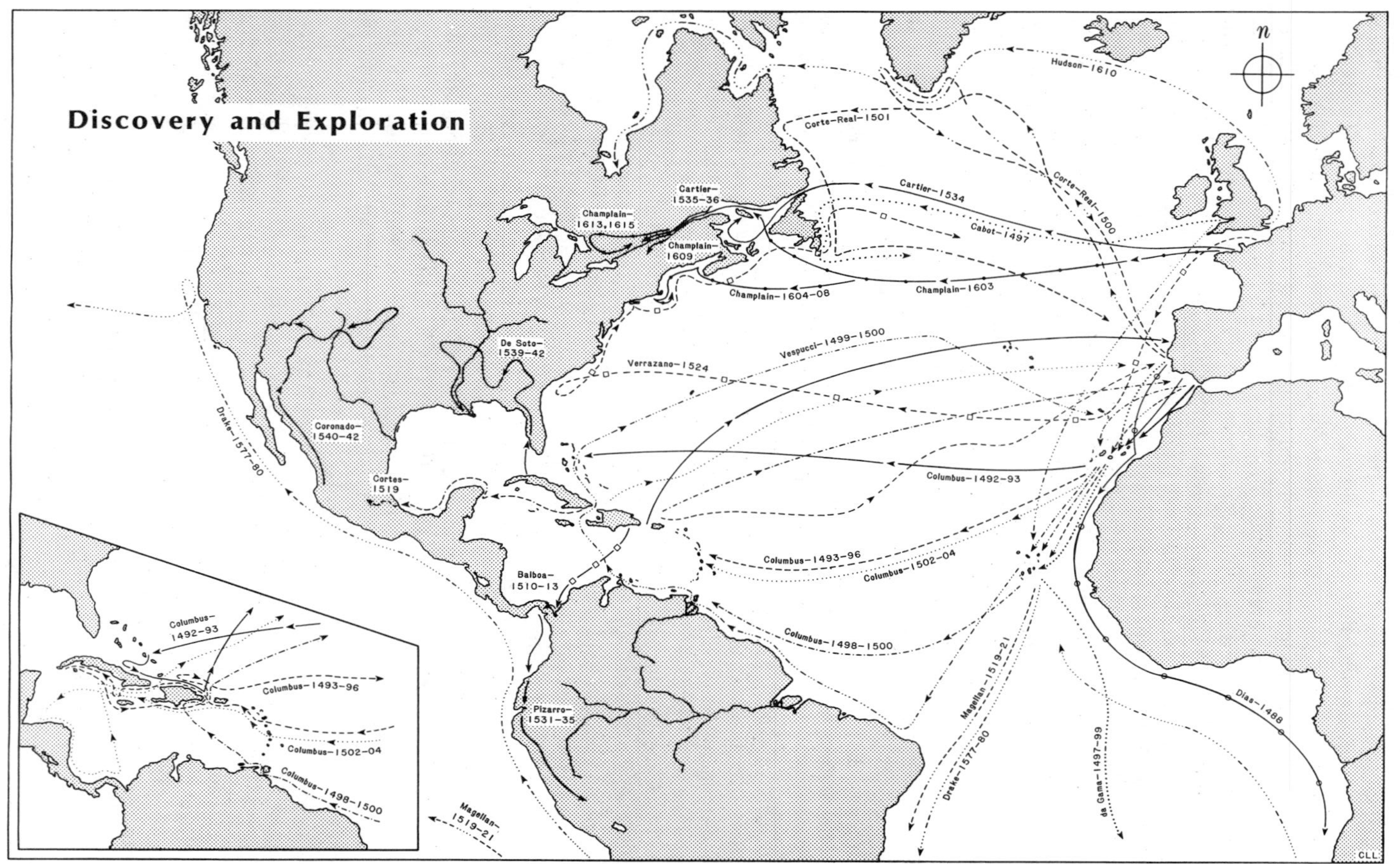
Discovery and Exploration
Hudson–1610
Corte-Real–1501
Corte-Real–1500
Cartier–1534
Cabot–1497
Cartier–
1535–36
Champlain–
1613,1615
Champlain–
1609
Champlain–1604–08
Champlain–1603
De Soto–
1539–42
Vespucci–1499–1500
Verrazano–1524
Coronado–
1540–42
Drake–1577–80
Cortes–
1519
Columbus–1492–93
Columbus–1493–96
Columbus–1502–04
Balboa–
1510–13
Columbus–1498–1500
Pizarro–
1531–35
Magellan–1519–21
Drake–1577–80
da Gama–1497–99
Dias–1488
Magellan–
1519–21
Columbus–
1492–93
Columbus–1493–96
Columbus–1502–04
Columbus–1498–1500
CLL

EARLY EXPLORATION

The Portuguese Venture South

Due to its early political centralization, commercial prosperity, and nationalistic zeal, Portugal became the first European power to explore distant lands and seas. One of the smallest nations in Europe—with a little over a million inhabitants—Portugal was a narrow strip of land bordered by the sea. Its extensive coastline had long sustained interest in ocean commerce; by the late fifteenth century it had developed a vigorous, prosperous merchant class. However, it was not until the reign of Prince Henry the Navigator (1394-1460), after the Moslems had been expelled, that the Portuguese embarked on extensive exploration. Then, they began sailing south, not west, down the African coast.

Like other European rulers, Henry no doubt hoped to find a quick route to the wealth and riches of the East. But perhaps more importantly, the Portuguese prince sought a Christian king called Prestor John who supposedly had built an empire in northwestern Africa. A devout, pious man, Henry hoped to form an alliance with Prestor John and defeat the infidel Moors, who had long preyed upon the Portuguese.

Beyond this, Henry proved a patron to scholars as well as a soldier and ruler. From the early fifteenth century until his death, he systematically encouraged the seafaring arts and sponsored numerous expeditions. During his reign the Portuguese limited their explorations to the coastline of Africa, never penetrating the interior; still, they greatly extended knowledge of those territories they investigated, which went as far south as Dakar. Perhaps even more significant, the Portuguese substantially enhanced the navigational arts with such developments as the quadrant, cross-staff, and compass. The Portuguese also improved the science of cartography, designed ship bottoms, and produced the faster, more maneuverable caravel.

Although interest in exploration waned for a time after Prince Henry's death, with the settlement of certain domestic and foreign difficulties the lure of the riches of the East proved too tempting. In 1487 John II of Portugal commissioned Bartholomew Diaz to find a route to India. Diaz sailed around the southern tip of Africa and up to the Indian Ocean before his crew forced him to turn back. In 1498, Vasco da Gama completed the journey, crossing the Indian Ocean to Calicut. The shipload of jewels, spices, and other exotic goods da Gama brought back from India ensured further expeditions. Two years later Alvarez Cabral, on the first leg of a voyage to the East, claimed Brazil for Portugal. Soon da Gama and other Portuguese captains established trading posts on lands near the Arabian Sea, the Bay of Bengal, and the South China Sea. For the first time the products of the East bypassed the Italian city-states, entering Europe through Lisbon. Portugal's major explorations soon ended, but the tiny seafaring nation had established commercial supremacy in Europe.

Spain

Having observed Portugal's successful exploration to the East, Spain was quick to follow its example. Ironically, Christopher Columbus, the man who launched Spain's century of exploration in the New World, was of Italian descent. Born to a weaver in Genoa about 1451, Columbus very soon developed a fascination with the sea. He spent his early adult years sailing in the Mediterranean as well as up and down the Atlantic, going as far north as Ireland and probably also down the coast of Africa. By the time he went to Lisbon to work with his brother in a chart-making shop, he had become a highly skilled sailor.

During these years Columbus may have come across Marco Polo's account of his trek to China; it is certain that he read and was strongly influenced by Cardinal Pierre d'Ailly's early fifteenth-century work, *Imago Mundi.* In *Imago Mundi* d'Ailly maintained that the Asian continent could be reached by sailing west of the Azores for only a few days. At any rate, by the 1480s Columbus had resolved to find a short western route to China. But before he could embark on such a journey, he needed the financial backing of a European ruler. For almost a decade Columbus attempted to persuade the Portuguese and then the Spanish courts to finance his venture. In early 1492, when Columbus had almost given up hope of persuading the Spanish monarchs, Ferdinand and Isabella, Spain defeated the Moors and took control of Granada. Shortly afterward the Spanish king and queen agreed to grant Columbus a commission as well as a portion of whatever riches he might uncover.

Columbus left Palos in August of 1492, with a convoy of three ships, and sailed for the Canary Islands. Although the expedition experienced fair weather and made rapid progress, the crew became increasingly uneasy and frightened as they faced three, and then four weeks of open sea. In mid-October, ten weeks after leaving Palos and with his crew on the brink of mutiny, Columbus sighted the coastline of an island in the Bahamas which he named San Salvador. From there Columbus went on to discover Cuba, which, as we have noted, he believed to be mainland China. From Cuba he went to Haiti. Although Columbus brought back many items unfamiliar to Europeans–such as tobacco, corn, sweet potatoes, coconuts–he uncovered little gold. Nevertheless, Spain and most of Europe hailed Columbus as the discoverer of a direct, western route to the East.

Because of discrepancies between the report of Columbus and those of his own explorers, John II of Portugal discounted the Spanish claim to have reached China. He insisted that Columbus had only landed on a few remote islands in the Atlantic lying within the area that Portugal had already explored. The Portuguese crown therefore proclaimed these islands Portuguese territory. Ferdinand and Isabella appealed to the Spanish-born pope, Alexander VII, to uphold Spain's right of conquest. In two statements or *bulls,* the pope granted Spain title to the lands Columbus had discovered and drew a demarcation line running north and south 100 leagues west of the Azores. This provision restricted Spanish rights of exploration to the area west of that line. The dispute between Spain and Portugal was finally settled in 1494 with the Treaty of Tordesillas. The treaty confirmed Spanish claims to the lands Columbus had discovered and divided the New World between the two powers with a line running 370 leagues west of the Azores.

Columbus made three additional trips to America. On the first (1494 to 1496), he explored the Virgin Islands, Puerto Rico, and Jamaica, and took a contingent of settlers to Haiti to establish a colony. Following a route slightly farther south on his next voyage (1498 to 1500), Columbus traveled to Trinidad on the northern tip of South America–a place he believed was the long-sought Asian continent. By the time he returned to Spain, however, Diaz, Cabral, and two other Portuguese explorers–Miguel and Caspar Corte-Real–had established that a new world, not Asia, had been discovered by Columbus. Undeterred by this news,

Columbus set out on one more voyage (1502 to 1504) in search of a passage to India. This last expedition ended in failure.

Up to his death in 1506, Columbus insisted that he had reached the Asian continent. Because of a dispute with Ferdinand, Columbus never received a share of the vast wealth that was beginning to pour into Spain from the New World. In addition, the continent Columbus had discovered took its name from Amerigo Vespucci, a Florentine merchant and voyager who claimed to have reached the American continent a year before Columbus landed on it in 1498. Vespucci's assertion was accepted by the German geographer Martin Waldseemuller, who labeled the new continent "America" in a work published in 1507, and the name stuck.

In the years following the discovery of the New World, Spain financed a series of expeditions there. In 1513 a party led by Juan Ponce de Leon explored the east and west coasts of Florida. Also that year another band of explorers, with Vasco Núñez de Balboa at its head, traversed the rugged isthmus of Panama and reached the Pacific Ocean. In 1522 a party headed by Ferdinand Magellan (who was killed in the Philippines before the end of the voyage) sailed around the South American tip, past Australia, through the Indian Ocean, and then around Africa to Europe. The Magellan group completed the first trip around the world, although it failed to discover a shorter, direct route to India. Spain's wealth and subsequent rise as the predominant European power, however, was tied directly to two expeditions. The first occurred between 1519 and 1521, when Hernando Cortés assaulted Mexico from Cuba. Assisted by Indian allies, the outnumbered Spanish force conquered the Aztec empire and along with it a fabulous store of gold and silver. The second expedition destined to reap a vast treasure for Spain was sent out in 1531 under Francisco Pizarro. Within two years Pizarro succeeded in crossing the Panamanian isthmus to Peru and subduing the powerful Incas. With this conquest Spain took control of the silver mines of Potosí and secured wealth even greater than that obtained from the Aztecs.

Spurred by the rich treasures it seized in Mexico and Peru, Spain continued to send out expeditions into the New World. In 1535 and 1536, Cabeza de Vaca established Spanish claims to the North American Southwest while Pedro de Mendoza reached Buenos Aires in Argentina. Between 1539 and 1542 Francisco Vásquez de Coronado led a party to the Grand Canyon and other areas of the Southwest in a fruitless quest for the fabled Seven Cities of Cíbola. About the same time Hernando de Soto headed an expedition from Florida, through the southeast section of North America, to the Mississippi River. By the middle of the sixteenth century, Spain had established a vast empire in America. But none of the territory to the north ever produced the wealth found earlier.

The imperial network Spain created in the New World to control its holdings was highly centralized. The vast lands of New Spain were theoretically considered the property of the king, whose councils managed the empire. In turn, these officials directed an intricate bureaucracy that stretched over numerous provinces, each headed by a governor. By and large, however, most political and economic decisions were made by governing bodies in Spain. The colonial administrative structure tended to rule New Spain in an authoritarian, inflexible, and often harsh manner. It imposed Spanish government, laws, and religion upon the natives. The Spanish empire employed the *encomienda*—a system of Indian servitude—and imported black slaves to supplement the labor force. While the nonwhites mined precious metals, cultivated tobacco and sugar fields, and raised livestock for shipment to Spain, the white population—which remained small and performed mainly administrative functions—grew rich off the profits of the colonies.

Although the Spanish empire exploited blacks and Indians, some things may be said to its credit. For example, the colonial administration of New Spain stopped the intertribal feuding that had characterized Indian life. Also, it established churches, universities, and cultural institutions in the New World. Certainly, it did not deserve the condemnation of the "Black Legend" which developed in Europe, in England, and in America from the sixteenth century on. This tale accused the Spanish of unspeakable cruelty and brutality toward the Indians in the days of conquest and the *encomienda.* Ironically, the impetus for the "Black Legend" came from a Spanish critic of Indian servitude, Bartolomé de Las Casas (1474-1566), who published *A Very Brief Relation of the Destruction of the Indies* in 1552. Las Casas characterized the Indians as "Lambs" who "were without fraud, without subtilty or malice, to their natural Governours most faithful and obedient." Toward the Spanish they were "patient, meek and peaceful, and who laying all contentious and tumultuous thoughts aside, live without any hatred or desire of revenge . . . ." As for his own people—the conquerors—Las Casas wrote:

> To these quiet Lambs, endued with such blessed qualities, came the Spaniards like most cruel Tygres, Wolves and Lions, enraged with a sharp and tedious hunger; for these forty years past, minding nothing else but the slaughter of these unfortunate wretches, whom with divers kinds of torments neither seen nor heard of before, they have so cruelly and inhumanely butchered, that of three millions of people which Hispaniola it self did contain, there are left remaining alive scarce three hundred persons. And for the Island of Cuba . . . . it lies wholly desert. . . . The islands of St. John and Jamaica lie waste and desolate. The Lucayan Islands neighbouring toward the North upon Cuba and Hispaniola . . . . are now totally unpeopled and destroyed; the inhabitants thereof amounting to above 5,000,000 souls, partly killed, and partly forced away to work in other places . . . . Other Islands there were near the Island of St. John more then thirty in number, which were totally made desert. All which Islands, though they amount to such a number containing in length of ground the space of above two thousand miles, lie now altogether solitary without any people or Inhabitant.[13]

Both as an administrative and economic experiment, the Spanish empire proved highly successful. When the French and English founded colonies in North America during the seventeenth century, they imitated the Spanish model in important ways. Both powers attempted, like Spain, to direct colonial political and economic development through governing boards at home. They also strove to transplant European institutions, customs, and laws to American shores. England's colonies in the South Atlantic followed the Spanish practice of importing African slaves in order to ease the labor shortage, while in the Northwest the French copied Spain's pattern of setting up a line of forts and trading posts in order to control its extensive holdings.

Still, the French and British empires differed markedly from New Spain. Neither France nor England succeeded in conquering and "civilizing" the native populations of North America. Lacking an indigenous colonial population, both built their empires upon the labor and industry of immigrants from Europe. That fact alone determined that the British and French North American colonies would evolve much differently from New Spain. By the end of the seventeenth century, the settlements of England and France had acquired considerable political sophistication and were beginning to approach in size and economic activity all but perhaps Spain's islands in the Caribbean.

Despite the continuous flow of wealth from its American empire throughout the sixteenth century, Spain's power began to wane by midcentury. The seeds of its decline were sown in part by the domestic and foreign policies pursued by Phillip II. Under Phillip, who came to the throne in 1556, Spain became increasingly weighted down by an inept, cumbersome, and costly bureaucracy. Also, Spain's continued dependence upon the riches of the New World seriously discouraged economic development and weakened domestic commerce. In addition, Phillip's foreign policies proved injurious to Spain's position in Europe. A zealous Catholic, Phillip attempted to exterminate Protestantism in the Spanish-controlled Netherlands. Sparked by religious fervor and growing nationalism, the Low Countries strenuously resisted Spain's attempts to suppress Protestantism there and revolted in 1566. For the next fifteen years Phillip expended vast amounts of gold prosecuting a war against the Netherlands—a war that ended in 1581 with Dutch independence.

The loss of the Netherlands and the depletion of Spain's bullion reserves seriously drained its economic vitality, while Phillip's support of the dynastic claims of Mary, Queen of Scots (a Catholic) against those of the Protestant Elizabeth (who acceded to the throne in 1558) earned him the enmity of the British crown. Elizabeth aided the Dutch in their revolt and encouraged English privateers such as Sir Francis Drake to plunder Spanish ships. Although Phillip succeeded in conquering Portugal in 1580, Spain's dominance in Europe soon ended. In 1588 the British defeated the Spanish Armada, a blow that proved decisive to Spanish military power. Throughout the seventeenth century Spain still represented a threat in Europe and the Americas, but after its defeat of 1588 Spain's preeminent position in Europe ended and its power in the New World gradually diminished.[14]

France Builds An Empire

During the century that Spain dominated the North American continent, other countries began to intrude into the New World and build their own empires. France first began exploration of America in 1524, when an Italian named Giovanni de Verrazano, who held a French commission to locate the Northwest passage to India, reached the North Atlantic coast. Ten years later, the French king, Francis I, sponsored a French contingent headed by Jacques Cartier. Cartier traveled through the Gulf of St. Lawrence and down the St. Lawrence River to what would become Montreal. Although he and a few other French explorers—such as Jean Ribaut, Gaspard de Coligny, and Rene de Laudonniere—embarked on expeditions in the New World during the 1500s, for the most part French explorations lagged until the seventeenth century.

In 1608, after a period of protracted religious conflict, France resumed her colonizing efforts in America. In that year the geographer and explorer, Samuel de Champlain, established a post at Quebec and then traveled north to Port Royal,

Nova Scotia. Champlain charted the territory along the North Atlantic coast south to Cape Cod. Although the French discovered no gold or silver, they soon built up a thriving fish and fur trade in North America. The waters off Newfoundland became popular fishing grounds, while trappers quickly established a booming fur trade with the Indians living along the Canadian coast. By 1635, when Champlain died, the French had erected military and trading posts throughout the St. Lawrence region.

During the rest of the seventeenth century, however, New France grew rather slowly. Although the prospect of precious metals and free land enticed a few to New France, for the most part the colony had difficulty attracting settlers because of its poor soil and severe climate. The Huguenots, or French Protestants, might have emigrated gladly to New France, but French policies prevented this. Hence, by the end of the seventeenth century, less than 7000 inhabitants populated the French North American empire, while rival British settlements boasted about 300,000.

In addition to difficulties in recruiting colonists, the development of New France was further hampered by the erratic policy of the parent country. Due to a variety of domestic pressures, the French government periodically made substantial changes in the administration of its colonial possessions. Up to the 1620s the fur-trading companies controlled the colony. Then, for a time colonial affairs fell under the management of Cardinal Richelieu. In an attempt to instill greater direction and encourage colonial growth, Richelieu revoked the old trading charters and created the government-sponsored Company of New France. But this agency proved no more successful than its predecessors. In their weakened condition, the French were no match for the British, who captured Quebec in 1629 and controlled the strategic fort for three years. Protracted conflict with the Indians hurt the colony even further. After the Company's failures the Crown finally assumed control of New France in 1663. Under royal direction the colonial empire expanded, but its government and economy continued to depend heavily upon the parent country.[15]

The Netherlands Enters the Race

Like their French neighbor, the Low Countries began exploration of the North American continent rather late. It was not until 1609 that Henry Hudson, himself English, discovered the Hudson River and claimed a part of North America for the Dutch East India Company he represented. Still, within a few years, Dutch vessels were carrying goods to and from the trading post that the United New Netherland Company had established on the southern tip of Manhattan Island. In 1626 Peter Minuit, governor of New Amsterdam, bought the island from the Indians. A few years later the Dutch West India Company, which controlled the colony, began selling large sections of land. In exchange for bringing colonists to New Amsterdam, as the settlement was called, the proprietors received almost feudal rights to land and over the tenants who farmed it. In the early seventeenth century Holland's settlements in the New World multiplied. The Dutch drove out a group of Swedes from the area that would become western New Jersey and spread out along the Hudson and Delaware rivers into the Hudson River Valley. Although the Dutch were more successful than the French in recruiting immigrants to

America, the Netherlands proved less skillful than France in maintaining control over its possessions. The autocratic rule of the *patroons* or large landholders, as well as the Dutch West India Company's emphasis on trade rather than farming, slowed the growth of a strong agricultural class. The diverse character of the Dutch population, along with the rigid nature of Dutch colonial practices, prevented New Amsterdam from developing into a strong, unified, prosperous colony. As the century progressed, the Dutch were unable to stop the intrusion of neighboring British settlers from New England. In 1664 the British defeated the Dutch and converted New Amsterdam into the English colony of New York.

The Advent of the Swedes

Along with other European nations, but particularly inspired by the Dutch example, Sweden also made forays into the New World. Although the noted Swedish military leader and king, Gustavus Adolphus, expressed some interest in colonizing America during the 1620s, it was six years after his death in 1638 before the Swedes established a foothold in the New World. Situated on the Delaware River, near present-day Newport and Wilmington, Fort Christina, as the settlement was called, was founded by the Swedish West India Company.

In the twenty-five or so years of its independent existence, New Sweden grew slowly from about forty to a peak of 400 people, and then declined. For much of the time, the colony was ruled by Johan Bjornsson Printz, a soldier whose military bent impressed itself upon New Sweden. The populace primarily trapped and farmed. The close proximity of Dutch settlements, along with rivalry between the two nationalities for the fur trade, eventually led to the takeover of New Sweden by the Dutch in 1655.[16]

2

England in America

In 1500 England was a tiny medieval kingdom and a second-rate power by almost any standard of measurement. Yet, by 1763, it had become Great Britain, the strongest nation on earth. The key to its later strength lay in its mighty colonial empire, its dominance over the Atlantic trade, and the strength and maturity of its domestic economy which was the product of both. England's rise to power and its worldwide expansionism were, in turn, the products of its rapid and profound transformation from a medieval to an essentially "modern" state. In that transformation, nearly all of the social, political, economic, and religious forces which we discussed in the last chapter played vital and easily discernible roles.

In the late fifteenth century the protracted War of the Roses—a dynastic struggle between the rival York and Lancaster families—exterminated a large portion of the nobility, hampered economic growth, and placed the government of the new king—Henry Tudor—on a precarious footing. Still, within the century, Spain found its position in Europe and its North American empire under challenge from the British. England's ability to establish permanent, prosperous colonies in the New World was due to several factors.

First, during the sixteenth and seventeenth centuries, the English economy underwent phenomenal change. Between 1500 and 1600 the population doubled. Also, a period of rapid inflation forced many of the aristocracy to sell off their lands to smaller landowners, resulting in what has been called the "rise of the gentry." It is not clear just how hard inflation hit the nobility, but it is certain that by the seventeenth century the gentry had secured substantial political and economic power based on the land it had acquired from the aristocracy and the Crown.[1] In various positions—such as representatives of Parliament or royal officials—merchants and gentry promoted government policies that favored their interests. Merchants sought and frequently received monopolies on certain products or areas of trade. For example, between 1550 and 1600 Elizabeth granted exclusive charters to several trading concerns, such as the Muscovy, Levant, and East India companies.

As the gentry grew more powerful and economically influential, two developments in particular proved enormously important in spurring English economic growth during the sixteenth century. One was the advent of the coal industry. The English mined coal because the fuel source upon which they had depended for centuries—wood—was disappearing. Coal burned hotter than wood. That fact not only helped existing industries like glass making but it led directly to the creation of new ones. Of these, none had greater long-range significance for England than iron production. The other development was the expansion of wool production and the wool trade. For years English wool growers had tried to meet domestic and continental demand for wool and wool products by draining marshes and converting tillable land into pastures for sheep (the latter was called the *enclosure* movement). By the end of the sixteenth century they achieved success and wool growers and merchants realized huge profits from the creation and exportation of wool and woolen products. Former agricultural workers and landless peasants provided the labor for the growing woolen industry. Mostly, they worked at home in what was known as the *putting-out* system. Employers found that it was easier and less expensive to have employees work on spinning wheels and looms in their own homes rather than to try to concentrate workers and equipment in a single building.

Second, besides rapid economic growth, England also experienced a significant change in its political order. Between 1500 and 1600 the Tudors succeeded in transforming Britain into a centralized national state. Like other European sovereigns, the Tudors and then the Stuarts slowly expanded royal power. They won over opponents by granting titles, offices, lands, and commercial favors. They also effectively used the royal administration, prerogative courts, and church hierarchy to extend further royal authority. By the early seventeenth century, James I was following the lead of other European monarchs and advancing the theory of *divine right of kings.*

Nevertheless, the English king did not acquire the absolutist power that continental sovereigns possessed. All the while royal authority was increasing, the gentry and commercial classes were also expanding their power through Parliament. During the early sixteenth century, Henry VIII allowed and even encouraged parliamentary activity because he could use it to promote his own ends. For example, in the 1530s Henry created the Church of England, dissolved the monasteries, and sold church lands by acting through parliamentary legislation. Although the English king probably could have achieved the same results through royal decree, he worked through Parliament in order to minimize his opposition. In shrewdly operating within the parliamentary structure, Henry VIII and then Elizabeth strengthened royal authority. At the same time, however, the assembly of nobles was evolving into a representative body that asserted its own independent, inviolable powers and prerogatives. By the end of the seventeenth century, the English political system had developed into a constitutional monarchy with legislative initiative residing mainly in Parliament.

Both political and economic changes laid the domestic foundation for England's eventual imperial dominance, but in the early seventeenth century, Britain still needed several ingredients essential for economic self-sufficiency and world power: an ample store of bullion to facilitate commercial transactions; a stable, reliable source of raw materials; and a permanent, expanding market for manufactured products. By establishing colonies in North America, England hoped to discover needed bullion, produce raw materials, and create markets for its finished goods. By 1700, its success in these areas led many English theorists, planners, merchants, politicians, and the like to dream of a self-sufficient Britain, economically dominant in the New World and the Old.[2]

THE ENGLISH REFORMATION

Despite its physical separation from the rest of Europe, Britain fell under the influence of Protestant ideas during the sixteenth century, and those ideas—together with the Protestant establishment which followed—provided a stimulus for overseas expansion. In Scotland, under the influence of John Knox, the church had been reordered along Calvinist lines, and in England the ideas of other reformers were spreading. Nevertheless, the English Reformation that occurred under Henry VIII resulted from political rather than religious motives. Henry VIII had originally adopted a hostile attitude toward Protestantism. In fact, in 1521 the pope had granted Henry the title of "Defender of the Faith" for writing *Assertio Septem Sacramentorum,* a work directed against Luther's treatises on the sacraments. And yet, thirteen years later, Henry Tudor refuted the authority of the papacy and declared himself to be "supreme head" of the English church. This dramatic turnabout in religious policy was precipitated by Henry's obsession to ensure Tudor dynastic rule through a male heir. Since his marriage to Catherine of Aragon had produced only a daughter and Catherine was now in her forties, Henry sought an annulment of his marriage. When the pope, bowing to pressure from Catherine's nephew, King Charles V of Spain, refused Henry's petition, the English king repudiated papal jurisdiction and established an "Anglican" Church under his sole authority. Following the break from Rome the English crown stopped payments to the pope, dissolved the monasteries, sold off many church lands, and initiated some changes in the worship service. Despite these actions, however, the Anglican Church created in 1534 differed little from the old institution. For the most part the clergy transferred allegiance from the pope to the king and continued much as before. Indeed, the doctrine of the English church, as set out in the Six Articles of 1539, retained many prescriptions of Catholicism.

Henry's death in 1547 brought his 10-year-old son, Edward VI, to the throne. Actual power, however, passed to Edward Seymour, Duke of Somerset, the uncle of Edward and regent until the young king came of age. Under Somerset, who held strong Protestant views, Thomas Cranmer, Archbishop of Canterbury, brought Protestant doctrines into the English church. The Protestant cause received a severe setback in 1553, when Edward died and Mary Tudor, daughter of Catherine of Aragon and a stern Catholic, acceded to the throne. Mary sought to reestablish Catholicism in England, and during her reign hundreds of Protestants fled to sympathetic religious centers on the Continent, such as Strasbourg, Geneva, and

Frankfurt. Only five years later, the pendulum once again swung back to the Protestant side. Upon Mary's death in 1558, Elizabeth, Henry's daughter by Anne Boleyn, assumed the reins of power. Under the influence of the "Marian exiles" who brought back strong Calvinist ideas, Elizabeth reestablished the Protestant religion in England. Her version of Protestantism, however, was unique. Seeking to create a national church that could accommodate a variety of religious beliefs and serve as a tool of royal policy, Elizabeth established a church government that retained the episcopal hierarchy and vestments of Catholicism, assumed a subordinate position to civil authority like Lutheranism, and sanctioned certain doctrines of Calvinism.[3]

THE RISE OF PURITANISM

Elizabeth's church settlement served her well during her forty-five year reign. The "middle way" she followed kept the majority of the English–including those with Protestant and Catholic tendencies–within the fold of the state church. Nevertheless, even Elizabeth's moderate approach to religious questions generated opposition. From about 1560 onwards, a small but influential group of Calvinists voiced strong opposition to the church settlement. Because they demanded that the church be "purified" from the remaining corrupt vestiges of Catholicism, these Protestants became known as *Puritans.* Puritans objected to the continued use of "Romish" ceremonies such as the liturgy, kneeling, and the wearing of robes. Even more strongly, they denounced the episcopal hierarchy as popish and unscriptural, urging instead the Calvinist form of church government that rooted authority initially in the congregation of saints and bodies of church elders called presbyteries.

A few early Puritans became so disgusted with the English church that they urged total separation from it. *Separatists* such as Robert Browne and John Robinson attempted to form separate "pure" congregations in England, but they were forced to flee to Holland in order to practice their religion. Most Puritans, however, maintained their ties to the existing state church while advocating a return to the pristine condition of the early Christian Church. The *Pilgrims* who settled in Plymouth in 1620 were Separatists, while the majority of the Puritans, who founded the Massachusetts Bay Colony ten years later and played a dominant part in the religious and political development of the colony, were "nonseparating" Congregationalists.[4]

EARLY ENGLISH SETTLEMENTS

Although one of the last European states to formally colonize the New World, England had sent out explorers as early as 1497, when John Cabot reached the shores of Newfoundland under a commission from Henry VII. Preoccupied with domestic problems, Henry sponsored no further expeditions to America. Nevertheless, Cabot's tales of New World bounty caught the attention of English seafarers who were quick to exploit the rich fishing grounds off Newfoundland and develop a prosperous trade.

The English Crown's interest did not return to America until the end of

Elizabeth's reign. The reason was that English "expansion" moved in other directions during the sixteenth century. Under Elizabeth, the English attempted to "pacify" and dominate the British Isles (especially Scotland and Ireland), to undermine the power of Imperial Spain, and to challenge the European commercial hegemony of the Netherlands and the great city of Antwerp. To accomplish these foreign objectives Elizabethans formed joint-stock trading companies to tap the potential of the continents of Asia and Africa as well as the Baltic and Mediterranean regions closer to home. The Muscovy Company was established in 1555 to develop Baltic trade and to find a northeast passage through Russia to the Orient. The Royal African Company was created in 1588 to develop the African slave trade while, four years later, the Levant Company organized to promote trade in the Mediterranean. In 1602, the East India Company was chartered to establish direct ocean routes to Asia. In each case the English borrowed from Spanish practice and founded coastal trading posts designed to siphon off the wealth of a particular region.

Then, in the 1580s, several individuals—most notably Sir Humphrey Gilbert, Sir Walter Raleigh, Richard Eburne, Sir Francis Walsingham (one of Elizabeth's most influential ministers), Sir Francis Drake, Richard Hakluyt the Elder, and his nephew, Richard Hakluyt the Younger—began a campaign to encourage British exploration and colonization of North America. In numerous writings these men helped to favorably condition English attitudes toward colonization. Tracts such as Gilbert's *Discourse of a Discovery for a New Passage to Catia,* for example, convinced many that the North American continent hid a direct "Northwest passage" to China. Both Martin Frobisher and John Davis set out to find such a route to the East. Although they failed to locate the mythical passage, the two men explored much of the North Atlantic coast, providing valuable information for later colonization attempts. The writings of Gilbert, the Hakluyts, and others developed arguments for colonization that were repeated and expanded upon well into the nineteenth century. Notions of planting New World military posts to assault Spanish power, of achieving economic self-sufficiency, of spreading the Protestant religion, and of creating American markets for English manufactured goods were advanced to support the exploration of the New World. These ideas won converts to colonization not only because of the promises they held forth but also because they fed the tide of rising English nationalism.

Other advocates of English colonization were captivated more by old legends of magnificent "lost" civilizations teeming with gold and silver. For them America's promise lay in discovering precious metals and providing England with a source of bullion equal to that of Spain. As early as 1516 Sir Thomas More combined mythology with Spanish tales of conquest in his work *Utopia.* More described a distant Eden where people had achieved social and individual perfection in an environment of material splendor. Although More's society was a creation of his imagination, as the century wore on English writers enlarged upon More's story of a remote paradise and placed it squarely in the New World. The existence of the New World made the mythological seem real. Indians became simple, honest, guileless people living in harmony with each other and with nature. Spanish colonies existed in lush, warm climes, and Spain's New World cities overflowed with gold and silver. Armed with such visions English writers advertised continually the likelihood that even greater and wealthier societies awaited discovery by the adventuresome. Hence, the idea of

America combined both the dream of individual wealth and power with the hope for national greatness.

The stories of New World wealth were made plausible by English ships and sea captains returning from voyages of plunder with holds filled with Spanish gold and silver from New World mines. One of the most famous of the English "sea dogs" was John ("Jack") Hawkins who made numerous voyages into Spanish West Indian waters looking for trade and plunder. A young man named John Sparke accompanied Hawkins on one of his voyages (1564 to 1565) and later published an account of what happened (1589). Describing the first visit by the English to Florida (and their first contact with tobacco) Sparke revealed typical attitudes of the Elizabethan English toward the New World when he wrote that, though Hawkins found little gold in Florida, the prospects of raising cattle for trade seemed excellent. "Here I haue declared the estate of Florida, and the commodities therein to this day knowen," he wrote,

> which although it may seeme vnto some, by the meanes that the plentie of Golde and Siluer is not so abundant, as in other places, that the cost bestowed vpon the same, will not bee able to quite the charges: yet I am of the opinion that by that which I haue seene in other Islandes of the Indians, where such increase of cattell hath been that of twelue head of beasts in 25. yeeres, did in the hides of them raise 1000. pound profite yeerely, that the increase of cattell onely would raise profite sufficient for the same. [However, he concluded,] because there is not the thing wee all seeke for, [gold] being rather desirous of present gaines, I do therefore affirme the attempt thereof [to establish trade with the Florida Indians] to be more requisite for a prince, who is of power able to goe thorow with the same, rather than for any subject.[5]

The "Prince" in question was Queen Elizabeth and, despite the tales of Sparke and the propaganda of the Hakluyts and others, her fear of Spanish power coupled with domestic problems and the feebleness of the royal treasury dampened her enthusiasm for exploration and colonization. Nevertheless, in 1578 she granted Humphrey Gilbert a six-year charter to found a colony in the New World. Armed with a force of over 400 Gilbert and Sir Walter Raleigh, his half brother, attempted to establish a military fortress in America as a prelude to planting a colony. Severe weather, however, caused the expedition's failure. Gilbert made another attempt to erect a colony in Newfoundland in 1583. Despite perseverance and enthusiasm, the second venture failed and Gilbert was lost at sea on the return voyage.

Undeterred by the Gilbert tragedy, Raleigh obtained a new charter from Elizabeth in 1584. Before embarking on a full-scale colonization attempt, however, Raleigh sent out a well-equipped advance party to survey the North Atlantic coast. The party returned with favorable reports on the land, climate, and natives. Raleigh named the newly discovered territory "Virginia" after Elizabeth, the "Virgin Queen," in hopes that the Crown would subsidize further exploration. Always in a precarious financial position, Elizabeth refused to do more than consent to further colonizing attempts. Raleigh therefore had to drum up private backing for the second expedition. In 1585 he again sent out a small force under Richard Grenville. The party explored the Chesapeake Bay area and approved of Roanoke Island as a conducive site for the colony. After all of these preparations, in 1587 Raleigh planted a small group of settlers on the island off North Carolina, leaving ample provisions for about a year. Due to the attack of the Spanish Armada on England, however, the governor of the settlement, John White, was prevented from returning to Roanoke with supplies until 1590. By that time his daughter, son-in-law, and granddaughter, Virginia Dare, along with the entire colony, had disappeared.

Early attempts by the English to colonize America failed miserably in part because the colonizers lacked the experience to adequately plan and finance such ventures. And yet, within seventy-five years of Raleigh's disaster, English settlements in North America were flourishing. There were several reasons why. First, the English learned ever so slowly that precious metals were not abundant in North America, that climate and geography were not the lush tropics of the legends or of much of Spanish America, and that colonies would have to survive for many years before they would show a profit from agriculture. Therefore, better planning and better financing were important aspects of seventeenth-century endeavors. Financing, in particular, proved critical, and it was supplied by the merchants—the paladins of an expanding England and a growing English economy. By the first decades of the seventeenth century their capital was such that through combined efforts (called joint-stock companies), they could support colonial ventures through dismal early years. Second, unlike Spain, France, or the Netherlands, England produced ordinary citizens who were willing to migrate to America and who did so by the thousands before 1650. Some were lured by the stories of the Hakluyts and others of fertile soil and a tolerable climate. Some considered it a reasonable alternative to debtor's prison. A few came hoping to find instant wealth through gold and silver. Most, though, left their homes and comfortable middle-level existences in the wake of religious and political conflict that increasingly characterized England during the first half of the seventeenth century.

In 1603 James Stuart—James VI of Scotland—ascended to the throne of England. He not only inherited the financial problems that had plagued Elizabeth, but he made his situation worse through imprudent spending and costly foreign wars. Unlike modern governments, the English monarchy was expected to assume costs for maintaining the government, for prosecuting wars, and for supporting the royal household. Within a few years, therefore, James found himself in serious financial straits. His difficulties were further exacerbated by dependence on Parliament. While James resisted Parliament's efforts to expand its own power at the expense of royal prerogative, the precarious financial position of the Crown continually forced him to seek money from Parliament.

In an effort to improve his situation, James began selling titles and granting charters to various individuals and groups in exchange for loans to the Crown. This practice indirectly proved a boon to colonization. It enabled promoters to receive royal sanction for such efforts and also provided a way for religious and political dissidents to find a climate more conducive to their beliefs. Other policies pursued by the early Stuarts helped spark colonization. Under the leadership of King Charles I (1625 to 1649) and William Laud, Bishop of London from 1628 to 1633 and Archbishop of Canterbury after 1633, the English church embraced a policy of conformity that made Puritan dreams of reforming the church look more and more remote. In addition, Puritans found it increasingly difficult to accommodate themselves to the established church. Many Puritan clergy were removed from their posts, while the church itself—under Laud's influence—seemed to be taking on the appearance of the Roman Catholic Church. By the 1630s, therefore, many middle-class landowners and merchants saw America as a refuge from the increasingly uncomfortable religious climate in England.[6]

VIRGINIA

England's expansion into North America began in earnest in 1606 when two groups of merchants—one from London, the other from the West Country—received permission from James I to settle in the New World. By their charter the London merchants, who formed the joint-stock Virginia Company of London, obtained rights to the southern half of Virginia. The other group, organized as the Virginia Company of Plymouth, or Plymouth Company, held rights to the northern half of Virginia. The London or Virginia Company (both names were used) was comprised of a select group of investors from the city of London who hoped their enterprise would either reap profits in gold and other precious minerals or locate a short route to the treasures of the East. With private financing more than 100 colonists left England in 1606 and headed for America. In early 1607 they arrived on the coast of Virginia and quickly moved inland up the James River to a site that would afford protection against an Indian or Spanish attack. Despite extensive preparations, the party made innumerable mistakes. The location of Jamestown, as the settlement was called, was wet and marshy and therefore unhealthy for the unacclimated arrivals. In addition, the contentious, faction-ridden ruling council was unable to organize the settlement, much less enforce discipline over the gold-hungry colonists. As a result the colony failed to build necessary shelters, and delayed planting too long to adequately replenish its food supply. By the time the new colonists arrived with supplies in early 1608, only thirty-eight settlers remained alive. The rest had died from exposure, disease, or starvation.

The next few years were crucial ones for Virginia. Without the firm discipline and planning of Captain John Smith, the settlement would undoubtedly have failed. In 1609 the company obtained a new charter. Under the leadership of Sir Thomas Smythe, the Company succeeded in attracting financial backing and additional settlers to Virginia. The influx of new people, however, created serious housing and food shortages and led to the "starving time" of the 1609 to 1610 winter. In order to improve the colony's chances of survival, governors Thomas Gates, Lord Thomas De La Warr, and Thomas Dale enforced a rigid code of behavior. By 1619 the severe discipline and control had relaxed with improved conditions. With such measures as the *head-right,* a system initiated in 1618 which granted fifty acres of land to immigrants who remained in the colony for three years, the Company was able to lure more settlers to Virginia. The experiments with tobacco by John Rolfe provided a real boon to the colony's economy. By 1627 planters were exporting a half million pounds of the crop.

Following instructions received from London in 1619, Sir George Yeardley, the new governor of Virginia, created a general assembly in Jamestown patterned after the company's governing board in London. Although the governor and counselors received appointments from the council in London, the assembly—soon called the House of Burgesses—was chosen by the colonists themselves. Despite the joint-stock company's success in Virginia, developments in the early 1620s indirectly caused the Company's demise. Virginia had maintained cordial relations with the Indians during the rule of Powhatan. However, Opechancanough, Powhatan's successor, resented the continuing encroachments of the white intruders. In 1622 he led an Indian attack in which 347 settlers were killed. The Indian uprising not only weakened the colony, but it pushed the Company into bankruptcy. In 1624 the colony's charter was revoked, and Virginia was placed under royal control.

The Indian rebellion in Virginia had a serious impact upon colonists elsewhere as well. European contacts with native Americans in the early seventeenth century slowly caused perceptions of the Indian to change. The image of a peace-loving, simple, "noble savage" of European heroic tales and folk legends was replaced by a more negative image of the Indian—one that was used to justify European expansion across the North American continent.[7]

PLYMOUTH PLANTATION

The Puritan movement under Elizabeth and James was characterized by two distinct attitudes toward the Anglican Church. The majority of Puritans believed that the Church of England needed to be purged of certain "popish" practices and sought to reform it from within. The other, small group of Puritans held "separatist" beliefs. Unlike the majority of Puritans, Separatists considered the English church too tainted with popish ways to be reformed. Hence, they felt obliged to withdraw or separate themselves from it.

The Pilgrims—the small party of religious dissenters who established Plymouth Colony—were Separatists. Originally members of a small congregation organized by William Brewster in Scrooby, Nottinghamshire, the Pilgrims left England in 1608 to escape the hostility and intolerance of their community. Under the leadership of their minister, John Robinson, over 100 members of the congregation migrated to Leyden in the Netherlands, where the populace was more tolerant of their religious beliefs. Although the Separatists were unmolested in Leyden, several aspects of their new life disturbed them. According to William Bradford's *History of Plymouth Plantation,* the Pilgrims feared, among other things, that Dutch influences would corrupt their children and that the Spanish might reestablish control over the Low Countries and again attempt to eradicate Protestantism. But in addition, Bradford wrote, the English Separatists in Leyden strongly felt the call of God to settle the New World and thus advance "the gospell of the kingdom of Christ in those remote parts of the world."[8]

Hence, after several years in the Netherlands, Brewster, along with a number of other Pilgrim leaders, approached Sir Edwin Sandys about settling the territory within the Virginia Company's charter. With Sandys' assistance, Robinson obtained permission from James I to settle in America. Having obtained both royal sanction and a patent from the Virginia Company of London, the Pilgrims still needed capital and supplies to launch their venture. Thomas Weston, a London merchant and promoter, offered to arrange the financing of the expedition, but only under the condition that a joint-stock company, modeled after earlier colonizing efforts and including non-Separatist members, be created. By September, 1620, when the *Mayflower* left Plymouth, less than a third of the 100 or so passengers were Pilgrims.

After a little over two months the party sighted the North American coast. However, weather had pushed them to Cape Cod, several hundred miles north of their intended destination and well beyond the area under their patent. Because they had landed beyond the territory delineated in the London Company charter, some of the colonists, as Bradford put it, by "discontente and mutinous speeches" argued that "when they came ashore they would use their owne libertie for none had power to command them."[9] Despite such dissension, wiser spirits prevailed and the Pilgrims drafted an agreement similar in form to the church covenants used to govern Separatist congregations. The result was the Mayflower Compact. In this document the colonists consented to "covenant and combine our selves togeather into a civill body politick, for our better ordering and preservation." Further, they swore to "enacte, constitute, and frame such just and equall lawes, ordinances, acts, constitutions, and offices, from time to time, as shall be thought most meete and convenient for the generall good of the Colonie, unto which we promise all due submission and obedience."[10] Although the Compact had no legality, nevertheless it rooted the colony government upon the principle of mutual consent and helped ensure order during the early days of settlement.

Having left England in the fall, the expedition arrived in America too late to prepare adequately for the coming winter. The bitter cold and rugged conditions of New England took their toll on the colony, and by spring only about half of the settlers were still alive. Nevertheless, with assistance from the Indians, the survivors planted corn and caught fish for the coming winter. Conditions remained bleak in 1621, with no supplies coming from England and winter again setting in. Still, after the harvest the Pilgrims, in the custom of the time, proclaimed and observed a day of Thanksgiving. Within a few years the hard work and struggle produced a thriving, if small, colony. In 1627 the colony paid off Weston and the London stockholders. Despite Plymouth's success in 1621 in obtaining a patent from the Council for New England (the old Plymouth Company) that legalized the colony's settlement, William Bradford, governor for most of Plymouth's early history, actively sought a royal charter that would guarantee the colony's autonomy and help ensure its survival. Bradford's efforts never succeeded and eventually Plymouth fell under the orb of its larger, more populous neighbor. In 1691 Plymouth was incorporated into Massachusetts Bay.

MASSACHUSETTS BAY

Although the Puritan migration to New England in 1630 turned out to be one of Britain's most impressive colonizing efforts, neither it nor Plymouth Plantation was the first enterprise aimed at settling the northern Atlantic shores. As early as 1607 the Plymouth Company, headed by Sir Ferdinando Gorges, Humphrey Gilbert's son Raleigh Gilbert, and Sir George Popham sent out a party to explore and settle New England. In the summer of that year the expedition established the garrison of Fort St. George on the Kennebec (or Sagadahoc) River in Maine. Leaving behind a small contingent to hold the fort, the rest of the party sailed back to England with the intention of returning with additional settlers and supplies the following spring. Popham, who was put in charge of the settlement, was past 70 and lacked the ability to exact discipline and control the colony. As a result, the small outpost was soon seething with factionalism and discontent. Problems in governing the colony, coupled with the deaths of Popham and his brother, Sir John Popham, the company's major investor, doomed the Sagadahoc experiment.

Despite this early failure, interest in *New England,* as Captain John Smith enthusiastically labeled the area, continued. Smith helped revitalize colonization efforts with his exploration of the region in 1614. Smith's tract, *A Description of New England,* which was published two years later, used glowing terms to characterize the area. In New England, Smith declared, "nature and liberty affords vs that freely, which in *England* we want or it costeth vs dearely." The land was so bountiful, he continued, "if a man worke but three dayes in seauen, he may get more than hee can spend, vnlesse he will be excessiue."[11] With such promises being held forth, it is not surprising that entrepreneurs and adventurers would find New England appealing.

In 1620 a number of English promoters, among them Gorges, Raleigh Gilbert, and Sir Francis Popham, revamped the old Plymouth Company into the "Council for New England." Operating under a new charter from James I, the Council began dispensing patents to various individuals and groups. Three years later, a party of West Country investors formed the Dorchester Company. Securing a patent from the Council for New England, the Company, under the leadership of the noted Puritan divine, John White, placed a small contingent on Cape Ann. Despite their high hopes and ambitions, the colonists lasted only a year. By 1626 the Dorchester Company had become defunct and only a few stalwarts, headed by Roger Conant, continued on at the small settlement they called Salem.

Spurred by growing religious conflict and increasing tension between king and Parliament, a second cluster of Puritan entrepreneurs formed the New England Company and obtained a patent from the Council for New England to colonize a northern portion of the Council's territory. In 1628, a small advance party led by John Endicott set sail for the post at Salem. There they began building shelters and collecting foodstuffs for a larger migration of Puritans expected later.

Meanwhile, several influential Puritans persuaded an unsympathetic king, Charles I, to grant them a royal charter. The old New England Company was reorganized into the Massachusetts Bay Company with the same territory and powers designated by the old patent. Profiting from the knowledge learned from previous colonizing attempts, these Puritans solicited solid financial support from merchants hopeful of rich profits and they were successful in obtaining adequate funding for the first group of about 400 colonists who embarked for Salem in 1629. A year later another 700 settlers followed. This larger body represented the core of hearty Puritan spirits and secular adventurers who would settle at Boston and fashion one of England's most successful colonies.

Although the Bay Company certainly reflected the commercial aspirations of the merchants who financed it, the Company enterprise nevertheless also evinced the strong religious motives of its first settlers. Many Puritans sought escape from religious persecution, but that represented only part of their religious quest. They also sought escape from the corruption of the Old World and the opportunity to create a second Jerusalem in the New. The men who became leaders of the colony —such as Sir Richard Saltonstall, Thomas Dudley, and John Winthrop—believed that they were engaged in a divinely inspired mission to establish a godly society in the midst of the wilderness. Winthrop, who was governor of Massachusetts Bay for almost twenty years, felt strongly that the Puritan settlement represented an essential part of God's final plan for the world. In his *Model of Christian Charity,* an address given while aboard the *Arabella,* Winthrop likened his small band to the Israelites of the Old Testament. He reminded his sea-weary troop that they had made a covenant with God to "be as a Citty upon a Hill" and to serve as a holy model for the rest of the world.

But even as Winthrop conveyed this sense of religious mission, in practical fashion he spoke to another, more immediate purpose. In this wilderness, this state of nature, he stressed, the colonists must remember that true Christian charity would be realized only through Christian obedience. Winthrop emphasized that the general good—indeed, the survival of the colony—would be threatened by unbridled individual freedom. He therefore admonished his company to subjugate personal goals and ambitions to the public welfare:

> We must be knit together in this work as one man, we must entertaine each other in brotherly Affection, we must be willing to abridge our selves of our superfluities, for the supply of others necessities, we must uphold a familiar Commerce together in all meakness, gentleness, patience and liberality . . . always having before our eyes our Commission and the Community in the work, our Community as members of the same body.

If the settlers did this, they would receive the Almighty's favor and assistance. But if they breached their covenant, they would provoke God's wrath. As Winthrop warned his fellow passengers, "when God giues a speciall Commission he lookes to haue it stricktly obserued in every Article."[12]

In its first decade Massachusetts Bay's political, religious, and social order to some extent reflected the sentiments of Winthrop. The colony limited and carefully governed the distribution of land, restricted the political franchise and office holding to church members, established a college to train godly ministers, and passed laws to regulate commerce. Still, as we discuss later, the Bay Colony was faced with powerful pressures from a flood of new settlers and from the lure of the frontier. The easy accessibility of land, the spread of settlements beyond the pale of authority, and the influx of secularly minded colonists unsympathetic to Puritan aims all caused continual modifications of the colony's structure and institutions. By 1640 Massachusetts was already manifesting the individualistic, commercial traits that would define the "Yankee" character of New England for later generations.

Ironically, one of the first challenges to the Bay Colony came from an individual who herself shared Puritan aims and aspirations: Mistress Anne Hutchinson. Hutchinson had migrated to Boston in late 1634 following the renowned Puritan minister, John Cotton, who left England in 1633 to fill the post of teacher at the Boston church. A strong-willed, outspoken, rather charismatic individual, Hutchinson soon won her own circle of disciples and began conducting weekly religious sessions at her home. Hutchinson's practices soon caused alarm, for her meetings progressed from discussion of the week's sermons into open criticisms of the

Massachusetts clergy. Hutchinson went so far as to imply that virtually all the Bay ministers were spiritually unfit to preach and teach the Gospel.

Hutchinson's doubts about the Massachusetts clergy were rooted in her Antinomian beliefs. Antinomianism, a term meaning against the word, exalted the voice of the spirit over the dictates of Scripture. Mistress Hutchinson believed that visible demonstrations of godliness–such as charitable works, church attendance, participation in the sacraments–were unreliable signs of an individual's inner condition. Further, she asserted that the Holy Spirit had revealed itself to her and that a "true believer" could ascertain whether or not another individual was saved. By replacing guidance through God's written word with personal revelation, Mistress Hutchinson not only challenged the basis of the congregational church but denied the validity of all human law, religious and civil. Logically, Hutchinson's position meant that an individual was obligated to follow the voice of the spirit, even if it called for him or her to violate holy Scripture.

Although Antinomian ideas flourished in England during the Civil Wars of the 1640s, particularly among the soldiery of Parliament's army, authorities in both England and Massachusetts recognized the danger such views posed to church and state. In England, following Parliament's victory, the new republic tightened control over sectarians. In Boston, the storm surrounding Hutchinson split the town into two camps, with Hutchinson winning the support of the young Massachusetts governor, Sir Henry Vane. After a protracted controversy–which resulted in Vane's departure back to England–the General Court convicted Hutchinson of sedition and expelled her from the colony. She moved to Rhode Island for a time and then to New York. In 1643 she was killed by Indians.[13]

RHODE ISLAND

Another exile from the Bay Colony preceded Hutchinson to Rhode Island and was primarily responsible for the survival of the colony's independence. Roger Williams, a mild yet fearless and devout man, had migrated to New England at the age of 27. Born to a London shopkeeper, Williams was nevertheless able to study divinity at Pembroke College, Cambridge, due to the generosity of the noted justice, Sir Edward Coke. At Pembroke Williams imbibed Puritan views. He served as a secretary to Coke, and then became the private chaplain of Sir William Masham of Essex. By 1631, when he arrived in Massachusetts Bay, Williams had not only become a staunch Puritan opponent of Archbishop Laud but an ardent Separatist. Because the Boston church continued to recognize the validity of the Church of England, Williams declined an offer from them and journeyed first to the "purer" climes of Salem and then Plymouth. Returning to Salem in 1633, Williams assisted in the congregation while continuing to criticize the condition of the Massachusetts churches. In 1635, after an ecclesiastical dispute, Williams withdrew even from the fellowship of his own congregation. His Separatist views eventually led him to accept the opinions of an English sect called the Seekers. Like his close friend and fellow Seeker, Henry Vane, Williams believed that the "true" church had been destroyed and would not be restored until the triumph of Christ over Antichrist.

Williams' political views matched in radicalism his religious opinions. Sympathetic to the Indians from the start, Williams argued that the American natives were true owners of the land and that the King possessed no legitimate authority to grant territory to the colonists. Understandably, his arguments greatly disturbed Massachusetts authorities, who were already highly sensitive about their title to the land. Of all Williams' opinions, however, he was perhaps most noted and feared for his insistence upon religious liberty. In Massachusetts and then later in England Williams argued persuasively through his *Bloody Tenant of Persecution* (1644) that the state possessed no authority over a person's conscience and so ought not force any individual to worship in a particular way. Further, he urged the separation of church and state.

Not surprisingly Williams' outspoken opinions led to his appearance before the General Court. Because of his repudiation of the colony's political and religious order, the Court banished Williams from the Bay Colony in October, 1635. Following the friendly hints of John Winthrop, Williams and a few stalwarts headed south to Rhode Island, purchased land from the Indians, and established the town of Providence. The first laws enacted by the plantation guaranteed liberty of conscience and separation of church and state.

Providence was but one of five towns that eventually formed the colony of Rhode Island. The others—Pocasset (later Portsmouth), Newport, Pawtuxet, and Shawomet (changed to Warwick)—were also settled by religious dissenters. Portsmouth (on Aquidneck Island) was founded in 1638 by Anne Hutchinson; Pawtuxet in 1638 by William and Benedict Arnold, who led a splinter group from Providence; Newport (also on Aquidneck) in 1639 by William Coddington, first a Hutchinsonian and then a Quaker; and Warwick in 1642 by Samuel Gorton, another Hutchinsonian who also championed English common law. In 1644 Williams went to England and obtained a charter for Providence, Portsmouth, and Newport. In 1647 Rhode Island drafted its famous Acts and Orders, which affirmed English law and created a federation of four towns (excluding Pawtuxet) governed by an elected assembly.

Williams' attempts to unify the plantations and thus strengthen Rhode Island against the encroachments of its neighbors met with resistance. The Arnolds submitted Pawtuxet to the jurisdiction of Massachusetts in 1642, hoping to fend off unification with Rhode Island. William Coddington sought to carve out a personal empire and succeeded, in 1650, in obtaining his own patent to control Aquidneck. Due largely to the efforts of Williams and John Clarke, the agent in England, Coddington's patent was revoked. Then, with the assistance of Henry Vane, now an important member of the Council of State, they received confirmation of Rhode Island's 1644 charter.

Despite Williams' success in England, disunity and dissension continued to plague the colony. Spurred by Coddington and others, the islands of Conanicut and Aquidneck acted independently, disregarding the 1644 charter. In addition the Arnolds continued their intrigues with Massachusetts. Upon his return from England in 1654 Williams worked to settle differences and two years later he succeeded. In 1656 Coddington was reconciled and Pawtuxet ended its isolation. With the restoration of Charles II, Rhode Island's status again became shaky. However, in 1663

Clarke again succeeded in winning confirmation of Rhode Island's charter, which included a guarantee of religious liberty.[14]

CONNECTICUT AND NEW HAVEN

Between 1630 and 1640 literally hundreds of settlers left the confines of the Bay Colony for regions beyond. In 1636 the noted Puritan preacher, Thomas Hooker, led most of his congregation down the Connecticut River and established the town of Hartford. About the same time sizable groups from Watertown, Roxbury, and Dorchester, Massachusetts, grew discontent over the proximity of their neighbors and their small grants of land. They, too, left Massachusetts for the Connecticut River Valley and founded the towns of Springfield, Wethersfield, and Windsor.

Colonists who left the Bay Colony for Connecticut did so for a variety of reasons. The Connecticut River Valley itself was attractive. It possessed a navigable river ensuring good transportation, excellent soil for farming, and abundant timber and furs. Some newcomers to Connecticut sought land they feared would become limited in Massachusetts. Others resented the control exercised by the Massachusetts General Court. Hooker's congregation had left because of the poor land allotted to them around Cambridge. Hooker himself opposed the growing practice of admitting to church membership only known "saints" who satisfactorily testified of a "conversion experience." Hooker, a strong evangelical, denied that one could discern the regenerate. He feared that stringent requirements for church membership would only split the church from the rest of the community.

In 1639 the inhabitants of Hartford, Wethersfield, and Windsor attempted to give their settlements legitimacy by formulating a government upon the *Fundamental Orders.* Following the model of Massachusetts, the *Orders* established a general assembly comprised of representatives from each of the towns. It also created an upper chamber or group of assistants. The questionable legal status of Connecticut became cause for worry, especially after the restoration of Charles II in 1660. Nevertheless, with the able assistance of John Winthrop Jr. Connecticut received a royal charter in 1662. Earlier, in 1638, the Reverend John Davenport and Theophilus Eaton had left Massachusetts and founded the town of New Haven. Five years later New Haven united with Fairfield, Guilford, Milford, and Stratford to form the colony of New Haven. The tiny colony lasted until 1662 when it was absorbed into Connecticut.[15]

NEW HAMPSHIRE AND MAINE

The last two colonies to be established in New England–Maine and New Hampshire –resulted from the almost compulsive urge by early colonists to settle new lands. These territories had been granted to Sir Ferdinando Gorges and John Mason in the 1620s by the Council for New England. Neither Gorges or Mason attempted to develop the region, however, and as a result of their neglect, settlers began moving into the area and forming illegitimate towns. As the population of New Hampshire grew, Massachusetts covetously eyed the region. By 1643 the Bay Colony absorbed it and controlled New Hampshire for thirty-six years. In 1679, however, New Hampshire became a royal colony. Massachusetts pursued a similar policy toward Maine. In 1647, with the death of Gorges, the Bay Colony tried to exert its authority over the settlements in Maine. It achieved success by 1652, and Maine remained a part of Massachusetts until 1820.[16]

MARYLAND

Unlike Virginia, which started as a commercial venture, Maryland grew out of the personal circumstances of George Calvert, Lord Baltimore. A favorite of James I, Calvert gave up the king's service in 1625 after he had converted to Catholicism. As a Catholic living in a Protestant country highly fearful of "popery," Calvert found it difficult to practice his religion. Furthermore, his beliefs placed his family's future in jeopardy. In seventeenth-century England normal avenues of occupation and advancement for the sons of the nobility, such as the law, military service, the clergy, and local offices, were closed to Catholics. In addition, Catholics were subject to fines for nonattendance and could not worship publicly. It was largely the desire to establish a religious haven for English Catholics and to guarantee land and wealth for his sons that led Calvert to seek land in the New World. Despite an unsuccessful attempt to colonize Newfoundland, Calvert's interest persisted. In 1632 he petitioned and received a patent from Charles I for about 10 million acres in northern Virginia. The first Lord Baltimore died before realizing his dream of establishing a permanent settlement in the New World, but in 1634 his son, Cecilius, transported about 200 colonists to America. The expedition itself was headed by Leonard Calvert, the second Lord Baltimore's younger brother. After planting a settlement near the mouth of the Potomac, the younger Calvert sectioned much of the colony into large proprietary manors and sold leases to other nobles. These landlords in turn rented smaller plots to farmers and tenants. In addition, Calvert sold freehold plantations, which ultimately proved more popular.

Despite some almost feudal characteristics of the Baltimore charter, Calvert attracted a steady flow of immigrants to Maryland. The colony possessed fertile land, excellent transportation, and wide religious toleration. Calvert attempted to exercise almost absolute control over the colony, but the colonial assembly created by charter continually challenged proprietary authority. Eventually, the assembly won greater power and divided into two houses along the parliamentary model. In 1649 the Maryland Assembly passed a Toleration Act guaranteeing religious liberty to all Christians who accepted the Trinity. The gradual influx of Protestants from other colonies, however, soon put Catholics in a minority in Maryland. Following the execution of Charles I and the creation of the Puritan Commonwealth in 1649, Puritan forces in Maryland assumed control of the colony. In 1655 they repealed the Toleration Act. A year later a brief civil war between Catholic and Protestant factions broke out in the colony. Through negotiations with Cromwell's government, Calvert managed to regain control over the colony in 1657. Despite constant friction with the Maryland legislature over political power, the Baltimore family continued to rule until 1691, when Maryland became a royal colony.[17]

THE CAROLINAS

Following the rather spectacular advances of the early seventeenth century, English colonizing activities stopped abruptly. The lag in colonization resulted largely from civil wars in England. The religious, economic, and political problems which marked England's evolution from feudal kingdom to early modern state climaxed in armed conflict between those English subjects loyal to the Crown and those tied to Parliament. Parliament won, Charles I was beheaded, and after a period of uncertainty, Oliver Cromwell, by then General of the Parliamentary forces, emerged as England's "Lord Protector" in the 1650s. However, more limited monarchy returned to England in 1660 with the restoration of Charles II. Charles' return also marked a new era in English expansion. Merchant ventures characterized by the old joint-stock company ended. The list of failures or semisuccesses was too long to attract the necessary capital. Religious and political dissenters who had fled England in earlier years and formed the core of many colonizing ventures no longer filled the holds of America-bound ships. Instead, the impetus for new expansion emerged among powerful representatives of the English nobility and from imperially minded statesmen and ministers. Perhaps reflecting the domestic calm that pervaded England following the Restoration, members of the gentry also grew keenly interested in expansion. The motives of the new generation of colonial adventurers were mixed: some were clearly profit oriented; others had devised schemes to reform society and saw America as a good place to try them out.

The return of monarchy in 1660 signaled the beginning of a colonial era dominated by the "proprietary" colony–that is, one settled by a noble or proprietor who had received a charter from the Crown. In 1663 important nobles like Sir William Berkeley, his brother Lord John Berkeley, and Sir John Colleton, along with five of Charles II's most important ministers (Edward Hyde, Earl of Clarendon; Sir George Carteret; Anthony Ashley Cooper, Earl of Shaftesbury; William, Earl of Craven; and Sir George Monck, Duke of Albemarle), set out to establish a colony in the Carolinas. Their goals were reform and profit. Since all eight men had contributed substantially to the restoration of monarchy, Charles was well disposed to grant their request. The royal charter they obtained extended considerable discretionary powers to the proprietors. It also freed colonists from paying customs duties on several tropical goods for seven years and guaranteed religious toleration.

Because a sizable population already inhabited England's North American colonies, the proprietors initiated a campaign to attract settlers from the Chesapeake and New England regions to Carolina rather than transport new colonists to America. In order to make Carolina appealing, they granted considerable legislative power to the colonial assembly and promised land to all colonists–including servants. In 1664 a contingent of small farmers left Barbados and migrated to the Cape Fear region, but after only a few years, the settlement collapsed. Despite the extension of greater privileges to settlers under the "Concessions and Agreements" the proprietors failed to draw many people to Carolina.

With their enterprise wavering, Shaftesbury convinced his fellow investors to pile further sums into the colony. In 1669 they equipped several vessels which sailed from England to Barbados where the ships picked up additional men. Because the

Caribbean economy had been transformed from small and medium farms to large sugar plantations dependent upon slave labor, many smaller farmers eagerly accepted the invitation to settle in Carolina. The immigrants reached the Carolina coast in 1670 and founded Charlestown. With the coming of new settlers, including a band of Huguenots (French Protestants), Charlestown became the most important city in Carolina. In 1680 the town was moved to its present site.

Although its development was less spectacular than that of other colonies, Carolina was notable for the idealism that Shaftesbury, its major promoter, infused into the colony's political organization. In 1669 he commissioned his philosopher friend and secretary, John Locke, to assist in devising a constitution for the colony. The result was the *Fundamental Constitutions.* This document, which borrowed many ideas from James Harrington's *Oceana,* aimed at establishing an American hereditary aristocracy that would maintain its position through the control of about 40 percent of the land. The rest of the territory was to be divided among the lesser colonists. The *Constitutions* also sought to regulate the pattern of settlement and prevent uneconomical, disjointed expansion that would result from scattered, isolated growth. Such provisions, however, could not stand under the strong contrary pressures of the New World, and after a series of revisions, the *Constitutions* were dispensed with altogether.

Despite the willingness of the proprietors to extend some political power to local areas, the colonists balked and resisted proprietary direction. Unable to regulate the colony effectively, the proprietors turned South Carolina over to royal governance in 1721. Thirty years earlier the northern counties of Carolina became the separate territory of North Carolina, although the area continued to be governed with South Carolina. Unlike its companion colony, the northern region with its rugged frontier attracted dissidents and malcontents from neighboring Virginia and developed an active smuggling traffic. In 1712 North Carolina was given a separate government, and in 1729 it too became a royal colony.[18]

NEW YORK

Originally settled by the Dutch, New York came under English rule in 1664, after the British captured New Netherlands. Upon winning the territory through the Second Anglo-Dutch War (1664 to 1666) Charles II granted the land of New Netherlands to his brother James, Duke of York. Although James theoretically possessed almost feudal rights to New York, as the territory was renamed, his deputy governor, Richard Nicolls, followed a conciliatory policy toward the colony's large Dutch population. In 1665 Nicolls issued a series of ordinances called the Duke's Laws. These laws guaranteed religious toleration, affirmed proprietary rights, exempted the Dutch from military service, granted them the right to vote in colonial elections, and devised liberal terms for acquiring land. In the years following, the Dutch responded far better to York's rule than did the English inhabitants, especially the settlers on Long Island. The paternalistic and somewhat autocratic characteristics of the old Dutch rule, along with York's tendency to maintain tight control over the colony, prevented the establishment of a representative assembly. As a result a colonial legislature did not meet until the 1680s. The Dutch regained control of the colony for a brief period in 1673, during the Third Anglo-Dutch War (1672 to 1674), but within a year the British reestablished rule. With the succession of James II to the throne in 1685, New York became a royal colony.[19]

THE JERSEYS

Shortly after obtaining New Netherlands from Charles II, the Duke of York granted a large tract of land between the Delaware and Hudson Rivers to John Berkeley and George Carteret, two of the individuals involved in the Carolina enterprise. In light of their recent colonial experiences, Berkeley and Carteret almost immediately implemented a variation of Carolina's "Concessions and Agreements" in hopes of drawing settlers into the colony. With the guarantee of religious toleration and representative government, a substantial number migrated from nearby New England into the territory, now called New Jersey after the island off the English coast where Carteret had acted as governor. In 1674 Berkeley relinquished his interest in the colony to John Fenwick and Edward Byllinge, both Quakers. After a series of transactions, the province was divided in 1676 into east and west halves, with William Penn and other Quakers acting as trustees to West Jersey and Carteret retaining control of East Jersey. After Carteret's death in 1680 Penn and several fellow Quakers acquired the East Jersey province. In 1677 the Quaker proprietors crafted a constitution which established freedom of conscience, created an independent legislature, and ensured many civil liberties including trial by jury. Following several decades of proprietary rule, the royal governor of New York assumed the administration of the Jerseys in 1702. New Jersey became a separate royal colony in 1738.[20]

PENNSYLVANIA AND DELAWARE

Besides playing an important role in the political development of East Jersey, William Penn was destined to exert even greater influence over a much larger part of North America. In 1681 he secured a charter from the king for a tract of land west of New Jersey and south of New York. Born into a rich, aristocratic family, Penn imbibed Quaker views while still a young man. The Society of Friends, as the Quakers called themselves, was an offshoot of the religious turmoil of the 1650s. A radical form of Puritanism, Quakerism not only denounced the hierarchical structure of the established church but also maintained that the true ministry consisted of all believers who had received the "inner light" of the Holy Spirit. Under the leadership of George Fox, the Society of Friends also rejected certain orthodox Calvinist doctrines. They emphasized the inner, mystical communion of each individual with God and insisted that salvation was obtainable to all people, not just the elect few. In addition they maintained that the state possessed no right to interfere in spiritual matters. Their egalitarian views, as well as their enthusiastic evangelicalism and their bold attacks on the social order of England, quickly made the Quakers a hated, feared, and persecuted sect. After the Restoration, however, the Friends evolved into a quietist group and lost much of their earlier radicalism. By the 1680s upper-class Quakers such as Penn had won tolerance.

Penn obtained a grant of lands in the New World in exchange for a sizable debt Charles II owed to the Penn family. Although his charter bestowed fewer powers than some of the earlier proprietary grants, it enabled Penn to establish one of the most enlightened governments in the colonies. Influenced, like Locke, by the political philosophy of James Harrington, in 1682 Penn erected a bicameral legislature in which the upper house debated the proposed laws and the lower house approved or rejected them. In addition, the broad voting qualifications in Pennsylvania made it the most democratic of the English colonies. Penn's willingness to purchase (rather than simply take) land from the Indians and his efforts to protect them from white encroachers kept the colony free from attacks.

While Penn actively helped govern the colony, it developed along the lines he had envisioned. Periodically, however, Penn returned to England to attend to business matters, and the non-Quaker population took such opportunities to resist Quaker rule. Penn's apparent sympathy for James II, the exiled Stuart, as well as boundary disputes with New York, resulted in the loss of his charter in 1692. The colony fell under the management of the New York governor for two years. Then, in 1694, King William restored Penn's charter. With his "Charter of Privileges" of 1701, Penn expanded the rights of the colonists even further. He also created a separate legislature for Delaware, a territory originally colonized by Sweden that he had obtained from the Duke of York in 1682. Delaware remained under the executive authority of the governor of Pennsylvania until the Revolutionary War.[21]

GEORGIA

By 1700 only one small portion of the North Atlantic coastline south of Maine remained uncolonized. That area, lying between South Carolina and Spanish-controlled Florida, became the object of widespread interest around 1730. Wealthy South Carolina planters as well as the British Board of Trade favored the establishment of a colony to defend against Spanish incursions into Carolina. At the same time a number of humanitarian-minded Englishmen conceived of the idea of populating the territory with unfortunates imprisoned for debt who would work in exchange for their freedom. Such a scheme would not only benefit the debtors but would give their creditors a chance to be repaid and would provide some relief from overpopulation in the British Isles. In 1732 a coterie of philanthropists led by General James Oglethorpe received a charter to settle Georgia, as the area was named. Unlike any of England's previous colonial ventures, this one was placed under the control of twenty-one trustees. These men were empowered to establish a colony and direct its management for twenty-one years. In addition, the enterprise received a substantial grant from Parliament along with considerable private financing to help ensure success.

In 1733 about 100 settlers, under the leadership of Oglethorpe, founded the town of Savannah. Oglethorpe quickly formed an alliance with the Indians and successfully defended the colony against the Spanish during the War of Jenkins Ear (1739 to 1742). His military exploits, however, were not paralleled by good management of the colony. Oglethorpe's severe discipline and a variety of impractical ideas promoted by the colony's trustees inhibited colonial development. For example, land allotments were restricted to fifty acres and were dispensed on a tenant, not ownership, basis. In addition, Oglethorpe ruled without an assembly and outlawed both slavery and rum. Inevitably, pressures from the German, Welsh, Scottish, and English populations for looser regulation led to change. In 1738 limitations on holdings were increased to 2000 acres. Within twelve years the trustees had opened the colony to slave labor and rum, and had removed restrictions on buying and selling land. Disappointed by the failure to establish their utopian dream in Georgia, the trustees relinquished control to the Crown in 1752.[22]

BERMUDA AND THE WEST INDIES

All the while the English settled the North American mainland, they and their European rivals realized the potential worth of the islands dotting the Caribbean. One of these islands, Bermuda, lay about 600 miles east of Charlestown. Also known as the Somers Islands, the territory was used as a military base against the Spanish. Although the island was originally included in the charter of the Virginia Company, in 1615 the Bermuda Company received a separate patent for it. Only five years later the first colonial assembly was formed. Initially, planters grew tobacco as a staple crop. When prices fell, however, they turned to livestock production; the scarcity of fuel prevented the development of a sugar trade. During its early history the island attracted a variety of religious nonconformists; indeed, one of its most influential stockholders and citizens, Robert Warwick, actively maintained Puritan-minded clergy and encouraged the spread of nonconformist views. In 1645 a victorious Parliament granted religious liberty to the colony. Despite the attractions of fertile land, religious toleration, and a warm climate, the small size and limited resources of the island prevented Bermuda from becoming as prosperous as other Caribbean colonies. In 1684, having successfully governed the island for almost seventy years, the Bermuda Company dissolved and turned the colony over to royal control.

In importance, English colonizing efforts in Bermuda were far overshadowed by activities in the West Indian Islands off the northern coast of South America. These included Barbados, Jamaica, and the Leeward Islands of St. Christopher (St. Kitts), Monserrat, Antigua, and Nevis. For most of the sixteenth century the area was controlled by Spain, but as Spanish influence declined in the last decades of the century, English privateers utilized the islands as bases in their attacks on treasure ships bound for Spain. No serious colonization began until 1624, when a contingent from East Anglia settled on St. Kitts. In 1625 the English claimed Barbados, and within a few years British adventurers, planters, and merchants were spreading throughout the islands.

Of all the West Indies, Barbados was one of the richest and most coveted agricultural spots. Its first colonists, who arrived in 1627, were sponsored by the Courteen Associates, a joint-stock venture, which initiated the expedition without benefit of a royal charter. Alert to the potential in the West Indies, the Earl of Carlisle obtained a proprietary grant in 1627 for a large portion of the islands. That set the stage for a clash of proprietary interests that caused political unrest in Barbados for years. Nevertheless, the colony's economic promise attracted large numbers of settlers, and by 1660 the population had surpassed 30,000. In its early years Barbados exported a variety of goods, including cotton, ginger, corn, tobacco, indigo, and dyewoods. Still, by 1650 sugar had begun to dominate the economy. During the midseventeenth century the ruling council and assembly took advantage of the civil turmoil in England and exhibited considerable independence. Planters traded openly with the Dutch despite the ban on such activity passed in 1651. The assembly attempted to expand its power at the expense of its governor, Daniel Searle. In 1660, however, Charles II assumed proprietary control of Barbados and leased the island to Lord Francis Willoughby. In 1673 Barbados was transformed into a royal colony.

The development of the Leeward Islands closely paralleled that of Barbados. These islands were ruled by governors, councils, and popular assemblies, and their inhabitants enjoyed considerable religious toleration. First tobacco, and then sugar became the staple crop of the islands. Although smaller and less populous than Barbados, the Leeward Islands shared in the prosperous trade between the West Indies and the North American mainland colonies.

Jamaica, the last of England's West Indian colonies to be discussed, had a much different history than its neighbors. Discovered by Columbus in 1503, Jamaica was settled and controlled by Spain until 1655. Under Spanish rule the island developed a diverse economy, exporting not only sugar, but cacao and livestock. As one of Spain's prized possessions, it became the target of English assault in 1654. Despite poor planning and direction, Oliver Cromwell's expedition succeeded in expelling the Spanish in 1655. It took the English five years, however, to subdue insurgents. In 1661, after the war with Spain ended, Parliament annexed Jamaica and made it a royal colony.

As the North American mainland colonies grew, the West Indies formed an integral part of the commercial network tying the British colonies together. After the decline of the tobacco trade, the islands became the primary producer of England's sugar as well as its important byproducts, molasses and rum. Because of their concentration on labor-heavy crops such as sugar, the West Indian planters soon sought a cheap, plentiful labor supply; and for that they turned to Africa and the slave trade. By the midseventeenth century large plantations worked by Negro slaves dominated the West Indian economy. Within another century the pattern of agriculture developed in the West Indies was being adopted by the southern colonies on the North American mainland.[23]

Part II
THE SEVENTEENTH-CENTURY COLONIAL WORLD

During the first century of English colonization in North America, the early settlers spent most of their energies simply trying to survive, a fact that is too often lost amidst tales of heroic deeds and noble ideals. For example, almost anyone who has had either public or private schooling in the United States can search old memories to evoke a few fleeting glimpses of the pathetic, starving, hopeless lot at Jamestown before Captain John Smith came to their rescue; yet most of us remember *only* that Smith saved the colony from extinction. This is because, traditionally, American history textbooks have emphasized the success with which the nation's first heroes overcame even the fiercest obstacles they encountered in the New World. In so doing, however, those books have downplayed the dominant characteristic of the seventeenth-century colonial world: the struggle for survival. Several generations of colonists fought a continual war against their hostile environment; and in that contest, more often than not they lost.

In the pages that follow, several ideas about the nature of seventeenth-century Anglo-America emerge. As was emphasized in the Prologue to this book, colonial society grew upon Old World values and culture, and yet became unique from them. Colonial institutions adopted or closely resembled their English/European models; but at the same time, they took on an appearance native to and reflective of the new land and people. There is no doubt that the first Anglo-Americans attempted valiantly to establish in the New World those institutions and cultural values they had left behind. But it is equally clear that only *segments* of the parent culture took root in the new land. This fact in and of itself ensured that Anglo-American society, from the beginning, would evolve differently from Europe and England.

In part, the North American British colonies were unique from England because they lacked several institutions that dominated English society. The most significant missing institutions were the Crown, the Anglican Church, and the aristocracy. Royal power and influence, so important for the development of European states, did not exist per se in the colonies until the late seventeenth century. During the 1680s King James II dissolved several colonial governments and created a single political unit, called the Dominion of New England, to govern them. By the 1680s, however, the American colonies had already established political patterns and habits which signaled the demise of the Dominion even as it was being created. Ironically, the absence of royal authority resulted from a conscious decision by the Crown. James I and then Charles I chose to leave colonial development in the hands of the companies and proprietors who initially financed colonization. As a result, Anglo-America evolved largely autonomous of English royal influence. Likewise, the Church of England expressed little interest in the dissenters who fled to the New World. Thankful to be rid of any nonconformists who chose to leave, the Anglican Church mostly ignored the various dissenting church establishments that formed in the colonies. Hence, colonial religious institutions became more tolerant, less politically active, and more pluralistic than their English counterpart. Finally, the aristocracy, perhaps one of the most powerful English institutions, never existed in Anglo-America. The primary base of aristocratic power was the possession of land, a commodity scarce in Europe but unlimited in Anglo-America. Whereas in England land was concentrated in the hands of the nobility and became the distinguishing mark of that class, in Anglo-America the abundance of land meant that virtually any enterprising individual could acquire it. Inevitably, the diffusion of land into the hands of many, rather than a few, had dramatic implications for the social structure of Anglo-America. The scattered attempts by proprietors, such as the Calverts in Maryland, to establish feudal-like estates failed miserably. The availability of land, therefore, ensured the demise of a hereditary aristocracy in America.

Besides the absence of certain key English institutions, another factor determined that Anglo-America would follow a course of development separate from England. That factor was the type of settler who came to America. Rather than being a cross section of English society, those who dared risk the Atlantic sea passage represented primarily the poor and the disaffected. Those with "nothing to lose" rather than those of wealth and position braved the dangers of colonization. Only in a few instances—such as the Puritan experiment in New England—did a sizable portion of higher-ranking and substantial English citizens decide to settle. But even then, as we see later, the Puritans had to recruit from the masses to make their venture succeed. It may not enhance American national pride to consider that its first heroes were more than likely the impoverished, the illiterate, the landless, and the alienated—in other words, the dregs of European society rather than the cream. But it is a fact that most of America's first settlers were men and women who had many reasons to leave the Old World and only a few to stay. They were among the lowest, most miserable, and most disaffected part of England's population.

A third factor helped ensure that the colonies would only partly mirror the Old World. America's first immigrants brought with them an English/European heritage, but one that exaggerated disproportionately certain features of Old World society. What were these features? The early colonists brought with them, first, a form of economic radicalism. Although their notions would not now be considered "radical," for the seventeenth century the concept that any individual might potentially attain property, social status, and political power was indeed radical. The seventeenth-century European world embraced the concept of a hierarchical class society, fixed by birth, in which each class performed certain functions. Without classes, it was believed, society simply could not exist. The first settlers of Anglo-America did not reject the ideas of a class society based upon property; rather they tended to endorse it. But when any individual, regardless of former rank or possessions, visibly possessed the opportunity to improve his wealth, position, and power through the ownership of property, inevitably the implications of such economic opportunity would be felt. Anglo-America began with a population drawn primarily from the lower or lower middle classes. By the end of the century the economic and social composition of colonial society became defined by English and European standards as a society of "middling" persons who were prospering—all because the colonial population revealed a large percentage of land owners as compared with Europe. Thus, by definition, the economic and social character of Anglo-America began to challenge the idea of a hereditary class society. As we see later, the political implications of this economic radicalism meant a more "democratic" form of government in the colonies.

Second, the early settlers brought with them a fairly well developed sense of their political and legal rights. Because many colonists were political or religious dissenters, they had known persecution or at least societal disapproval for their beliefs. As dissenters, they necessarily developed both strong convictions and an abiding will to defend those convictions. From the start, then, Anglo-American society attracted people who both demanded and exercised greater freedom of expression than their compatriots in England. The struggle with the American wilderness as well as the absence of much governmental control over their lives encouraged colonials to develop an independence of mind and an individualist outlook. This is not to say that the first settlers exalted the individual above society; to the contrary, they believed the opposite. But, for the time, the types of settlers and their reasons for colonization encouraged the growth of and respect for individual freedom.

Finally, probably one of the most significant aspects of Old World culture brought to Anglo-America was the heritage of Protestantism. Again, rather than representing a cross section of European religion, the British portion of the New World championed a peculiar brand of religious nonconformity. That is, North America—and especially the colonies north of the Chesapeake—attracted men and women who not only opposed Catholicism, but who also refused to "conform" to the beliefs and practices of certain Protestant state churches in Europe and particularly England. Often persecuted or at least disdained for their beliefs, many nonconformist Protestants fled to America to find religious freedom. But in addition, they sought to escape the evil and corruption they saw within European Protestant churches. Convinced that they were living in the final days before the end of the world, they viewed themselves as God's chosen remnant who had a Christian duty to preserve the true, pure church from taint and corruption. In this sense, then, Protestant nonconformists carried with them a positive Christian mission. Not only seekers of religious liberty for themselves, they aspired to create a Christian fortress that would hold forth God's truth against the forces of Satan and Antichrist. When times grew prosperous and dangers distant, colonial millenarian fears no doubt subsided. But when life turned rough and dangers threatened, the old visions of America as a bastion of religious truth resurfaced. In the harsh environment of the American wilderness, the besieged, warrior mentality of the early settlers became embedded into the colonial frame of mind. This element of Protestant ideology permeated and influenced Anglo-American thought throughout the colonial era.

From what has been written, the seventeenth-century world of British North America appears as a world shaped by forces that would cause it to develop quite differently from England and Europe. Both the absence of crucial Old World institutions, as well as the mutant character of the colonial populations and the ideas they brought with them, all ensured that Anglo-America would trek a future course far from that staked out by the Old World. But even if the colonists had successfully transplanted their English/European culture intact, colonial society would have deviated from the old pattern simply because the colonies were created to serve a specific purpose. The seventeenth-century colonial world was defined in large part by both personal ambitions *and* English imperial goals. Those who risked the perils of colonization did so because they had dreams of a better life. They sought wealth, or higher social status, or religious freedom, or perhaps a godly society. But, whatever the dream, America gave them a chance to realize it, a chance not available to them in England. At the same time that settlers worked toward personal goals, however, they also perhaps unknowingly began to achieve an imperial goal: the transformation of England into a supreme world power. While initially economic ventures of a few enterprising businessmen, the North American colonies became the central instrument through which England acquired wealth, economic independence from its European rivals, and world power. The imperial mission, like the personal mission of each settler, proved highly successful. As we examine more closely the patterns of colonial economic, political, social, and religious life, we see how the various factors just discussed influenced the development of seventeenth-century Anglo-America.

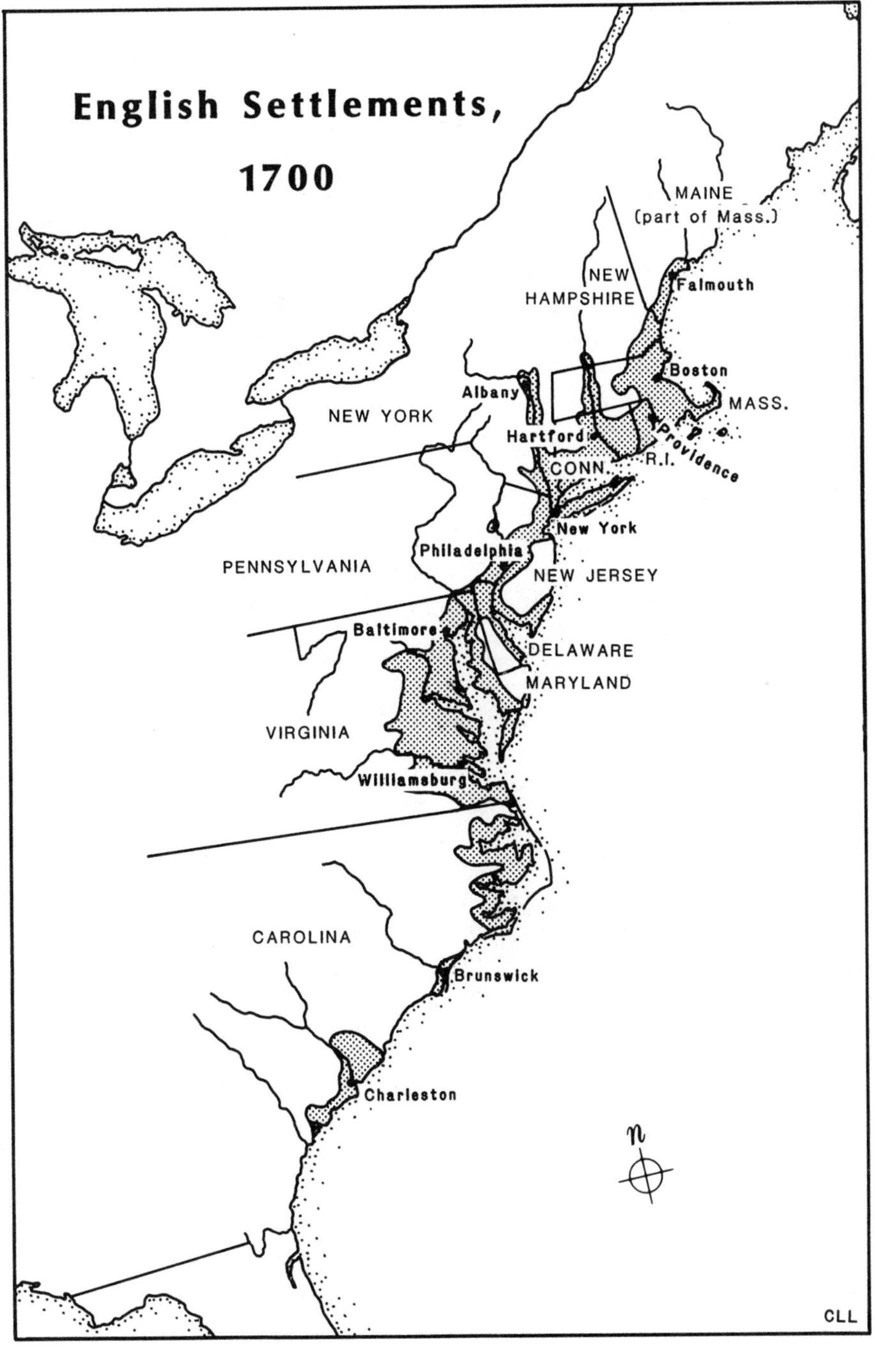
English Settlements, 1700
MAINE
(part of Mass.)
Falmouth
NEW
HAMPSHIRE
Boston
MASS.
Albany
NEW YORK
Hartford
Providence
R.I.
CONN.
New York
Philadelphia
PENNSYLVANIA
NEW JERSEY
Baltimore
DELAWARE
MARYLAND
VIRGINIA
Williamsburg
CAROLINA
Brunswick
Charleston
n
CLL

3

Forming an Empire

England's North American colonies were founded by joint-stock companies, proprietors, and small groups of land-hungry immigrants. Sooner or later every successful colony received a royal charter, and most eventually lived under a royal governor. Still, the role of the English government in the formation of a colonial empire was haphazard at best. Gradually, that changed. After 1660, a revived Stuart monarchy became active in formulating colonial policy and directing colonial affairs. With guidance from the Crown, Parliament passed legislation regulating colonial trade. In addition, considerable sums of time and money were spent trying to reverse the results of early colonizing practices in order to bring all or most of the colonies directly under the control of the Crown. That policy received a near fatal blow in 1688 with the "Glorious Revolution" against the Stuart king, James II. With the Crown's power even further limited by Parliament, control of the colonies and colonial policy gradually shifted to Parliament in the eighteenth century. Parliament proved ill-suited for its role. Besieged by powerful economic "interests" and the demands of almost continual warfare with the French and Spanish, Parliament had little inclination or vision to formulate coherent policy for Anglo-America or to watch over the day-to-day operations of an empire. Those jobs were left to a growing, creaky, occasionally self-defeating colonial bureaucracy.

Though miniscule by modern standards, a colonial bureaucracy developed to administer various regulatory acts, to monitor the activities of colonial officials abroad, to assess the strengths and weaknesses of colonial possessions, and to make suggestions for policy shifts. By 1763 almost every colony had colonial officials, some English and some native born. Yet, despite the growth of colonial administration and regulation in the lives of Anglo-Americans, the English failed to create an efficient centralized government for their overseas possessions. Thus, from the beginning of settlement, Anglo-Amercans enjoyed a degree of autonomy not duplicated in other imperial systems.

Since to a great extent the patterns for colonial government, social structure, religion, and economic life were established in these early years, the gradual creation of an administrative bureaucracy did not change the direction of colonial development; it only altered it somewhat. In most areas of life the English imperialists were content to let the colonists decide their own destinies. In those areas in which British officials were active—such as trade or colonial politics—the English pursued an erratic, often contradictory course. As a result, Anglo-Americans learned to live comfortably as members of an expanding empire. Certainly, some friction between colonial interests and those of England occurred, but it rarely amounted to much. The colonials learned quickly that aside from the inconveniences of bureaucratic red tape and of dealing with a government thousands of miles away, most resolutions benefited them. Those that did not could be circumvented or ignored.[1]

MERCANTILISM AND THE EMPIRE

From hindsight it may appear that the English ought to have exerted greater control over the colonies sooner—possibly avoiding the fateful events of the 1770s. But at the beginning England was ill-equipped for colonizing ventures and relied primarily upon private financing and organizations to undertake settlement of the New World. What is more, the character of English colonial policy in the eighteenth century was largely a product of the theories and practices that evolved over two centuries of imperial thought, experience, and struggle. A Scottish philosopher named Adam Smith wrote and published one of the earliest studies of the rise of the "modern" states of the West in the sixteenth, seventeenth, and eighteenth centuries. His book, entitled *An Inquiry into the Nature and Causes of the Wealth of Nations* (1776), was a seminal work in economic history and economic theory and a classic defense of the competitive ethic, enlightened self-interest, and laissez-faire in economic matters. Smith surveyed European expansion and used the phrase *mercantile system* to describe the assumptions and ideas which motivated England and other European powers to colonize. Though no friend of those ideas or many of the practices they spawned, Smith conceded that the mercantile system formed the foundation for the national wealth and power of the important states of his era. "Political œconomy," he wrote, "considered as a branch of the science of a statesman or legislator, proposes two distinct objects." One was to "provide a plentiful revenue or subsistence for the people." A second was to "supply the state or commonwealth with a revenue sufficient for the publick services." Over the years, Smith went on:

> The different progress of opulence . . . has given occasion to two different systems of political economy with regard to enriching the people. The one may be called the system of commerce, the other that of agriculture. I shall endeavour to explain both as fully and distinctly as I can, and shall begin

> with the system of commerce. It is the modern system, and is best understood in our own country and in our own times.[2]

For Smith the "system of commerce" was the mercantile system. Later commentators shortened the term to simply *mercantilism* and the new name stuck. Most agreed that mercantilist assumptions and practices grew from medieval notions about the organic nature of society and the state and the need for the state to regulate both individual and economic behavior. They agreed as well that mercantilism provided much of the rationale for the centralized state, the expansion of Europe, the creation of far-flung colonial empires, and the great imperial wars of the seventeenth and eighteenth centuries.

Some commentators defined mercantilism narrowly, others broadly. Bullionism, or the quest for precious metals, was the narrowest definition. "A rich country," wrote Adam Smith, "in the same manner as a rich man, is supposed to be a country abounding in money: and to heap up gold and silver in any country is supposed to be the readiest way to enrich it."[3] We adopt a much broader definition. We suggest that mercantilism described the methods employed by nation states of the "age of expansion" to achieve a dominant world position. However, those methods—and the ideas which lay behind them—changed over time. During the period of England's imperial growth, we can discern four basic stages of mercantilist thought and action, all reflecting changing circumstances within colonial empires and among European nations. First, as European powers unified small provinces into centralized, national states, they saw economic growth through trade as the major avenue to world dominance. To those early European states, national wealth meant economic power (trade) which in turn produced world power. Influenced by this equation, countries such as Portugal and Spain initiated explorations to find quick, direct trade routes to the wealth of the East. Likewise, England pursued markets in northwestern Europe in hopes of increasing its wealth and power. At this stage, then, mercantilism meant the state's regulation of economic activity and the pursuit of trade in order to increase national greatness.

Then, as European states searched for a route to the wealth of the East, something totally unexpected happened. Explorers discovered the New World. More importantly, Spain in particular uncovered and tapped a vast supply of gold and silver. Adam Smith observed that:

> For some time after the discovery of America, the first enquiry of the Spaniards, when they arrived upon any unknown coast, used to be, if there was any gold or silver to be found in the neighborhood? By the information which they received, they judged whether it was worth while to make a settlement there, or if the country was worth the conquering.[4]

Smith hated bullionism, considering it to be the folly of his age. He mocked the Spanish and all gold and silver hunters and hoarders by comparing the Spanish to the Tartars. "Among the Tartars," he wrote:

> as among all other nations of shepherds, who are generally ignorant of the use of money, cattle are the instruments of commerce and the measures of value. Wealth, therefore, according to them, consisted in cattle, as according to the

> Spaniards it consisted in gold and silver. Of the two, the Tartar notion, perhaps, was the nearest to the truth.[5]

But Adam Smith recognized the role precious metals played in European expansion. He understood that with the influx of New World treasure into Spain and the subsequent growth of Spain's power, envious mercantilists modified their ideas about the way to achieve national greatness. They began advocating bullionism, or the acquisition of a large, independent supply of precious metals. Believing that the Earth possessed a finite amount of precious metals and that all gold and silver would be found one day, they argued that the nation which could accumulate the largest stock of bullion would be able to maximize its economic power and eventually dominate other states. Reflecting the rise of this mercantilist theory, elements of England's landed and commercial elite supported colonizing ventures into North America during the late sixteenth and early seventeenth centuries, primarily in search of gold and silver. With the Spanish imperial success in view, English monarchs increasingly permitted and encouraged overseas colonies.

Of course, we all know that England found no cities of gold or plentiful supplies of any precious metals. What it did find, however, was abundant, fertile land and numerous raw materials. Geographer and mercantilist Richard Hakluyt the Younger had predicted as much as early as 1584 in a private report to Elizabeth I calling for state support of Walter Raleigh's proposed Virginia colony. Though not published until 1877, Hakluyt's report circulated widely and became known as *A Discourse of Western Planting.* In it he told Elizabeth that in America "the soyle yeldeth, and may be made to yelde all the severall comodoties of Europe, and of all kingdomes, domynions and Territories that England tradeth withe, that by trade of merchandize cometh into this Realme . . . ."[6] Hakluyt intended to make two points: first, that colonies would expand England's trade immensely by providing English manufacturers with new markets and raw materials, and second, that colonies would decrease England's dependence upon other "kingdomes, domynions and Territories" for certain products, thus allowing the English to export more than they imported. The latter would lead to vast quantities of foreign bullion filling English coffers.

Elizabeth liked Hakluyt's report but refused to finance Raleigh's project. Nonetheless, Hakluyt's ideas formed a basic text for later English expansionists, for he made colonization a key to national glory, domestic tranquility, and economic growth and development. Besides increasing England's manufacturing, trade, and bullion supply, Hakluyt argued that colonies would "staye the spanishe kinge from flowinge over all the face of that waste firme of America" just as they might provide a home for "wandringe beggars of England, that growe upp ydly and hurtefull and burdenous to this Realme," or "men of excellent wittes and of divers singuler giftes overthrowen by suertishippe by sea or by some folly of youthe." Benefiting from "excellent trees for mastes," and "goodly timber to builde shippes," England's navy would grow strong to challenge Spain, "the supporter of the greate Antechriste of Rome." As for Protestantism, "wee shall by plantinge there inlarge the glory of the gospell and from England plante sincere relligion, and provide a safe and a sure place to receave people from all partes of the worlde that are forced to flee for the truthe of gods worde . . . ."[7] Slowly at first, the fledgling colonies in North America began providing needed goods, such as lumber, grain, tar, and sugar, to England. In addition, English manufacturers and merchants quickly recognized and exploited the colonies as markets for manufactured goods. What England lost by failing to establish gold and silver mines it gained tenfold in commerce stimulated by its colonies.

This experience set the stage for further modifications in mercantilist theory in Europe and England. Adam Smith described those modifications when he observed that the main effect of the discovery of America and "a passage to the East Indies by the Cape of Good Hope" was "to raise the mercantile system to a degree of splendor and glory which it could never otherwise have attained to." It became "the object of that system to enrich a great nation rather by trade and manufactures." Moreover, England and parts of Europe became "the manufacturers for the numerous and thriving cultivators of America, and the carriers, and in some respects the manufacturers too, for almost all the different nations of Asia, Africa, and America." Smith concluded that "Two new worlds" had been "opened" to the "industry" of England and Europe, "each of them much greater and more extensive than the old one, and the market of one of them growing still greater and greater every day."[8] Consequently, as Smith recognized, the value of an "empire" came to be defined by its utility as both a supplier of raw materials and as a market for finished products—and especially the latter. The relationship between colony and parent country emerged as one of subservience and dominance. Colonies existed to enhance the national greatness and power of the parent country. Likewise, each European state's colonies became the target for conquest and/or destruction by its competitors. If a state could subvert and control its rival's colonial system, it could weaken that rival and increase its own power.

Over the course of the seventeenth century, then, mercantilist thought became a powerful blend of economic theory, political nationalism, and to a great extent, religious ideology. The result was constant economic, religious, and military conflict among the competing states. Moreover, in their rush to encourage trade and to exalt exports over imports, mercantilists began to sense that wealth did not necessarily equal bullion and that power could encompass more than simply hoarding precious metals. As Adam Smith understood, the expanding markets of "Two new worlds" undermined bullionists' theories of the finite character of the world's wealth. Thus, as the seventeenth century gave way to the eighteenth, affairs between nations of the Atlantic world were characterized by attempts by the major powers to dominate each other. Sensing that victory might involve more than grabbing up most of the available bullion, England and part of Europe began to prepare for a very long struggle in which the size and health of colonial empires could prove critical. This led to the fourth stage of mercantilist theory: the dream of self-sufficiency (Adam Smith believed it to be more of a pipe dream). Not only the expansion of commerce, but also economic independence from other countries became the goal of England and some European states in the eighteenth century. Disruptions in trade brought on by frequent wars had made England and many European nations painfully aware of their economic dependence upon both allies and enemies for supplies and markets. Therefore, in England's bid for dominance, its colonies assumed ever greater importance. They provided England with raw materials and markets for its economic well-being. In addition, they held out the possibility of self-sufficiency by freeing England from its previous economic dependency upon Europe. The Board of Trade, one of the chief sources of British colonial policy in the eighteenth century, spoke directly to these new mercantilist goals in a report entitled the *State of the British Plantations in America,* issued in 1721. The Board wrote that:

> notwithstanding the advantages, at present arising from the Plantation trade, are so very considerable, it is not to be doubted, but that they might still be rendered much more useful, if sufficient encouragement were given to induce them [the colonists] to turn their industry to the production of Naval Stores of all kinds, & of such other commodities as our necessities required, & which are purchased by us with great disadvantage from foreign Countries. . . .[9]

By the eighteenth century, English and continental mercantile thought had meshed together old medieval notions about the state's right and obligation to regulate economic activity with newer ideas regarding the role of trade and economic self-sufficiency in achieving national greatness.

In one important respect, however, English mercantile practice differed from that of other European states. For a variety of reasons, the English colonial experience produced a high degree of autonomy for colonies within the empire. In contrast, Spain and France created more centralized imperial systems. Like its European rivals, England built its empire upon the premise that the colonies existed to promote the parent country and help it achieve national greatness. But in England's case, national greatness came through allowing the colonies to develop relatively free from control. Eventually, many English mercantilists criticized this freedom and called for reform. But few wanted to imitate the Spanish imperial system. They affirmed that giving colonists some freedom of action was important because they believed that an individual's pursuit of wealth and power advanced the nation's cause as well. Consequently, even an avowed critic of mercantilism like Adam Smith gave England its due when he wrote that "There are no colonies of which the progress has been more rapid than that of the English in North America . . . Plenty of good land, and liberty to manage their own affairs their own way, seem to be the two great causes of the prosperity of all new [Anglo-American] colonies."[10]

Mercantilism in the Anglo-American Colonies

From what has been said, it should be clear that mercantile theories not only conditioned much of the English government's attitude toward colonization, but they also influenced the leadership in the colonies and the individual colonists themselves. From the outset, private, not public, enterprise, embodied in England's commercial trading classes, provided most of the capital and labor for early English colonization. Both the English merchants who financed colonial experiments and the settlers who came to Anglo-America viewed the New World as a place to realize their personal dreams for wealth and power. But they rarely saw their commercial and individual successes in opposition to or in conflict with the goals of the state. Rather, as Anglo-Americans transformed the early settlements into thriving, prosperous colonies, their experiences reinforced their conviction that such success was the basis for England's national greatness and world power. In that sense, both the colonial leadership and colonists themselves were good mercantilists. They accepted the right of the state to regulate economic activity, and saw the colonies benefit and grow as a result of imperial regulation.

The operation of mercantilist principles was readily evident within the colonies. For example, Massachusetts Bay was founded pa. tly to prevent what John Winthrop and other Puritans saw as the gradual erosion and decay in England of the mercantile notion of an ordered, conformist society. While Winthrop suggested supplanting state coercion with Christian love as the guiding force in human affairs, the government of the Bay Colony used legislation to try to control most aspects of human behavior. This was especially true in the economic realm. Individual commercial initiative was not outlawed–far from it–but the colony made an attempt to control it. Legislation regulated the economic behavior of the Bay residents. In particular, the government discouraged activities which were considered marginal or frivolous while it encouraged those pursuits deemed necessary for the survival and prosperity of the colony. An example of the latter occurred in 1645. John Winthrop's son, John Winthrop, Jr., approached the Massachusetts General Court with plans to establish an "iron work." Representing a group of investors, Winthrop, Jr. had gone to England and brought back with him "1000 pounds stock and diverse workmen." The prospective "iron work" was approved by the Court "as a thing much conducing to the good of the country." John Winthrop, Sr. recorded in his *Journal* that, although the Court had no money to give to the "adventurers," it gave them "near all their demands, as a monopoly of it [mining and iron production] for twenty-one years, liberty to make use of any six places not already granted [for mining], and to have three miles square in every place to them and their heirs, and freedom from public charges, trainings, etc. . . ."[11]

Despite the Puritans' reputation for interfering in the lives of individuals, their colonies practiced little that was not duplicated elsewhere. Initially, mercantilism regulated economic activity everywhere. In most colonies laws were passed governing all sorts of human endeavors, especially when they pertained to the economy. Laws controlled prices, wages, where people could live, and what they could do. One of the severest examples of this mercantilist approach took place in early Virginia when, after the near collapse of the Jamestown settlement in 1610, the Virginia Company put the colony under the control of Sir Thomas Gates and Sir Thomas Dale. Seeing the low morale and the low productivity of the colonists, Dale and Gates instituted some of the toughest regulations ever seen in America. Called "Dale's Laws," these regulations invoked martial law and much more. They made swearing a capital offense and required regular church attendance. For the latter the first offense meant loss of rations; the second led to whipping; and the third meant the gallows. In addition, trading with the Indians without first obtaining a license from colonial authorities carried the death penalty, as did failing to work–if the offense was repeated more than once. Finally, anyone opposing the government or fomenting opposition could be broken on the "wheel" and then chained to a tree until dead. Needless to say, after a time the measures were suspended, but they achieved what they were meant to achieve, and Virginia never again faced collapse.

Most colonies moved from subsistence to sufficiency so quickly that government regulation tended to impede economic development and was gradually dropped. It was not an easy process, however, as the case of Robert Keayne of

Boston illustrated. In 1639 Keayne, a merchant and leading citizen, was brought before the Massachusetts General Court and fined for violating the old medieval notion of a "just" price by profiteering. At one time it had been common for communities to set a "just" or fair price for a product without paying attention to supply or demand. Massachusetts had no specific law "to limit or direct men in point of profit in their trade," although not for want of trying to implement one that was effective in practice. Apparently, Keayne had a well-earned reputation for buying goods cheaply and then selling them at the highest possible price. Also, it was hinted that from time to time he loaned money at "excessive" interest rates—a practice known as usury.[12]

Besides a General Court conviction Keayne was "admonished" by the elders of his church and was forced to publicly ask for forgiveness from the members of the congregation. His minister, John Cotton, attacked Keayne in an address delivered on "lecture day." Cotton, as well as the magistrates, knew that it was common in other countries for men "to make use of advantages for raising the prices of their commodities." He knew also that Massachusetts men were not above charging the highest possible prices for cattle, corn, and labor. Nevertheless, Cotton proclaimed to his audience that Keayne and others conducted their business affairs according to "false principles."[13] He then summarized those false principles:

1. That a man might sell as dear as he can, and buy as cheap as he can.
2. If a man lose by casualty of sea, etc., in some of his commodities, he may raise the price of the rest.
3. That he may sell as he bought, though he paid too dear, etc., and though the commodity be fallen, etc.
4. That, as a man may take the advantage of his own skill or ability, so he may of another's ignorance or necessity.
5. Where one gives time for payment, he is to take like recompense of one as of another.[14]

Cotton then listed the correct "rules for trading":

1. A man may not sell above the current price, i.e., such a price as is usual in the time and place. . . .
2. When a man loseth in his commodity for want of skill, etc., he must look at his own fault or cross, and therefore must not lay it upon another.
3. Where a man loseth by casualty of sea, or, etc., it is a loss cast upon himself by providence, and he may not ease himself of it by casting it upon another. . . .
4. A man may not ask any more for his commodity than his selling price. . . .[15]

John Cotton was neither a mercantilist nor a capitalist but a Christian moralist. The philosophy he espoused was an old one but it assumed the civil government's and the community's right to intervene and regulate individuals' economic affairs. In that sense it was the immediate ancestor of the mercantilism of the seventeenth century. Robert Keayne was both a good mercantilist and a good capitalist. He believed that the state could regulate individual moral, political, and economic behavior for the good of society. At the same time he felt that a merchant had the right to make a fair profit. To his dying day he refused to believe that he had sinned against his God or broken a civil law. Instead, he argued that he had only done what any good businessman would do: He had set his prices according to supply and demand. Adam Smith would have understood Keayne's dilemma perfectly, for he affirmed that the "laws" of supply and demand should govern economic affairs and he knew that mercantilistic state regulation often twisted, distorted, and frustrated those laws. That was the crux of his argument against the mercantile system.

Robert Keayne, of course, only dimly recognized this contradiction between mercantilism and capitalism. He concluded–and probably correctly–that he was the victim of those who envied his success. His rise had been rapid and he was plagued by those who hinted that he made his money by cheating his customers. So convinced was he that he had been victimized unnecessarily that, when he died, he left behind an extraordinary "will" of 50,000 words. Written in 1653, his will not only disposed of his property but it analyzed and defended his highly successful career as a businessman. It was more like an audit than a last testament because Keayne explained his bookkeeping procedures and many of his business transactions to try–one last time–to prove that he was a just and moral man. "I have been the longer and more particular in this relation," he concluded:

> to ease my own oppressed spirit which hath not been a little burdened about this thing and to leave a testimony of my innocency, so far as I was innocent, to the world behind me and [to show] how apprehensive I was and still am of the injury I then received therein.[16]

Robert Keayne's "crime" indicated how mercantile assumptions contributed to Anglo-America's growth; it also illustrated how quickly some assumptions were rendered obsolete and were replaced by others more conducive to colonial development. As the seventeenth century progressed colonial governments made fewer efforts to manage economic growth, especially as legislatures became battle grounds for competing economic interests. Nevertheless, even these colonials continued to accept basic mercantile assumptions about the right of the state to regulate commerce and the role of the colonies in building England into a world power. By choice colonists had become producers of raw materials and consumers of English manufactured goods. However, they expected the empire to protect their interests and allow them to pursue wealth basically unfettered by bureaucratic restraints.

ENGLAND AND THE AMERICAN COLONIES

Although mercantilism fashioned the basic relationship between England and its American colonies, another factor–England's domestic development–also influenced the course of colonial policy. England's attitude toward the colonies during the seventeenth century was fundamentally affected by the struggle between king and Parliament during the 1640s which produced civil war. Constitutional and religious issues were settled for a time at least with the execution of Charles I and the dissolution of the Church of England. After a brief period of rule through Parliament alone, the hero of the Puritan cause and leader of Parliament's army, Oliver Cromwell, assumed control of the government.

Cromwell, Lord Protector of England between 1653 and 1658, was the first English ruler to see the potential of the colonies and the first to endorse a mercantilist notion of empire. Cromwell had read and digested a host of mercantilist tracts published in England and on the Continent. Among the most important was a book manuscript, *England's Treasure by Foreign Trade,* written by Thomas Mun. This book summarized most of the arguments advanced by mercantilists everywhere. Like the writings of the Hakluyts, it emphasized the value of colonies as an important source of national wealth and power by their producing raw materials, consuming finished goods, and, above all, stimulating commerce. Also like the Hakluyts, Mun combined economics and nationalism and offered a blueprint for England's drive to the status of a world power. Trade was the key. The nation that dominated trade dominated the world. Exports had to exceed imports, Mun argued, for through such a favorable "balance" of trade bullion would flow to the exporting nation.[17] To English mercantilists of Cromwell's era, the Dutch provided a perfect example of the truth of Mun's thesis. A small, insignificant area only lately emancipated from Spanish control, the Netherlands had become Europe's foremost power by dominating Atlantic commerce. For England to rise that power had to be broken. Equally important to mercantilists of the 1650s was the conviction that the development of England's colonial system required more stringent supervision and regulation. Colonists enjoyed too much political and economic freedom. A necessary first step was to end their trade with foreign nations, especially the Dutch.

Cromwell believed Mun's argument and tried to follow it, though he added a few very important wrinkles of his own. He revitalized England's imperial mission and made it a legitimate goal of state policy. He maintained a strong army, built up the navy, and used both to pacify the British Isles and make war on the Dutch. Cromwell, however, had little enthusiasm for a war with Protestant Holland, and he pulled England out at the first opportunity (1654), settling nothing between the two countries. In Catholic Ireland Cromwell sent his armies against the natives, and after a series of bloody battles and ruthless campaigns which left a legacy of hate down to the present time, Ireland was temporarily pacified.

Cromwell saw the need to regulate the infant trade of the colonies and draw them politically closer to England, but again, he was reluctant to move against them since so many colonists had supported the parliamentary cause during the Civil Wars. He had much greater interest in breaking the power of Catholic Spain in the New World. In 1654 he sent a large expedition into the West Indies to capture Puerto Rico, Hispaniola, and hopefully the great Spanish port in Central America, Cartagena (the port for many treasure fleets). The expedition failed, capturing only the island of Jamaica. Nevertheless, though Cromwell could not foresee it, Jamaica would become a principal cog in England's New World empire.

The restoration of monarchy under Charles II, in 1660, brought internal tranquility to England for the first time in over half a century. It also brought a nationalistic and imperialistic king to the throne. Charles and his principal advisor, Edward Hyde, first Earl of Clarendon, continued Cromwell's expansionist policies, although they shifted the emphasis considerably. Serious attention was given to curbing the power of the Dutch in the New World and on the high seas. An expedition sent against New Amsterdam in 1664 succeeded in bringing that colony into the British fold. Charles provoked a war with the Dutch (1665 to 1667) but it achieved meager results, largely because the English fleet had not been maintained well since Cromwell's death in 1658. In 1667, Charles was trying to secure peace when a Dutch fleet entered the Thames River and broke a great cable protecting English warships anchored in the Medway. Three of England's largest ships were destroyed and two more–including the *Royal Charles,* the flagship of the fleet–were towed to Holland. "So God help us!" wrote Samuel Pepys, the Secretary of the Acts in the Navy Office and chronicler of the early years of Charles II's reign.[18] As it turned out, Clarendon needed the help, for he was impeached in order to cover the incompetence of Charles' brother James–the Lord High Admiral–and much of the naval establishment. Parliament and the nation wanted a scapegoat and Charles gave them Clarendon. Samuel Pepys viewed the charade from close quarters and, like a loyal employee, tried to minimize the importance of the dismissal. In his diary, he gave the final act little more space than he allowed for his own wife's music lessons:

> At the office all the morning–where, by Sir W. Penn I do hear that the Seal was fetched away to the King yesterday from the Lord Chancellor by Secretary Morrice–which puts me into a great horror, to have it done after so much debate and confidence that it would not be done at last . . . . This day, being dissatisfied with my wife's learning so few songs of Goodgroome, I did come to a new bargain with him, to teach her songs at so much, *viz.,* 10 *s.* a song, which he accepts of and will teach her.[19]

However, Charles exacted retribution for both Clarendon and the naval disaster in the Medway in 1674 when the English defeated the Dutch in a series of decisive naval engagements and ended Holland's reign as a commercial power in the western hemisphere.

The Navigation Acts

Part of England's tactics against the Dutch included denying Dutch ships access to colonial ports. That practice began in 1651 when Parliament passed an act which specifically excluded Dutch ships from Anglo-American ports, though its enforcement provisions were so vague that very little was accomplished. Charles and Clarendon did much more. They developed a twofold policy toward the American colonies that characterized official British thinking and behavior until 1763. One aspect involved the creation of a legislative and regulatory apparatus to control and stimulate colonial trade while keeping foreign ships from trading in colonial ports. This policy developed through the passage of important Navigation Acts in 1660, 1662, 1663, 1673, and 1696. Of course these acts were meant to deal with much larger issues and problems than those represented by the British North American colonies but, nonetheless, they had important implications for Anglo-America. The early acts passed between 1660 and 1663 established the basic character of British regulatory policy for the next century. Besides reaffirming the Act of 1651, the 1660 act, usually referred to as the First Navigation Act, specified that henceforth

> noe Goods or Commodities whatsoever shall be Imported into or Exported out of any Lands Iselands [sic] Plantations or Territories to his Majesty be-

> longing or in his possession . . . but in such Ships or Vessells as doe truely and without fraude belong onely to the people of England . . . or are of the built of, and belonging to any of the said Lands Islands Plantations or Territories . . .[20]

In addition, the 1660 act required that colonial ships carry crews "wherof [sic] the Master and three fourthes of the Marriners at least are English." Also, the First Navigation Act created a class of "enumerated" products which could be shipped only to England, Ireland, or one of the other English "plantations." The first enumerated items included all of the important colonial "money" crops such as tobacco, sugar, indigo, and cotton. The notion of an enumerated product had developed over four decades through various degrees, but the First Navigation Act placed it in law for the first time.[21]

The act of 1663 ordered that "noe Commoditie of the Growth Production or Manufacture of Europe shall be imported into any Land Island Plantation Colony Territory or Place to His Majestie belonging . . . but what shall be bona fide and without fraude laden and shipped in England . . . and in English built Shipping."[22] Just as the First Navigation Act meant to give England control over colonial exports, the 1663 law intended to keep foreign merchants from operating directly with Anglo-American agents, thus encouraging colonials to buy English goods and guaranteeing England's control over colonial imports. As a byproduct of all the trade legislation passed by Parliament during the late seventeenth century, an enlarged bureaucracy emerged to handle colonial affairs, including a special advisory board to the Crown established in 1675 and designated as the Lords of Trade and Plantations.

Few of the provisions of the early Navigation Acts were enforced rigidly. In part they met some colonial resistance and in part the British government lacked adequate enforcement machinery. The situation changed with the passage of the Navigation Act of 1696. In contrast to the laws of 1660 and 1663, entitled respectively "An Act for the Encourageing and Increasing of Shipping and Navigation" and "An Act for the Encouragement of Trade," the 1696 act declared its intent, as "An Act for Preventing Frauds and regulating Abuses in the Plantation Trade." One of the most important pieces of legislation dealing with colonial affairs before 1763, the 1696 act expanded the English customs service to include Anglo-America. It also provided for the appointment of customs officials in every major port in the colonies. Customs officials were to

> have the same Powers and Authorities for visiting and searching of Shipps and takeing their Entries and for seizing and securing or bringing on Shoare any of the Goods prohibited to bee imported or exported into or out of any the said Plantations for which any Duties are payable or ought to have been paid . . . as are provided for the Officers of the Customes in England . . .[23]

At the same time, and most important for the enforcement of maritime laws and regulations, the Navigation Act of 1696 extended the jurisdiction of England's admiralty court system to America, giving it the power to try cases involving violations of the navigation acts, especially smuggling. England had long maintained a tradition of specialized courts, and admiralty courts–which dealt with all maritime affairs—were a prime example. Their extension to America proved a significant step in the regulation of colonial trade. Finally, in the same year—1696—King William created the Board of Trade and gave it prime responsibility for making colonial policy and monitoring colonial affairs. The Board of Trade replaced the Lords of Trade and Plantations.[24]

Royal Government

The other component of colonial policy developed by Charles II was the attempt to bring the mainland colonies under closer English political supervision—primarily through the creation of royal governments in each colony. English officials were appalled by the degree of independence shown by colonies like Massachusetts (especially since New England had supported Parliament, not the King during the Civil War era). Further, they were disgusted by some colonial institutions (such as dissenting churches), by the existence of illegal colonies (such as Connecticut), and by the colonials' occasional disregard for existing maritime restrictions. But it was not easy to revoke a charter, even if it had been issued in earlier times and under suspicious circumstances. Neither Crown nor Parliament could simply void a charter. The Restoration settlement that returned Charles II to the throne outlawed government by fiat and affirmed the rule of law. This meant not only parliamentary supremacy but also the sanctity of the courts. The charters of the colonies were contracts, and as such they were protected by centuries of English legal practice. The only way the government could void a colonial charter was to prove in court that the colonists had violated their responsibilities under the contract. If such a breach could be proved, the court would issue a writ of *quo warranto,* voiding the charter and paving the way for the establishment of royal government.

Charles and his advisors worked to amass damaging evidence against the colonies still outside the rule of the Crown. Massachusetts Bay drew special attention because of its history of intransigence. In the first years of his reign, Charles and his Chancellor, Clarendon, made a determined effort to void Massachusetts' charter at the same time New Amsterdam was taken from the Dutch. The English expeditionary force to North America included four "commissioners" whose instructions specified that they gather evidence relative to allegations of charter violations by Massachusetts. The Commission received little cooperation during its stay in New England, mostly because the commissioners did not attempt to hide their dislike for the colonials. In 1665 the Commission wrote a very critical report calling for the nullification of Massachusetts' charter because of repeated violations. Charles ordered Massachusetts to send representatives to England to answer the Commissions' charges. The colony refused, voting to send Charles a gift of two large masts for the Royal Navy instead. One member of the General Court, probably Daniel Dennison, tried to cool tempers on both sides by putting Charles' action in the best light possible. "The king may accept any complaint, and require an answer thereto," Dennison observed, "so that our absolute power to determine must not abate the king's prerogative." Deputy Governor Francis Willoughby responded to the situation with words that seemed almost prophetic: "How easily may the king in one year undo all that he hath done," thundered Willoughby, "for if the king may send for me now, and another to-morrow, we are a miserable people."[25]

The Dutch War diverted Charles' attention and saved Massachusetts from legal proceedings against its charter. That diversion, however, proved only temporary. Enemies of the colony continued to charge that it considered itself independent of English control and that it ignored the Navigation Acts and traded with whomever it pleased. The Crown moved toward a new confrontation with the Bay Colony in the mid-1670s. Agents for Massachusetts in London warned the government in Boston of its peril. In 1677 the Massachusetts General Court endorsed all the Navigation Acts and declared that Massachusetts would follow both the letter and the spirit of the various laws. That did not slow the momentum building to overturn the Bay Colony's charter.

In May, 1678, Lords of Trade and Plantations recommended quo warranto proceedings against the Massachusetts' charter. The Lords' recommendation was based, in part, upon information coming from New England from Edward Randolph. For two years Randolph had acted as the Lords' agent in New England and he had filed at least two reports documenting many examples of violations of the Navigation Acts by Massachusetts' shipping and trading interests–violations which were neither reported nor prosecuted. In June, 1678, Randolph gained an official position as the first collector of customs for New England. By 1680 he was firmly settled in Boston. In 1681 he received a commission giving him full responsibility for the enforcement of the Navigation Acts in New England. Randolph was motivated partly by a desire to advance himself and partly by a belief in England's imperial destiny and the small role that he could play in fulfilling it. He continued to call attention to alleged violations of the Navigation Acts by Massachusetts and to urge action against the colony. In this he was joined by powerful men in the royal bureaucracy in England–men like William Blathwayt, Secretary to the Lords of Trade and Auditor-general for the customs' revenues.[26]

Finally, in the last years of Charles' reign the Lords of Trade and various royal officials, members of Parliament, merchants, and other mercantilists who favored tighter political and economic control over the colonies achieved some notable successes. In 1679, New Hampshire, up to that time a part of Massachusetts, became a royal colony with its own governor. In 1681, Charles gave a proprietary grant to his friend, William Penn, but the power of the Penn family over the proposed colony of Pennsylvania was weakened somewhat by the insertion in the charter of a provision for an elected assembly. (Charles angered and frustrated those wanting tighter control over the colonies by making several proprietary grants to friends during his reign.) In 1682 plans for a proprietary colony in Florida were scuttled. Then, in 1684, the charter of Massachusetts Bay was declared null and void by an English court–an event which owed much to the unceasing efforts of Edward Randolph. In the following year the charters of Connecticut and Rhode Island were disposed of in the same fashion.

The zenith of these actions against the North American colonies came in the creation, in 1685, of the Dominion of New England. A pet project of Charles and the product of a suggestion made years earlier by the Lords of Trade, the Dominion placed all of the New England colonies and New York under a single royal governor, Edmund Andros, who resided in Boston. A lieutenant governor received authority to administrate the affairs of New York. This proved to be one of the most unpopular measures enacted by the British before 1763. By the time Andros arrived in New England, Charles II had died and his brother, James II, had assumed the throne.

Andros attempted to introduce a number of radical changes in the institutional structure of New England society, making the governor and the King he represented despised.

The Glorious Revolution of 1688

Events in England thwarted the attempt by English mercantilists to tighten their control over Anglo-America. In 1688 James II was deposed by an angry Parliament and charged with arbitrary rule and the attempted subversion of the English government. But equally important, James' sympathies for France and his preference for Catholicism alienated his late seventeenth-century Protestant subjects fearful of Catholic domination. The news of James' overthrow arrived in New England at about the same time that a popular revolt in Boston placed the hated Andros in jail and a similar rebellion in New York did the same to Lieutenant Governor Francis Nicholson. From Cambridge, Massachusetts, in July, 1689, former Bay Colony magistrate Thomas Danforth wrote to Rev. Increase Mather in London to tell him of the revolt in Boston (Mather would soon act as Massachusetts' agent in negotiations with the new King and Queen, William and Mary): "We are eased of those great oppressions that we groaned under," Danforth wrote:

> The business was acted by the soldiers that came armed into Boston from all parts, to the great amazement of all beholders, being greatly animated by the Prince's [William's] declarations . . . and heightened by the oppressions of the governor, judges, and the most wicked extortion of their debauched officers. The ancient magistrates and elders, although they had strenuously advised to further waiting for orders from England, . . . yet were they now compelled to assist with their presence and councells for the prevention of bloodshed, which had most certainly been the issue if prudent councells had not been given to both parties.[27]

The New York rebellion was quelled forcibly by English troops and Massachusetts' leaders waited fearfully to see what would happen to the Bay Colony. "I am deeply sensible that we have a wolf by the ears," Thomas Danforth told Increase Mather.[28] The wolf did not bite, however. The Massachusetts rebels quickly professed loyalty to William and Mary and their "revolution" was excused. Under the new monarchs, Mary (James' daughter) and William of Orange (a noted Dutch political and military figure), at least part of the colonial policy of Charles and James was overturned. The Dominion died quietly and liberal charters guaranteeing some self-government went to colonies like Massachusetts. While the Bay Colony retained a royal governor, New Jersey, a colony made royal under the Dominion, returned to the control of a proprietor. Ironically, at the same time, responding to a rebellion against proprietary rule in Maryland, Parliament revoked Lord Baltimore's charter and turned Maryland into a royal colony with a representative assembly.

Although the Dominion failed, the goals of mercantilists and imperialists were served well by the Navigation Act of 1696, which provided both the bureaucracy and regulatory machinery for colonial affairs. Moreover, the Dominion's failure did not destroy the long-range goals of greater external regulation of colonial commerce and tighter control over colonial governments. Concerning the latter, the Board of Trade's 1721 report, *State of the British Plantations in America,* not only called upon the colonies to aid England's drive toward self-sufficiency but it also urged a complete reorganization of the administrative structure of the empire. Observing that "some of the Proprietary and charter Governments have shewn too great an inclination to be independent of their Mother kingdom," the Board recommended that all of the colonies be put "under the Government of one Lord Lieutenant, or Captain General, from whom all other Governors of particular provinces should receive their orders . . . . "[29] England never went that far but, as we see later, by 1763 most of the colonies were led by royal governors. Together with customs officials and admiralty court judges, they formed the core of England's overseas colonial administration until the American Revolution.[30]

4

Economic Growth and Social Change

The establishment of colonies in the New World resulted from the profound commercial and political "revolution" which transformed Europe between 1350 and 1750. This transformation launched an even greater series of changes and technological advances known as the Industrial Revolution in the years after 1750. Initially, the New World was discovered during Europe's quest for a new, shorter route to the riches of the Orient. Once discovered, America held out the prospect of wealth closer to home. Early European explorers, therefore, established outposts in the New World to pursue trade with alien civilizations and to look for gold and silver.

Against this background, Richard Hakluyt, Humphrey Gilbert, and others wrote treatises on trade and national glory. But, initially, only a few English people saw the New World as adding much to England's rise. Spanish gold and silver production had already declined by the end of the sixteenth century, and few new mines were found. Future discoveries of precious metals seemed unlikely. Moreover, prospects for lucrative trade with indigenous Indian civilizations appeared slim as well. Limited contact with North American Indians, along with the tales of European explorers, suggested that the natives in North America were inferior to the Aztecs and Incas and offered little to the English capitalist.

A few men, such as Humphrey Gilbert, pushed England into America despite the early skepticism of England's government and some of its great traders. But the early expansion efforts were ill-conceived and poorly financed, and the English compiled a record of dismal failures. As get-rich-quick ventures the colonies were a bust for virtually all of the speculatively inclined merchants and landed gentry who financed them. Investors in early Virginia, for example, lost £200,000 by 1620.

Joint-stock enterprises such as the Plymouth and London Companies lasted only a short time. Proprietors did not fare much better. Even later in the seventeenth century, when the colonies of Massachusetts and Virginia flourished, proprietors such as William Penn or the backers of the Georgia and Carolina experiments either pulled out because of the financial burden or learned to live with mounting debts.

How then did Anglo-America and the West Indies become the basis for England's great eighteenth-century empire? Through persistence and trial and error, the English learned that extracting precious metals and trading with natives need not provide the only avenue to wealth and power or the only reason for expansion and colonization. They borrowed ideas and practices from their imperial rivals in the West Indies and Latin America. They also applied, experimented with, and modified English ideas and practices. In the end, they learned the art of *creating wealth* in an alien environment—that is, of producing raw materials from farms, forest, and sea for English, European, and other colonial markets, and then constructing the ships and marketing mechanisms to handle them. Sending raw materials to England for processing and resale fueled England's commercial and economic development. At the same time, economically successful Anglo-Americans became the prime consumers of English manufactured goods, thus stimulating England's industrial revolution in the late eighteenth century. As a result, when the new imperial powers—France and England—conducted their great struggle for hegemony of Europe and control of North America in the eighteenth century, the real motives for overseas expansion had changed. Administrators and promoters of North America no longer expected to reap wealth through precious metals. Instead, they measured an empire's worth by its capacity to produce raw materials needed by the parent country and to consume manufactured goods.

Building a new kind of colonial empire based on production of raw materials and consumption of finished goods required thousands of colonists with the strength and ingenuity to exploit the resources of a lush continent. England found it had them in abundance—not in the Court nor the Parliament, nor in the counting houses, nor in the great estates of the countryside; but in the villages among land-hungry yeomen and in the cities among the expatriates of the countryside who showed a willingness to go almost anywhere and do almost anything offering the opportunity for a better life. By 1670, about 100,000 Britons lived in scattered settlements along the Atlantic seaboard. Most lived in either Virginia or Massachusetts, and in the development of those colonies lay the key to England's economic success in North America.

Jamestown (Virginia) was the critical colony. Founded by the joint-stock Virginia Company, Jamestown was intended to prosper through trade with the Indians and the discovery of precious metals. Initially, all land was held in common and ruling authority remained in England among the investors. As we have seen, a "starving time"ensued for the Jamestown colonists as neither gold nor silver nor Indian trade emerged. Continually teetering on the verge of financial disaster, the Company experienced reorganization upon reorganization. In the most significant shift, the colonists searched for agricultural stability through a money crop. John Rolfe's introduction of tobacco plants from the West Indies provided the answer. Still, the English seemed reluctant to go to the infant colony, probably because it had a reputation in many circles as "an unhealthy place, a nest of Rogues, whores, desolute and rooking persons; a place of intolerable labour, bad usage and hard Diet."[1]

A money crop required land under production and labor to work it. That produced a series of innovations which secured Virginia's future. Colonists were lured to the colony when they were promised their own land and assured considerable local control over their own affairs. They were drawn, also, by promises that hard work would be rewarded with a comfortable life and high social position—something which would be denied them if they stayed in England. "It is knowne," wrote a pro-Virginia pamphleteer in 1656, "that some from being wool-hoppers and of as mean and meaner imployment in England have there [in Virginia] grown great merchants, and attained to the most eminent advancements the Country afforded. If men cannot gaine (by diligence) states in those parts," he concluded, "I speake not only mine owne opinion, but divers others, . . . it will hardly be done."[2] Those too poor to pay their own way were accommodated by inventions like the headright and indentured servitude (discussed shortly). Another answer to the labor problem arrived in 1619 with the first boat load of African slaves. By 1624 the Virginia Company lay in shambles, its investors bankrupt; but Virginia prospered. Though the Crown was forced to assume control of the colony, Virginia had shown the English how to colonize and thrive. The way to prosperity lay through money crops or their equivalent: raw materials with utility in English or European or other colonial markets. Moreoever, to create such wealth required thousands of laborers and Virginia's experience showed that private property and local control were necessary prerequisites to attract them. In Virginia and adjacent areas the results were impressive. During the initial stages of settlement Virginia's settlers experimented with cotton, indigo, sugar, olives, oranges, and tobacco; but only tobacco became a staple money crop. Although the market was small at first, tobacco soon became immensely popular in Europe. Virginia's production of tobacco expanded from 2500 pounds in 1616 to 30 million pounds per year at the end of the seventeenth century, to 100 million pounds annually by the mid-eighteenth century. Besides cultivating tobacco, the South as a whole developed rice and indigo as money crops in the pre-Revolutionary period.

The English learned slowly—but they learned. To the north of Virginia another joint-stock venture, the Massachusetts Bay Company, started a colony in 1630. Years earlier, in 1616, John Smith published *A Description of New England,* warning potential investors that while the region had no precious metals or luxuries like figs, spices, and silks, it offered much to the industrious. He wrote,

> The ground is so fertill that questionless it is capable of producing any Grain, Fruits, or Seeds you will sow or plant . . . . All sorts of cattel may here be bred and fed in the Iles, or *Peninsulaes,* securely for nothing . . . . Salt vpon salt may assuredly be made, if not at the first in ponds, yet till they bee prouided this may be vsed: then the Ships may transport Kine, Horse, Goates, course cloath, and such commodities as we want.[3]

Smith went on to utter other prophetic words about the promise of the sea and the forests and concluded that "who euer as they are able to subsist of themselues may beginne the new Townes in *New England* in memory of their olde: which freedome being confined but to the necessity of the generall good, and the euent (with Gods helpe) might produce an honest, a noble, and a profitable emulation."[4]

The English *were* learning, and a "profitable emulation" began with the arrival of John Winthrop's Puritan band in 1630. The nonconformists who arrived with Winthrop, and the thousands more who joined them during the "Great Migration" to New England during the 1630s, established tiny agricultural villages based on an ancient English and European model. In addition, they trapped for furs, traded with the Indians, fished for cod, and built small ships for coastal trade, using lumber, fish, and corn and cattle from their farms as saleable items. Over all this activity, however, hung the mantle of covenanted communities, "congregational" churches, religious zeal, and the communalism so specifically outlined in Winthrop's "Modell of Christian Charity" speech given aboard the Arbella.

Was Massachusetts Bay a denial of the individualism and opportunism so apparent in early Virginia and the young English settlements in the West Indies? Was a "better life" in Massachusetts and New England to be found only in religiosity and communality? Apparently it was, at least as long as nonconformists fled religious persecution in England in the 1630s and provided willing colonists and laborers for the New Zion. New Englanders never found a money crop like Virginians or West Indians. Instead they practiced near-subsistence agriculture in the European "peasant" tradition. Winthrop and a handful of former "country gentlemen" tried to control the affairs of the Bay Colony through the General Court, a body originally intended to include only those who owned shares in the Massachusetts Bay Company. The Court granted parcels of land to the towns, and the towns decided the allocation of lands among the inhabitants. Land was meant to be held by the towns in common, with individuals' receiving some "private property," but only what they needed with much held aside for future generations. Growth of the colony and the towns was meant to be controlled. For example, the founders of Springfield, Massachusetts, specified that "our town shall be composed of forty families or, if we think meet to alter our purpose . . . not to exceed the number of fifty families."[5] Laws were passed by the General Court touching all aspects of human behavior and severely limiting individual aggressiveness. The towns sought common standards of behavior through town and church "covenants" signed by all. The settlers' search for social cohesiveness shows clearly in the following excerpts taken from the covenant or agreement signed by the founders of Dedham, Massachusetts, in 1636:

> One: We whose names are here unto subscribed do, in the fear and reverence of our Almighty God, mutually and severally promise amongst ourselves and each other to profess and practice one truth according to that most perfect rule, the foundation whereof is everlasting love . . . .
>
> Two: That we shall by all means labor to keep off from us all such as are contrary minded, and receive only such unto us as may be probably of one heart with us . . . .
>
> Three: That if at any time difference shall arise between parties of our said town, that then such party and parties shall presently refer all such difference unto some one, two, or three others of our said society to be fully accorded and determined . . . .
>
> Four: That every man that . . . shall have lots in our said town shall pay his share in all such . . . charges as shall be imposed upon him . . . as also become freely subject unto all such orders and constitutions as shall be . . . made now or at any time hereafter . . . .
>
> Five: And for the better manifestation of our true resolution herein, every

> man so received (into Dedham is) to subscribe hereunto his name, thereby obliging both himself and his successors after him for ever, as we have done.[6]

The Puritans did apply, immediately, one lesson from the Virginia experience—the utility of local control—by taking the charter of the Bay Company with them to New England. Thus, the remaining investors in England played no role in the colony's affairs (except to aid prospective immigrants during the 1630s) and reaped no profits from their investments.

At first, Winthrop's Massachusetts appeared to be a reaction to the changes sweeping Europe and England and a throwback to a real or imagined earlier, more sanguine era. Some writers have called it a *Bible commonwealth.* Others have marked it a series of Puritan/peasant communes. Whatever it was, it began as an experiment definitely out of step with what England and especially Anglo-America would become. But the Bible commonwealth lasted only about a decade. The revolt of Parliamentary and sectarian forces in England crippled the "city upon a hill" by curtailing its flow of immigrants and ending its role as an alternative to English religious and civil "tyranny." In response, some Puritan leaders tried to redefine and broaden Massachusetts' and New England's collective mission. They emphasized a special messianic role the region and its people were meant to play in the final struggle between the forces of good and evil which marked the thousand-year rule by Christ and the eventual end of the world (millennialism). In 1654 Captain Edward Johnson of Woburn, Massachusetts, published the first history of New England. In it he echoed the thoughts of many when he urged his compatriots to do battle with Antichrist (the personification of evil in the biblical prophecies of the last days). "But to come to the time of Antichrists fall," he wrote:

> and all that expect it may depend upon the certainty of it: yea it may be boldly said that the time is come, and all may see the dawning of the day: you that long so much for it, come forth and fight: who can expect a victory without a battle? the lordly Prelates that boasted so much of these great achievements in this work, are fled into holes and corners: Familists, Seekers, Antinomians and Anabaptists, they are so ill armed, that they think it best sleeping in a whole skin, fearing that if the day of battle once go on, they shall fall among Antichrists Armies: and therefore cry out like cowards, If you will let me alone, and I will let you alone; but assuredly the Lord Christ hath said, *He that is not with us, is against us*: there is no room in his Army for toleratorists . . . now is the time, seeing the Lord hath set up his standard of resort: now, *Come forth of her, and be not partakers of her sins*: now is the time, when the Lord hath assembled his Saints together; now the Lord will come and not tarry.[7]

Edward Johnson's call for united action against Antichrist was not heeded. To survive after 1640, Massachusetts and the other New England colonies had to become more like Virginia. The communal zealousness of the Bay Colony and its towns gradually faded. Though covenanted, subsistence-level agricultural communities continued, their slow growth owed more to limited resources than to legal restrictions. Private property, decentralization, and greater personal freedom emerged as New Englanders defined their mission more in economic than religious terms.

Massachusetts' saintly glow continued but the New England colonies worked hard to guarantee their economic success by appealing to the desire for material gain and well-being among inhabitants and potential immigrants alike. Trade based on an agricultural surplus and the products of forest and sea became the key to the area's future. "This year corn [wheat] was very scarce and so it was in all countries of Europe," John Winthrope wrote in 1648. "Our scarcity came by occasion of our transporting much to the West Indies, and the Portugal and Spanish Islands."[8]

Indian corn, however, proved to be the major agricultural product produced for trade by New Englanders during the seventeenth century. Most of it went to other mainland colonies or to the rapidly developing sugar plantations of Barbados or the Leeward Islands in the West Indies. In addition, Rhode Island exported wool, mutton, and horses and tiny Connecticut, easily the least expansive of the early New England colonies, managed to export some wheat, rye, peas, beef, pork, barley, hemp, wool, and flax, as well as Indian corn. All of the New England colonies exported wood and wood products. In 1680, for example, Connecticut listed its wood exports as "parry and tar, deal boards, and pipe staves."[9] Finally, most New England colonies exported fish, especially cod.

Still, nothing New Englanders grew, or took from their forests, or fished from the sea ever made much of an impact on ledger books in England during the seventeenth century. There, the most important colonial products were West Indian sugar and Virginia tobacco, and those two products created most of the Anglo-American colonies' wealth during the era. However, New Englanders did make an important contribution to colonial development that had nothing to do with a product. Instead, they provided a service: shipping. Thanks mainly to the early Indian corn and wheat surpluses, enterprising colonials living in coastal communities like Boston, or Salem, or Ipswich began building small ships for coastal trade almost as they built houses to live in. Within a few years New England ships sailed regularly to New York, Virginia, the West Indies, Newfoundland, and even to England and Europe. For example, in 1645 one of New England's finest ships, the *Seafort* (over 400 tons), ran aground and sank off the coast of Spain with the loss of many lives. The *Seafort* was a large ship by both English and European standards. Moreover, the fact that New Englanders' had built the ship for the Atlantic carrying trade as early as 1645–only fifteen years after Massachusetts' founding–was amazing. John Winthrop reported that the *Seafort* was constructed at Boston by Captain Thomas Hawkins, "a shipwright of London, who had lived here divers years." He "had set her out with much strength of ordnance and ornament of carving, painting, etc. and . . . he set sail from Boston, accompanied with another ship of London." Both ships were "laden with bolts, tobacco, etc. for Malago."[10] (Malaga was located near the port of Cadiz on the Costa del Sol in Spain.) A few years after the *Seafort* disaster came the important mercantile regulations of the 1660s, which specified "enumerated goods" but also made it mandatory for English goods–and all goods going in and out of English and colonial ports–to be transported by English (which included colonial) ships. That proved to be a tremendous boon to New England shipping and ship building. By 1700, New Englanders had 2000 ships plying the waters of the Atlantic, with many going regularly to ports in England and Europe.

Still, for all the bustle, the seventeenth century was characterized by little rise in the per capita income of Anglo-Americans. Except for a handful of Boston merchants, a few Virginia and Maryland tobacco planters and South Carolina rice planters, and the spectacular activity of sugar planters on the island of Barbados, most colonists engaged in subsistence agriculture—that is, they consumed what they produced with only a little left over for trade. What were the reasons? One school of thought suggests that subsistence was all that was intended; that the peasant mentality of many of the colonists, especially in New England, dictated a continuation of the medieval agricultural village and a live-according-to-the-cycles-of-nature, no-growth mentality. Actually, the problem was much more complicated. Frontier conditions, which were faced by all colonists almost continuously through the seventeenth century, dictated a static economy and subsistence-level activity. To go beyond that required basic economic change. For example, there had to be population growth. As we have seen, seventeenth-century Anglo-America had that; but it was small compared to what would follow in the eighteenth century. Actually, immigration from England picked up after the English Civil War period, remained steady until about 1675, and then dropped to practically nothing after 1689. Outside the Chesapeake region, colonial population expansion was fueled mainly by a phenomenal birth rate and a low infant-mortality rate compared to European figures for the same era.

Another problem was land. This might seem odd considering that land was the most plentiful resource in North America, but one must remember that English colonists were used to centuries of land *scarcity* and *overpopulation.* They were not prepared mentally or technologically to put hundreds of thousands of fallow acres into production in a manner that would guarantee yearly increases in production and constantly rising personal income. They were used to scarcity; to working small plots—owned by someone else—for a meager crop with little or no hope of increasing either production or holdings. Even if they had been prepared to exploit the land for all it was worth, they lacked the labor to achieve much growth. Colonists wanted their own land; they did not want to work for someone else. Finally, even if labor had been plentiful, markets and capital were not. Early colonists were chronically short of capital, and they had to create markets for their products as well as the means to move those products before they could ever hope to rise above subsistence to specialization.

Then, of course, other problems like hostile Indians, hostile foreign powers, and climatic and geographic barriers had to be met. All things considered, seventeenth-century English colonists did remarkably well. They lived good lives—better than they could have expected in England—while they solved the problems we have just outlined. Though their economic growth was slow, they paved the way for the growth which would follow in the eighteenth century, making America what Pennsylvanians liked to call the "best poor man's country." Life in seventeenth-century Anglo-America was no economic bonanza or get-rich-quick paradise and, as we see later, it was especially hard for indentured servants and slaves, but many colonists would have agreed with German Mennonite leader, Francis D. Pastorius, who wrote in 1700 that:

> Although this far-distant land was a dense wilderness—and it is only quite recently that it has come under the cultivation of the Christians—there is much cause of wonder and admiration how rapidly it has already, under the blessing of God, advanced, and is still advancing, day by day.[11]

LAND AND LABOR

The prosperity of Anglo-Americans resulted from some critical decisions made by the first colonists. Those decisions reflected a trial-and-error period in which the colonists discarded some of the beliefs and institutions brought from England and Europe, modified others, and even created a few of their own. That selective incorporation of European culture into Anglo-American life gave colonial institutions a hybrid character. Although they resembled parent institutions in some ways, at the same time they possessed distinctive "Americanized" features of their own. The process was not willy-nilly, however. It reflected the conscious choices of the colonists as they tried to determine what would best guarantee the fulfillment of the main goals of settlement. Nowhere was the rational, pragmatic character of the process more apparent than in the methods adopted by colonists to partition, distribute, and farm the lands they settled.

During the Middle Ages, only a few persons actually owned the land they inhabited or cultivated. Indeed, most property was held by the established church or the aristocracy. The king, who was theoretically considered the "lord of the realm," bestowed title to land upon his nobles who in turn granted the right to cultivate their lands to others in exchange for special duties, such as military service, and annual fees (called quitrents). The tenant's "right" to use the land versus that of the lord varied considerably, depending upon local customs and traditions. Because of those local variations, the medieval world possessed a complex system through which it regulated the possession and use of the land.

Two basic systems of utilizing land for agriculture prevailed in England and Europe. In the first, the *open-field* system, the right to use the land was considered a privilege available to the members of the community. With virtually the entire population engaged in agricultural pursuits, and with the amount of fertile, tillable land in short supply, all land–barren and fertile–was possessed in common by the community. Villagers shared hay grown in the communal meadows, timber cut from the surrounding forests, and pasture land used to graze livestock. Likewise, those areas suitable for cultivation, usually adjacent to the village, were partitioned into small strips of an acre or so in size. The community allotted each farmer a certain number of pieces. Because each villager generally received some good and some bad land, his parcels were frequently scattered throughout the village holdings.

In the *closed-field* system, the other major form of agricultural organization, a somewhat different pattern of land distribution was employed. In England, this system was most prevalent in the southeastern area, such as East Anglia, where the ground was more fertile than the land further north or west. Under the closed-field system, farmers received large single blocks of land surrounding the village. Typically, a limited amount of *common land* was set aside for the benefit of the entire community. Although this practice helped build some common ties among farmers in a given neighborhood, the closed-field system tended to weaken rather than strengthen communal bonds. As tenants moved out of the village to live closer to the land they farmed, they grew less communally oriented and more independent.

Both the open- and closed-field systems, as practiced in England and also in Europe, reflected the medieval concept of land tenure. In fact, the practice of the King's granting a charter–the practice which stimulated England's early colonial expansion–itself reflected the traditional notion of holding and using, rather than owning, land. In general a colonial charter bestowed a parcel of land to a company or proprietor in exchange for a yearly rent (usually one-fifth of any gold or silver discovered). In turn, the company or proprietor conferred permission to individuals to settle and farm pieces of land in exchange for quitrents. Throughout the early years of settlement, proprietors, joint-stock companies, and the royal government considered the settlers renters or users of the land, not "owners."[12]

Almost immediately, however, the early Anglo-American settlements began departing from the medieval concept of land tenure. When the General Court of Massachusetts, acting as the official representative of the Massachusetts Bay Company, sold or otherwise granted land to colonists, it soon treated the purchasers as owners—that is *freeholders* or *freemen.* Colonists paid no quitrents and provided no services to the Bay Company. The rest of Anglo-America slowly moved toward the New England pattern of private ownership, though tenancy and quitrents persisted in many areas. In some of those areas, proprietors and company representatives attracted poor settlers with offers of tenancy on wilderness land. The Calverts, for example, took about £4000 a year from Maryland through quitrents during much of the seventeenth century, and other proprietors tried to do the same (as did the royal officials of Virginia, for example). But quitrents were never popular and as more and more land lay in private hands it became increasingly difficult for tenants to accept the obligations of their tenancy. The legal and administrative structures of most colonies were too weak and inefficient to force compliance and the presence of available unsettled land made it easy for individuals to escape the bounds of the law by moving to the frontier. The quitrent survived until 1776, but its utility diminished to almost nothing.

Despite the challenge the frontier posed to the old ways and institutions of Europe, the first colonists nevertheless succeeded in establishing both the open- and closed-field systems in America. Many of those who settled Massachusetts Bay came from areas of England where the open-field system dominated. Not surprisingly, therefore, groups of communally inclined immigrants were quick to obtain land from the General Court, erect central villages, and partition the surrounding areas into the familiar small patches of land so that all their members received some fertile and some barren land. At the same time, they also reserved other lands in common ownership for future generations and for new settlers. The New England open-field system did deviate somewhat from that in England, not in the pattern of distribution (land parcels continued to be spread out over a large area), but in that individuals owned their land.

At the same time that the open-field system was established in many New England towns, settlers in the southern colonies tended to stake out individual, isolated farms, adopting a pattern of distribution resembling the closed-field system. That traditional form of land utilization as much as the geography of the region (with its multitude of inlets and rivers) encouraged settlers to forsake village life for the remoteness of the plantation.

By the end of the seventeenth century, private property became the norm for Anglo-America. Along with it, the family "farm," a small, independent, self-sufficient agricultural unit, gradually replaced other forms of land utilization. Even in New England, where the communal instincts of the early settlers and the institutional arrangements of the colonies tended to encourage the old patterns of settlement, the economic practicality of consolidating land into large, single units and the need to move out of the village to work the farm overcame the community-oriented traditions of the first generation of settlers. In addition, the birth rate was so high that the reserves of common land originally set aside for subsequent generations proved inadequate. The limited amount of land prompted newcomers as well as the sons of the first settlers either to move to the outskirts of a village—weakening the community's control over them—or to settle elsewhere and establish a new village. The trend of settlement gradually eroded the power the community exercised over the individual and encouraged an acquisitive, independent, individualistic ethic rooted in private property.

During the seventeenth century, the size of an average farm was about 200 acres, of which about fifty were cultivated or used for pasture, while the rest was left for children. Because the holdings in North America were considerably larger than those of small, open-field farmers in England, and the land far more fertile than overworked English farmland, colonists soon produced goods for trade as well as for subsistence. In both the North and South, however, the impulse to expand agricultural production suffered from a shortage of labor. Few colonists wanted to work another man's land when they could readily obtain their own. Proprietors tried to maintain a balance between the supplies of land and labor through devices such as tenancy or the *headright.* In the former, as we have seen, the proprietor divided his holdings into small pieces which he then rented to new arrivals lacking cash to purchase their own land. The inability of the proprietor or company to prevent colonists from squatting on unsettled land, however, made tenancy a marginal system for Anglo-America. Colonial authorities achieved more success balancing the availability of land with the labor supply through the headright. That system offered a landless immigrant a parcel of land (usually fifty acres) for each "head" or family member who came with him. In return for a headright, the colonist paid a yearly quitrent. The headright system did draw people to unsettled areas of Anglo-America, but it did little to solve the labor problems on existing farms and plantations.[13]

Indentured Servitude

In order to remedy the labor shortage, proprietors and joint-stock companies began to employ a system of *indentured servitude.* Essentially, they promised to pay an individual's transportation to the New World in exchange for a contract to work for a set period (usually from three to seven years). After the period of servitude expired, the indentured servant received freedom and sometimes a small amount of land as well. Joint-stock companies and proprietors were not the only ones to encourage indentured servitude. The great demand for labor induced many well-to-do colonists to pay for the passage of new settlers to America. They not only profited from the labor they obtained but frequently they received a headright for each person they transported to America.

The indenture system began in Virginia and spread to the other colonies. It never became very significant in New England because of the small farms which dominated that area. In the Chesapeake region, however, its importance cannot be overstated. In Virginia alone, the majority of English immigrants between 1635 and 1689 came as indentured servants. For Virginia and Maryland in the seventeenth century, perhaps a quarter of all English immigrants arrived as indentures. Most were of very humble origins. Their experiences in America varied considerably. If they arrived before 1660 their chances of achieving success were very good. If they arrived after 1660 they found fewer and fewer opportunities. For example, Stephen Sealus and Miles Gibson both came to Maryland as indentured servants in the 1660s. After serving their indentures they gained their freedom and bought land. Sealus lost his "plantation" in the 1670s and became a tenant farmer, a position he held the rest of his life. In 1691 he petitioned his county court for relief, saying he was "both weake and lame" and could not "worke whereby to maintaine himselfe nor his wife." The court accepted his claim, but, apparently, there was little that could be done to overcome his poverty. He died in 1696 and left an estate worth only £18 6s. Miles Gibson, however, prospered. Aided by two good marriages he built his holdings to 2000 acres of land and a personal estate worth over £600 (including nine slaves) by the time of his death in 1692. Considered part of the gentry, he served as sheriff, justice of the peace, and a member of the House of Burgesses during his lifetime. Obviously the careers of Sealus and Gibson differed radically; research suggests that, in late seventeenth-century Maryland, Stephen Sealus' experience typified that of many indentured servants.[14]

The situation was similar in neighboring Virginia. High mortality rates among emigrants meant that a large number of indentured servants poured into Virginia in the early years. Gradually, the life span of Virginians increased, but at the same time opportunities for indentured servants to own land and prosper dwindled. That situation owed something to the activities of masters who exploited their servants and then devised ways to keep them in bondage. Consequently, many potential servants grew wary of Virginia, and Virginia masters had to expand recruiting among exconvicts who had been imprisoned for either criminal acts or indebtedness. Thus, given the ruthlessness of many masters and the unsavory character of many servants, the two became antagonists, with each fearing and perhaps hating the other. The pathetic situation was revealed in a letter concerning a possible Dutch invasion of Virginia written by Virginia Governor William Berkeley to Charles II in 1673. "Virginia," Berkeley explained,

> is intersected by so many vast rivers as makes more miles to defend than we have men of trust to defend them. For by our nearest computation we leave at our backs as many servants (besides Negroes) as there are freemen to defend the shores of all our frontiers . . . which give men fearful apprehension of the danger they leave their estates and families in, whilst they are drawn from their houses to defend the borders. [As to the available freemen] at least one third are single freemen whose labor will hardly maintain them, or men much in debt, both of which may reasonably expect, upon any small advantage the enemy may gain upon us, would revolt (and join the enemy) in hopes of bettering their condition by sharing the plunder of the country with them.[15]

In other words, neither servants nor many former servants could be trusted.

Throughout much of the seventeenth century indentured servants from England provided the colonies with most of their labor. Unfortunately, the supply of indentured laborers directly reflected economic fluctuations in Europe and England. When depression or hard times struck, many people volunteered to go to America; when times were prosperous, the supply of indentured servants dried up.

On the whole, in the last quarter of the seventeenth century, the English economy—spurred by the expansion of overseas trade—entered a period of rising prosperity that greatly reduced the numbers of English men and women willing or eager to become indentured servants in North America. (Declining opportunities in America probably had something to do with it as well.) In addition, at the same time that the English economy was expanding, Anglo-American tobacco producers faced declining prices and fierce competition from Mediterranean tobacco growers. In order to offset low prices, colonial southerners put more land into production. But the increased acreage under cultivation meant that more labor was needed. The Royal African Company (formed in 1672) provided a partial solution to the southern labor problem. It brought black Africans to the West Indian islands where thousands were reexported to the mainland to be used to fuel the agricultural specialization—the cash crops—of the South. Later, as the demand for slaves on the mainland grew, slave ships went directly from Africa to mainland ports.

Slavery

As we mentioned, the first Africans came to the North American mainland in 1619, when a Dutch ship brought a load of blacks to Jamestown. The absence of written statutes regarding the legal position of blacks has led some historians to question whether the first Africans were considered slaves or indentured servants. Regardless of their initial status, however, by the middle of the seventeenth century laws had been passed clarifying the status (or nonstatus) of the slave, and the "peculiar institution" of humiliation and debasement had begun to take root in Anglo-America.

Historians will probably never resolve the question of whether slavery in Anglo-America resulted from economic necessity or from prejudice. Slavery was *not* an indigenous English institution. Nonetheless, along with other Europeans, the English possessed a strong prejudice against non-Christian Africans. That initial bias was made worse by the Africans' skin color, which the English equated with evil and death. In addition, the rise of national, centralized states in Europe sparked a crude form of nationalism and a sense of national pride. As they began to expand overseas, the English embraced nationalism with a passion. Moreover, they were an introspective people, and much of the history of English colonization reveals their obsession with themselves. In the New England town the trait appeared everywhere: in religious beliefs, communal, social, and political attitudes, hostility to strangers and foreigners, general reluctance to admit new persons into the community, and finally, schizophrenia regarding the environment. At one moment they viewed the wilderness as Eden; in the next they condemned it as the source of all evil and corruption.

Because of their self-centeredness English mainland colonists were reluctant to accept Africans among them. Nevertheless, the Spanish and Portuguese used black slave labor many years before the introduction of slavery into Anglo-America, and the success of those nations was well known to the English. Probably, knowledge of the slave system in Latin America and the Indies, coupled with its availability, led the English to embrace slavery to solve their labor shortage.

English slavery developed first in the West Indies, especially Barbados. On the mainland the term *slave* began to appear frequently in the laws of Virginia in the

1650s and, during the 1660s, a "system" of slavery emerged in that colony as the distinctions between white servants and black slaves were spelled out. Blacks were characterized as a white person's "property" whose period of bondage was for life. For example, in 1662 Virginia lawmakers noted that "Whereas some doubts have arisen whether children got by any Englishman upon a negro woman should be slave or free, be it therefore enacted and declared by this present Grand Assembly, that all children born in this country shall be held bond or free only according to the condition of the mother."[16] Seven years later (1669) the reality of the slave as property was affirmed by another law:

> Whereas the only law in force for the punishment of refractory servants resisting their master, mistress or overseer cannot be inflicted upon Negroes, nor the obstinancy of many of them be suppressed by other than violent means, be it enacted and declared by this Grand Assembly if any slave resists his master (or other by his master's order correcting him) and by the extremity of the correction should chance to die, that his death shall not be accounted a felony, but the master (or that other person appointed by the master to punish him) be acquitted from molestation, since it cannot be presumed that premeditated malice (which alone makes murder a felony) should induce any man to destroy his own estate.[17]

At that time there were only about 2000 slaves in the whole colony.

As the demand for laborers among Chesapeake tobacco planters and Carolina rice and indigo planters increased dramatically in the late seventeenth century, independent British and colonial shipowners and merchants challenged the monopoly of the Royal African Company in the slave trade and successfully broke it in 1698. After that, the slave trade with West African "trading" posts or slave stations opened to any industrious entrepreneur, and it quickly grew to astounding proportions. Curiously, at the very time angry English "whigs" were overthrowing a "tyrannical" James II and establishing William and Mary in a Glorious Revolution designed to preserve English liberties, and at the same time New Englanders overthrew another supposed "tyrant," the royal governor of James II's Dominion of New England, Edmund Andros, no English man or woman decried the quickening of traffic of black cargoes into North America or the system of bondage which awaited them. Ironically, the first protest against slavery and the slave traffic in Anglo-America came not from the English but from German Mennonites in Pennsylvania. In the year revered by all the liberty-loving English–1688–a Mennonite congregation in Germantown, Pennsylvania, adopted and published a resolution which follows in part:

> These are the reasons why we are against the traffick of mensbody as followeth . . . we hear that ye most part of such Negers are brought heither against their will & consent, and that many of them are stollen. Now tho' they are black, we cannot conceive there is more liberty to have them slaves, as it is to have other white ones. There is a saying, that we shall doe to all men, licke as we will be done ourselves: macking no differences of what generation, descent, or Colour they are. And those who steal or robb man, and those who buy or purchase them, are they not all alicke? Here is liberty of Conscience, wch is right & reasonable. Here ought to be lickewise liberty

> of ye body, except of evildoers, wch is an other case. But to bring men hither, or to robb and sell them against their will, we stand against.[18]

By the early eighteenth century, slavery surpassed indentured servitude as the dominant labor system on large farms and plantations in the southern colonies. But during the seventeenth century, at least, slavery remained an untypical solution to the colonial labor problem. By and large agricultural units in all of the colonies were small and relied upon family members or an occasional indentured servant to work the land. Likewise, commercial and industrial enterprises, such as shipping or various trades, utilized hired or indentured help throughout the colonies, North and South. As we see later, the rise of single, labor-intensive cash crops as the dominant fact of economic life in the southern colonies was required to bring about the proliferation and heavy utilization of black slavery.[19]

5

Political Thought and Political Practice

Because the colonial era ended in armed revolt and led to a republican government based on a written constitution, the character and evolution of government and politics remain among the most distorted and controversial aspects of the American Odyssey. No historian can forget that the political experience of Anglo-America produced rebellion. The temptation is great to explain colonial government and politics solely as a prelude to the events of the 1770s. During the nineteenth century in particular, historians dealt with the colonial period in precisely those terms. Freedom, democracy, and love of liberty preoccupied them. American history became a chronicle of people and events showing that Anglo-America's development preceded in a straight line to independence. Britain's rulers represented intolerable tyranny, while American colonists became the saviors of liberty and democracy.

By the early twentieth century, however, scholars reexamined this view and put forth some rather different interpretations of the colonial era. Some historians contended that modern concepts and practices such as political democracy were alien to the experience of colonial America. Instead of being considered single-minded exponents of freedom and political liberty, colonials were characterized as happy members of the British Empire until a series of structural changes in that empire during the 1760s placed them in an intolerable position. Even then, revolution represented the final alternative for colonials after the last hopes for redress of grievances were extinguished in 1774 or 1775.

Other historians adopted a contrary view of America's early experience. They argued that Anglo-America had evolved away from European and English norms into a new, unique society. To them the American Revolution was inevitable because at some point colonials had to recognize and assert their special status. The events of the 1760s provided the catalyst which led Anglo-Americans to realize fully their distinct and superior qualities and seek independence. Actually, this view offered a more sophisticated version of the liberty-versus-tyranny explanation of early America's growth discussed previously. In both interpretations, the prime ingredient was the notion of Anglo-America's unique character.[1]

As we see in this and subsequent chapters, neither the notion of America's history as the triumph of liberty over tyranny, nor the view of the Revolution as a peculiar aberration from the rest of the colonial experience, nor the theory of the Revolution's inevitability fits logically into the general evolution of Anglo-America by the mideighteenth century. Instead, the course of colonial development we outline suggests a basic harmony between Anglo-American and English ways. As in other aspects of colonial life, the story of government and politics in early America was a continuing attempt to adapt English ideas and practices to a New World environment. By 1763 the colonists had produced a replica of the English system as they understood it and as conditions permitted. If they departed from their English model—and they did in some important ways—they did so because of necessity or because they had several English models from which to choose. Ironically, the very Anglo-American beliefs and traditions that led ultimately to revolution were precisely those colonists had gleaned from their English heritage.

Probably nothing affected the character of colonial government and politics more than two decisions made by the English early in the seventeenth century. One was the willingness of James I to leave the character of American settlements to the companies, proprietors, and colonists who founded them. The other was the move by a desperate, near-bankrupt Virginia Company to shift ruling authority for the Virginia colony from London to Jamestown. The first decision gave Anglo-Americans most of the seventeenth century to develop institutions to suit their needs. The second brought to the New World a horde of middle-level English people for whom self-government was as important as owning their own land. Together these two decisions ensured that a vital part of the colonial's cultural baggage, *localism,* would influence markedly the government and politics of Anglo-America.[2]

In the Middle Ages local government—dominated by the lord of the manor—was far more important than king or Parliament. The great nobles with their private armies and large land holdings comprised a force stronger, on the whole, than the power of the Crown. Parliament was a weak agency and was dominated by the great nobles who sat in the House of Lords. Thus, ordinary English citizens looked to "their" nobles as the most important political force in their lives. Even the centralization of the state and expansion of monarchical power did not substantially alter the character or importance of local government. The nobility continued to rule the countryside, except for some areas of southern England where depression or war had undermined its power. There, self-governing towns grew from the old agricultural villages of the Middle Ages. These towns were controlled by councils similar to the ones that would be established in New England. Thus, a strong tradition of local control continued, despite the rise of the national state, a vastly strengthened monarchy, or a more active Parliament.[3]

Some things did change, however. Broad economic forces caused instability in English society at the local level. The rise of trade, the expansion of the woolen industry, the enclosure of common lands, and rapid population growth (creating overpopulation in some areas) all helped fuel the "price revolution" of the late sixteenth century. That in turn caused an upheaval in the countryside which drove thousands of English people off the land and into the cities. Some historians have argued that the price revolution also produced a fundamental realignment in England's social structure: a "rise of the gentry" and a decline of the aristocracy as many landowners were compelled to sell their lands. In addition, by the early seventeenth century England experienced rising crime rates and extensive poverty, with nearly half of the population among the ranks of the poor.

Few ordinary English citizens, however, understood the causes of their misery. All they knew was their own poverty—or the threat of impending poverty—and the unsettling, insecure nature of the times. Historian Carl Bridenbaugh called these people "vexed and troubled Englishmen,"[4] and they proved the most willing to settle America. They were attracted by the possibility of owning property and managing their own affairs. But as much as anything, significant numbers of these English people migrated to America during the seventeenth century hoping to recapture in the wilderness the ideal agrarian society they felt they had lost in England. At the basis of this society would be both law and order.

ENGLAND'S LEGACY

Although the first English colonists endorsed the English system of government, it must be remembered that North America was colonized at a time when the English divided and fought a bloody civil war over the character of their civil and religious policies. With the *Petition of Right* in 1628, England began thirty-two years of debate and violence, highlighted by war, the execution of Charles I, the abolition of both monarchy and the Church of England, the rule of a Lord Protector, and finally the restoration of a more limited monarchy and the Church of England. Even a return to monarchy in 1660, however, did not end England's constitutional turmoil. James II was deposed in the Glorious Revolution of 1688, the supremacy of Parliament was declared, and the power of the Crown steadily eroded until the emergence of cabinet or ministerial government in the eighteenth century.[5]

The first English colonists reflected at least some of that political turmoil. Even after the Civil Wars all of the English—colonists included—endorsed the conception of *mixed government.* That concept—manifested in the English system of Crown and Parliament—suggested that the best form of government was one in which all of the elements of society were represented. That did not imply either representative government as we know it (most English citizens were only symbolically represented in Parliament) or universal suffrage (few adult white males could vote). Society, it was believed, was divided into two great classes, nobility and commoners. The English system was a mixed government since the House of Lords represented the nobility and the House of Commons represented all commoners. Those who could vote were represented directly; the rest were "virtually" represented. The Crown represented either everyone or no one, depending upon which of the competing theories of the time one followed. Suffice it to say that the Crown was an important symbolic figure in the English constitution, reflecting the "interests" of the people and the unity of the nation, both contemporaneously and historically.[6]

What was the English *Constitution*? It was a term used to describe the unwritten, accumulative, governmental and legal arrangements as they existed and as they had evolved. Thus, it represented a source of endless confusion as well. English political theorists constantly proclaimed their version of the true "spirit" of the Constitution. The basic problem was that the English Constitution *was* in a state of flux and change. The rise of the modern secular state had thrown many of the assumptions of medieval political theory into a cocked hat. Those assumptions—strangely at odds with the reality of a continental Catholic Church and a multitude of kingdoms and principalities—declared two distinct realms of authority, one secular and one spiritual. Both were God's creations, and both were subject to God's law. Both realms were intended for the governance of the individual. The spiritual kingdom, ruled by the Church, cared for the soul. The secular kingdom, ruled by the state, regulated the flesh.

The functions of state and church were at the same time both regulatory and educative. The individual had the obligation to obey. The instrument of obedience was the law. Human law, whether issued by the state or the church, was a reflection of God's law. God's law was natural law—a term inherited from the ancients and implying rules governing the conduct of the universe. The political theory of the Middle Ages had no coherent notion of individual "rights" as something different from the claims of the state. Liberty was often divided into "natural" and "civil" components, as it was by New England Deputy Governor John Winthrop in his famous "Little Speech on Liberty" given before the Massachusetts General Court in 1645. Natural liberty was the freedom to do anything, or anarchy. Civil liberty meant the freedom to obey the magistrate and, by association, the will of God.[7]

The swift development of the secular state broke the power of the church by the midsixteenth century. In England, the Tudors and then the Stuarts became the supreme earthly heads of church and state and utilized both religious and secular arms to expand the might and prestige of monarchy. In light of what historians have termed the *rise of absolutism,* some men scurried to justify and legitimize the increased power of the monarchy, while others sought ways to curb it. Of the former, the zenith was the theory of the divine right of kings—that is, the assertion that the king was God's spokesman on earth and thus derived his right to rule only from God. The most famous and successful practitioner of that theory was Louis XIV of France (1660-1720). In England James I (1603-1625) tried unsuccessfully to emblazon the Stuart dynasty with the light of divine approbation. Partly as a result of his efforts, two theoretical debates ensued: one over the question of the ultimate source of sovereignty in the state, and the second over the rights of citizens against the claims of the state.[8]

While kings such as James I asserted sovereignty, other English citizens looked to Parliament and the people for final authority. In the process—and again borrowing heavily from the ancients—a new version of natural law began to evolve. It suggested that natural law led to natural rights for individuals. Natural rights were, in turn, immune from the claims of the state. As early as the fifteenth century Sir John Fortescue, an English jurist, argued that natural law made the people sovereign, and that their sovereignty passed to Parliament through the act of election. Fortescue accomplished several things. First, he separated natural law from divine law. Second, he rested sovereignty in the people and made an elective assembly their spokesman. Third, he championed the rule of law and laid the foundation for the claim that an Englishman's "rights" were superior to the claims of the state.

That more or less set the stage for England's seventeenth-century constitutional crisis over the issues of rights, liberties, and sovereignty. It also molded the climate of opinion that shaped the thoughts of the first English colonists in the New World. An additional factor in the debates over liberty and sovereignty was the place of law and the courts. There was a growing clamor that the majesty of the law superseded both the edicts of kings and the prerogatives of Parliament. That law, especially the common law, was characterized as the single greatest source of liberty for the English and their best defense against the tyranny of the state. English common law—or customary law—developed in the Middle Ages from the decisions of local courts. It was unique because it used custom and reason as its source, not legislation. As the centuries passed, the common law expanded through judicial decisions until it found its champion in the early seventeenth century in Sir Edward Coke. As Chief Justice of the King's Bench under James I, Coke argued for the supremacy of the common law and the common law courts. Also, in his *Institutes of the Lawes of England* and his *Reports,* Coke asserted that English justice and English liberties—embodied in common law—originated with *Magna Carta.* Coke's writings and ideas were among the most important sources of legal theory in eighteenth-century Anglo-America.[9]

But the common law and the common-law courts represented only one system of law and one set of courts in England. Parliament, for example, was not simply a legislative body but also acted as a court. The early dual roles of colonial assemblies—legislative and judicial—reflected the duality of Parliament. In addition, acts of Parliament composed part of the tradition of statute law which included both parliamentary legislation and royal decrees.

Besides statute law there was also equity law administered by equity courts, especially the Chancery. As their name implied, these courts arose to remedy "injustices" which resulted from gaps in the existing laws. In addition, Tudor and Stuart monarchs created prerogative courts, so named because they were outside the common-law system and were rooted instead in royal edict. By the early seventeenth century prerogative courts were numerous, and many performed important functions. But prerogative courts became a symbol of tyranny among opponents of the Stuarts in the seventeenth century. Of these, the most notorious was the Court of Star Chamber, which was used to stifle political and religious dissent. Most of the prerogative courts were abolished during the civil-war period. Finally, there were church courts and admiralty courts which utilized other kinds of specialized laws. For example, violations of marine law on the open seas came before the admiralty courts, whereas wills fell under the jurisdiction of ecclesiastical courts.[10]

Still, by modern standards the English lived with almost no government. For most Britons, life moved quite smoothly with only token reminders of the government's power. The English learned through word of mouth, books, and pamphlets, but their knowledge of governmental activity—except for local government—was fuzzy and often weeks or months out of date. Thus, seventeenth-century colonists knew that some government was necessary to manage their collective affairs, but they desired to minimize its role. For them, by far the most important level of government was local administration. Studies of early colonial institutions demonstrate quite clearly that Anglo-Americans carefully reconstructed many of the institutions of English local government while paying relatively little attention to the precise character of colonial government.[11] They *knew* what was essential for the security and success of their settlements. To them a board of selectmen, a fence viewer, a justice of the peace, or a captain of the local militia was far more important than a chancellor of the exchequer or a parliamentary committee. The same yardstick applied in law. Most of the colonists were familiar with common law and common-law courts. Most also had an aversion to lawyers and judges and cared little about admiralty, ecclesiastical, or prerogative courts or statute law. Their lives had proceeded without constant litigation, and they created a very modest court system rooted in the legislature and the magistrate in New England, and the justice of the peace and the county court in Virginia.

As we have mentioned, most of the English colonists endorsed mixed government. However, since the trading companies used local control as a lure to attract colonists, they landed settlers with a strong sense of their liberties and rights versus the power of government, with a dislike for "arbitrary" rule, and with a belief in the sovereignty of the people and the value of representative assemblies. Most sided with Parliament in the struggle with the Crown and applauded some of the results of the Civil War. Regarding the institution of monarchy, they were ambivalent. As patriotic, nationalistic English subjects, they understood and respected the historic tie between monarchy and the essence of the English nation. Yet they looked upon the growth of royal power as a mixed blessing. Many endorsed the notion that Charles I had been a tyrannical, corrupt king, and accepted his execution. But they accepted also all of the governments which followed, including the restoration of monarchy.[12]

We cannot carry this antimonarchist argument too far because seventeenth-century colonists left few records of their thoughts. Mostly, concern for their own security muted any political radicalism which might have existed. For example, New Englanders welcomed political exiles from Restoration England, including several judges who had passed sentence on Charles I, but they declared their allegiance to his son, Charles II. In Massachusetts, the most recalcitrant of the Anglo-American colonies, some wanted to snub or at least ignore Charles II in the early 1660s, but cooler heads prevailed and the colony accepted the reality of a Stuart's return to power.

One of the most fascinating aspects of England's political history between the death of Charles I in 1649 and the restoration of monarchy in 1660 was the growth of republican ideology. In part a response to the perceived "failures" of Cromwell, that republicanism envisioned an England governed only by Parliament and devoid of any single person executive. Based in part on classical republican theories as resurrected by the Italian Renaissance, English republicanism also contained a healthy dose of religious radicalism which presumed the imminent return of Christ and the millennium. It viewed the seventeenth century as the long-awaited age of struggle between Christ's forces and those of Antichrist. Republicans believed that the English monarchy had become a tool of Antichrist to oppress Christ's people. Charles I was executed for his tyranny, but it was a tyranny which had its origins in Rome. Although republicans failed to achieve their goals in the 1650s, republican ideals along with fears of Catholicism and an Antichristian monarchy evolved into an ideology of the "Whig" opponents of Charles II, James II, and the eighteenth-century ministry of Robert Walpole.[13]

Historians do not know the extent to which republican ideals may have influenced seventeenth-century Anglo-American colonists. However, as heirs of the same radical Protestant tradition which produced republicanism in England, it is likely that at least a segment of the colonial population, especially in New England, absorbed the republican's distrust of monarchy. Certainly, we know that millennialism took root in America, and with it came a fear of Antichrist and a belief that Catholic nations were following the Pope's (Antichrist's) bidding.

COLONIAL GOVERNMENT: VIRGINIA AND MASSACHUSETTS

Neither mixed government, nor the doctrine of parliamentary supremacy, nor millennial fears of Antichrist determined the character of colonial government in the beginning. Rather, as we noted earlier, the trading company, proprietor, or royal authority established the form most colonial governments assumed. In Virginia, government developed according to the dictates of the company charter. From 1607 to 1618 ruling power centered first in a council, then in governors. Neither system was especially popular, though the latter was successful. So harsh were both the physical and political conditions in early Virginia that although the colony seemed on solid footing after 1612, few people could be convinced to immigrate. To make the colony more attractive and to quiet the complaints of colonists who had spread out, away from Jamestown, in 1619 the Virginia Company created a representative body, the House of Burgesses, to help rule the colony. The first assembly, meeting at Jamestown, repealed the severe laws stemming from the governorship of Thomas Dale (1611 to 1616) and passed new statutes reflecting English common law. The Burgesses proved so popular that when Virginia became a royal colony in 1624, the assembly was allowed to continue.

It is important to note that the formation of a representative assembly in Virginia did not imply endorsement of mixed government or parliamentary rule. Although the Burgesses copied certain procedures of Parliament, they did not exercise the same authority. They sat with a governor and his council, and all decisions were subject to review by the company in London or later by the English government. Further, the composition of the Burgesses was unique. No hereditary distinctions separated them into houses; rather, they represented all freeholders. Actually, the position of the governor—and later the royal governor—as well as the Burgesses followed no fixed pattern. Governor Yeardley, the governor in 1619, represented the Virginia Company. The royal governors after 1624 represented the interests of the Crown in a commercial/political venture, not the interests of the nobility or commoners.[14]

Several significant facts can be gleaned from the creation of the House of Burgesses. First, the Company established the assembly for the betterment of the colony after it grew too large to be ruled by a governor alone. Moreover, the Burgesses offered colonists a voice in the determination of policy, even if that voice meant nothing more than debating Company or Crown orders and sending petitions to London for consideration. Finally, the Burgesses performed a function familiar to the English: It acted as a buffer or filter separating colonists and the center of political power. Virginians had not liked either the distant governance of a London-based company or the naked power of a Thomas Dale. Neither democrats nor adherents of a primitive system of checks and balances, they wanted protection as well as participation. The Burgesses provided both. Abraham Persey, an early

Virginian, summed up the colonial attitude toward the Burgesses when he said he "sawe the authority [of the London Company] was good, yet was he unwilling to yield till suche time as the Gov.r & the Assembly had layd their commandement upon him."[15]

If colonial government in Virginia evolved in no predetermined fashion, local government did. Reflecting the importance of local institutions to English-born Virginians, colonials carefully reconstructed much of England's system of county, precinct, and parish. At the county level, most governmental decisions were made by justices of the peace who met monthly as a court. The county court served as the first layer below the Burgesses and provided another institutional buffer against the power of the English government. Before too long it was common for burgesses and justices of the peace to be the same persons. Below the county lay the precinct. The principal officer was the constable, who along with the sheriff collected taxes, maintained the peace, and did the bidding of the county court. Then came the parish, which was the name given to the ecclesiastical jurisdiction of the church. Ruled by a group of laymen known as the vestry, the parish in Virginia became as much a political as a religious unit. Over a period of years, the members of the vestry gradually assumed powers having little to do with their ecclesiastical jurisdiction until, by the late colonial period, the vestry was the most important unit of local government.

At the colonial level, Massachusetts Bay, like Virginia, gradually moved toward representative government. Massachusetts carefully made its first central government conform to the dictates of its charter. (Remember, the Bay colonists took their charter with them!) That was difficult since the charter was an economic document meant for a corporation rather than a political entity; but its measures worked nonetheless. Stockholders were renamed freemen and they became the core of the body politic. Administrators, or officers of the corporation, were chosen by the stockholder/freemen. They included the governor and a council of magistrates.

John Winthrop, a member of the English gentry, and the other magistrates (most of whom were gentry as well), attempted to limit ruling authority to themselves. Their reasons were mainly practical. In a frail, struggling colony there was little to be gained by organizing a debating society. Besides, the magistrates were well schooled in the arts of government. Winthrop cloaked himself in the theory of the "Christian Magistrate," but his attitude was pure English country gentleman. His training, from boyhood until 1630, had centered on how to order the affairs of his estate and its people.

For thinking like members of the gentry, Winthrop and his colleagues have earned the condemnation of historical writers for the past several hundred years. Called representatives of a "Puritan oligarchy" by some and "theocrats" by others (though none of the rulers were clergy and clergy never had a formal role in Massachusetts government), the leaders of the Bay Colony have been accused of creating a society controlled by a political, social and religious elite, while their opponents have been portrayed as defenders of nascent democracy.[16] Actually, what transpired in early Massachusetts had little to do with democracy as we understand the term. Yet it was significant that in a colony known for its religiosity, there was considerable squabbling between rulers and ruled during the first two decades.

Simply stated, if Winthrop and the other magistrates behaved like English gentry, then their subjects behaved like "middling" Englishmen. They simply refused to accept the arbitrariness of Winthrop's magistracy. It violated their political ideas and their political experience. They demanded a share of governmental authority and, like their Virginia neighbors, they demanded the filtering system which, to them, typified English government. Thus, they sought an enlarged number of freemen, which they received. Then they demanded direct election of magistrates by the freemen, which they received as well. Then they requested or demanded that representatives of the growing number of towns be allowed to sit with the magistrates in the "General Court." They won that too.

Then, in the late 1630s, the *deputies*–the representatives of the towns–began to argue with the magistrates over the latter's assumption of a "negative voice"–that is, a veto on all measures passed by the General Court. The vehicle for their dispute proved to be a pig–Goody Sherman's pig. Goodwife Sherman, a widow, claimed that merchant Robert Keayne stole her prize sow and butchered it. Keayne declared his innocence, and the matter went to the General Court. The Deputies ruled for Goody Sherman but the Magistrates exercised their negative voice and the case began to loom as a constitutional crisis. The Deputies pressed the issue and the rhetoric soared accordingly. The Magistrates were accused of denying rights sacred to the English. Winthrop responded with allusions to classical definitions of government coupled with appeals to an Englishman's love for mixed government. He argued that under the system in use, Massachusetts was a "mixed aristocracy" (mixed government) while the Deputies wanted "democracy" (a pseudonym for anarchy or rule by mob at the time). Winthrop insisted:

> That which makes a specificall difference betweene one forme of Government and another is essential and fundamental. But the negative vote in the magistrates does so in our government; therefore, it is essential and fundamental.
>
> The assumption is proved by this: That if the negative vote were taken away, our government would be a mere democracy, whereas now it is mixed. This I prove thus; Where the chief ordinary power and administration thereof is in the people, there is a democracy. This I prove thus: If it be in the deputies, it is in the people, but it will be in the deputies, governor, etc., for they are but the representative body of the people, and the matter lies not in the number of the people assembled, but in their power.[17]

Winthrop lost the argument, and the Goody Sherman Sow Case ended with the magistrates and deputies agreeing to sit separately, each with a veto over the decisions of the other. Thus was the American bicameral legislature born in Massachusetts–not by intent, but more by accident. It resembled Parliament and, Winthrop's arguments notwithstanding, it seemed to employ the essence of mixed government. Yet, there were neither lords nor commoners. Persons were chosen more for their reputations and, later, their wealth than for their birth. Any fundamental differences in function that separated the two houses of government in the Bay Colony were not readily apparent at first. Gradually, though, the idea of the superiority of a bicameral legislature developed–a forerunner of the constitutional principle of checks and balances.

The evolution of two houses in the Massachusetts General Court may not have conformed to any existing English model, but it did provide the filter for the governing process that Massachusetts colonists deemed essential. At the same time another component of that filter emerged in a demand from many deputies that

Massachusetts draft a statement codifying the laws and liberties of the inhabitants so that the citizens would be further insulated from arbitrary government. The movement resulted in the Massachusetts *Body of Liberties* (1641) and in *The Book of the General Lawes and Liberties* (1648). Both documents reflected common-law principles and circumscribed the power of the government, not just the magistrates. Although no early *Bill of Rights*–as some historians have suggested–or no direct link to American constitutionalism and democracy–as others have argued–the *Body of Liberties* and *The Book of the General Lawes and Liberties* did reflect the concerns of the aggressive, somewhat individualistic English of the time. They demonstrated the sensitivity of colonials to the citizens' "rights" before the power of the state.[18] John Winthrop had read Sir Edward Coke and knew the import of his writings. Still, Winthrop opposed the codification of laws and liberties as excessive legalism in a tiny colony supposedly composed of friends and neighbors. In Massachusetts, he argued, it was not necessary to resurrect the essence of the English Constitution. His opponents, who had also read Coke, disagreed.

While there is a danger of reading too much into the early histories of Massachusetts and Virginia, there is also the danger of reading too little. Fear of arbitrary rule, desire for a filtering system to dilute the governmental process and to create distance between rulers and ruled, and concern for the liberties of the English–all basic elements of the English political experience–appeared in the early days of colonization, twisting and distorting the intent of trading-company charters. Moreover, as in Virginia, Massachusetts Bay Colony residents exhibited another trait which was typical of Englishmen of their station at that particular time: a sense that local governmental institutions were more important in their daily affairs than were the activities of a distant "national" or colonial government. Thus, Bay Colonists in particular, and New Englanders in general, paid considerable attention to resurrecting their version of English local government in the wilds of America.

New Englanders created counties, townships, and so forth, but because so many of the colonists had come from agricultural villages (at least some of which were self-governing), they placed the greatest share of the burden of local government on the town. The town's authority for governing came from the General Court (as did its land and the right to distribute it) and townspeople chose to exercise their authority through a town meeting of all the inhabitants. Gradually, the town meeting delegated authority to run the day-to-day affairs of the village to an elected board of *selectmen.* The activities of the town meeting were diverse and, in many ways, innovative. The town meeting distributed land and monitored the economic progress of the village; it elected local officials (fence viewers, constables, overseers of the poor, etc.). In addition, it assumed the ecclesiastical functions of the English and Virginia vestries by maintaining the meeting house (which was also the church), by hiring and firing ministers, and, on occasion, by even serving as a forum for the discussion of ecclesiastical issues. Later, as towns grew larger, and their business more complicated, and as more than one church appeared in each community, the town meeting created separate parishes for each church, and the functions of church maintenance and business passed to a vestry like corporation of the church known as the *society.*

Equally significant, the town meeting served as an important part of the filtering process described earlier. The meeting elected deputies to serve in the

General Court as representatives of the town and, from time to time, issued instructions to its representatives or submitted petitions to the General Court reflecting the town's opinions on issues confronting the assembly. Also, the town meeting acted as the recipient, interpreter, and enforcer of acts passed by the General Court. And, as was the English practice, from time to time the town meeting chose to ignore acts passed by the General Court, as any casual survey of the minutes of the Court will reveal. The town meeting also functioned as a kind of law court to resolve disagreements which arose among the inhabitants. Most local legal matters, however, wound up before one of the colony magistrates who traveled about holding court as itinerant justices. Really sticky problems went, eventually, to the General Court. Gradually, Massachusetts created a permanent county-court system, and the legislature divested itself of legal duties by creating a *supreme* court.[19]

The governments of Massachusetts and Virginia worked so well that they were copied in all subsequent mainland colonies. Once offered the possibility of a large degree of local control, English colonists would accept no less. Moreover, they used their freedom to infuse their governmental institutions with ideals and practices they considered an essential part of their political and constitutional heritage: rule by law, freedom from arbitrary rule, representative government, the primacy of local government, protection for their English liberties, and the sovereignty of the people. To the notion of popular sovereignty, they added several components which went beyond even the theory and practice of England at that time.

In their successful efforts to establish representative assemblies, codify the law, rework the essentially economic character of company and proprietary charters into political systems, form church and town covenants, and legitimize settlements with "compacts" such as those of Plymouth and Connecticut, English colonists inadvertently developed two important governmental principles. One legitimized institutions through a written document, either in the form of a contract with a sovereign agency like the Crown, or through a covenant or mutual agreement to create sovereignty where none had existed. The second presented society and its institutions as a voluntary association established through an implicit or explicit social contract among all inhabitants and conferring freedoms and obligations upon each person. Both principles were contained in this paragraph from the *Mayflower Compact* (1620):

> We whose names are underwritten . . . , do by these present, solemnly and mutually, in the presence of God and one of another, covenant and combine ourselves together into a civil body politic, for our better ordering and preservation and furtherance of the ends aforesaid; and by virtue hereof to enact, constitute, and frame such just and equal laws, ordinances, acts, constitutions, offices from time to time as shall be most meet and convenient for the general good of the colony; unto which we promise all due submission and obedience.[20]

The first English colonists developed these procedures and principles in part from desire and in part from necessity. They did not realize fully the novelty or the revolutionary nature of their actions. Later generations of English, European, and Anglo-American colonists would.

TOWARD REPUBLICANISM

While noting the revolutionary character of the Mayflower Compact, we are not arguing that seventeenth-century political attitudes led directly to the American Revolution. There is no evidence that Anglo-Americans ever seriously considered independence before the mid-1770s. Nevertheless, we are suggesting more coherence in Anglo-American political ideas and practices over the whole colonial era than what most historians are willing to admit. Scholars have tended to argue that a revolutionary mentality emerged from fundamental changes in political thinking and behavior during the eighteenth century.[21] Although eighteenth-century Anglo-American thought evolved in directions not foreseen by the early colonists, it expanded upon, but never violated, the assumptions and beliefs the founders brought with them.

In observing an element of continuity between seventeenth- and eighteenth-century political ideology, it must be added that colonials spent relatively little time worrying about or debating political theory except when events forced them to do so. However, it is apparent that in the years between 1607 and 1763, events moved in ways which were not always hospitable to the predispositions of the colonists. The power of the English state expanded, and with it the restrictive apparatus of empire expanded also. Economic growth and commerce drew the colonies toward Europe and England. Hostile Catholic enemies prowled along colonial borders amidst the increasing clamor of international imperial rivalries. Hundreds of thousands of Protestant non-English swelled the colonies, bringing with them the scars of the religious, political, or economic oppression that ravaged Europe in the eighteenth century. Their arrival brought mixed reactions from older English settlers and immigrants alike. In a negative vein, many immigrants demonstrated little love for the English and only slight understanding of English institutions or beliefs. On a more positive note, quite a few new arrivals distrusted monarchies and aristocracies. They feared the growing power of the European state and knew of the renewed vitality of European Catholicism and the declining vigor of European Protestantism from first-hand experience. Consequently, many could and did endorse Anglo-American political ideals and institutions, just as they fought for a place in colonial society.

Such local and international developments in the late seventeenth and early eighteenth centuries had the effect of exaggerating some of the Anglo-Americans' more paranoid tendencies. More and more, colonials conceived of America as a haven or oasis in a world governed by and subject to the whims of malevolent forces. Increasingly, they sensed an inability to control their own destinies. That in turn provoked a wistful retrospective look at the optimism and creativity of the founders. It also led them to develop and expand upon some of the political radicalism inherent in early colonial beliefs and experiments. Anglo-Americans grew convinced that the legitimacy of their institutions reflected the intent of the English Constitution and owed more to charters and compacts—and the popular sovereignty implied therein—than to parliamentary statute or royal decrees. They also grew more sensitive to criticism of colonial institutions and more wary of "designs" aimed against their civil and religious polities. Above all, they grew more jealous of their rights and liberties and vastly more sensitive to real or imagined abuses of power by governmental officials—especially those across the sea. As a rule, colonials believed the more distant the official, the greater the likelihood of his venality. In short, the deeper Europe entered the "age of absolutism," the more Anglo-Americans embraced principles and practices which can best be labeled *republican.*

The movement was slow, halting, and at times barely discernible, but it was there. It was not a conscious trend as much as a series of reactions by Anglo-Americans to a world they viewed with caution and not a little distress. Also, the movement tended to follow the meandering course of fluid frontier societies in which men sometimes rose and fell in power and prestige in only a few months and in which politics was often the personal struggles of crude and greedy men whose behavior seemed to conform to no known set of rules. The late 1670s and the 1680s signified a watershed. First, in Virginia in 1676, angry colonists rebelled against royal Governor William Berkeley. It was the first time that Anglo-Americans had mounted organized opposition to English authority in America using guns rather than petitions and it sent shock waves throughout England and its fledgling empire. The leader of the rebels was Nathaniel Bacon. No political ideologue, Bacon was an ambitious young man who had come to Virginia to make his fortune. He and his followers were mostly frontierspeople who were angry because they felt Berkeley and the Tidewater planters who supported him were not willing to protect the Virginia frontier from Indian raids. Bacon captured Jamestown and the government for a time before he became ill and died. His followers were then routed and many were subsequently executed.

Even though some of Bacon's "rebels" may have held radical political and religious beliefs, Bacon himself was an opportunist and the movement he led reflected Virginia's economic, political, and social instability, not widespread colonial opposition to English rule. Still, it cannot be forgotten that Bacon's men fired upon representatives of the Crown and temporarily unseated the duly appointed royal governor of the colony of Virginia. The people of Virginia did not miss the significance of the event and in the decades following Bacon's upheaval a romantic legend grew up about the events of 1676 in which Bacon was cast a popular leader and Berkeley was labeled a "tyrant."[22]

A few years after Bacon's Rebellion a remarkable series of events took place in the colony of New York. Ruled by the representatives of the proprietor James, Duke of York (soon to be King James II), New York was the only colony without a legislative assembly. Since 1664, many New Yorkers had resented deeply the "arbitrary" character of proprietary rule and had made repeated demands for an assembly. They were rebuffed. The result was the development of a "popular" party demanding an assembly and greater rights and power and an "aristocratic" party siding with the interests of the proprietor. The factions threatened to tear the colony apart. Finally, in 1683, James gave in to his opponents and granted new Governor Thomas Dongan the authority to call an assembly.

The most vocal advocates of representative government in New York were ex-New Englanders living in the towns on Long Island. Those towns had once been counted as part of Connecticut and had sent representatives to the Connecticut Assembly. The malcontents met Dongan soon after his arrival and demanded an assembly, arguing that they had long been denied the rights enjoyed by ordinary English citizens as well as by most Anglo-Americans. They also declared that they had a verbal "compact" with the first English governor, Richard Nicolls, promising them a legislature. Dongan called the Assembly which met in October 1683. The Assembly quickly created a *Charter of Libertyes,* an extraordinary document which cited the arbitrary nature of the Duke of York's rule, and spelled out, in unusual detail for the day, the "rights" of ordinary English citizens. The *Charter* placed ruling authority in "A Governor, Councell, and the people mett in Generall Assembly," while it restricted executive authority (the Governor and his Council) with the caveat that they were to act "according to the Lawes." It listed in detail both the individual liberties and the property rights of citizens and their exemptions from the claims of the state. In so doing it cited the "fundamental rights of Englishmen" embodied in the common-law tradition and documents like *Magna Carta* and the *Petition of Right* as its source of authority. Finally the *Charter of Libertyes* gave considerable power to the legislature. It never became law, for it was squashed by English officialdom, but as a republican document it left its mark.[23]

More important than the *Charter of Libertyes* was the impact of the Glorious Revolution in 1688 against the "tyranny" and Catholicism of James II, the triumph of parliamentary supremacy, and the arguments of James' "Whig" opponents. The Whigs claimed that Parliament's sovereignty stretched back to the days of Saxon antiquity, that Parliament was the inherent guardian of the rights of Englishmen, and that it had finally crushed nearly a century of Stuart attempts to usurp power and trample on English liberties. Most Anglo-Americans were natural Whigs, and they staged several versions of the Glorious Revolution themselves by sacking Edmund Andros, the unpopular royal governor of the Dominion of New England, and his aide Francis Nicholson, lieutenant governor and chief executive officer of the colony of New York. At the same time that John Coode and a faction which called itself the *Protestant Association* rebelled successfully against the Calverts in Maryland, several groups challenged the proprietary governors of the Carolinas, Seth Sothell and John Colleton, and eventually secured their dismissal, and a small faction in Virginia denounced an alleged Catholic plot involving the royal governor of that colony. The governor, Lord Francis Howard, Baron of Effingham, was a Catholic and he had made patronage appointments of numerous Catholic friends while in office. Also he quarreled continuously with the Burgesses. Ironically, though the rebellion against him fizzled, he was eventually replaced by a new governor, the ill-fated Nicholson of New York.

After the rebellions, most of the colonies of the old Dominion of New England busied themselves with the arduous process of trying to retrieve lost colonial charters and the autonomy they had granted. For Anglo-Americans as a group, the significance of the Glorious Revolution was twofold. First, it fixed forever in their minds the character of the English Constitution. To that point a changing mixture of institutions, customs, and laws, it became to colonials a fixed system revolving around parliamentary sovereignty and the rights of English citizens as guaranteed by law, custom, and parliamentary statute. Second, the Glorious Revolution confirmed the legitimacy of colonial assemblies. Massachusetts retrieved its charter and, though a royal governor came with it, the Bay Colony recovered most of the elements of self-government and representative government that it had possessed in the days before Andros. Connecticut and Rhode Island fared even better. In Maryland the members of the Protestant Association, after dispensing with proprietary rule, elected an assembly and then asked Parliament for approval of their actions. Parliament responded by making Maryland a royal colony *with* a representative assembly. A similar process took place in New York. After Lieutenant Governor Nicholson's collapse, Jacob Leisler, leader of the rebels, ruled New York aided by his son-in-law Jacob Milbourne. Though Leisler's political ideology was somewhat confused, his son-in-law was a Protestant religious and political radical who held views reminiscent of the English republicans of the 1650s. Together Leisler and Milbourne organized an elected assembly to rule New York. Both men eventually died for their roles in the insurrection but their achievements were confirmed when William and Mary agreed to a permanent legislature for New York. Thus, as a consequence of events in New York, Massachusetts, Maryland, and elsewhere, by the end of the seventeenth century political conflict in the British North American colonies had reaffirmed the "rights" of English citizens in America as well as the legitimacy of elected colonial assemblies. Moreover, numerous precedents had been established for both peaceful and violent resistance to royal control.[24]

One of the leading English "Whig" theorists of the late seventeenth century was John Locke. His *Second Treatise of Government,* though written in the early 1680s, appeared just after James' overthrow and was widely hailed as a defense of what had transpired. Locke elaborated a theory of the individual's *natural rights*—that is, universal rights reflecting natural law—in contrast to the rights of English citizens, which were restricted to a particular culture. Locke argued that government existed only to protect and nurture rights such as life, liberty, and property. He also created a theory that men and women moved from a state of nature to a state of society through a social contract of all people. The move was occasioned by the danger that *natural liberty*—liberty unrestrained by any power—posed to natural rights. In the same contract, Locke concluded, individuals created government and agreed to give up a portion of their natural liberty in return for protection of their natural rights.[25]

Locke's treatise, brilliant as it was, capped a century of political speculation in which mainly Protestant theorists in both Europe and England had altered traditional medieval notions of natural law, the divine origins of society, and the contract between rulers and ruled into a notion of society as an artificial construct reflecting people's concern for their natural rights as they flowed from natural law. In the process, these theorists developed an ideological weapon which could be used against the secular state by making government an artificial byproduct of the social contract instead of the divine institution of the Middle Ages.

However, not all contractarians adopted Locke's view of limited government. Earlier thinkers like Thomas Hobbes found such ideas equally useful to justify absolutism and arbitrary rule. Locke reacted violently to Hobbes and others of his ilk for what he considered to be their perversions of contract theory. In response, he created a new synthesis reflecting libertarian tendencies stretching back to Thomas Aquinas but inherent, he thought, in the arguments of seventeenth-century thinkers and movements ranging from the republicans of the English Civil War era to the recently published works of one of his contemporaries, German Protestant jurist and philosopher, Samuel Pufendorf. The immediate object of Locke's scorn was Robert Filmer, a popular English writer, critic of contractarianism, and supporter of what Locke considered to be absolutist tendencies. Filmer argued that government was an extension of the family, and in the family the father's rule was complete and unquestioned.[26]

Although Locke's arguments for natural rights represented a break with the

English tradition of civil rights and really had little to do with the arguments of many Whig opponents of James II, his theories spread quickly. Anglo-American colonists—who were uncertain that appealing to the rights of Englishmen was a sufficient hedge against arbitrary rule—began to use the arguments of the natural-law-natural-rights contract theorists. Even in New England, the supposed bastion of "Puritan" conservatism and John Winthrop's arbitrary though benevolent Christian magistrate, the lure of Lockeian views proved irresistible. Samuel Willard, one of the most important Massachusetts ministers of the seventeenth century, delivered an election-day sermon in Boston in 1694. No Lockeian, Willard characterized government in terms familiar to his time, his place, and his profession. Civil rulers, he argued, were "God's Viceregents here upon earth . . . Government is God's ordinance." But God ordained no particular form of government. Sometimes, Willard concluded, He placed his faith in monarchs and sometimes He blessed a representative government growing out of a contract among the people.[27]

The significance of Willard's sermon was not that he endorsed Locke or contractarian views, but that he indicated familiarity with the arguments and seemed to contend that both English and Anglo-American governments could be satisfactory in God's eyes. At about the same time, Gurdon Saltonstall, young minister of the church in New London, Connecticut, and soon to become governor of the colony, adopted a position similar to Willard's. In a Connecticut election-day sermon in 1697, Saltonstall first characterized rulers as having a divine mission, and then told his listeners that "the Power of Choosing, and Liberty . . . of Electing Persons into any Office of Civil Rule and Government" was blessed by "divine Providence" as well.[28]

Less than two decades later, a New England minister endorsed Locke's contractual synthesis completely. Entering an argument among clergy over church government, John Wise of Chebacco parish in Ipswich, Massachusetts, supported Congregationalism. At the same time Wise argued that civil government and civil society were based on contracts and the end of government was to maintain "the common peace, security, and well-being of all."[29] Although this was not quite Locke's natural rights of life, liberty, and property, it placed Wise squarely in the contractarian tradition and made him an advocate of limited government whose purpose was to serve the people. No mention was made of civil rulers as "God's viceregents."

It is argued commonly that many seventeenth-century Anglo-Americans, especially Puritan New Englanders, endorsed absolutist theories of government. But, as we have seen, nothing could have been farther from the truth. Given their heritage and experience, they could not have been absolutists. No democrats or libertarians either, they believed in order, conformity, and deference as the fundamentals of society and government. But they were tinged with republicanism, and their experience in the New World further encouraged republican attitudes and practices. Thus, though endorsement of Whig principles or John Locke's natural rights or contractarian views of society and government represented an important shift for colonials, it was not quite the revolutionary change many writers have suggested.

As we see later, events of the eighteenth century produced many more colonial "republicans." Not all followed John Locke or his apologists and imitators. Some looked to David Hume and the "Common Sense" school of philosophers and political theorists in Scotland. Others followed the evolution of Whig arguments in England and adopted a "neo-Whig" posture, following "coffeehouse" radicals and opponents of arbitrary government like John Trenchard and Thomas Gordon, who published *Cato's Letters* and the *Independent Whig* in the early eighteenth century. Still others, clergy especially, resurrected the millennial republicanism of the English Civil War and the Protectorate and called for republican governments based on liberty to usher in the Kingdom of Christ and defeat the forces of Antichrist.

Most colonials, though, followed no ideology. They simply pursued their own private affairs, seeking to enjoy their lives and advance their "interests" within the matrix of their own representative institutions. In that context, local government continued to be the most important layer of government for most colonists. Still, some changes occurred. As society became more economically stratified, wealthy elites of planters, or merchants, or farmers used their wealth to gain stature in their communities, counties, or colonies. They emerged as the dominant economic and political forces in every colony. In the process, they took control of political institutions, and colonial legislatures became battlegrounds for competing elite factions seeking their own narrow interests. This development placed colonial elites in direct contact with Parliament, the Crown, and the apparatus of a growing imperial system. The contact was not an unhappy one for most colonists, but one of its unforeseen results was to advance the cause of republican principles and practices among Anglo-Americans everywhere.

6

Toward a Protestant Pattern of Culture: Religion and Society

During a 1976 public lecture celebrating the Bicentennial of the American Revolution a distinguished scholar was asked how the Spanish had viewed America's struggle with England. "Just another fight among Protestants," he replied quickly. The attentive audience, which had heard a series of speakers relate the timeless quality and near-universal appeal of American revolutionary rhetoric, was stunned by this attempt to reduce one of the supposedly pivotal events in human history to a religious squabble. After a few moments of silence, laughter filled the lecture hall as the audience decided the scholar had made a joke. The speaker smiled, but when the laughter had died down, he made his point again. The Spanish, he explained, had imperial ambitions, international alliances, and hatreds, which brought them into America's revolutionary struggle. But colonial rhetoric mean nothing to them, for Americans were a thoroughly Protestant people. When colonials or their English enemy talked of human rights and political tyranny, they spoke from a common tradition of political theory which assumed that liberty existed only in Protestant areas of the world, and that the greatest source of tyranny and evil lay with the Catholic Church and its pope. A thoroughly Catholic country, Spain could hardly be expected to applaud or endorse such rhetoric. No one laughed this time. Instead, a vigorous debate ensued in which several critics charged the speaker with overstating the continuing importance of religious differences in the late eighteenth century and overlooking the secular basis of the Revolution as expressed through manifestos like the Declaration of Independence. When the debate concluded several important points had been made. Among them was the tremendous impact of Protestant thought on Anglo-American culture as well as the widespread acceptance by most colonials of a Protestant world view. Our problem in this chapter is to understand how and why these developments took place. In a later chapter we return to a consideration of the role of Protestant ideology in the era of the American Revolution.

PROTESTANT IDEOLOGY

By the end of the colonial era, the attitudes, behavior, and institutions of British North Americans not only reflected material goals but also a heavy dose of religious idealism. This was true, in part, because religion played a vital role in all Western societies during the seventeenth and eighteenth centuries. It provided a unifying force in the lives of most men and women. It explained their origins, their places in the scheme of things, and their destinies. It served as the basis for most theories of political, economic, and personal behavior. But religious idealism in Anglo-America reflected something more than this. It echoed the continuing thunder of the Protestant Reformation.[1]

The superficial unity of Western Christendom had shattered with the Protestant revolt of the sixteenth century. Protestantism spread rapidly throughout much of western and eastern Europe in the years following Martin Luther's excommunication in 1521, but then retreated almost as quickly before the onslaught of a revitalized Catholicism. By the early seventeenth century, Spain and France were the dominant Catholic powers facing England, the Netherlands, and Scandinavia, the major Protestant areas. The seventeenth century produced near continuous international conflict and intranational strife in which religion was a potent factor. Not only England, but France, Germany, and Holland experienced internal political turmoil sparked in part by religious differences. At the same time, England and the seaboard nations of western Europe engaged in a struggle for European hegemony and imperial world domination which would go on for more than a century.

All of the protagonists made forays into North America as Protestant and Catholic idealism, nationalism, and simple greed combined into a cant of conquest. In addition, the English Civil Wars (1641 to 1648), plus more or less constant warfare in Europe, produced thousands and thousands of refugees during the seventeenth and eighteenth centuries. Most were Protestants who looked to North America (and other regions like South Africa) for survival. They thought they saw glimpses of a "new Eden" where they could live, prosper, and start anew in relative safety. English colonizers needed labor to cut timber, plant crops, and take fish from the Atlantic. So, they encouraged Protestant refugees to settle within the expanding confines of North America. During the seventeenth and eighteenth centuries, men and women did this by the tens of thousands. Beginning with the migration in the 1630s of English "Puritans" to New England, Barbados, and other locations, and culminating with the huge migration of German Lutherans and German Mennonites as well as Scotch-Irish Presbyterians to the middle and southern colonies during the eighteenth century, Anglo-America attracted Protestants from all parts of Europe, Scandinavia, and the British Isles. They settled from Maine to Georgia and as far west as the rough terrain, the French, and the native Americans would allow.

The new world of British North America, then, became a haven for Protestants who found freedom not available in Europe or England. Who were these Protestants? They had many names, and those groups who settled during the seventeenth century differed in religion and nationality from those who came during the eighteenth century. But because this chapter concerns the first century of settlement, the discussion of later migrations of religious dissenters is relegated to a later chapter. During the seventeenth century most of the major Protestant groups who braved the Atlantic for the New World were English nonconformists—that is, people who for religious reasons could not accept or conform to certain doctrines and practices of the Church of England. If they shared an opposition to the Anglican Church, they nevertheless differed considerably from one another on doctrinal and organizational questions. As is explained in more detail shortly, the very nature of Protestantism led to divisions among Protestants. Hence, English nonconformity had many faces both in England and Anglo-America.

The largest group of English nonconformists to settle North America during the seventeenth century was the New England Puritans. Although in England the term *Puritan* described a variety of groups, in New England the majority of Puritan settlers were Congregationalists. Followers of the doctrines of John Calvin (as were most English Puritans), Congregationalists believed that the early "primitive" Christian Church, the only right model of church organization, had placed religious authority in the hands of the individual congregations. Another segment of English Puritans called Presbyterians (who incidentally were probably the largest group in England) also settled Anglo-America in the seventeenth century, although their numbers were considerably smaller. Although they agreed with Congregationalists on doctrinal issues, such as the sacraments, predestination, and so on, they differed strongly over proper church organization, or *polity*. Instead of giving individual congregations power to decide many religious matters, Presbyterians favored a hierarchy of councils, or *presbyteries,* to govern the individual churches.[2]

Puritan nonconformity also spawned two types of Baptists, some of whom settled in North America. The General Baptists rejected Calvin's doctrine of predestination, the belief that God had preordained that certain people would be saved. They argued that a righteous God would never permit only a few select people to be saved and insisted instead that all people could be redeemed. The group earned the label Baptist because it advocated adult, rather than infant, baptism. Despite these doctrinal differences, the General Baptists, like the Congregationalists, adhered to a congregational church order. The other type of Baptist was called the Particular Baptists. This group also opposed infant baptism, but it accepted Calvin's predestination views. Particular Baptists also advocated a congregational church polity.[3]

Two other groups that arose out of the religious strife in England during the seventeenth century also need to be mentioned. First, the "separatist" Pilgrims, who migrated from the Netherlands and England to Plymouth Colony, held doctrinal and organizational views similar to their neighbors in Massachusetts. However, they denounced the Anglican Church as a false church. Separatists believed that the only way to uphold the purity of Christ's church was to separate themselves completely from the corrupted Church of England and admit only proven regenerate Christians into the body of Christ's earthly church. As was noted in the discussion of the founding of Massachusetts Bay, the Puritans there clung to the hope that the English church would be reformed. Therefore, they never broke completely from it, nor did they reject the idea of an established, state-supported church governing the individual congregations in the colony.[4]

The other group, the Quakers, was insignificant in numbers and impact until the late seventeenth century. George Fox, its founder, did not organize the Society of Friends until 1652. During the early stage of the Quaker movement, Fox and other leaders shook both the political and religious establishment of England by challenging all forms of authority and calling for political and social, as well as religious, change. Strongly millenarian, the Quakers differed from other Puritan groups by completely spiritualizing the final conflict between Christ and Antichrist. The key doctrine of Quakerism was the belief in an experiential revelation of God to each soul, what Fox termed the *inner light.* This exaltation of personal revelation was viewed by others as an attack on Scripture as the only true source of divine revelation. The doctrine of the inner light, coupled with Quaker disregard for authority, their active proselytizing, and their intensely militant, millenarian language made them feared, shunned, and denounced by other Puritans. By the 1680s, however, when William Penn's experiment in Pennsylvania attracted large numbers of Quakers to Anglo-America, the Quaker movement had evolved out of its militant, almost revolutionary posture into a quietist stage.[5]

English nonconformists—most of whom settled north of the Chesapeake and especially in New England—comprised the bulk of Protestants who migrated to the New World during the seventeenth century. Nevertheless, there were also scatterings of other groups as well: Anglicans, Dutch Reformed (the Calvinist state church of the Netherlands), Swedish Lutherans, and French Huguenots (French Calvinist Protestants, also called French Reformed), to name a few. Considering the wide range of issues that divided Protestants, one might well wonder how historians can speak with any accuracy of a Protestant ideology. Indeed, when one goes even further and argues that this single ideology seeped into the fabric of colonial life and thought and conditioned the attitudes and behavior of thousands of colonials, most of whom were probably not even particularly religious, then some explanation is certainly in order.

The answer to the first dilemma is that even if some doctrinal and ecclesiastical issues divided Protestants, an even larger body of common Christian beliefs and practices united them. In response to the second dilemma, British North America emerged as the Protestant bastion described earlier by our Bicentennial scholar not because every colonial went to church or exhibited intense religiosity, but rather because the Protestant ideology they identified with Anglo-American culture had as much a secular as a religious character.

Three key concepts which defined the heart and gave power to Protestant ideology are described next: opposition, authority, and conscience. These threads of ideology grew out of the religious controversies of the sixteenth century and therefore are explained in that context. As we examine the religious life of seventeenth-century Anglo-America in more detail, we see manifestations of these ideas in the character of colonial religious institutions. But beyond that, as the religious context of Protestant ideology became blurred or even faded in the minds of the colonists, a secular as well as religious version of the ideology remained to color and define the shape of Anglo-American culture.

Opposition

The Protestant reformers of the sixteenth century earned their opprobrious name for their "protest" against certain doctrines and practices of the Roman Catholic Church. As such, Protestantism was born and took root as an ideology of opposition. By the end of the sixteenth century, especially after the resurgence of

Catholicism marked by the Counter-Reformation, Protestants had developed a common, abiding fear of Catholicism. Although many European states, including England, had firmly established, generally recognized state churches, Protestants in England and Europe nevertheless trembled at the sound of the word *Catholic.* Indeed, England in particular experienced periodic rumors of popish plots, and even an occasional panic prompted by fear that Catholic conspirators would overthrow the government and enslave the people. This fearful, apprehensive climate arose simultaneously with and in part out of a renewed interest in eschatology (a word meaning the doctrine of the last times, or doctrines relating to the end of the world). By the seventeenth century, virtually all Protestants came to identify the pope as Antichrist and the Catholic Church as the false church foretold in the Bible that would deceive people during the last days.

Although some Protestant groups became more preoccupied than others with theories of the last times and the coming millennium (a period of a thousand years during which Christ would reign on earth), Protestants in general shared the belief that they were living in the final days and would witness and perhaps even act out part of the ultimate struggle between Christ and Antichrist. What made this millennial view so powerful and appealing was its appearance coincidently with the wars in Europe that raged between Protestant and Catholic countries, and also its coincidence with several internal civil conflicts within Protestant countries. It is not hard to imagine a Protestant Englishman, Swede, or German witnessing the international and civil wars, and then interpreting them as lesser manifestations of the greater cosmic battle between God and Satan. Given this millennial perspective, it is not surprising that the early Protestant settlers, especially those in New England, viewed themselves as part of God's chosen remnant that had been commissioned to "be as a city on a hill," as John Winthrop phrased it. They had left the corruption and evil of Europe not only to find a better material life but also to build a Protestant fortress to withstand the onslaught of the Catholic Antichrist and his forces.[6]

What Protestants found in America only served to confirm their sense of being in opposition to the rest of the world. The early years of settlement were harsh, cruel ones for the neophyte colonies. Life was hard and death constantly at the doorstep. Armed with little but their own wits and courage, the first settlers battled Indians, disease, famine, and the elements to carve out a new society free from the taint and corruption of the old. Equally worrisome, British colonists were surrounded by people they considered the pope's henchmen. They faced Spaniards to the south and French to the north and west. On the east the sea offered no escape. So, even if many colonists had only passing acquaintance with Protestant ideology, the years of struggle against the frontier coupled with constant threats from Catholic forces around them gave substance to the Protestant concept of living in opposition to the world.

Authority

Second, as an ideology of opposition, Protestantism by definition rejected the authority of one of the building blocks of European society, the Catholic Church. By implication, Protestantism challenged the basis of society itself. Ironically, Protestant leaders initially sought to reform or purify the Catholic Church, not denounce it or break from it. But their activities against the Church and eventually their position toward the functions and role of the church undermined both the Catholic Church's spiritual and political authority. The Catholic Church had long justified its existence by maintaining that it was the only means through which sinful men and women could obtain salvation. People were too evil, too corrupt, to speak directly to God or to expect God's forgiveness. Therefore, people needed the institutional church to act as their representatives or intermediaries before God. From this basis the Catholic Church developed an exalted concept of the clergy and also the doctrine of saint worship. The priest, or St. Peter, or the Virgin Mary would hear the sinner's confession or prayer and intercede for him with God.

In contrast, Protestant reformers, particularly Martin Luther, gave primacy to a personal, direct relationship between God and each individual. When Luther examined the Catholic view of the church in light of his doctrine of "justification by faith alone," he concluded that each believer could essentially act as his or her own priest and obtain salvation by repentance and faith. An individual did not require a priest or the office of the church to intercede for him or her with God. Further, like a priest, each person could read the Scriptures and find God's truth for him- or herself. Luther pioneered the translation of the Bible from Latin into German and encouraged its distribution specifically to give ordinary people access to God's Word. Logically, Luther's doctrine, called the "universal priesthood of all believers" negated the fundamental purpose for an institutional church.

Despite the implications of his argument, Luther himself steadfastly upheld the need for an institutional church and vehemently denounced radical elements of the Reformation movement who rejected both religious and political authorities. The mainstream reformers supported a state church that would train the clergy, educate the people about God's truth, and ensure the maintenance of pure doctrine and discipline. They both feared religious anarchy and believed in the importance of the institutional church to ensure that the Gospel in its purity would be preached. As a result, Protestants behaved no more tolerantly toward people of differing beliefs than their Catholic rivals did toward them. Further, most Protestants viewed the institutional church as essential in leading the unregenerate to salvation and in encouraging the faith of the already saved. Although the left wing of the Protestant Reformation denied the need for a formal institution to accomplish these purposes, most of the English nonconformists who settled Anglo-America adhered to the concept of a state-supported church.

Ironically, even while Protestant settlers in North America attempted to create religious institutions of the mainstream Reformation mold, they were confronted with an environment that threatened to undermine the church's authority. As we see shortly, the pressures of the frontier, coupled with the inherent tendency within Protestantism to challenge, if not reject, institutional authority, meant that the history of colonial religion during the seventeenth century would be rocky, indeed.

Conscience

The Protestant position on the authority of the institutional church revealed a fundamental dichotomy within Protestant ideology. The source of this dichotomy was the Reformation's substitution of conscience for the church in the process of salvation. As noted earlier, Protestants conceived of salvation as a personal affair between the individual and God. This emphasis not only eliminated the need for the church, but it enthroned the "enlightened" conscience as the final authority in determining personal conduct. On the one hand, then, Protestant ideology unleashed a revolutionary force—that each person was the final judge of right and wrong, regardless of what the church or state decreed. But on the other hand, Protestantism affirmed the need for both church and state to control man's depraved nature.

This tension between two concepts of Protestantism splintered the movement as people chose different paths to resolve the fundamental struggle between internal authority and external authority. Some Protestant reformers turned the decrees of conscience into a justification for political and social revolution (such as the Munsterites) or a withdrawal from society by banding into little groups or by migrating to places where the dictates of conscience could be followed unmolested by an established church or state (such as the Mennonites). In contrast, other Protestants called for rigid control of the unregenerate masses by the chosen elect. This position produced dogmatism and intolerance for any other beliefs. John Calvin's model Christian society in Geneva is remembered most for its tight, almost repressive governance of personal behavior.

Between the extremes were most of the English nonconformist groups discussed earlier. They attempted to walk the fine line between revolution and repression. Although they challenged aspects of Anglican doctrine, polity, and worship, they attempted to work within the church, not destroy it from without. They conceived of the church primarily as a voluntary gathering place for those already marked for salvation. "The Church visible," wrote Reverend Thomas Hooker of Connecticut in 1648, "results out of that relation which is betwixt the professors of the faith, when by voluntary consent they yield outward subjection to that government of Christs exerciseth by his word, spirit, and discipline, by his ordinances and officers over them who have yielded themselves subjects to his Headship and Supreme Authority."[7] Hooker, like other English nonconformists, identified the church as a group of equals separate and distinct from the generality of society. And yet, the same English nonconformists advocated a state church—encompassing all citizens—that would ensure religious purity, maintain a high moral standard for society, help bring into the fold those elect who had not reached a regenerate state, and finally, control the behavior of the unregenerate many. They exalted the concept of conscience and upheld the individuality of the Protestant version of salvation, but they also desired an institutional church to curb the anarchic tendencies inherent in Protestant ideology.

In reconciling this dichotomy of Protestant ideology, the mainstream of Protestantism postulated a harmony between the individual and society. One's individuality would emerge from one's participation in society. Most Protestants, and especially English nonconformists, assumed that the moral dictates of individual consciences would not differ among right-thinking persons. There was, they believed, a single correct moral code. What they sought was not a society of libertarians but a society of persons instinctively behaving correctly. They sought moral conformity, not individuality. Moral conformity was essential for a godly society. They recognized that tension often developed between group loyalties and individual desires, but they did not view that tension as either inevitable or desirable. It simply happened and had to be resolved. Nor did they automatically assume that the demands of the group took precedence over the needs of the individual or vice versa: neither libertarian nor totalitarian, neither free spirits nor conformists—they were much more pragmatic. Individuals had to live in society in a position of interdependence with one another; therefore they had to work out harmonious relationships between individual desires and group goals.

This is one of the most difficult aspects of seventeenth- (and eighteenth-) century Protestant thought for modern students to grasp: that people could posit a certain freedom for the individual while ruthlessly suppressing other freedoms; that people could leave England to avoid religious or political oppression and then turn and oppress others; that people could talk of liberty for themselves while their slaves worked their fields. Yet, Protestant ideology postulated both, and in the environment of the New World the Protestant notions of opposition, authority, and conscience would color dramatically the face of religious institutions.

RELIGION IN THE COLONIES

When we wrote earlier about the church as one of the twin pillars of European society, it was not simply an acknowledgment of the importance of religion for the seventeenth- and eighteenth-century Western world; it was also a recognition that the church performed several secular as well as religious functions in society. In addition to supervising the doctrines and practices of the individual congregations (called parishes in England) and setting the moral standards for society, the institutional church served as a kind of welfare department. It fed the poor, sheltered the old and disabled, and cared for the widowed, orphaned, and homeless. The parish vestry (a local council that supervised the running of many town and church services) as well as other church bodies also acted as courts. The church legally registered births, deaths, and marriages. It probated wills and handled the affairs of minors. Further, as one of the largest landowners, the church employed thousands of people to cultivate its crops and tend its livestock. Hence, it represented a significant economic force in England and Europe. Finally, in England the bishops, as ecclesiastical peers, comprised a large bloc in the House of Lords and through this office exercised considerable influence over political affairs. In short, then, the functions of the European/English church extended far beyond those activities related to the spiritual welfare of the country.

When Protestants arrived in North America, they attempted to create religious institutions that fulfilled some of the same functions performed by the established church they had left behind. But the environment of the New World weighed heavily against this aim. Instead, it encouraged the anarchic or individualist tendency inherent in Protestantism to take root. Within fifty years the colonies witnessed the proliferation of autonomous, self-governing congregations relatively free from external religious and political authorities. By 1700 Anglo-American churches faced a unique situation. By European standards the populace demonstrated considerable piety and concern for spiritual matters. The harsh, rugged life of the frontier no doubt made people deeply conscious of the precariousness of their existence and thus more attuned to spiritual concerns than might otherwise have been the case. But many of the religious resisted organizational bonds. At the same time, literally hundreds of churches in the colonies lacked ministers to attend them. Those congregations which secured clergy often had to settle for men poorly trained or totally lacking any formal university education. It was specifically to provide for a learned clergy that Massachusetts Bay established Harvard College in 1636, only six years after the founding of the colony. Furthermore, as Anglo-America experienced rapid population growth during the latter half of the seventeenth century, the general population quickly outdistanced the growth in church membership, thus further diminishing the influence of religious institutions over colonials. The end result, then, was a society with a strong religious base but with a fragmented, weak religious structure that was struggling to define its proper role in society.[8]

New England

When discussing religion in seventeenth-century New England, it is customary for historians to generalize about the congregational church structure in Massachusetts and talk about the *New England Way.* In one sense this term is misleading because it seems to imply religious consensus among the various English nonconformist groups who migrated to the area. Massachusetts, of course, was settled primarily by nonseparating Congregationalists, with a trickle of Presbyterians, Baptists, and Separatists. In Connecticut Congregationalists also dominated, although the colony drew in a sizable number of Presbyterians as well. In Plymouth and New Haven, however, Separatists comprised the bulk of settlers, and the situation in Rhode Island was truly unique. Its charter guaranteed religious freedom to all who "doe not actually disturb the civill peace of our sayd colony" or did not use "this libertie to lycentiousnesse, and profanenesse, nor to the civill injurye or outward disturbeance of others."[9] This policy attracted all sorts of groups, but primarily General and Particular Baptists, Separatists, and Quakers, with even a few Catholics and Jews.

Rather than intending to show the dominance of Congregationalism over other branches of English nonconformity in New England, however, historians have used the term the New England Way to describe a religious structure comprised of autonomous congregations that formed the centers of the New England communities. Whether in Plymouth, Rhode Island, New Haven, Connecticut, or Massachusetts, the churches served as the locus for most community activity. The meetinghouse was also the town center for activities ranging from road repair to setting local taxes, to electing representatives to the colony legislature. The New England Way also meant a congregational church order that restricted church membership to the elect, or to "visible saints" who could profess a conversion experience. With a little variation, the concept of the church as the body of the elect became the norm for all of New England. Finally, the New England Way implied an active, powerful clergy who through the force of persuasion and personality—not legal authority—influenced the conduct of church affairs. But even though New Englanders, particularly the first generation, revered their ministers, there was no doubt that religious authority rested finally in the congregation. When Plymouth Colony determined that one of its ministers was unsatisfactory, it expelled him. Likewise, churches throughout the seventeenth century discharged clergy at will.

Even as the churches of New England operated as autonomous, self-governing bodies, the desire to maintain religious purity remained strong. Puritans, after all, had left England because they believed Anglican practices had become corrupted.

Although they had left England to seek freedom of worship for themselves, they proved no more tolerant of other religious beliefs than the Anglican Church had been of them. Hence, except for Rhode Island the New England colonies passed laws officially "establishing" Congregationalism and outlawing other beliefs.

In the end, however, the legal installation of Congregationalism proved no instant recipe for guaranteeing a strong institutional church order in New England. During the first two decades of Massachusetts Bay's existence, the colony experienced a series of troubling incidents: the Antinomian controversy in 1636 (over the teachings of Mistress Anne Hutchinson), the expulsion of Roger Williams in 1637 for his religious unorthodoxy, and Robert Child's petition to establish a Presbyterian Church order in 1645. These events caused ministers and laypeople alike to look for a way to ensure religious orthodoxy in New England. The result was a call for a synod (a council of ministers and elders) in Cambridge. Although some Connecticut town representatives attended, and Plymouth sent "messengers," by and large the Cambridge Synod was a Massachusetts affair. In 1648 the Synod produced the Cambridge Platform, a document that both set out church doctrines and practices and gave church councils "advisory" power—but no legal authority—over the congregations. The Cambridge Synod tried to encourage uniformity among New England's churches, but it met with only small success.[10]

Church councils made several additional attempts to exert some control over the congregations and the general populace. As noted earlier, during the seventeenth century the colonies, including New England, experienced population growth that far outdistanced increases in church membership. The clergy diagnosed part of the problem as increasing materialism and lack of piety, but they also recognized that New England membership practices created difficulties. In the early 1630s Massachusetts, under the guidance of John Cotton, had instituted a religious test—that is, testimony of a religious conversion experience—as necessary for admittance to church membership. Many New England churches adopted it. Over the years the test caused the gap between churches and towns to increase. Many baptized individuals, often the children or grandchildren of first-generation Puritans, simply failed to experience such a visible sign of God's grace. By the 1650s this situation created great concern. To counteract this trend, in 1657 a ministerial council composed of Massachusetts and Connecticut clergy endorsed a "half-way" practice. Those baptized Christians who practiced a godly life would be admitted to a half-way membership if they made a profession of faith. Still, full-membership status, which included voting rights and admittance to communion, was reserved for the visible saints. In 1662 a larger synod sanctioned what became known as the Half-Way Covenant.

Although the Half-Way Covenant spoke to those individuals basically within the fold but lacking a conversion experience, it did nothing to allay fears of growing materialism and a decline of piety within New England. These concerns, coupled with the traumatic aftermath of King Phillip's War (1675 to 1676), prompted a call for a third synod, the Reforming Synod of 1679. This council issued a confession of faith patterned closely after the Savoy Declaration of 1658, a document drafted by English Congregationalists. But despite this attempt to bolster further uniformity and strengthen the church's position in the colonies, the problem of New England's churches remained the Protestant problem. Colonists continued to develop a variety of ideas about religious truth and sought to practice them, either within or outside of organized religion. The synods called during the seventeenth century strove to forge a common governing association among the churches and to spur religiosity throughout the colonies, but all in all the synods were not terribly successful. The Protestant thrust toward autonomy, which blossomed in the New World environment, simply doomed their attempts to failure. As a result, even in New England, where the established church was the strongest in the colonies, a pluralistic, autonomous pattern of church order prevailed.[11]

The Southern Colonies

In contrast to New England, Virginia's religious history was molded by its secular climate and the early intervention of the Crown. The first decades of the colony's existence saw little attention to religion. In 1624, however, the House of Burgesses called for "an uniformity in our church as neere as may be to the canons in England,"[12] and after the Crown assumed control of the colony in 1625, Anglicanism became established. But even with official sanction, the Church of England languished in Virginia for much of the seventeenth century. Bemoaning the scarcity of both churches and clergy in Virginia, one pamphleteer wrote in 1662, "Many Parishes as yet want both Churches and Gleabes, and I think not above a fifth part of them are supplyed with Ministers."[13]

It was not until 1693 that a college to train clergy (named William and Mary) was founded in Williamsburg, and as late as 1730 David Humphreys estimated that Virginia had only about forty parishes, and lacked ministers for nearly half of them. With no resident bishop and only a handful of ministers to watch over the rowdy, scattered populace, seventeenth-century Virginia became noted for its lack of religiosity.[14]

The weakness of Anglicanism in Virginia encouraged New England Puritans to move into the colony. Despite a 1643 law ordering that "all nonconformists upon notice of them shall be compelled to depart the collony with all conveniencie,"[15] by 1649 a sizable group of non-Anglicans lived in Virginia. Thirteen years later the number of Quakers and Baptists in Virginia had increased so substantially that the House of Burgesses passed severe laws against them. As a result, many of these dissenters moved south into what would become North Carolina. Some Quakers, however, still refused to leave Virginia. In 1672 the Quaker population was significant enough to prompt a visit from George Fox. As we see shortly, it was only in the eighteenth century that the Church of England reasserted its influence and became the dominant religious force in the colony.[16]

The Carolinas, like Virginia, also established Anglicanism as the state church, but in the thinly populated, raw frontier society that characterized the region, the Church of England's growth was very slow. David Humphreys reported that until 1701 South Carolina had "no Minister of the Church of England Resident in this Colony" for its population of 7000. North Carolina's situation was even worse. Its 5000 inhabitants, Humphreys declared, all lived "without any Form of Divine Worship publickly performed, and without Schools for the Education of their Children in the Elements of Learning and Principles of Religion."[17] In the south the Church of England did form several parishes, but those were mostly around Charlestown. In the north, no parishes were organized until the eighteenth century. Like Virginia, the Carolinas lacked sufficient ministers or a church hierarchy to build a religious network in the colony. So not surprisingly, the region attracted nonconformists. North Carolina became a haven for Quakers and Baptists, and drew a few New England Congregationalists and Presbyterians as well. South Carolina attracted Congregationalists, Baptists, Huguenots, and some Quakers. By the end of the seventeenth century the Carolinas were dominated by the non-Anglicans within their borders.[18]

As noted earlier, Maryland was founded by Lord Baltimore in part as a religious haven for Catholics. It must be kept in mind, however, that officially Maryland possessed an Anglican establishment. Because of the intense fear and hatred of Catholics by the English, Catholicism was tolerated but not officially sanctioned by the colony. The Calverts encouraged the migration of Catholics to the colony, but few chose to come. The rich land coupled with religious toleration attracted large numbers of Protestant nonconformists to Maryland during the seventeenth century. Indeed, in the 1670s, when the English government investigated Calvert's rule with an eye toward bolstering the Anglican establishment there, the second Lord Baltimore reminded the English authorities that the "greatest part of the Inhabitants (three or four at least) doe consist of Presbiterians, Independents, Anabaptists and Quakers, those of the Church of England as well as those of the Romish being fewest."[19] Britain postponed actions to strengthen the Anglican Church in Maryland, and it remained weak throughout most of the seventeenth century. After the Glorious Revolution and royal takeover of the government in 1691, however, the Church of England began to take root and grow, so that by the time of the American Revolution the colony, next to Virginia, had become the largest stronghold of Anglicanism in North America.[20]

The Middle Colonies

During the seventeenth century, the middle colonies were populated primarily by the Dutch, Swedes, Puritans, and Quakers. New York was originally settled by the Dutch East India Company, which established the Reformed (that is, Calvinist) Church of Holland (or Dutch Reformed Church) in the 1620s. Holland's tolerant religious policies, however, provided little impetus for migration to the New World for the Dutch, so by the midseventeenth century only a few ministers and a dozen or so Dutch Reformed Churches existed in the colony. In 1664 the defeat of the Dutch by the British brought in Anglicanism. But, as elsewhere in the colonies, its influence was almost nonexistent until the eighteenth century. David Humphreys wrote that "there was no Face of the Church of England here till about the Year 1693."[21] Four more years passed before the first Anglican Church was founded in New York City. The colony attracted some French Reformed, Lutherans, and an element of New England Puritans (who settled primarily in Long Island).

Delaware, and to a lesser extent New Jersey, were first settled by Swedish Lutherans, but their numbers remained small. More important in the religious history of New Jersey was the influx of New Haven Puritans into East Jersey in 1666 and then the settlement of Quakers in West Jersey during the mid-1670s. Later on, the founding of Pennsylvania signaled a sizable migration of Quakers into that colony. Because of its policy of religious toleration, in the eighteenth century Pennsylvania experienced a dramatic influx of non-Quakers, particularly Scotch-

Irish Presbyterians, German Mennonites, and German Lutherans. But that comes later in our story. For the middle colonies, the portrait of religious institutions was much the same as elsewhere in Anglo-America. The diversity of religious beliefs, coupled with the ineffectiveness of the established church, produced a pluralistic, variegated religious structure.[22]

PROTESTANTISM AND ANGLO-AMERICAN CULTURE

Because society remained so primitive for much of the seventeenth century, and because so many Anglo-American ideas and institutions were derived from England and Europe, many historians find it difficult to refer to a distinct "Anglo-American" culture during the seventeenth century. Yet that is what we find. Anglo-America did, indeed, copy many of the features of England and Europe, but it did so imperfectly. The result was a derivative culture which was, at the same time, unique. Protestantism played an important role in shaping this paradox. We saw it at work in the unusual religious establishments which emerged in the colonies. Earlier, we noted its mark in the economic and political ideals and behavior of the colonists. It remains to note how the Protestant character of Anglo-America influenced some other facets of seventeenth-century colonial life. Let us use education and literature as our examples.

Education

Education in early America is usually associated with New England grammar schools and Harvard College. In truth, these represented only minor aspects of colonial education. Among the English, formal education was reserved for the upper classes. The liberal-arts curriculum, which formed the core of the English university of the time, was meant to provide the sons of the nobility with the learning that befit their station. Except for legal training at the Inns of Court and theological studies at the universities, higher education had little practical intent. Much the same was true of the English grammar school. Reading, writing, mathematics, classical languages, and a smattering of rhetoric and logic were taught to the sons of the upper classes to prepare them for entry into the universities. Once there, they might stay a year or two before returning to the family estate to learn the more important business of managing family affairs and promoting its interests in the Houses of Lords or Commons.

Such formal education was far from the world of common English citizens. For them education meant the transmission of the principal components of culture from one generation to another—in other words, passing on the knowledge and attitudes necessary for sons or daughters to assume proper places in the world. As such the home formed the center of education, and the family, the principal educating unit. The curriculum usually had two parts: preparation for a trade or for homemaking and moral instruction. Only in the latter did reading or writing play a role, usually through a half-literate parent's teaching the child enough to read and understand the Bible.

That view of education was predicated on the notion that a thin veneer of civilization, called society, separated men and women from barbarism. Modern theories of social "progress" were unknown to the seventeenth-century English. Rather, man had to struggle constantly to suppress his baser instincts, avoid evil, and survive natural occurrences such as sickness or starvation that plagued the common folk of every country. Society was man's defense against barbarism and the cruelties of nature. It was a composite of attitudes and institutions which reflected centuries of human wisdom on how to survive in the world and how to do it with an element of grace.

Society's principal function, then, was an educative one—the transmission of culture. The family, the central unit of society, performed the primary role in education and, as such, had the support and protection of other social institutions. The structure of the family was authoritarian and paternalistic. The child was often considered a miniature adult with strong moral and physical responsibilities for the family's success and survival. As many modern students have observed, no "childhood" existed in the seventeenth century.

In Anglo-America this concept of education formed the basis for its social order and helped explain, for example, the tightly knit, family-oriented, communal structure of the early New England town. Separated from the kinship ties of the Old World, first-generation New Englanders drew institutions like the church and state even closer and made them provide more protection and support for the family than they did in England. The New England Congregational Church began as a kind of extended family, nurturing, protecting, and disciplining its members. In every colony, but especially in Puritan New England, the state exercised considerable control over individuals. From the vantage point of courts and rulers, nothing was protected more zealously than the obligations and duties of parents toward children, and visa versa.

In that seventeenth-century environment. formal education was largely an accident and played only a minor role. Harvard College, founded in 1636 to train a learned clergy, produced some remarkable graduates in its formative years; but they represented a very small minority of the populace. The famous New England grammar schools were established by high-minded, religiously inspired leaders who feared that the family could not perform the tasks asked of it. The first Massachusetts school law (1642) expressed the General Court's deep concern over "the great neglect of many parents & masters in training up their children in learning, & labor, & other implyments which may be proffitable to the common wealth." The Court went on to charge magistrates in each community "with the care of the redresse of this evill." It empowered local officials not only to "take account from time to time of all parents and masters, and of their children, especially of their ability to read & understand the principles of religion & the capitall laws of this country," but also "to put forth apprentices the children of such as they shall not be able & fitt to imploy and bring them up."[23] Formal schools emerged from a statute issued five years later. "It being one chiefe piect [project] of y^{t} ould deluder, Satan," declared the General Court in 1647,

> to keepe men from the knowledge of ye Scriptures, as in form^{r} times by keeping y^{m} in an unknowne tongue . . . It is therefore ord^{r}ed, y^{t} ev^{r}y township in this iurisdiction, aft^{r} ye Lord hath increased y^{m} to ye number of 50 house-

> holdrs, shall then forthwth appoint one wthin theire towne to teach all such children as shall resort to him to write & reade . . . & it is furthr ordered, yt where any towne shall increase to ye numbr of 100 families or householdrs, they shall set up a gram̄er schoole, ye mr thereof being able to instruct youth so farr as they may be fited for ye university . . . .[24]

In truth, however, most towns considered schools a luxury they could not afford. Despite the stern prodding of the legislatures, schools in early New England lived perilous and often short existences.[25]

Literature

During the Middle Ages and into the seventeenth century, creative writing was a luxury usually associated with the upper class. Shopkeepers, farmers, artisans, merchants, and fishermen had neither the time nor the education necessary to engage in abstract speculation, or to write treatises on law, politics, or religion. This distinction between "high" and "low" culture was transported to the New World. The first Anglo-Americans were, on the whole, poorly educated as befit their humble origins. Moreover, for most of the first century of their life in America, colonists were preoccupied with battling the forces of geography, climate, and wilderness. Not surprisingly, therefore, they did not produce much literature, or any of the forms of expression usually associated with "higher culture."

Most of the literary activity in seventeenth-century Anglo-America took place in New England. It had a well-educated clergy and a sizable population of English nonconformists–introspective people who placed considerable emphasis on rudimentary education. The clergy published many of its sermons as well as a few books which dealt with pastoral concerns and with applied theology. Several Puritans, such as Anne Bradstreet and Michael Wigglesworth, wrote some rather memorable poetry. Bradstreet composed love poetry from a religious perspective, while Wigglesworth wrote his epic poem *Day of Doom,* describing New England's fall from grace. Several histories were written by early New Englanders, but they too dealt with religious themes–principally how God's plan for the redemption of mankind was unfolding in the development of New England. Among these the most significant were William Hubbard's *History of New England* (1680) and Edward Johnson's *Wonder-Working Providence, or A History of Sion's Saviour in New England* (1654). Aimed primarily toward an English audience, the histories portrayed New England as a place where God's will had been acted out–where with divine aid, Christian men and women had succeeded in creating a purer, more God-pleasing society than that of Old England. "The Souldiers of Christ in N.E.," declared Johnson

> are resolved (the Lord willing) to keepe the government our God hath given us, and for witnesse hee hath so done, let this History manifest: for we chose not the place for the Land, but for the government, that our Lord Christ might raigne over us, both in Churches and Common-wealth, and although the Lord have been pleased by an extraordinary blessing upon his peoples industry to make the place fruitfull (as at this deed indeed it is) yet all may know the land in it selfe is very sterrill, but the upholding of the truths of Christ, is the chiefe cause why so many hitherto come . . .[26]

Another, rather more notable historian of New England was the Boston minister, Cotton Mather. Product of a family of ministers, Mather was one of the most remarkable people in American history. Active in nearly all phases of colonial life (even a member of London's prestigious Royal Society), but probably best remembered for his unfortunate role in the Salem witch trials, Mather produced several hundred books and pamphlets dealing with various religious and secular subjects between 1680 and 1720. He wrote on topics as diverse as inoculation for smallpox and the paths of comets. His writings included an enormous and remarkably good religious history of New England whose Latin short title was *Magnalia Christi Americana* (1702).[27]

Mather's activities and diverse interests, however, made him unusual in colonial life. In general, the early colonists led rather isolated and insular lives and did not communicate with each other through the printed word. Although a substantial number of them could read and perhaps write, they owned few books. Typically a library contained the Bible and very often *The Whole Duty of Man,* an English book of manners and morals written by an Anglican, Richard Allestree. In their forms of cultural expression, seventeenth-century Anglo-Americans behaved similarly to the English of the same station. If anything, the New World situation tended to exaggerate some traditional English attitudes. The colonials' preoccupation with religion, their denouncement of idleness, their exaltation of work and of things practical, their suspicion of lawyers, courts, and practitioners of medicine—all those reflected biases and virtues of the struggling, individualistic, striving English middle classes.

Part III
THE EIGHTEENTH-CENTURY COLONIAL WORLD

The previous chapters have outlined how colonial society during the seventeenth century was confronted by and preoccupied with the struggle to survive. In contrast, the tone and tenor of the eighteenth century proved strikingly different. Having moved beyond the survival stage, colonials were able to devote their labor and energies into expansion, both economic and territorial. The primitive frontier outposts of the first century of colonization gave way to bustling commerical centers. Raw, pristine forests were transformed into plowed fields. The impetus for such dramatic change came from several sources: notably, rapid population growth, economic expansion, and the maturation of colonial political institutions.

In light of such developments, it could be argued that the history of the colonial period should be viewed as a study of contrasts between the two centuries. Certainly the social, political, and economic changes of the eighteenth century often made it appear far removed from seventeenth-century Anglo-America. Indeed, in part many of the trends discussed earlier became muted after 1700. But in another sense the changes that transpired during the eighteenth century more accurately reflected a shift in emphasis upon old patterns, not a move away from them. As we see shortly, eighteenth-century colonial society achieved economic prosperity, the beginning of native literary and artistic production, a revival of religion, and political independence—all by refashioning and building upon the heritage of the seventeenth-century world.

Earlier sections of this book identified several themes that helped to explain the nature and direction of colonial development during the seventeenth century. It was argued, first, that Anglo-America imitated many of the features of the Old World but copied them imperfectly. As a result, colonial society from the beginning possessed a uniquely American character that increasingly influenced colonial institutions, ideas, and values. The absence of certain crucial English/European institutions as well as the character of the first generations of settlers determined that Anglo-America would follow a course of development far different from its parent.

Second, it was noted that from the outset Anglo-American society fostered a type of economic radicalism. The early settlers were economic radicals in part because they allowed an unprecedented degree of individual freedom in economic as well as religious and social pursuits. In addition, the colonists almost inadvertently created a society that measured social status on the basis of wealth, not birth. Although Anglo-Americans believed that individual desires must, if need be, take second place to the public good, in practice the pursuit of individual gain simultaneously worked for the good of the community. For most of the seventeenth century, the example of Robert Keayne notwithstanding, colonial society viewed individual goals as harmonious with the goals of the community. The economic radicalism of the colonists had significant implications for the social structure of Anglo-America. The standard of wealth as a basis for social status doomed to extinction the notion of a hereditary class society. Further, because economic opportunity fell within the grasp of most individuals, Anglo-America afforded unprecedented upward social mobility.

Third, the scarcity of labor and abundance of land led to the introduction of black slavery into North America. Although the institution existed to some extent in all colonies, it took root primarily in the southern colonies. But even there, only a few owned slaves, and the number of slaves in the mainland colonies remained quite small until the eighteenth century. During the first century of colonization, settlers relied primarily upon indentured servitude or family help to solve the labor problem.

Fourth, because of the availability of land, Anglo-America experienced a certain degree of "democratization" of its political institutions. When the traditional voting qualification used in the English counties—that is, the possession of property valued at 40s. or more—was applied to the colonies, it worked a small revolution. It extended voting rights to a far greater segment of the colonial population than that comparable in England. Whereas the imposition of property qualifications in England served to limit severely the number of men allowed to vote, in Anglo-America, where land was abundant, the opposite effect occurred.

Fifth, those who left England for the New World during the seventeenth century included a large number of Protestant reformers. In New England, where Protestant ideology was especially pervasive, the early settlers identified themselves not just as a godly people, but as a people in opposition, whose lives and ideas were threatened by the corruption and ungodliness of the Old World. Having left England for a purer land, they sought to create a fortress in the wilderness that would preserve a godly society from the evil and corruption that surrounded it. The harshness of frontier life, coupled with the reality of Indians, uncommodious climate, disease, and threats from the Catholic powers of France and Spain, conditioned people to view their lives in the very light that Protestant ideology purported. Hence, even as Anglo-America grew more prosperous and materialistic, the Protestant seige mentality became imprinted in colonial culture, not only in religion but in secular activities as well. In addition, ideas within Protestantism led colonists in two conflicting directions: toward conformity to a "pure" established church, and also toward freedom to follow the lead of one's conscience. Both tendencies made their mark upon Anglo-American religious institutions during the seventeenth century, but by 1700 the impulse toward autonomy had become the dominant force in Anglo-America.

Finally, the seventeenth-century colonial world reflected the determination and purposes of its founders. Some of the colonies began as economic ventures, others as religious experiments; but by the middle of the century all of British North America felt the impact of the imperial purpose that justified the colonies' existence to England. Insofar as individual success contributed to the general prosperity of the colonies, it became a welcome enterprise. From the start, almost naturally, colonists sold available raw materials to England and purchased British manufactured goods—an arrangement beneficial to both colonial and English development. What distinguished British North America so markedly from the French and Spanish empires was simply the harmony with which personal goals achieved imperial ends. The prosperity of each colonist enhanced the general prosperity of the British empire. Because they succeeded so well, the North American colonies were largely left to their own devices. Some imperial regulations sought to define the "proper" activities of the colonies, but those laws that might limit or inhibit natural colonial economic activity were largely ignored. The remaining regulations tended to protect and encourage colonial economic ventures. In general, then, the seventeenth century witnessed the development of an imperial net of regulations which allowed the colonies to grow almost free of British control.

All of the themes just outlined to some extent helped mold eighteenth-century colonial society. But new influences, circumstances, and conditions produced a society that in most ways departed from the patterns established during the previous century. In what ways was this true? First, Anglo-America continued to pursue a course of development that reflected its mutant English/European heritage. Surprisingly, however, eighteenth-century colonials clung to an illusory image of themselves and England. They came to believe that their society indeed embodied—if imperfectly—the same values and experiences of the parent society. As we see shortly, eighteenth-century Anglo-America identified its society with institutions and attitudes it simply did not contain. Although Virginians, South Carolinians, and Bostonians did not have a hereditary aristocracy, they manufactured a nobility of wealth. Although colonial political institutions permitted considerably more popular expression than their English counterparts, colonials were convinced that their rights "as English citizens" were the same exercised by compatriots across the sea. The illusion that Anglo-America was a little England, a true "New England," bred strong expectations among colonials that their own interests and wishes would (or should) be reflected in the economic and political decisions of the imperial government. They soon learned, however, that England's king and Parliament would not always serve colonial interests. To the contrary, colonials would painfully awaken to the reality that their rights as English citizens—as they saw them—were clearly inferior to the rights of native Britons. Only when this realization became widespread among the colonies would the move for independence gain strength.

Second, the economic radicalism identified earlier created an emphasis on wealth that led to social stratification during the eighteenth century. Although the availability of land, and hence the more equal distribution of wealth, permitted considerable social movement during the eighteenth century, the advent of a new brand of immigrant—the Scotch-Irish, German, Swede, and Swiss—caused a tightening within the social structure of the colonies. The first century of colonization witnessed the rise of a group of wealthy elites who established a power hold upon the political and economic life of the colonies. This colonial "aristocracy" looked unfavorably upon newcomers and made it increasingly difficult for immigrants to rise to higher social positions. Although the colonies continued to exhibit greater social mobility and less class strictures than Europe, during the eighteenth century Anglo-America saw the gulf between classes widen.

Third, without question one of the most significant developments of the eighteenth century was the phenomenal acceptance and spread of black slavery. Whereas slavery represented an insignificant labor alternative to indentured servitude on the North American mainland during the seventeenth century, the increased concentration upon several labor-intensive crops—that is, rice, indigo, and tobacco—during the eighteenth century caused large landowners to rely upon slavery increasingly as a way to produce crops cheaply. The growth of slavery in the colonies had an irrevocable impact upon the society of the southern colonies.

Fourth, the eighteenth century experienced two apparently contradictory yet reinforcing developments in the political structure of the North American colonies. On the one hand, the royal governor, who was either relatively powerless or nonexistent during the seventeenth century, grew increasingly powerful and significant. At the same time, however, the lower houses of the colonial legislatures began to control or strongly influence the decisions made by the royal governor. By exercising the power of the purse, colonial legislatures made many governors more dependent for power and influence upon them than the governor was upon the Crown. This development marked the coming of age for the political institutions of Anglo-America and provided the basis for the protests against the British government during the 1760s and 1770s.

Fifth, eighteenth-century colonial America witnessed a resurgence of the conflict between the conformist and autonomous impulses within Protestantism as well as an intensification of the Protestant sense of being in opposition. By the beginning of the eighteenth century, religious leaders had come to view much of the population as either indifferent to or only mildly concerned with religion. Many colonial clergy feared what they perceived to be rampant materialism and irreligion. Surely, they worried, such behavior would arouse the Lord's wrath and bring destruction upon the colonies unless people turned back to God. Sparked by the efforts of a new, charismatic generation of ministers—notably George Whitefield, Samuel Davies, Gilbert Tennent, and Jonathan Edwards—the colonies experienced a "great awakening" of piety and religious fervor. Although the evangelical efforts of the churches reaped converts, they also produced dissension and conflict that fractured the churches and ensured religious pluralism in America. The Great Awakening also intensified the Protestant mentality of opposition. That attitude, coupled with radical Whig and Enlightenment ideas, set the stage for American revolutionary fervor in the 1760s and 1770s.

Finally, earlier chapters described the imperial purposes behind the founding of the Anglo-American colonies. Although some of England's leaders of the seventeenth century envisioned an all-powerful worldwide British empire and directed colonial policy to that end, it was during the eighteenth century, when England fought the decisive wars for empire, that the imperial purpose of the colonies came to be felt. The result of England's attempt to control colonial affairs was a breakdown in the harmony between imperial and personal goals that contributed so significantly to colonial development. In the mideighteenth century, then, Anglo-Americans—for really the first time—felt the weight of imperial regulations. British edicts that sought to control economic and political behavior in the colonial view unduly and unfairly hampered their pursuit of private goals. The erosion of the harmony between personal and imperial ends, perhaps as much as any of the other factors mentioned, fueled the revolutionary temper in the colonies and led Anglo-Americans ultimately to challenge British authority.

7

The Eighteenth-Century British Empire

The administration of Charles II developed a twofold colonial policy which would remain in effect until 1763. One aspect concerned the regulation and stimulation of trade while the other involved tighter political control over the mainland colonies in North America. Still, in some important ways the shape of the British Empire of the eighteenth century would stand in marked contrast to the imperial structure that evolved in the seventeenth. The diverse origins of the colonies, coupled with English preoccupation with domestic affairs for much of the seventeenth century, resulted in a loosely structured, often inconsistent colonial policy. Even the few attempts to tighten British control over colonial commerce—such as the series of navigation acts passed under Cromwell and then Charles II—were only mildly effective; and they were directed at the Dutch as much as they were intended for North American colonists. The English governments of the seventeenth century differed not only in their attitudes toward the colonies, but also in their depth of concern for colonial development. Besides, Britain failed to employ a sufficient number of colonial agents to enforce imperial policy anyway. Thus, despite the early navigation acts and attempts at tighter political control like the Dominion of New England, by 1688 Anglo-America enjoyed a measure of autonomy and self-direction unmatched in other colonial empires.

In the late seventeenth century, however, England's domestic turmoil ended and, for the first time, Britons made a concerted effort to control colonial trade and development. This new attitude in England—and the resulting behavior—can be attributed to several factors, but one of the most significant was a growing consciousness of the importance of national economic self-sufficiency. King William's War (1689 to 1697) forcefully impressed England with its economic vulnerability. Heavily dependent upon the European mainland states for foodstuffs and raw materials, as well as for a major outlet for Britain's manufactured goods, the English economy suffered substantially from the interruption of trade caused by war. The only bright spots during that time were the American colonies. Their economic success led the British government to a new definition of empire based on the theory of self-sufficiency. The new emphasis led to some fundamental changes in the basic relationship of the parent country to the colonies. Also, it tied economic nationalism more closely to political nationalism.

In many ways the new definition of empire was the logical conclusion to the original justification for colonies: acquisition of precious metals. As it became apparent that North America would not produce the silver and gold the Spanish had gleaned in Latin America (and as those mines played out), a struggle developed over existing supplies of bullion. This in turn led to the seventeenth-century notion of the necessity for colonies to stimulate trade by producing raw materials, for those could be processed and sold to other nations. Selling raw materials and finished goods would create a favorable balance of trade and would ensure that more gold and silver flowed into the state treasury than flowed out. But as the North American and West Indian colonies proved phenomenally profitable, many theorists began to conceive of even grander schemes based upon colonial possessions. Particularly, they began to suggest that a country might become totally self-sufficient—that is, no longer forced to rely on any country, friend or enemy, for materials vital to the country's well-being. Eighteenth-century mercantilists argued that no country could become a world power so long as vital resources were controlled by a potential enemy or by a country which might fall under the domination of a potential enemy.

This kind of thinking led directly to England's nearly century-long struggle with France. Both countries sought to become self-sufficient through colonial empires which were nearly identical in content and geographic location. Neither country possessed the domestic resources to achieve the aim. Each needed many products that either had to be purchased elsewhere or produced in the colonies. Actually, every European nation was in the same situation—an obvious reason why expansionism became a dominant feature of European affairs from the sixteenth century to the twentieth.

By the middle of the eighteenth century the New World had already provided abundant evidence of being an economic success. At the same time the English domestic economy was experiencing an unparalleled period of prosperity, due in part to manufacturing based on colonial production and consumption. To mercantilists England appeared on the verge of achieving self-sufficiency. Planners conceived of a not-too-distant future when England would be the manufacturing center of the world, importing needed raw materials from the colonies and turning them into finished products for sale everywhere. The prospects were staggering. England seemed to have a mercantilist dream almost at hand: It would export all it produced and face no imports of consequence from its competitors; and gold and silver would flow into English coffers in quantities greater than those enjoyed by Spain a century or so earlier.[1]

INTEREST POLITICS

Such speculation might now seem to be absurd economic thinking, but for eighteenth-century nationalists, it made good sense. In pursuing the goal of self-sufficiency, though, Crown and Parliament chose somewhat different means. Increasingly, Parliament's vision was clouded by the growing demands of various economic "interests" within the realm. The great trading companies (like the British East India Company), the sugar planters of the West Indies, and various combinations of merchants, landowners, and manufacturers within the British Isles competed for legislation favoring their interests. The mainland colonies also represented diverse economic interests and, throughout the seventeenth and eighteenth centuries, various colonies maintained their own representatives in England. These agents monitored Parliament's activities, reported back to colonial officials, and lobbied for their colonies when necessary.[2]

However, the influence of colonial agents in Parliament tended to dwindle in the eighteenth century. Mainland colonial interests were frequently overwhelmed by the demands and power of the British East India Company, or Jamaican planters, or London merchants. Also, though Parliament continued to recognize the tremendous value of North American possessions, it feared their growing wealth and assertiveness. Thus, in the first half of the eighteenth century, many bills emerged from Parliament regulating colonial trade and manufacturing. Particularly dangerous in the eyes of British interests were the growing dominance over colonial trade by colonial merchants, illegal smuggling by those same merchants, and the likelihood that colonists would turn their profits from commerce into manufacturing, thus competing with Britons (which Northerners were beginning to do in some areas by the time of the Revolution).

But it should not be thought that Parliament's treatment of North America was entirely punitive or that its behavior reflected only the partisan concerns of the moment. On the contrary, from a mercantilist posture bent on achieving self-sufficiency, Parliament believed that what it did was necessary for the welfare of the realm. Between 1695 and 1713 the British national debt increased 500 percent. Elements within the country debated over how the debt should be paid. Almost everyone agreed that the most likely solution was greater wealth through manufacturing and trade. William Wood, secretary to the commissioner of the customs, published the leading mercantilist tract of the era. His *Survey of Trade* (1718) covered the place of the colonies in the empire more thoroughly than any previous book or pamphlet. Above all, he argued that the colonies' interests should be suborned to those of England and that colonial trade should exist for one purpose: to enhance the wealth and power of England. He prophesied that the colonists' eighteenth-century role—the one that would lead to England's self-sufficiency—would be to supply raw materials to the empire while they consumed England's manufactured goods. He urged Parliament to pass whatever legislation was required to ensure that role.[3]

For the most part, members of Parliament accepted Wood's assessment of the importance of colonies and endorsed his recommendations for regulation. Parliament proved especially interested in stopping any colonial manufacturing operations which might compete with English industries. Thus, Parliament passed the

Wool Act of 1699, for example. Although aimed mainly at Irish wool producers, the Wool Act also hampered a growing Anglo-American industry by prohibiting the intercolonial trade of wool or its export to the British Isles or foreign countries. A number of similar acts followed. Of those, one of the more important was the Felt Act of 1732, which made colonial exportation of felt hats illegal. This hurt another growing colonial industry. Even more important was the Iron Act of 1750. That piece of legislation forbade colonists to erect new iron mills (about 100 small ones then existed, mostly in Pennsylvania) or to make iron hardware. It did, however, encourage colonials to ship bar iron to England by allowing them to do so duty free. The Iron Act requires some explanation. Since about 1717 English merchants and iron products producers had complained to Parliament that American-made iron tools and implements were hurting them in Anglo-American markets. That explained the restrictive provisions of the Act. But why encourage the shipment of bar iron to England? The answer was that England produced no iron ore of its own. For years England depended primarily upon Swedish iron. Colonial iron would replace Swedish iron. English manufacturers would then convert colonial iron into hardware and ship iron products to America to be sold to the colonists—a perfect example of the mercantilist notion of the colony as a producer of raw materials and consumer of finished products.[4]

William Wood told the readers of his *Survey of Trade* that, in building a self-sufficient empire, the English should pay close attention to those colonial resources which were most important. None placed higher on his list than sugar. Members of Parliament shared Wood's belief in the importance of sugar. Thus, concern for West Indian sugar producers and the sugar trade led to one of the most famous pieces of legislation and regulation to emerge from Parliament before 1763, the Molasses or Sugar Act of 1733. Declaring that

> the welfare and prosperity of your Majesty's sugar colonies in America are of the greatest consequence to the trade, navigation and strength of this kingdom: and whereas the planters of the said sugar colonies have of late years fallen under such great discouragements, that they are unable to improve or carry on the sugar trade upon an equal footing with the foreign sugar colonies, without some advantage and relief be given to them from Great Britain,[5]

the Molasses Act prohibited colonials, especially New Englanders, from importing French molasses from West Indian islands like Guadeloupe, Martinique, or St. Domingo (Haiti). The legislation resulted from the demands of London-based West Indian planters angered by French incursions into the molasses trade with the mainland colonies. French West Indian planters sold molasses to New Englanders at cut-rate prices because officials in France feared that rum produced from molasses would compete with French brandy.

One area of mercantilist and imperial concern for which neither William Wood nor any member of Parliament had the correct answer was the problem of a colonial money supply. Mercantilist theory foresaw trade's filling English coffers with bullion so Parliament refused to scuttle that dream by coining money for the colonies or allowing them to coin their own. The result was that bullion did flow from North America to England. North Americans loved hard currency, also, and as their trading empire flourished in the eighteenth century they demanded and received gold and silver coin for their products. That money, in turn, was hoarded and eventually sent to England where it was sold to pay debts. The result was that most British North Americans never saw much hard money. Consequently, in the early eighteenth century some of the New England colonies began to print paper money. The practice spread. Parliament repeatedly tried to prevent the colonies from issuing paper money, a sore point for colonials who needed money to pay debts or finance new ventures. The zenith of parliamentary intervention in colonial monetary affairs came in 1751 when Parliament banned paper currencies in New England. In 1764 it extended the law to the other colonies. Parliament's monetary restrictions hurt many Anglo-American colonists but, as we see in the next chapter, not as badly as historians once assumed.[6]

WALPOLE, NEWCASTLE, AND SALUTARY NEGLECT

The success of Parliament's attempts to regulate colonial trade and manufacturing depended entirely upon the Crown's willingness to enforce Parliament's will, since prime responsibility for the administration of colonial affairs remained with the king. In such matters the attitudes of the monarchs (Queen Anne, and then George I, II, and III) were less important than those of their advisors or ministers. During the eighteenth century royal advisors gained a larger and larger voice in determining the Crown's interests, in working with Parliament to create legislation, and in overseeing and directing the vast bureaucracy. Of those ministers, two exercised considerable influence over imperial affairs between 1713 and 1763. One was Robert Walpole (1674–1745), First Earl of Orford, First Lord of the Treasury, Chancellor of the Exchequer, and the King's chief advisor from 1722 to 1742; the other was Thomas Pelham-Holles (1693–1768), Duke of Newcastle, Walpole's Secretary of State for the South (all colonial correspondence from and to royal governors passed through his hands), and First Lord of the Treasury from 1754 to 1762. Walpole was the more important of the two. He entered Parliament in 1700 and grew in power and prestige until 1712 when his political enemies drove him from office and managed to get him thrown in prison for a time on a charge of corruption. He made a dramatic return to public affairs with the accession of George I in 1714. Named First Lord of the Treasury and then Chancellor of the Exchequer, he served only three years before resigning. Then, in 1720, he gained national attention again during a great political scandal and financial disaster known as the South Sea Bubble.[7]

The *South Sea Bubble* was a label applied to the collapse of a large trading organization known as the South Sea Company. The Company had formed in 1711 when a group of wealthy, influential men agreed to lend the British government large sums of money at low rates in order to receive special trade concessions. Robert Harley, then Chancellor of the Exchequer, saw the scheme as a way of paying off England's national debt. Thus, the Company was formed, chartered by Parliament, and, in 1713, given the exclusive right to Spanish-American trade concessions negotiated from Spain as part of the Peace of Utrecht in 1713. This privilege fueled expectations of vast wealth for the company and, as a result, its stock rose rapidly in value. In truth, however, the company never realized any profit from its monopoly over the Spanish-American trade. In part, this was due to the considerable restrictions Spain had placed over the trade. The number of both slave and cargo ships given legal access to Spanish-America was severely limited. Spain, after all, expected to retain the bulk of its colonial American trade for itself. In addition to such restrictions, however, the South Sea Company also suffered fierce illegal competition from other British and New England ships. The result was that the value of Company stock crashed in 1720, ruining many investors and endangering England's financial structure. A number of politicians' careers were ruined by the Bubble, among them Charles Spencer, Third Earl of Sunderland, and Robert Walpole's main political opponent.[8]

Walpole made many friends and reversed some of the negative effects of the South Sea Bubble by convincing the British East India Company and the Bank of England to assume £18 million of South Sea Company stock. Subsequently, he returned to his old positions—First Lord of the Treasury and Chancellor of the Exchequer—and when Sunderland died Walpole became the most powerful minister serving the King.

Walpole maintained his position as the "prime" minister from 1722 to 1742. Unlike in the modern British cabinet, however, his power had no constitutional basis but was founded upon influence. He had the support of George I and, later, George II, and he could mold majorities in Parliament for the Crown when he needed them. His control over the House of Commons, especially, stemmed partly from patronage but mostly from his abilities as a politician and a persuader. A good mercantilist, Walpole concerned himself mainly with England's domestic financial and economic situation and its foreign policy on the continent. He dealt, as well, with the immense problems associated with securing the Hanoverian succession (George I was the first king from the German line of English succession known as the House of Hanover) and protecting it from real and rumored attacks by supporters of the Stuarts and others. Along the way he made many enemies. Some envied his power and influence. Some disliked his flamboyant, often gaudy style of living. Others simply opposed his person and his policies. Despite his enemies, though, he was the most effective politician of the eighteenth century. According to his biographer, J. H. Plumb, "an excellent administrative ability, an outstanding parliamentary skill, the unshakeable favour of the King, these factors gave Walpole an eminence in English life unparalleled since Burleigh [Elizabeth's chief minister]."[9] Historian Dorothy Marshall surveyed Walpole's career and wrote that "under his peaceful, practical rule the economic resources of the country had grown steadily and the Hanoverian dynasty, if not much loved, was firmly established."[10]

Though the two feuded often, Walpole and Newcastle created an approach to colonial affairs now known as *salutary neglect.* Essentially, this phrase meant leaving the colonists alone whenever possible. The reasoning behind their thinking was threefold. First, the colonies provided huge profits for English interests and greatly stimulated the English economy, and both men believed that a good relationship should not be tampered with. Second, the English were either at war with France and Spain through much of the period or they were involved in a fragile truce with them. In either case England needed friendly, happy colonists as allies. Third, although Walpole was master of the House of Commons for two decades and much of the trade legislation of the period originated with the Crown, Walpole could not control everything Parliament considered or enacted. Inside and outside of Parliament he contended with imperial and commercial factions which wanted tighter control exerted over the empire and war with England's main rivals, Spain and France. At times he could not control these factions. At other times he compromised with them in order to temper their bellicosity. Also, he placed continental considerations above colonial affairs. The result was that, although Parliament was very active in passing legislation pertaining to Anglo-America and the empire during the first half of the eighteenth century, the Crown was occasionally lax and always selective in its enforcement. This meant that commercial interests in Anglo-America enjoyed the benefits of British protection and the advantages of trade within the British imperial system, while they avoided many of the restrictions aimed at them. In other words, much of the time they simply did as they pleased.

HALIFAX

Not all royal officials were happy with salutary neglect. Many wanted parliamentary regulations strictly enforced and urged tighter control by the Crown over colonial affairs. Of these, no one was more important than George Montague Dunk (1716-1771), Earl of Halifax, who took control of the Board of Trade in 1748 and quickly began to undermine Newcastle's dominance of the colonial bureaucracy. Halifax's early career was marked by opportunism. His ambition was fired by his family's relatively meager circumstances. Thus, at about the same time he entered the House of Lords (1742) he married Anne Richards, the heiress to a huge fortune which had come to her family from the estate of Thomas Dunk, a merchant. Anne's dowry was £110,000. Her father's stipulation was that she marry a merchant. To qualify, Halifax joined a London-based trading company. Then, after his marriage he added the name of Dunk to his own.

From that point on Halifax was a major spokesman for England's mercantile interests and especially the more radical elements which were demanding expanded trade and colonization, tighter control over the empire by the government, and war with Spain and France if necessary. At the same time, Halifax pursued a career in the Army. It began in 1745 when he was made a Colonel in the forces raised to fight the small army of Highland Scots Charles Stuart ("Bonnie Prince Charles") led in a doomed attempt to wrest England from the Hanoverians. Halifax never saw action against Charles Stuart or anyone else but, by 1759, he held the rank of Lieutenant-General.

Becoming head of the Board of Trade gave Halifax the career opportunity he so eagerly sought. Not only could he promote and secure his own future but he could advance the beliefs and promote the interests of the merchants who supported him. Thus, he worked to enlarge the importance of his own position and that of the Board. Within a few years, all colonial officials were expected to communicate with the Board of Trade, not the Secretary of State for the South. Then, thanks to Halifax, the Board became an official government agency (not an advisory body as before). Thenceforth, its chairmanship carried cabinet status and it received the power to nominate men for colonial office. Halifax used his new cabinet position to lobby for an Anglican bishop in America. Also, he used his post to plant an English colony in Nova Scotia (Halifax, Nova Scotia, was named for him) and he tried to get the West Indian sugar colonies placed under the control of the Board.[11]

Some of Halifax's schemes worked, some did not. He streamlined the administration of colonial affairs and is generally credited with enhancing trade with North America as a result. He worked very hard to enlarge the powers of British officials in America—with mixed results. He tried to secure tax support for colonial officials, something royal governors had sought for years. He tried also to curtail the activities of rambunctious colonial assemblies. For example, in 1753 the new royal governor of New York, Sir Danvers Osborne, took these instructions from the Board of Trade with him to his post:

> Whereas it hath been represented to us that . . . our royal prerogative and authority [have been] trampled upon and invaded in a most unwarrantable and illegal manner; and whereas the assembly of our said province have not only refused to comply with the powers and directions which we thought it expedient to give by our commission and instructions to our governor of the said province with respect to money raised for the supply and support of government, but have also in open violation of our said commission and instructions assumed to themselves . . . the disposal of public money, the nomination of all officers of government, the direction of the militia . . . and many other executive parts of government . . . which by law belong to our governor only . . . having called the council and assembly of our said province together, you are to signify to them in the strongest and most solemn manner our highest displeasure for their neglect of and the contempt they have shown to our royal commission and instructions . . .[12]

The power of Halifax and the Board began to slide in 1754 with the advent of the French and Indian War. In 1756 Halifax resigned from his position in a spat with Newcastle. A year later, however, he was back as head of the Board, a post he held until he was named Lord-Lieutenant of Ireland in 1761.

After Halifax's departure, the Board of Trade slipped back into oblivion, but the momentum for change which Halifax and the Board had started no longer depended upon one person or agency. The proof of that was exemplified by the rise in the 1750s of William Pitt, First Earl of Chatham. Newcastle's opponent at first, Pitt joined him in early 1757 to form a new ministry to fight the French and Indian War. Pitt believed in England's destiny to dominate the world's trade, and he believed that war was a legitimate way to do it. Time and again, he informed Anglo-American colonists that he would accept nothing less than their complete adherence to all relevant imperial laws and regulations.

The new hard line of royal officials was very evident in the last years before 1763. Upon learning that the colonials had traded with the enemy throughout the French and Indian War, in 1760 Pitt ordered all colonial governors to crack down on the illicit traffic and to enforce the Molasses Act of 1733. Armed with "writs of assistance," the governors did as they were told, and colonial merchants everywhere were arrested for illegal smuggling. The writs were general warrants which allowed English officials to search private property without showing cause. In use since 1751, they had been ignored by colonials until they were utilized to quell the French trade. In 1760 a group of Boston merchants went to court to test the legality of the writs. James Otis, a fiery young lawyer, pleaded their case using an argument that would soon become very familiar to all colonists. The writs, he insisted, violated basic rights guaranteed in the British Constitution (he referred not to a

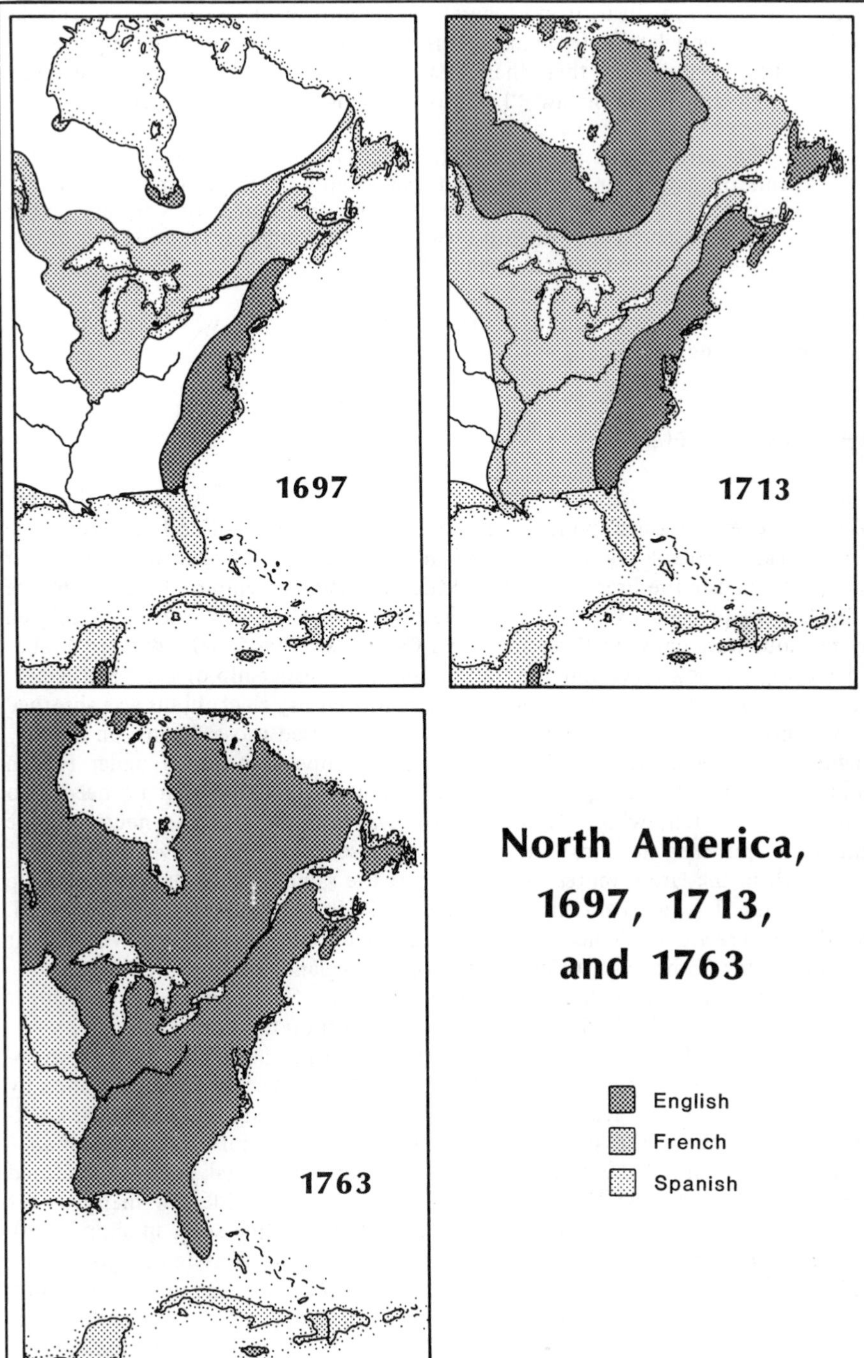
1697
1713
1763
North America, 1697, 1713, and 1763
English
French
Spanish
CLL

document, but to the history and general character of British governing institutions, both political and legal). If, indeed, Otis went on, the writs were supported by parliamentary legislation, then that legislation had to be declared null and void because it violated common law. "I will to my dying day," Otis announced,

> Oppose with all the powers and faculties God has given me all such instruments of slavery on the one hand and villainy on the other as this Writ of Assistance is . . . It appears to me the worst instrument of arbitrary power, the most destructive of English liberty and the fundamental principles of law, that ever was found in an English lawbook.[13]

The merchants lost their case and the writs stood, but the whole episode was a harbinger of things to come.

THE WARS FOR EMPIRE

Through the last years of the seventeenth century and the first half of the eighteenth, the expansionist policies of the English and French collided. Although France had sent explorers and colonists into the New World as early as, or earlier than, the English, the French had done little to develop an empire. Before 1660 the French were plagued by their own domestic problems: dynastic struggles colored by religious wars between Protestants and Catholics. After 1660, however, France rid itself of domestic turmoil and united under the leadership of the "Sun King," Louis XIV. In many ways the model seventeenth-century ruler, Louis was absorbed by dreams of personal and national glory, and he based those dreams on military might and overseas trade. Louis envisioned a European continent under French domination with French armies marching unmolested. To do that he needed to conquer the Dutch, whose military power was considerable, and neutralize the English. In pursuing his aims Louis undertook a series of military ventures against the Dutch in the late seventeenth century. At the same time he built a friendship with Charles II (who spent his years of exile in France) and then with James II. Both men were ardent Francophiles and Louis used their sympathies as well as their admiration for Catholicism to create turmoil in England. He hoped to occupy the English with continuing domestic quarrels over the Stuart kings and the threat of Catholicism while he fulfilled his plans of conquest on the Continent.

Louis also hoped to hide his intentions in America, where the French intended to build an empire similar to England's. Following a blueprint outlined by his minister of finance, Jean-Baptiste Colbert, in the 1660s, Louis envisoned a self-sufficient empire as the prerequisite for French domination of Europe. France would be the heart of the empire, supplying leadership, capital, and manufactured goods. The French islands in the West Indies would provide raw materials for French manufacturers (the islands would eventually provide sugar in abundance). French slave farms in Africa would supply slaves for the West Indian plantation, and finally, New France (Canada) would send furs to France, and lumber and foodstuffs to the West Indian islands. New France's role had changed considerably since the days of Cardinal Richelieu and the Company of New France whose charter, issued in 1627, had maintained that the Company's main purpose was to convert

Indians to Christianity and, especially, Catholicism. To accomplish that end the directors and associates of the Company had intended to send to America only the most pious individuals so that vice and wickedness would not develop in the colony. In that way it was hoped that New France would become "a New Jerusalem, blessed by God and made up of citizens destined for heaven."[14]

In the late seventeenth and early eighteenth centuries the French and British empires developed along parallel lines. Sugar from the West Indies became the most important money crop for the French, just as it was for the British. Both empires relied heavily on African slaves for labor, and both sought to support their island plantations with crops grown on the mainland. There, however, the similarities ended, for New France simply did not live up to French expectations. The French government sent colonists in abundance (many were soldiers) into New France in an attempt to build up agriculture to the point at which food could be exported. But that did not happen. Partly the climate and geography hindered such development, and partly the French colonists had little incentive because they had little freedom and lived in a semimilitary outpost controlled directly from France through several layers of bureaucracy. Partly, New France's potential was reduced by the aggressive and highly successful policies of England's Hudson Bay Company (chartered in 1670). The result was that French island possessions turned more and more to the Anglo-American colonies. Soon, much to the horror of the French, English colonial merchants dominated the French West Indian trade.

New France never paid for itself in the eyes of many members of the French government. By the 1750s, some French officials had just about decided to let the British have the region if they wanted it. New France did play several important roles in the empire, however. First, it was the source of a lucrative fur traffic, especially in beaver. Second, it served as a staging area for French priests and traders who worked the Ohio Valley, the Mississippi Valley, and the Great Lakes region. These priests and traders built friendships and alliances with various Indian tribes, traded with them, established "forts," and effectively slowed the westward expansion of Anglo-American colonists. Nevertheless, these successes could not disguise the overall economic weakness of New France in the eyes of French planners.

French attempts to avoid conflict with England on the European continent worked well until the Glorious Revolution of 1688, when James II was overthrown. The Crown then passed to Mary, James' daughter, and the Dutch leader, William of Orange. Their accession to the throne immediately drew England into war with the French (the War of the League of Augsburg or King William's War, 1689 to 1697). After numerous campaigns on sea and land–including deprivations inflicted by the French and their Indian allies against frontier settlements in Anglo-America–the war ended indecisively in 1697.

Anglo-French Conflict

France and England now settled in for sixty years of more or less continuous warfare. The struggles amounted to three additional wars fought between 1702 and 1763. The first two involved English, Dutch, and German attempts to thwart French aims and maintain a balance of power on the European continent. The Anglo-American colonies were involved only to the extent that France and England tried to harrass one another in America, hoping to force men and material needed in Europe to be sent overseas. Not surprisingly then, most of the fighting on the North American continent was done by French and English colonists, aided by Indian allies. The tribes, especially the Iroquois, played their own territorial games. They hoped to keep the French and English fighting so that neither would further encroach on tribal territories. However, the last war–the French and Indian or Seven Years' War (1756 to 1763)–began in the colonies and was fought primarily for control of North America.

The French and English were fairly evenly matched. The French generally had superior ground forces while the English had a better navy. If the English possessed an advantage, it lay in the character of its Anglo-American colonies. English mainland colonists were stubborn, proud, and willing to fight to protect and extend their homelands. More or less used to operating on their own, they could conduct war without much reliance upon English direction, though they needed English supplies badly. That strength, however, also proved to be a weakness, for the Anglo-American colonists fought only when they wanted to and made rather unreliable allies. Then too, of course, the colonials made considerable profits from trade with French colonies and were not eager to see those profits disappear. The French, on the other hand, knew the vulnerability of their colonies to English naval blockade. Moreover, their colonists were fewer in number and, save for the sugar planters, somewhat less interested in risking life or property for the glory of France. The great French asset in the New World proved to be the numerical strength of Indian allies. The alliances, however, resulted from no great love by the Indians for the French, but rather from a greater fear of English expansion than French expansion.

The second Anglo-French war lasted from about 1702 to 1713 and was as indecisive as the first. It ended in the Peace of Utrecht in 1713. Called the War for the Spanish Succession (Queen Anne's War in the colonies), it began when the King of Spain died leaving no direct heir. Louis XIV tried to claim the throne for a Bourbon relative, a tactic which, if successful, would have placed Spain and its empire under Louis' control. The conclusion of the war inaugurated a nearly thirty-year period of uneasy truce. That was broken in 1739 when a group of English merchants, eager to move against Spanish interests in the Caribbean, promoted a short-lived war with Spain called, rather facetiously, the War of Jenkins Ear.

This war was an outgrowth of tension between England and Spain stretching back to the era of the South Sea Bubble. Competition between South Sea Company ships and other British and New England ships for the limited access to Spanish America granted England through the Peace of Utrecht resulted in smuggling by all the parties. This, in turn, led Spain to initiate repressive measures against English smugglers. Unfortunately, the Spanish made little effort to distinguish a smuggler from an English or Anglo-American ship involved in legitimate trade either with English possessions in the West Indies or with Spanish colonies. The issue was a sore point between the imperial powers for over two decades.

Finally, in 1739, a scheme was hatched which was designed to lead to war with Spain. A ship captain named Jenkins appeared before a parliamentary committee and told a story of Spanish cruelty and insolence. Jenkins reported that he had just returned from the Caribbean where his ship had been stopped by a Spanish cruiser and his ear had been cut off by the Spanish captain. Jenkins alleged that he was told to return to England with the message that his fate would be the fate of all Englishmen who traded illegally with Spanish possessions. He then held up a box supposedly containing his ear (apparently he had lost an ear in the manner described but in 1731, not 1739). Admiral Edward Vernon, a member of Parliament and a party to the plan, announced to his colleagues that he would take a force and clean the Spanish out of the Caribbean. Robert Walpole opposed the idea but the plan carried. Vernon captured the weakly defended port called Porto Bello on the Isthmus of Panama, but when he took a greater force and attacked Cartagena, the largest Spanish port in the Caribbean, his expedition was nearly destroyed by disease and Spanish arms.

War between Spain and England evolved into a new war between France, Spain, and England over the question of dynastic succession in Austria (The War for the Austrian Succession or King George's War, 1744 to 1748). Again, the French attempted to place a Bourbon in a vacant throne, and again, the enemies of France combined to stop it. Also, as before, the war ended with little accomplished by either side. In America, a large colonial force did attack and capture Fort Louisbourg, a bastion which controlled the mouth of the St. Lawrence River and, hence, the entrance to Quebec City and all trade to and from New France. The treaty of peace which ended the war, however, returned the fort to the French.

The French and Indian War

The War for the Austrian Succession—or King George's War as it was known among irreverent Anglo-American colonists—ended in 1748. Six years later began the last, and in many ways the most furious, of all the struggles, the French and Indian War. England's commercial interests generally favored war and their friends in government, including political rivals like the Duke of Newcastle and William Pitt, pushed for new campaigns against the French. In 1754, hostilities began when colonial land speculators tried to push the French out of the Ohio Valley to open that area to English settlement. The French promptly built a number of forts in the region, including a great fort at the junction of the Ohio and Monongahela Rivers, Fort Duquesne (present day Pittsburgh). George Washington led a force of Virginia militia against the French, but he was driven back.

After that the fighting gradually expanded. The British and colonials decided that a single decisive campaign would clear the French from not only the Ohio Valley but America as well. They devised a plan whereby one army under General Edward Braddock would move against Fort Duquesne; a second under Colonel William Johnson would take the French fort at Crown Point on Lake Champlain; a third under Governor William Shirley of Massachusetts would take Fort Niagara; and an English fleet would capture Louisburg and destroy the French fleet on the St. Lawrence River guarding Quebec City.

Nothing worked. Braddock's army was routed; Shirley turned back, and Johnson was driven back. Braddock's defeat was a particularly bitter pill since his army outnumbered the enemy by a margin of at least five to one. George Washington, a Colonel of Virginia militia assigned to Braddock's staff, wrote to his mother to describe the defeat and the subsequent death of Braddock. In the letter he expressed feelings about British soldiers and American militia that were shared throughout the colonies. The British, he wrote, "were struck with such a panick, that they behav'd with more cowardice than it is possible to conceive . . . . The

Virginia Troops shew'd a good deal of Bravery, and were near all kill'd; for I believe out of 3 Companys that were there, there is scarce 30 men left alive."[15] For the moment Anglo-American military power was broken and the French took the initiative. They turned their Indian allies loose, and from Maine to the Carolinas, the back country resounded to gunfire amidst the glare of burning farms and towns. Louis-Joseph de Montcalm-Grozon, Marquis de Montcalm, commander of French regulars in Quebec and one of France's better soldiers, ranged far south winning a string of victories over the British between 1756 and 1758. In August, 1757, he captured a 2500-man English garrison at Fort William Henry in northern New York. Having lost only thirteen men he was in an excellent position to move into the heart of British North America. But he turned back instead, arguing that he was moving too far from his sources of supply. Most historians feel that, at that moment, the French lost their chance to win the war, for there was little to have kept Montcalm from moving on Boston, New York, or Philadelphia.

England declared war on France in 1756. In desperation George II turned to his political enemy, William Pitt, to become "prime" minister and direct the war effort. Pitt, a member of Parliament since 1735, was 48 years old and at the height of his power and popularity. Known as the "Great Commoner" he pledged that he would commit all available resources to defeat the French. England's Prussian allies moved against the French on the European continent. Elsewhere, English naval detachments and troops were sent to attack French outposts everywhere: in India, the Caribbean, and North America. To Anglo-America went thousands of the best British soldiers and some of England's ablest generals. The French countered with similar measures, including preparations to invade England.

Once committed to an all-out war, the British began to score victories. The British fleet tried to blockade New France by sea while warships patrolled the Caribbean attacking French vessels and possessions. With 14,000 men, Lord Jeffrey Amherst captured Fort Louisbourg (Nova Scotia) in 1758 and the St. Lawrence River, the water route to Quebec City, was threatened by the British. In 1758 and 1759 Amherst commanded a large colonial force which cleared the French from the Ohio Valley. At the same time Anglo-colonial armies moved north. They suffered a disaster in 1758 when Montcalm, with less than 4000 men, routed a 15,000-man Anglo-colonial army at Ticonderoga, near Lake Champlain. The following year, 1759, the British undertook the siege of Quebec City by water and land. The last French supply ships reached Quebec in May, 1759. After that the province was sealed off by the British. Command of the 8500-man invading British army went to James Wolfe, only 22 years old and something of the boy wonder of the British officer corps. Vain and arrogant, but a courageous soldier and field commander, Wolfe had risen quickly through service in Europe and Scotland. He led Amherst's forces successfully at Fort Louisbourg but ill health forced him to go back to England shortly after the victory. He returned to America in 1759 to execute the capture of Quebec.

Wolfe's army was ferried to Quebec City by a British naval detachment under Admiral Charles Saunders. At the same time a second Anglo-colonial army moved against the French stronghold at Crown Point, New York. Montcalm defeated the Crown Point expedition, then returned quickly to Quebec City to await the British advance. For all practical purposes the French and Indian War ended when Wolfe defeated Montcalm. The defeat was unnecessary, however, and became a classic example of how a single error in judgment could change the course of history. Wolfe's forces outnumbered Montcalm's by two to one but the French fortress of Quebec, lying on hills high above the St. Lawrence River, was well defended. Wolfe lay siege to Quebec throughout the summer of 1759. He hoped to draw Montcalm out of his defensive position into a battle on open ground. Montcalm would not move. Finally, Wolfe told the French that unless they surrendered he would destroy the city and burn the farms in the surrounding countryside. Still Montcalm refused to budge. Wolfe did as he promised. American rangers, whom Wolfe called "the worst soldiers in the universe," were ordered to destroy crops and any buildings they encountered in parishes up and down the river. They did. Fourteen hundred farms were burned and leveled. Included in the destruction were some of the oldest stone buildings in the province. At about the same time Wolfe's cannon began a bombardment of Quebec City that destroyed or badly damaged nearly 80 percent of its buildings. Montcalm held out.

Finally, sick and growing desperate, Wolfe decided to try to scale a nearly vertical rock wall above the St. Lawrence and place part of his army behind Montcalm's defenses on the Plains of Abraham. His plan succeeded. At daybreak on September 13, 1759, Wolfe had 4400 troops within hailing distance of the city. Montcalm discovered the ploy and rushed troops to meet Wolfe. By midmorning he had 4500 troops facing the British. Then he made a tragic mistake. Instead of waiting for more reinforcements (a French army of 3000 was less than ten miles away) or moving back into the city to await Wolfe's advance, he ordered an attack upon the British troops. In the ensuing battle, which lasted less than a half hour, the French were routed. Both commanders, Wolfe and Montcalm, received fatal wounds. In the hours that followed the battle, however, fresh French troops arrived. Thus, despite their defeat, the French continued to hold Quebec City and actually outnumbered the British troops commanding the Plains of Abraham. Incredibly, the victorious British could neither retreat nor attack. But there would be no more fighting that day. In a final act of folly, Montcalm signed a document surrendering Quebec City and most of the French empire in North America to the British. He died minutes later.[16]

The Peace of Paris ended the war in 1763. Tired of war and saddled with heavy war debts, England proved rather lenient. Caribbean possessions (sugar islands) taken from the French during the war were returned. New France became a part of Anglo-America except for the region west of the Mississippi, which was given to Spain as "compensation" for its losses. Considering that the wealth of the French empire was in the sugar islands and the French had just about given up on New France anyway, the treaty certainly did not end France's position as a colonial power. It did remove the French from the mainland, but, in light of the problems New France would cause the British, that proved a mixed blessing.

For American colonials, the end of the war produced warm, patriotic feelings toward Britain. Still, there were ominous signs. The British, disgusted by the behavior of the colonials during the war—especially the illicit trade with the French—were in no mood to be charitable toward the Anglo-Americans. The British economy groaned from war-produced inflation while the government faced bankruptcy from seventy years of nearly constant hostilities. Powerful men argued that since the last war had been for the benefit of the colonists, they ought to pay its bills. Also, the war had given the British a land mass twice as large as before to govern. Quickly, the Proclamation of 1763 closed the area west of the Appalachian region to settlement. Colonial land speculators, for whom the war had begun, felt cheated and embittered. But the British, fearful of the consequences of pell-mell settlement, wanted time to consider how to proceed.

Above all, the French and Indian War demonstrated the political and economic weakness of the British empire. Colonials had refused to cooperate with English generals and administrators. Colonial merchants traded with whomever they pleased, and wherever they pleased. A loud hue and cry developed in England for a rapid reordering of the empire with new taxes and tighter political and economic control. Some of the English even wondered aloud if the colonials were not maneuvering to secure their independence. Benjamin Franklin scoffed at the idea. "There are so many causes that must operate to prevent it [Union]," he wrote,

> that I will venture to say a union among them [the colonies] for such a purpose is not merely improbable, it is impossible. And if the union of the whole is impossible, the attempt of a part must be madness, as those colonies that did not join the rebellion would join the mother country in suppressing it. When I say such a union is impossible, I mean, without the most grievous tyranny and oppression. People who have property in a country which they may lose, and privileges which they may endanger, are generally disposed to be quiet, and even to bear much, rather than hazard all. While the government is mild and just, while important civil and religious rights are secure, such subjects will be dutiful and obedient. The waves do not rise but when the winds blow . . . .[17]

8

Economic Growth and Social Change

By the end of the seventeenth century, the Anglo-American economy already reflected certain regional differences. In the eighteenth century, these differences would grow even more pronounced. The New England area exported wood and wood products, fish, and some grain, but it grew prosperous primarily from shipping. Commerce far more than agriculture characterized that region. In contrast, the middle colonies became the breadbasket for Anglo-America and provided most of its neighbors with foodstuffs, primarily wheat, rye, beans, and pork. As they had from the first decades of settlement, the southern colonies and West Indies continued to concentrate their resources on the production of a few cash crops, notably tobacco, rice, indigo, and sugar. Although the colonies succeeded in producing sufficient surpluses to export some goods to England, during the seventeenth century the Anglo-American economy nevertheless attained a level only slightly above subsistence.

Several factors had inhibited economic development in Anglo-America during the seventeenth century, but the major causes could be traced to slow population growth, lack of capital and markets, and significant shortages of labor in some regions. The colonial population grew mainly from natural increase rather than immigration. Even though the harsh conditions of the frontier and especially a damp, buggy climate produced high infant mortality rates and low life expectancy in the Chesapeake region in its formative years, these were more than offset by the low infant-mortality rates and the long life expectancy to be found north of the Chesapeake. For the colonies as a whole during the seventeenth century the percentages of children surviving infancy and adults reaching old age surpassed those of both England and Europe.

Immigration reflected conditions in England. The end of domestic strife and an improvement in the economic condition of England in the last few decades of the seventeenth century slowed the flow of immigrants to the colonies compared to what had transpired earlier (there was very little English immigration between 1689 and 1763). Opportunity still beckoned the restless and poor to Anglo-America, but the wild tales of a Garden of Eden which had lured the first generations to the colonies had been replaced by more realistic accounts of life in America: stories emphasizing the dangers of Indian attacks, the risks of disease, and the generally harsh frontier life. As a result, Anglo-America experienced a steady, but rather slow population growth during the seventeenth century.

Second, from the beginning the colonies lacked the capital resources and the markets needed to expand. In part, Anglo-America did not possess a sufficient supply of hard currency to make the exchange of goods and services easy or rapid. Barter or local credit was the rule, and hard cash the exception. The small supply of currency slowed the rate at which goods were bought and sold and accordingly restricted the speed at which the Anglo-American economy expanded. But even if capital had been plentiful, markets were not. The early colonists had to create markets for their products and then had to build roads and develop river systems to move them from villages or plantations to seaports. Finally, once on the coast, the colonists had to construct ships to carry their products where they were wanted.

Third, as noted earlier, the colonies' greatest asset, an abundance of land, indirectly created one of Anglo-America's most serious problems, a shortage of labor. As soon as possible, the indentured servants left their masters' service and began working their own small farms. The availability of land thus diffused the labor resources of Anglo-America and forced colonists into agricultural practices which limited production. In addition, the economic boom the English economy experienced in the late seventeenth century virtually dried up the supply of indentured servants migrating into the colonies. A few Anglo-Americans, primarily southerners, imported slaves in an attempt to command an adequate labor force, but during the seventeenth century slaves provided only a small fraction of labor in Anglo-America.

To be sure, the problems just outlined posed serious obstacles to the economic development of Anglo-America. Nevertheless, during the eighteenth century the colonies experienced significant economic growth. Their success in doing so resulted from rapid population growth, expanded agricultural and timber production, increased immigration of both Europeans and black slaves, the use of credit as a substitute for currency, and the creation of markets for their products and the ships to get them there.

COMMERCE

By the middle of the eighteenth century, the North American mainland colonies and the West Indian islands were the economic heart of the vast and ever-growing British empire. England was in the early stages of an industrial revolution triggered to a great degree by wealth derived from its American colonies. England's overseas trade had increased dramatically since the midseventeenth century, especially exports. From a net worth of about £4,000,000 in 1669, exports had grown to £15,671,000 in 1774. A considerable amount of that trade came in the form of colonial goods reexported to other markets. For example, by the time of the American Revolution, more than four-fifths of the tobacco entering English ports from the southern colonies was reshipped to Europe and elsewhere. Also, exports of English manufactured goods increased rapidly in the eighteenth century with much of that production going to the American colonies. Between 1700 and 1774, the value of English manufactures exported yearly rose from £3,583,000 to £8,487,000. In 1774, nearly half (£3,981,000) of those products went to Anglo-America.[1]

From commerce England and Anglo-America prospered together. Peter Kalm, a Swedish naturalist who visited Anglo-America between 1748 and 1751, caught the importance of the relationship. "England and especially London, " he wrote,

> profits immensely by its trade with the American colonies; for not only New York but likewise all the other English towns on the continent, import so many articles from England that all their specie, together with the goods which they get in other countries, must altogether go to Old England, in order to pay the amount to which they are however insufficient. From hence it appears how much a well-regulated colony contributes to the increase and welfare of its mother country . . . .[2]

Clearly, however, the colonies also benefited from the commercial relationship with England. Beginning as a string of isolated agricultural and trading settlements in the midseventeenth century, by the American Revolution the Anglo-American colonies were burgeoning, prosperous societies that enjoyed a standard of living equal to or above those of England and Europe. The abundance of good land and other resources allowed the early colonists to produce what they needed for self-sufficiency and a little beyond; and in that premodern time, being self-sufficient put the colonists ahead of most people.

After a modest rise in the per-capita income of colonists in the seventeenth century, the standard of living increased steadily in the eighteenth century. The annual rate of per-capita income growth in Anglo-America averaged around .4 percent to .5 percent between 1700 and 1775. That was roughly equal to or slightly greater than England's own growth for the same period, but considerably less than the 1.6 percent per year figure that the United States achieved in the nineteenth century. Thus, Anglo-America experienced sizable but not particularly startling economic growth for the colonial period.

What was startling, however, was that Anglo-America sustained a population growth rate of 3 percent per year (to about 2.5 million colonists by 1776) while raising the colonists' standard of living at the same time. In some respects, the colonial population grew too fast in the eighteenth century. For example, by 1776 large areas of the coastal regions of Anglo-America were overcrowded. As early as 1748 Peter Kalm noted crowded conditions in the colonies. "The country, especially all along the coasts, in the English colonies," he wrote, "is inhabited by Europeans, who in some places are already so numerous that few parts of Europe are more populous."[3] This statement becomes particularly significant when it is remembered that, as late as 1750, colonials in many regions of Anglo-America had not ventured much farther inland than 100 miles.[4]

How then does one explain the overall prosperity and the steady economic growth of Anglo-America in the eighteenth century, given the likelihood that the population increased a little too quickly and produced overcrowded conditions in some areas? An important part of the answer may be found in the constant process of putting new land into cultivation. Another important part was the rising demand for colonial raw materials in England, especially after 1745. But colonial supply would not have met England's demand had it not been for the growth of colonial commerce. By the end of the seventeenth century, colonial ships made regular runs to Europe and England. By 1770, colonial ships and colonial merchants—operating from Boston, Philadelphia, New York, and a host of smaller ports—had more than their share of the trade of the British empire, much to the chagrin of some English merchant competitors. New Englanders owned the West Indian trade. In fact, they even succeeded in controlling the trade of the French and Spanish West Indian islands as well. Moreover, colonial ships roamed all over the Atlantic and the Mediterranean. They moved into the slave traffic in Africa, often carrying blacks to the West Indies or directly to the Anglo-American mainland.

The volume of colonial shipping and commerce grew for a variety of reasons. First, Anglo-Americans benefited from a protective blanket of imperial regulations. Statutes passed by Parliament and enforced by the British Navy kept most foreign competitors from colonial ports. Second, American producers received the highest possible prices from English firms and, in addition, enjoyed the privilege of trading in foreign ports when price advantages dictated it. Some of that trade constituted smuggling in the eyes of British officials, but few attempts were made to stop it before 1763.

Two important factors in the growth of colonial commerce—the phenomenal productivity of colonial shipbuilders and the development of American "money" crops like tobacco, rice, and sugar—were discussed in an earlier chapter. However, neither of those factors would have been terribly significant had not Anglo-Americans made colonial products competitive by lowering shipping costs. They succeeded in doing that in part by shortening the length of voyages, and in part because decreased losses from piracy significantly reduced insurance rates. But more importantly, colonial and British shippers cut costs by specializing in certain products. Anglo-American and British merchant ship owners transported tobacco, or rice, or slaves, or forest products and carried nothing else. Consequently, in the century before the American Revolution freight rates on the trans-Atlantic run between England and Anglo-America were cut by almost 50 percent.

For many years historians assumed that colonials concentrated on a series of "triangular" trading routes in the eighteenth century. Consider the African route, for example. It was believed that ships cleared Boston with cargoes bound for the African coasts. They traded these cargoes for slaves and then transported blacks to the West Indies. There slaves were exchanged for a cheap sugar product, molasses. Finally, ships brought the molasses to New England where it was distilled into rum. That was a triangular route. However, recent research has shown clearly that triangular routes were rare simply because they would have been too expensive. Analysis of port records indicates that two-way direct shipping was much more common. Considering data for the years 1768 to 1772, economic historians Gary Walton and James Shepherd have found that most colonial exports went directly to Great Britain (55 percent). The West Indies were second with 27 percent, while southern Europe was third with 14 percent.

English Settlements, 1760
MAINE
(part of Mass.)
NEW
HAMPSHIRE
Falmouth
Ft.
Stanwix
Boston
MASS.
Albany
NEW YORK
Hartford
Providence
CONN.
R.I.
PENNSYLVANIA
New York
Philadelphia
NEW JERSEY
Ft. Bedford
Ft. Cumberland
DELAWARE
MARYLAND
Richmond
VIRGINIA
Williamsburg
Salem
Hillsboro
NORTH CAROLINA
Camden
Wilmington
SOUTH CAROLINA
Ft. Augusta
Charleston
GEORGIA
Savannah
n
CLL

Most of New England's commodities went to the West Indies. For the middle colonies, easily the largest exporter of foodstuffs, 44 percent went to the West Indies, 33 percent to southern Europe, and 23 percent to Great Britain. About 75 percent of the products from the southern colonies (mainly tobacco and sugar) was exported to Great Britain. In this export trade, English ships dominated commerce with the southern colonies, while colonial ships carried the overwhelming majority of all other goods. Tobacco and rice accounted for almost two-thirds of colonial exports. Bread and flour from the middle colonies came in second, while New England products, principally fish, represented a distant third.

The colonial import trade, which came principally from Great Britain, averaged £3,083,000 per year for the 1768-1772 period. By region, 66 percent of New England's imports came from England, while 32 percent came from the West Indies. Seventy-six percent of all imports to the middle colonies came from England, with 21 percent from the West Indies. For the South, over 85 percent came from England and less than 14 percent from the West Indies. Even though these figures represent the most complete statistics available for any single period of the colonial era, they must be used cautiously, especially in relation to earlier years. Nevertheless, they do suggest the clear dominance of direct colonial trade with Great Britain and the West Indies.

For the 1768-1772 period Shepherd and Walton found that the value of coastal trade was about one-fourth that of the overseas trade—a considerable amount, but lower than historians had believed. The coastal trade was most important to New England and the middle colonies, whose own merchants and shippers dominated that trade. For New England, exports averaged about £304,000 per year while imports averaged about £289,000. The figures for the middle colonies were £220,000 in exports and £178,000 in imports. Due primarily to the self-sufficiency of its tobacco planters, the Chesapeake coastal trade amounted to very little: £88,000 in exports and £73,000 in imports.[5]

During the eighteenth century tobacco, along with sugar and rice, constituted the great money crops of the British Empire. Although just about everyone in Virginia planted tobacco, by the mideighteenth century about half of the tobacco was produced by 100 or so great planters owning thousands of acres. They lived mainly in the Tidewater and eastern Piedmont regions of Virginia. To the west smaller farms populated by English, Scotch-Irish, and other nationalities dominated the landscape. Nevertheless, throughout the South tobacco was the single most important crop.

In the early eighteenth century the European demand for tobacco increased substantially. In response colonial planters eagerly turned additional land into cultivation. That created a large supply of tobacco which flooded the market and in turn caused tobacco prices to plunge sharply in the 1720s. Thereafter, prices increased only slightly until about 1750, when they then rose slowly. Despite low prices planters continued to overproduce. The competition among them was so fierce that cooperation, which might have led to price fixing, proved impossible. Instead, planters continued to place more and more land into production to offset low prices. As they purchased additional land and slaves to grow tobacco, and as they spent more and more on English manufactured goods to maintain their standards of living, they became increasingly indebted to English and Scottish merchants. After 1745, factors—representatives of Scottish merchant houses—appeared in the southern colonies to handle the growing paper work of an economy more and more a product of credit. By the eve of the Revolutionary War, English merchants and Scottish factors were buying tobacco crops that would not be grown for several years (called futures) in order to keep capital flowing into the Chesapeake region. Although the economy in the southern colonies expanded steadily during the eighteenth century, it became highly dependent upon English capital and commercial talent.

The northern economy grew even more rapidly than the southern. Expansion resulted in part from British capital and in part from the growing commercial and shipping activities of merchants in Boston, Newport, New York, and Philadelphia. In addition, the lush farming regions of the middle colonies developed a variety of agricultural products for export. The most important of these were wheat and livestock. Although some northern colonies, particularly those in New England, experienced a serious agricultural slump during the early part of the eighteenth century, by 1750 agriculture in colonies like New York and Pennsylvania showed significant profits. Even larger profits were being reaped by merchants. They often reinvested profits in manufacturing endeavors such as shipbuilding, textile factories, iron foundries, and shoe-making plants.

The agricultural boom in the middle colonies owed something to the English, but even more to the Scotch-Irish, Welsh, Lowland Scots, Swedes, Swiss, Dutch, and immigrants from southwestern Germany. In southeastern Pennsylvania, one of the most productive agricultural regions of the eighteenth century, English, Scotch-Irish, and Germans predominated. By 1790 the area supported 92,000 English; 57,500 Scotch-Irish, Scots, and South Irish; and 128,000 German-speaking peoples. These non-English immigrants moved beyond subsistence-level farming quickly. Indeed, by 1750, farmers in southeastern Pennsylvania consumed only about 60 percent of what they produced. These figures suggest why the middle colonies exported sizable amounts of wheat and livestock by the end of the eighteenth century.

Although English and Dutch estates in New York reached considerable size, by and large farms in the middle colonies averaged about 125 acres. As a result, no farmer "aristocracy" emerged; rather the aristocrats of the North were the merchants. By 1770 northern merchants controlled 95 percent of the West Indian trade as well as all of the mainland coastal traffic. In addition, they maintained smaller commercial connections just about everywhere colonial products were bought and sold. Wealthy and powerful, they lived in a world as remote from the countryside of western Massachusetts or northern New York as that of their kinsmen in London or Portsmouth. Although less enamored with the English aristocracy than their southern brethren, northern merchants adopted some of the habits of the English nobility. The wealth and activities of the northern mercantile class fostered the growth of colonial urban centers that dominated society and politics on the eve of the Revolution. Yet, the North was anything but an urban society. Only about seven percent of the population lived in towns larger than 2500 by 1775.[6]

While comprising only a small fraction of the population, wealthy merchants became the symbols of success in much of Anglo-America during the eighteenth century. Benjamin Franklin's famous *Advice to a Young Tradesman* (1748) showed the way to wealth in a series of homilies reflecting his own and probably many other colonial experiences as well. The self-made man worked hard, wrote Franklin, but wealth and success lay not just in labor but in the judicious use of credit. "Remember," he observed,

> that CREDIT is Money. If a Man lets his Money lie in my Hands after it is due, he gives me the Interest, or so much as I can make of it during that Time. . . . Remember that Money is of the prolific, generating Nature. Money can beget Money, and its Offspring can beget more and so on. The more there is of it, the more it produces every Turning, so that Profits rise quicker and quicker.[7]

Based on the economic situation in the colonies during the eighteenth century, Franklin's advice hit the mark. Riches had to come through credit since there was very little hard currency. For the most part, imperial restrictions prevented colonies from coining or printing their own money. What currency Anglo-Americans obtained (mostly Spanish coin from West Indian sales) passed to England to pay for manufactured goods. The British wanted it that way, for the scarcity of coin and the increased use of credit for capital ensured colonial dependence and helped ease Britain's own currency problems. Apparently, a few colonials wanted it that way too. Some merchants in both New England and the middle colonies demanded and received bullion as payment for goods sold to West Indian planters. Those merchants, in turn, hoarded the bullion, thus contributing to the shortage of hard money in the colonies. The merchants treated the bullion as a commodity, shipping it to England only when necessary and selling it at the highest price to pay their debts.

The imperial restrictions on currency have led some historians to assume that Anglo-Americans were a debtor people whose revolution was as much an assertion of economic as political independence. They interpreted the often-rancorous debate over currency in the eighteenth century as an important component in the emerging desire for independence. Periodically, colonies printed paper money in defiance of British restrictions (or occasionally when restrictions were relaxed) to help finance land speculation or pay soldiers engaged in the continuing Anglo-French conflict. British merchants, who feared depreciation of the currency and enormous losses as a result, complained bitterly. For example, when Virginia printed paper money during the French and Indian War to pay its soldiers, British merchants protested to Parliament, which had sanctioned the printing. In 1759 the Virginia House of Burgesses responded to those complaints with a ponderous tome which seemed to reveal a rebellious spirit. In a challenge to the power of British mercantile interests, the Burgesses wrote Parliament stating their case for paper money:

> We are informed that the Merchants of Great Britain are much alarmed at our Assembly's passing some Acts for emitting large Quantities of Paper Money . . . and they are very apprehensive that they may be great Sufferers thereby in collecting their Debts due here. . . No Loss can arise to the Merchts from making this paper Money a legal Tender for Sterling Debts as the Law now stands, and they are in a much better Condition & less liable to Losses in collecting their Debts than if nothing but sterling or lawful Money of Great Britain were held a Tender for such debts. . . .[8]

Actually, research now suggests that Anglo-Americans were much less in debt than was once assumed. It appears that the scarcity of currency had little relationship to sentiments for independence and that the colonials managed fairly well without large supplies of hard coin. The steady growth of the British economy in the first half of the eighteenth century stimulated colonial production and increased the profits on colonial goods. Also, the prices Anglo-Americans received for their exports rose faster than the prices paid for English manufactures. For example, 100 bushels of colonial wheat purchased 150 yards of woolen cloth from England in 1740. By 1763 the same amount of wheat bought 250 yards of cloth.

Because the southern colonies were the greatest direct exporters of products to England, one might expect them to have benefited most from increased colonial purchasing power. Actually, they did not, primarily because about 80 percent of the rice and tobacco was promptly reexported to Europe. Since much of the agricultural export trade of the northern colonies went to the West Indies, demand for northern foodstuffs was closely tied to the demand for West Indian sugar. In the early eighteenth century sugar and rum prices slumped due to a lagging English market. As a result, northern farmers faced a somewhat uncertain and erratic market for their crops. After 1745, however, English demand for West Indian sugar increased substantially, and the market for northern agricultural goods in the West Indies rose accordingly, increasing colonial purchasing power.

Other factors also influenced colonial economic prosperity. Sizable increases in colonial exports to Scotland and southern Europe, for example, produced considerable trade surpluses for the colonies during the mideighteenth century. In addition, colonial merchants reaped significant profits from shipping charges. One estimate puts revenues to colonial merchants and ship owners (most of whom were in the North) at £600,000 annually. That figure offset about three-fifths of the colonial trade deficit with England. Other profits, such as those from the sale of bullion and ships in England, reduced the deficit even further. Thus, the economic picture of colonial relations with England was one colored by a fundamental dependency upon the parent country, but one characterized as well by economic expansion, diversity, capital investment, and general economic prosperity.

Slavery

As noted earlier, one of the ill effects of increased production of cash crops such as tobacco was the phenomenal growth of black slavery in the colonies. Between 1700 and 1775 black immigration into the mainland colonies matched white immigration (about 300,000 of each), and by 1776 there were around 600,000 blacks in Anglo-America. Of course, they were more heavily concentrated in some areas than others. Rising to about 20 percent of the total population by 1775, blacks accounted for 70 percent in South Carolina, 47 percent in Virginia, 33 percent in Maryland, 15 percent in North Carolina, and only 5 percent in all northern colonies. But the five percent figure was somewhat deceiving, for blacks living in the North were clustered in such a manner that they were very visible in some colonies, while virtually nonexistent in others. For example, in New York and Rhode Island they comprised 15 percent of the population, in New Jersey about 8 percent, and in Connecticut and Massachusetts only 4 percent. In addition, black population density differed by locale. Some areas had no blacks whereas other areas, especially certain cities such as Providence, Rhode Island, contained sizable populations of blacks. Like their southern counterparts, most northern slaves were employed as agricultural workers and not simply household servants.[9]

Just as the pattern of life in the colonies was diverse and changed over time, so, too, the character of slavery varied. In the West Indies, society rather quickly developed a racial character. During the seventeenth century, Barbados proved to be one of England's fastest-growing possessions. Begun as a colony of small farmers, Barbados turned to sugar as its money crop. Following the advice and the example of the Dutch between 1640 and 1660 Barbadians created an economic "revolution" which saw the emergence of the first English colonial "aristocracy" of large wealthy sugar planters. They owed their success in part to borrowed knowledge regarding the growing and processing of sugar cane and in part to the massive infusion of cheap West African slave labor. This system was quickly exported to the Leeward Islands and to Jamaica.

As sugar production increased and planter elites grew smaller and wealthier, the black population surpassed that of the white (in Barbados, for example, there were only 20,000 whites in 1680). The slave system which emerged was especially cruel. Slave mortality was high, both during the Atlantic passage and afterwards, as a result of overwork, poor nourishment, and disease. High mortality forced planters to continually import new slaves. This situation led to slave revolts and an exaggerated fear of slave uprisings among whites. For blacks, the experience was disastrous. As property, slaves were dehumanized by the system, while all of their familiar African institutions–family, religion, marriage–were either destroyed or rendered impotent.

During the eighteenth century the English societies on Barbados and Jamaica changed somewhat. Due to soil exhaustion, sugar production on Barbados declined. Consequently, many whites turned to raising livestock. The concentration of wealth and land leveled off with about a third of the white population owning about half of the land. The white population increased vis à vis blacks and the living conditions of blacks improved accordingly. Fewer Africans were imported, while creoles (blacks born in the West Indies) learned to adapt to their system of bondage. Mortality rates diminished and the slave family stabilized. Life was never easy, but it improved markedly over the preceding century.

On Jamaica, sugar production reached its peak between 1740 and 1775, and the island became England's most important source of sugar. Production outstripped Barbados by a ten to one margin, and the value of the economy neared £15 million by the time of the American Revolution. Though Jamaican society was divided along racial lines, it never developed the sugar monoculture found on the other islands. Nearly half the slave population was involved in activities other than sugar production and many slaves were able to grow some crops and raise a few cattle for their own consumption and sale. Also, more free blacks lived on Jamaica than on any other British Caribbean island. All these factors created a slave system considerably less harsh than that on Barbados or the Leeward Islands in earlier years. Consequently, Jamaican slaves were able to establish their own culture and social system which, because of the legal and psychological gulf separating blacks and whites, preserved much of their African heritage.[10]

Of the mainland colonies, South Carolina came the closest to duplicating the social structures and slave systems of the English West Indies. We noted earlier that most of the first settlers of South Carolina came from the West Indies, often bringing their slaves with them. However, throughout most of the seventeenth century the immigrants worked small farms and owned only a few slaves. At no time did the number of blacks approach the number of whites. These conditions greatly softened the effects of slavery on blacks; some won their freedom and others escaped. Those who did neither often taught their masters about survival in a semi-tropical climate. Consequently, restrictions on slaves were few and relatively mild and an Afro-American culture—containing elements of both Anglo-American and African beliefs and institutions—developed among blacks.

Then, in the last years of the seventeenth and the early years of the eighteenth centuries, South Carolina underwent a profound transformation as the English turned more and more to rice and indigo as their "money" crops for export. Small farms disappeared as the swampy lowlands became great plantations. To provide labor for rice growing, new slaves were imported by the thousands each year. By about 1720, South Carolina had become the first and only mainland colony in the colonial era to have a black majority.

Throughout the eighteenth century rice production increased dramatically and a rich planter elite dominated South Carolina society. Seeking to escape the malaria-infested swamps where their rice flourished, many planters moved to Charlestown, building great houses and developing a style of life to rival that of the gentry of England. In the process, the character of slavery in South Carolina changed dramatically as well. In Charlestown, and other cities, slaves by the thousands lived on the fringes of white society, emulated white ways, and perpetuated an Afro-American culture. On the plantations, though, a vastly different situation developed. The paternalism of West Indian slavery emerged as did the awesome chasm between black slaves and white masters and overseers. Alienation and degradation marked the lives of the plantation slaves. Though they had a measure of independence due to minimal contact with whites, long hours of gang labor in malarial swamps, poor health care, inadequate diet, and dismal housing crippled family life and contributed to an ever-increasing mortality rate. Black resentment grew, resulting in frequent attempts to escape and occasional acts of violence.

Ultimately, in September, 1739, a group of Angolans in St. Paul's parish, twenty miles from Charlestown, gathered along the Stono River and killed about twenty-five whites before they were stopped. Most of the slaves were killed, although a few escaped to the swamps. The result was paranoia among white colonists. Laws were passed outlawing the importation of new slaves from Africa. Also, slave gatherings were prohibited. In general, the authority of whites over blacks increased, and South Carolina slavery grew more repressive. According to historian Peter Wood, the legacy of the "Stono" Rebellion determined the character of slavery in South Carolina down to the Civil War and established a pattern which was copied in many areas of the nineteenth-century antebellum South.[11]

Like South Carolina, society in neighboring Virginia and the Chesapeake region came to be organized around racial divisions. Still, as historian Ira Berlin points out, slavery in Virginia differed considerably from slavery in South Carolina. The reasons were several. First, blacks never outnumbered whites in Virginia so the conditions of the rice plantations were not duplicated. Second, though Virginians placed more and more land into tobacco cultivation, the slave population grew more from natural increase than from importation of African slaves. For a time in the early and middle years of the century, when Virginians were clearing land west of the Chesapeake, large numbers of Africans were imported to do the heaviest work. But that was a temporary measure, and Virginia masters encouraged natural increase, even importing large numbers of black women to achieve a sexual balance. This meant that most Virginia slaves were creoles (blacks born in Virginia) who had learned the English language and customs and knew how to get along in white society. This Afro-Americanization of the slave was no accident but a deliberate design of white masters. Consequently, the gulf that separated whites and blacks in South Carolina never emerged in Virginia. Third, as a wealthy and powerful planter elite developed in the upland and Chesapeake regions of Virginia during the eighteenth century, white planters lived *on* rather than away from their plantations. They tended to the housing, health care, diet, and complaints of their slaves, and generally were sympathetic to their needs. Occasionally they worked alongside them. Also, Virginia planters employed slaves in a variety of skilled occupations in addition to the manual labor of the fields. As a result of these factors, the slave system produced a slave class whose culture was decidedly Anglicized and whose skills differentiated slaves nearly to the same degrees as in white society. Despite its benevolent paternalism, slavery in eighteenth-century Virginia was still dehumanizing; but it never achieved the repressiveness that characterized the English West Indies or post-1740 South Carolina. In fact, even in the middle of the eighteenth century, many Virginians sensed the inherent immorality of slavery and refused to justify it along racial lines. Instead, they argued that it persisted out of economic necessity.

One such Virginian, the Reverend Peter Fontaine of Westover (the plantation of the famous Byrd family), explained slavery to his brother, Moses, in 1757, utilizing language which Thomas Jefferson might have understood. First, he blamed the continued importation of slaves on English officials and the Royal African Company. "Our Assembly," he wrote,

> hath often attempted to lay a duty upon them [incoming slaves] which would amount to a prohibition . . . but no governor dare pass such a law, having instructions to the contrary from the Board of Trade at home. By this means they are forced upon us, whether we will or will not. This plainly shows the African Company hath the advantage of the colonies, and may do as it pleases with the Ministry.[12]

Fontaine then attributed the persistence of the institution of slavery to the poverty of Virginians—a condition he believed was brought about by perpetual warfare with the French and their Indian allies. He also offered a glimpse of the situation of blacks in Virginia:

> Before our troubles [the Anglo-French wars], you could not hire a servant or slave for love or money, so that unless robust enough to cut wood, to go to mill, to work at the hoe, etc., you must starve or board in some family where they both fleece and half starve you. There is no set price upon corn, wheat, and provisions, so they take advantage of the necessities of strangers, who are thus obliged to purchase some slaves and land. This of course draws us all into the original sin and curse of the country of purchasing slaves, and this is the reason we have no merchants, traders, or artificers of any sort but what become planters in a short time . . . . A common labor, white or black, if you can be so much favored as to hire one, is a shilling sterling or fifteen pence currency per day.[13]

North of the Chesapeake slavery took on yet another form. As we have noted, most blacks in the North worked as agricultural laborers but rarely in gangs, as did their brethren to the south. Those farmers wealthy enough to own slaves owned only one or two. No great planters emerged in the North. Consequently slave-owning farmers in the North prized their slaves as highly as any possession they had, and the slaves benefited accordingly. They ate better, had better housing and health care, and were closer to their masters. Often, bonds of deep and mutual affection developed. Also, slaves performed all of the tasks of the farm, not the single job expected of plantation slaves. They raised and tended the animals, plowed the ground and nurtured the crops, maintained and repaired implements and buildings, and often performed household tasks as well. Like their masters they were both agriculturists and semiskilled artisans.

Many northern slaves, both urban and rural, worked in burgeoning industries such as iron foundries or tanneries. In ports such as Boston, New York, and Philadelphia, slaves worked as longshoremen, teamsters, and even sailors. One of New England's best-known eighteenth-century ministers, the Reverend Benjamin Colman of Boston's Brattle Street Church, observed that "we are serv'd here in this Town very much by blacks or Negro's [sic] in our Houses. Scarce a House but has one, excepting the very poor."[14] His comment was only a slight exaggeration, for slaves were very prominent in every urban area by the eighteenth century. Nearly 25 percent of all blacks in the colony of New York lived in New York City. Boston had about a third of the blacks in Massachusetts, and Newport, Rhode Island, had one of the largest concentrations of blacks anywhere in the North.

In the middle colonies, except for New York, the majority of blacks worked in small industries in the countryside. In Pennsylvania, which had the only large number of iron foundries in the colonies during the eighteenth century, blacks formed the basis of the labor force for the iron industry. A few Pennsylvania farmers also owned slaves, but they were placed in skilled trades rather than field work. Prosperous German, Scotch-Irish, and Quaker farmers in Pennsylvania preferred indentured servants to slaves throughout the eighteenth century. In fact, a majority of Europeans migrating into that colony came as indentured servants, thus keeping alive a labor system that had all but disappeared in the South.

Two important facts emerged from the character of slavery in the North during the colonial period. First, though not accepted as members of white society, rural slaves nonetheless mastered the complexities of white culture. Second, urban slaves, because they rarely lived with their masters, possessed a degree of autonomy not enjoyed by slaves anywhere else. Like their rural counterparts, they absorbed the ways of white society and moved in it almost as easily as whites. For the slave, the end product was an Afro-American culture that combined the ways of the English and Europeans with the remnants of an African heritage.

The institutions of northern slavery never took on the edge of cruelty and ruthlessness that developed elsewhere, simply because blacks and whites lived too closely together. The "Africaness" of the slaves was muted by their apparently total acceptance of white culture. Conversely, the solidarity and resilience of black or Afro-American culture owed much to the fact that before 1730 few blacks entered the North directly from Africa. Most had spent time in the West Indies and were partially "Americanized" before coming to the mainland. Moreover, the northern slave family proved exceptionally stable and remarkably similar to its white counterpart. Consequently, blacks reproduced at a rate more than sufficient to satisfy the demands for their services.

Similar to the experience in South Carolina, slavery in the North changed radically after 1730. The phenomenal growth of commerce and agriculture created a demand for labor unprecedented in the history of the region. As a result—and for the first time—Africans were imported directly to the North, many winding up in port cities. The character of northern slavery grew more repressive as the "strangeness" of the African became apparent to white masters. For the Africans, too often their fate paralleled that of blacks who were the first to encounter the lowlands of South Carolina. Large numbers died as they experienced northern winters and previously unknown diseases. By the time of the American Revolution, jittery northerners, especially those in New York and Pennsylvania, had stopped importing Africans, once again turning to European indentures. Most of the surviving African slaves accepted the Afro-American culture of the region. But, they also helped reawaken the interest of northern blacks in their African origins.[15]

A CHANGING SOCIETY

As Anglo-America evolved from the simplicity of a frontier existence in the seventeenth century to the complexity of agricultural specialization, commercial sophistication, and a position as a vital, even dominant, component of a vast imperial system centered in England in the eighteenth century, the individual and institutional relationships which characterized Anglo-American society changed dramatically as well. From primitive, even egalitarian beginnings—when all colonists more or less labored together to overcome climate and geography, when differences in wealth were slight, and when social distinctions were blurred—social and economic classes emerged, separating the rich from the poor. Moreover, men and women adopted deferential attitudes toward those above them. Further, most of the professions and other nonagricultural occupations found in England also appeared in America. Above all, like the colonial economy, as colonial society matured, it conformed to and reflected most of the salient features of social organizations everywhere in the preindustrial world.

Still, as noted before, Anglo-American society also developed important traits which differentiated it from Europe and England: traits which reflected the fulfillment of some of the hopes and aspirations of the founders. Of these, none surpassed in importance the fact that wealth, not birth, became the prime arbiter of social and economic position in Anglo-America. Every colony developed its social and economic elite. Although many colonials tried to imitate the life of the English gentry, none could escape the basic fact that money or property—not hereditary class differences—meant power and status. Only in the South, around Chesapeake Bay and in the lowlands of South Carolina, did society even faintly resemble the ancient European pattern of a landed aristocracy. There, through intermarriage and the distribution of wealth among their children, the large tobacco and rice planters of the mideighteenth century integrated political power, economic wealth, and social status and tried to pass this combination on to succeeding generations. But, lacking the distinctions associated with titles and the sanctions of law and custom, they achieved only limited success.

Georgian England

In contrast, perhaps the most significant feature of English society in the eighteenth century was the presence, persistence, and power of heredity and class. For modern-day Americans who live in a society free from hereditary class differences, the idea of attributing superior social and political position to a person solely on the basis of birth seems alien and contrary to common sense. However, for the English who lived in a society that for centuries had fixed one's place by birth, the notion of class was both accepted and approved. Put simply, English society recognized and reinforced a hierarchy of divisions that separated and defined an individual's function, responsibility, opportunity, and freedom. The English believed that class distinctions preserved order, ensured stability, promoted the public good, and reflected the natural pattern of things.

England had evolved out of a feudal existence in which the cultivation of land was virtually the only means to acquire wealth. Land equaled wealth. The feudal and manorial systems had provided a kind of quid pro quo arrangement. A king or great lord would receive obedience, military aid, and other forms of service from his vassal in exchange for land; likewise, the lord of the manor obtained labor and services from his tenants and serfs in exchange for giving them protection and economic sustenance. Class differences grew out of this medieval heritage and were rooted in the possession of land. Even with the advent of the Industrial Revolution in the late eighteenth century, agriculture and land-related activities continued to serve as the mainstay of the English economy. Despite the increasing importance of manufacturing and trade, landed interests dominated England's political and social life as well. Possession of land still meant wealth, social respectability, economic opportunity, and political power. Hence, as soon as a merchant acquired wealth, he sought to confirm a new, higher social and political status by purchasing land.

Even as alternative avenues for accumulating wealth opened, land continued to be valued highly. This was primarily because of its scarcity. Historians of colonial America have long observed that the availability of land encouraged the spread of democratic social and political ideas and blurred class distinctions. Conversely, in England the scarcity of land upheld class differences and limited political rights to a few. Given England's population of approximately 5.5 million by 1700, there was simply an insufficient amount of land within its boundaries to permit all its people to own real property. In addition, the rapid increase in population (historians estimate an increase to about 9 million by the end of the eighteenth century) tended to reinforce the political, social, and economic inequities already part of England's past. It is not surprising, then, that eighteenth-century Britain continued to be ruled and dominated by the propertied classes.

At the top of English society was the nobility. This group consisted of those who possessed a hereditary title to land and who perpetuated this title by primogeniture, or the passing of all land to the eldest son without division to other heirs. The members of the aristocracy, by virtue of birth, automatically sat in the House of Lords and exercised substantial power in the government. Also, the great families controlled the territory surrounding their landed estates. This control not only extended to local government, but to the social and economic life of the community. On the fringe of the nobility was the upper gentry. They too were landowners, but they usually held smaller estates. This group—composed of the younger sons, daughters, cousins, relatives by marriage, and so on, of the aristrocracy—traditionally entered the army and navy, law, medicine, the church, or other professions that assured them of certain social esteem. Although less important than the aristocracy, the upper gentry too possessed substantial political, social, and economic power. In those localities where they held sway, they provided the leadership similar to that of their noble kinspeople.

Beneath the upper gentry was a group we identify as the squirearchy. This section of society also owned land, occasionally as much or even more than their aristocratic betters, but they had no direct connection with the nobility. Often the squirearchy represented men who had made fortunes in trade, acquired land with their wealth, and by the second or third generation won respectability. After the Restoration of Charles II these "country gentlemen" played an important role in national as well as local affairs. They fiercely guarded their independence from aristocratic control and were courted by parliamentary leaders for their votes. Held in high esteem in the communities where they lived, they often bought or won the right of presentment (that is, the right to appoint local clergy) for the parish, served as justices of the peace, held other local offices, and acted as lesser patrons in the community.

Below the upper classes was a layer in society that has been called the *middling sort.* Generally it included such groups as successful tenant farmers, small freeholders, prosperous tradespeople and shopkeepers, and a variety of lower professions such as civil servants and schoolmasters. They owned little or no land, but they did possess other types of property. In the counties and boroughs many of the middling sort had the franchise and exercised some political power in their communities.

Finally, at the bottom of the social hierarchy was the mass of the population. These were the wage earners and manual laborers. They included craftsmen and artisans—such as blacksmiths, shoemakers, weavers, and cooks—as well as agricultural laborers. These people were poor. Most eked out a living but generally kept just above subsistence. Typically, they lived in overcrowded, unheated dwellings that provided little more than shelter from the elements. A sizable portion of the lower class included those who could not or would not work, such as the elderly, disabled, orphaned, widowed, and vagrant. This group existed through public charity administered by the local parish. If they had no place to live, they were put in workhouses (not always as harsh and cruel as the one described in Charles Dickens' *Oliver Twist*). Because by the Poor Law each community had responsibility for the unfortunates within its boundaries, the local parishes discouraged the influx of any unemployed laborers or migrants who might become a burden upon the community. Generally, society blamed the condition of the poor upon the individuals themselves, not upon the circumstances in which they were born. The lower class possessed no education and little opportunity for it, no political rights, no status, and virtually no chance to improve their condition.

Despite great inequities in wealth, station, and rights between the aristocracy and the poor, the bulk of English society upheld or at least tolerated class distinctions. In part they did so because notions of class were deeply imbedded, in part because society afforded little chance to alter the status quo, and in part because the prevailing social ethic justified class by tying high position to greater social responsibility. The nobility and landed gentry received deference, privilege, political rights, and economic opportunity, but at some cost. They acted as a kind of hereditary civil service. The upper classes were expected to assist the poor, oversee the administration of local services, maintain the local clergy, ensure the operation of the courts, and in general look after community interests. By accepting extensive public obligations as the duty of their high station and by maintaining personal ties with the communities they represented, the propertied classes helped mitigate social tensions that rose from the inequities of society.

Class divisions were also perpetuated by English institutions. In the eighteenth century land provided the avenue for social mobility and conveyed the right to vote and hold office. The Act of 1710 required county MPs (Members of Parliament) to own £600 annual worth of property and borough MPs £300. Likewise, though qualifications varied from place to place, only the propertied classes had the franchise. In all the counties, the 40s. freeholder possessed the vote. In the boroughs, where a large portion of the population lived, voting qualifications tended to be more restrictive and varied widely. Some boroughs excluded all but members of the corporation; some tied the vote to residency or payment of local taxes; still other admitted men who held a freehold, leasehold, or other type of tenancy. In addition to a variety of voting requirements, there was also wide disparity in the size of electorates. In certain "rotten boroughs" perhaps only a half dozen individuals might elect one or two MPs, while in some densely populated areas several thousand might vote. Robert Walcott, a historian of eighteenth-century English politics, has estimated that in the 203 boroughs that elected representatives in the early eighteenth century, two-thirds had electorates of 500 or less, and two-fifths of 100 or less. Also, because balloting was conducted openly rather than secretly, the election process was highly subject to political manipulation. As a result, even in areas in which a substantial percentage of the population might have the vote, elections were largely contests between leading families who swayed voters through bribery, influence, or social pressure.

Through parliamentary legislation and management of governmental offices, the upper classes not only maintained class privileges but also advanced their economic interests. For example, through Parliament individuals might obtain monopolies, receive authorization and moneys to drain fens, enclose common lands, or dredge rivers, influence the amount and placement of customs duties on goods, and in general exercise power over wide areas of the economy. Parliamentary influence therefore meant economic influence. In addition to parliamentary legislation, numerous government posts carried with them revenues from and powers over economic activity. The king and his ministers distributed these choice plums to their supporters and through a network of patronage directed domestic and foreign policy. The operation of both politics and the economy worked to the tune of the propertied classes and served to reinforce class distinctions.

Despite the social, political, and economic domination of the propertied classes in England, one aspect of British society–its localism–mitigated some of their power. The population as a whole possessed little direct control over affairs, but they nevertheless exercised considerable indirect influence upon the ruling classes. The relationship between rulers and ruled was mutually dependent. Although the aristocracy and gentry governed Britain, they held power through centuries-old political, social, and economic ties with their local constituencies. Fierce competition among governing families, juntos, and parties for political influence meant that the chief power in a county or borough had to be somewhat responsive to local interests or else risk defeat in parliamentary elections. This dependency upon the electorate kept governmental outlook and concerns highly local. The ruling family in a county was attentive to local problems, cultivated a close, personal relationship with the community, and in a multitude of ways made its presence felt. In that respect, the ruling classes did indeed represent and serve the constituencies that elected them. If society was paternally oligarchic rather than democratic, it nevertheless required some accountability from those who governed. This localism, coupled with the relative smallness of Britain, enabled English society to retain many of its traditional class characteristics, even as it moved steadily toward an industrial, modern, democratic order.[16]

Mobility in Anglo-America

Anglo-America departed from England, then, in the degree of social and economic mobility possible for the enterprising colonial. In general, colonial society was considerably more open than either Georgian England or Europe. At the same time, however, it did not offer all of its citizens the same degree of economic opportunity popularized by Benjamin Franklin and others during the eighteenth century. In fact, most historians agree that as colonial society moved away from its seventeenth-century origins, vertical mobility—at least in certain areas—became more and more difficult. In Virginia, the "great families" solidified their power and position around 1720, and entrance into that class became very difficult by the Revolution. In colonies like Massachusetts, Pennsylvania, or New York, mobility proved considerably easier; but there too, it became more difficult to move up the social and economic ladder as the eighteenth century progressed. In Maryland, indentured servants usually acquired land in the seventeenth century; by the eighteenth century, however, they were more likely to become tenant farmers. Moreover, for the colonial era as a whole, recent studies indicate that as the colonies matured, fewer people held an increasingly larger share of the wealth. By the American Revolution, the top 10 percent of white property owners in the middle colonies possessed one-third of the aggregate wealth; in New England, the top 10 percent owned about 40 percent. In both regions the bottom half of the population owned less than a quarter of the total wealth: New England had 11 percent, compared to 23 percent for the middle colonies. In the South the concentration of wealth was even greater, with the top 10 percent owning more than half of the available total wealth. For Anglo-America as a whole, one scholar estimates that the highest 10 percent of the population may have held nearly 50 percent of the wealth by 1770.

As indicators of mobility, however, these figures can be a bit misleading. Colonial America had an expanding economy, and new wealth was being created all the time. For this reason, in western frontier areas—where the early patterns of colonization were duplicated, and institutional and social restraints still lacked form—enterprising people easily rose above their economic and social stations. Two students of economic and social mobility in eighteenth century Anglo-America, Jackson Turner Main and Charles S. Grant, for example, have found very high rates of upward mobility in the frontier regions of eighteenth-century Virginia and Connecticut.[17]

Even in the older, established areas where the concentration of wealth was the greatest and inequalities the most obvious, the expanding colonial economy led to a rise in income levels for all layers of society, poor as well as rich. However, while limited advancement was easy, great jumps up the economic and social ladders proved difficult. Historian Aubrey Land shows this clearly in his research on the northern Chesapeake Bay region. Surveying the period from 1690 to 1760 he finds just four men who rose from indentured status to great wealth—that is, from "rags to riches." Most persons improved their positions only slightly. Between 1690 and 1699, nearly 75 percent of the population possessed estates worth less than £100. By 1740, this group had shrunk to about half (54.7 percent) of the population. At the same time, persons in the next level of wealth (£100 to £500) grew from 21.7 percent of the population in 1690 to 35.7 percent in 1740. But, Land cautions, the significance of this movement must be placed in perspective. Between 1690 and 1700 the wealthiest planters in the northern Chesapeake region (about 1.6 percent of the population) had estates valued between £1000 and £2000. By 1740, however, the rich had grown much richer. Many planters had estates above £2000 and one man, Amos Garrett, was worth £11,508. Thus, Land concludes, while all the people seemed to improve their lot somewhat, the rich did much better than the poor and the gap between the two increased greatly. His statistics suggest that social and economic mobility in a populous, established region like the northern Chesapeake was far less than on the frontier.[18]

Despite the emergence of slavery, the exploitation of the Indians, and the development of wealthy, powerful elites in the colonies during the eighteenth century, Anglo-America remained one of the most egalitarian societies of its age. Ironically, this characteristic grew out of the very notions which had produced such entrenched class distinctions in Europe. Like their ancestors eighteenth-century colonials believed that the possession of property ensured a stable social order because those with a vested interest would protect it. In England and Europe, as noted earlier, this idea reinforced class distinctions. In Anglo-America, however, the abundance of land and the richness of natural resources caused a wider distribution of property and hence a more egalitarian society. Following English practices, Massachusetts, for example, required voters in the eighteenth century to own a "40s. freehold" (land, which if rented, would produce a yearly income of 40s.) or other property worth £40. Applied to European countries, this qualification would have effectively eliminated much of the populace from voting; but in Massachusetts it did not. Most male inhabitants met one or both of those requirements. In Virginia the situation was similar. Colonial society was not *democratic* as we understand and apply the term. Social and economic distinctions existed in abundance and were both accepted and embraced by the overwhelming majority of the inhabitants. Still, if Anglo-America was not quite the land where everyone could expect to become rich and powerful, it was a world where political and economic opportunity existed to a much greater degree than in either England or the rest of Europe.[19]

Social and Sectional Conflict

Sharp conflict occasionally punctuated the evolution of the relatively fluid social systems of the Anglo-American colonies. Part of it resulted from western jealousy and eastern snobbishness, but much had more concrete origins. For example, because a considerable portion of the wealth and political power in the colonies was concentrated along the coast, westerners often felt their interests were neglected by the colonial assemblies. As early as 1676 such a grievance led to an armed revolt in Virginia. An enterprising young colonial named Nathaniel Bacon led an uprising composed mainly of frontiersmen against Tidewater planters and the royal governor, William Berkeley. Bacon's supporters were angry over the Virginia government's failure to protect them from Indian raids. They also resented a poll tax levied by Berkeley some years earlier. Although Bacon himself was no poor frontiersman, he used western distrust of Tidewater planters to pursue his own ambitions. In the revolt Bacon captured the seat of government at Jamestown. Shortly afterwards, however, he died of fever, the uprising collapsed, and many of his followers were hanged.

For generations, historians believed that Bacon's Rebellion represented an early warning of how American colonials would react to a "tyrannical" ruler. Modern scholarship, however, portrays Bacon as an opportunist who capitalized upon the social, political, and economic instability in Virginia. Berkeley has lost the tryant's mantle and is now characterized as a somewhat pompous, arrogant man caught up in circumstances over which he had little control. Whatever the truth, there developed quickly in colonial Virginia a rather romantic view of Bacon as a popular leader and Berkeley as a narrow-minded aristocrat. Thirty years after the events, Thomas Mathew, a Virginia planter, commented upon the growing Bacon legend and added something to it himself. Reflecting upon an incident in which Bacon pardoned a known Berkeley spy, Mathew observed: "upon this manifestation of clemency Bacon was applauded for a mercifull man, not willing to spill Christian bloud; nor indeed was it said, that he put any other man to death in cold bloud, or plunder any house." Concerning Berkeley, however, Mathew revealed that a friend had overheard the governor say he "would have hang'd half the countrey, if they had let him alone." In concluding, the writer repeated a remark attributed to Charles II, that the "old fool [Berkeley] had hang'd more in that naked country than he [Charles] had done for the murther of his father."[20]

Questions of land policy and Indian policy most often turned West against East. In the eighteenth century particularly, rapid expansion westward created a demand for land that increased speculation to mammoth proportions on the frontier. Speculation, in turn, proved a source of considerable social ferment. Although generally wealthy already, land speculators were often not members of the economic elites controlling the legislatures. This situation caused friction if not antagonisms between the two groups. For years, for example, the Susquehanna Company battled Penn family representatives over territory in western Pennsylvania that became Ohio. In addition, whites who poured west were met by the French and their Indian allies. Settlers turned to the colonial governments for help. When they did not receive it, as in Bacon's case, or when they did not obtain sufficient assistance, they resorted on occasion to violence. In 1763, the "Paxton Boys," a group of Scotch-Irish immigrants living on the frontier of Pennsylvania, turned into vigilantes when the Quaker-dominated Pennsylvania legislature failed to give them sufficient protection from Indian raids resulting from the French and Indian War and a postwar rebellion led by Pontiac, an Ottawa chieftain. The Paxton Boys slaughtered a peaceful village of twenty-four Conestoga Indians whom they suspected of providing aid and information to other tribes loyal to the French or to Pontiac. Then, they marched on Philadelphia to state their grievances to colonial officials. They complained of underrepresentation in the legislature (western legislators, though representing five counties, had eight fewer representatives than Bucks and Chester, the two eastern counties), inadequate protection from Indian forays, lack of compensation to wounded veterans of the Anglo-American armies, failure to provide a bounty on Indian scalps, failure to negotiate the release of "our nearest and dearest relatives" held captive by the Indians, and English trade with hostile Indians during the war. It was a list of grievances which might have come from frontierspeople in any of the colonies during hard times. It was punctuated by the belief that "We apprehend that as Freemen and English Subjects, we have an indisputable title to the same privileges & immunities with His Majesty's other Subjects who reside in the interior Counties of Philadelphia, Bucks and Chester . . . ."[21] A delegation from Philadelphia, led by Benjamin Franklin, met the frontierspeople, listened to their grievances, and promised that, at the very least, the legislature would create a bounty on Indian scalps.

As the incident of the Paxton Boys suggested, some of the friction in colonial society involved the non-English. This is not to say that the English were law abiding and peace loving while others were not. Actually, most of the non-English immigrants of the eighteenth century coexisted with each other and with the older English inhabitants with remarkable harmony. But, as newcomers entering an alien world the non-English were naturally wary and defensive. Also, the English often reacted to them with indifference or contempt, treating them as outsiders or, at best, second-class citizens. Finally, the immigrants usually sought the open land of the frontier because of its opportunity as well as its distance from the older English settlements. That placed them in danger of attack by the French or the Indians, or both, and also made it difficult for them to gain the attention or the interest of colonial officials or English royal governors or the representatives of English proprietors, many of whom were happy to have them form buffers between themselves and their enemies.

Germans, Scotch-Irish, Dutch, French, Swedes, Highland and Lowland Scots, Portuguese, and a smattering of other nationalities entered Anglo-America in the eighteenth century, mostly because of deteriorating economic and social conditions in Europe and parts of the British Isles. Of these groups the two largest were the Germans (about 100,000) and the Scotch-Irish (about 250,000). Most Germans entered the colonies through Philadelphia and settled in Pennsylvania. Many Scotch-Irish did the same. Large numbers of Scotch-Irish, however, arrived at New York City, then moved west into Pennsylvania, southwest into the Shenendoah Valley, or farther south into the western portions of the Carolinas. There they encountered the same official indifference which prompted the uprising of the Paxton Boys in Pennsylvania. In the early 1760s the frontierspeople of North and South Carolina complained loudly of their vulnerability to Indian attack and protested, as well, their legislatures' failures to create satisfactory local governmental institutions for them. By 1767, the frontierspeople formed "Regulator" associations to provide law and order.

While they dispensed vigilante justice, they petitioned their legislatures to resolve their grievances. In South Carolina, one of these petitions, written by an itinerant Anglican clergyman named Charles Woodmason, recited a litany of lawless acts perpetrated by an "infernal Gang of Villains, who have committed such horrid Depredations on our Properties and Estates–Such Insults on the Persons of many

Settlers, and perpetrated such shocking Outrages thro'out the Back Settlement as is past Description."[22] Included in the litany was cattle stealing, looting, burning, murder, and rape.

> The Chastity of many beauteous Maidens has been threat[e]ned by these Rogues. Merchants Stores are oblig'd to be kept constantly guarded (which enhances the Price of Goods) And thus We live not as under a British Government (ev'ry Man sitting in Peace and Security under his own Vine, and his own Fig Tree), But as if [we] were in Hungary or Germany, and in a State of War. . . .[23]

In addition, the Regulators of South Carolina complained of corrupt officials, poor and inadequate courts (or none at all), and, like the Paxton Boys, underrepresentation in the South Carolina legislature. "The South Side of Santee River," Woodmason noted, elected "44 Members, and the North Side, with these Upper Parts of the Province (containing 2/3 of the White Inhabitants) elected only six. It is to this Great Disproportion of Representatives on our Part, that our Interests have been so long neglected, and the Back Country disregarded." Woodmason's petition asked for action by the legislature on twenty-three different proposals. "We are *Free-Men*–British subjects–not born *Slaves*," he declared. "We contribute our Proportion in all Public Taxations, and discharge our Duty to the Public, equally with our Fellow Provincials, Ye[t] We do not participate with them in the Rights and Benefits which they Enjoy, tho' equally Entituled to them."[24] The South Carolina legislature did create a new court system but it also sent troops to disperse the Regulators. Pitched battles followed, and loss of life was heavy on both sides until the Regulators were beaten. The legislature's action created such a legacy of bitterness in the South Carolina backcountry that, when the Revolution broke out a few years later, few ex-Regulators or their sympathizers could bring themselves to support the Patriot cause. The same was true of frustrated ex-Regulators in North Carolina.

Although specific grievances occasionally provoked hostility between nationalities, it should be remembered that those enmities often antedated settlement of the colonies and were not simply a product of eighteenth-century conditions. For example, as early as 1689, when Edmund Andros, royal governor for the Dominion of New England, was imprisoned in Boston, a German, Jacob Leisler, led an uprising in New York which overthrew Francis Nicholson, Andros' lieutenant governor for the provinces of New York and New Jersey. Leisler established himself as governor and declared his (and his provinces') loyalty to the new regents, William and Mary. Leisler governed well but he could not obtain the official approval of King William, who appointed Colonel Henry Sloughter to be New York's governor. Leisler refused to vacate his office, and he and several of his followers were arrested and tried for treason. Leisler and his son-in-law, Jacob Milborne, were found guilty and hanged.

For many years afterward, New York politics followed the lines of division formed between Leislerians and anti-Leislerians between 1689 and 1692. Why this occurred reflected the reasons Leisler had managed to take power in the first place. New York suffered from deep enmity between many of the old Dutch families and the new English interlopers. Thus, though an English colony since 1664, New York was a microcosm of international Anglo-Dutch rivalry in the seventeenth century. Also, a number of the appointees serving under Lieutenant Governor Nicholson were Roman Catholics, sparking the hostility of both the Protestant Dutch and the English against the Andros and Nicholson regimes and injecting another major European and English conflict into New York life. Finally, in the 1680s New York politics was dominated by a small number of wealthy Dutch and English families and Leisler, a wealthy man and relative newcomer in New York, represented the antagonisms of the "outs" against the "ins," just as Nathaniel Bacon had led the "outs" in his revolt in Virginia a decade earlier. Leisler and his followers took advantage of all of these grievances—as well as the power vacuum created by Andros' fall—to take control of New York. That was why hostility between Leisler's followers and his detractors continued long after his death.[25]

For the most part the greatest source of conflict in Anglo-America grew out of a desire for wealth and power. Generally, this kind of social discord did not generate violence but was absorbed by the political system in each colony. Ambitious men did not shoot each other or form armies. Instead, they organized political factions and jockeyed for advantage in the legislature or they curried favor with the royal governor. Such conflict became thoroughly institutionalized in the eighteenth century and was the most important single reason why politics became the vocation of many colonials and the avocation of many more. Although violence punctuated the history of early America, episodes such as Bacon's and Leisler's Rebellions, or the Paxton Boys and the Regulators were exceptions, not the rule.

9

Political Thought and Political Practice

In earlier discussions of colonial politics, two divergent yet complementary themes were emphasized. First, during the seventeenth century, the model of representative government established in Massachusetts and Virginia was copied by later colonial settlements, so that by 1700 virtually every British colony in North America boasted of a colonial legislature and executive. Some colonies had one representative body and an executive council. Most patterned the parliamentary model and established an executive council, with an assembly composed of two houses: a lower chamber elected by localities, and an upper chamber appointed by the governor or proprietor, or occasionally elected by the lower house. Although the "mixed-government" form varied slightly from colony to colony, the early success of the Massachusetts/Virginia model prompted later colonies to adopt it. Second, even though the Massachusetts/Virginia example set the standard followed by the other colonies, still, the governments of the colonies differed considerably. The diverse character of Anglo-America produced variations in the internal structure and operation of the shared political model. The representative form hid a wide range of differing political activities and divisions of power that lay beneath the surface.

In part, these differences can be traced to the diverse origins of the colonies themselves, some of which grew from a strong religious base, others of which reflected a commercial or proprietary origin. For example, the Puritan influence in Massachusetts Bay led to the restriction of the franchise to church members.

In addition the early strength and autonomy of the New England towns resulted in colony governments for both Massachusetts and Connecticut that were dominated by the legislature rather than the executive. In contrast, Virginia's political institutions initially reflected its joint-stock charter. After 1625 the change to royal government cemented the governor's position as the central political force in the colony. At its inception Plymouth Colony established a communal order rooted in the towns. Even after their absorption by Massachusetts Bay, Plymouth's towns continued to exercise considerable political autonomy. Rhode Island placed political power first in the hands of family heads, and then transferred control to the towns. The efforts and influence of Rhode Island's founder, the religious dissenter Roger Williams, determined that Rhode Island would practice some of the most tolerant and liberal religious and political policies in Anglo-America. In New York and Maryland, the proprietors first held almost feudallike authority. Even after circumstances prompted them to create representative bodies, proprietary interests continued to dominate the legislatures.

In addition to differing origins, the colonies also developed various political habits and operations because of the diversity of geography, climate, soil, and the traditions and nationalities of their settlers. In New England, cultural as well as environmental factors contributed to a more concentrated population and the rise of the town as the main political unit. In contrast, the marshy, inlet-filled coast of Virginia and South Carolina, coupled with a climate and soil suited for labor-intensive, single-crop agriculture, resulted in a far more diffused population and the development of an English countylike system of political representation that concentrated power in the hands of the wealthy, land-owning upper class. In Pennsylvania strong Quaker and German elements exerted a powerful influence within the legislature, whereas in New York, the lingering Dutch heritage had a significant impact on politics well into the eighteenth century. In summary, then, even though the colonies shared a common political form, in practice the governments operated differently from colony to colony and represented a varying array of religious, national, cultural, and economic groups.

This dual nature of seventeenth-century colonial political institutions—that is, the establishment of a representative form of government on the one hand, coupled with the diverse composition and operation of this model on the other hand—produced two interesting phenomena that had significant consequences for colonial politics during the eighteenth century. First, after 1700 the assemblies became the main vehicle for both concurrence with and resistance to British imperial policy. Second, the cultural and economic diversity that existed within each colony made factionalism dominant within colonial political institutions.

In part, the rise of the legislatures as voices of popular dissent developed through the auspices and encouragement of the imperial government itself. During the latter half of the seventeenth century, English policy makers recognized the vast potential of Anglo-America for building Britain's national power. Therefore, they sought to increase imperial control over the colonies. In attempting to do so, however, the Crown was thwarted by its own earlier policies. Initially, royal charters extended considerable discretionary powers to proprietors and joint-stock companies. Later on, however, the prerogatives of the proprietors in particular inhibited imperial efforts to direct colonial development. As a result, the Crown embarked upon a campaign to reduce the powers of proprietors.

One of the key elements used by the imperial government to counterbalance or limit proprietary authority was the colonial assembly. Compare, for example, the charters given to Cecil Calvert in 1632, Sir George Carteret and his associates in 1663, and William Penn in 1681.[1] Calvert received powers over his lands in America almost equal to those of the Crown in England and ruled through an appointed proprietary council. When the Crown issued the Carolina group's charter in 1663, it still gave the proprietors considerable latitude in constructing the government, but required them to obtain "the advice, assent, and approbation of the Freemen of the said Province" to any laws that were established.[2] By 1681, when William Penn received his charter, his proprietary powers were severely circumscribed by rights given to the colonial assembly. As it granted new charters, then, the Crown provided for the creation of an assembly and gave that legislature certain counterbalancing powers. Further, in colonies already established by liberal proprietary charters, the Crown encouraged the creation of colonial assemblies to offset proprietary authority.

If the Crown fed the growth and power of colonial assemblies in proprietary colonies, it pursued a radically different policy toward colonies established under commercial charters. There, British policy makers worked to rein in the legislatures. Ultimately, in most nonroyal/nonproprietary colonies, the Crown succeeded in revoking charters and converting the colonies to royal control. By 1686, Massachusetts, New Hampshire, Plymouth, Rhode Island, Maine, Connecticut, New York, and New Jersey were all consolidated into the Dominion of New England. This single government ruled by an executive council only. But even the conversion of these colonies to royal control ultimately produced an affirmation, rather than a denunciation, of the rights and powers of legislatures.

The confirmation of colonial assemblies occurred primarily as a byproduct of the Glorious Revolution in England (1688). At the same time that the English replaced James II with William and Mary and affirmed the sovereignty of the elected, representative branch of government—Parliament—various elements within the colonies seized the opportunity posed by English political revolution to initiate similar challenges to executive authority in Anglo-America. In Maryland, John Coode and the Protestant Association overturned Calvert's rule, elected a convention, and then quickly appealed to Parliament to sanction their actions. Parliament obligingly revoked Lord Baltimore's charter—destroying most of Calvert's power in the process—and then converted Maryland into a royal colony having a representative assembly. In Massachusetts, a successful revolution expelled Governor Edmund Andros, destroyed the Dominion of New England, and reasserted the government of the old charter. In New York Jacob Leisler followed suit and called an assembly to govern the colony. Even though Leisler was eventually hanged for leading the insurrection, the British government affirmed the results of Leisler's Rebellion by installing a permanent legislature. Although the assemblies of North and South Carolina did not totally reject proprietary rule during that period, they nonetheless banished their proprietary governors. By the end of the seventeenth century, therefore, political conflicts produced an affirmation of the "rights" of colonial assemblies and established a precedent for resistance to royal control. In addition, the strengthened position of the legislatures set the stage for the conflict that would occur between assemblies and governors during the eighteenth century.

The other legacy of seventeenth-century colonial politics was the continuation and expansion of factionalism within colonial political institutions. The people who settled Anglo-America came from many areas of Europe and possessed a variety of religious, social, and cultural traditions. The diversity of the population produced an intense localism throughout the colonies. During the eighteenth century, the situation grew even more complex with the influx of additional national and religious groups, all of whom seemed to share little but a common dislike for one another. Besides cultural and religious differences, the colonies became further divided by the rise of various competing agricultural and commercial interests. As subsistence agriculture gave way to surplus production in some regions, farmers sold off their goods to merchants in Boston, New York, and so on, creating in the process a clear conflict of economic interests. One could not very well work for higher grain prices for farmers and lower grain prices for merchants at the same time. The end result of increased cultural and economic diversity within the colonies was the spread of factionalism within their political institutions. Representing as they did various local and economic groups within each colony, the lower houses of the legislature became the battlegrounds for competing factions, each of which sought to advance its own interests. Although the colonies' assemblies in one sense grew more powerful, their effectiveness was continually hampered by intense inner quarreling and conflict.

In addition to the two factors just mentioned, a third element had a substantial impact upon the course of colonial politics during the eighteenth century. This was the rise of *real-Whig* ideology. In the earlier chapter on religion and culture, it was noted that much of colonial culture could be defined as "Protestant." Two central stands of colonial Protestant culture defined earlier were a sense of being in opposition and a deep fear of or resistance to external authority. Both themes appeared, interestingly enough, in certain real-Whig political tracts published in England during the late seventeenth and early eighteenth centuries. Although these tracts had a relatively minor impact upon English politics, in America the polemics appealed strongly to the colonial mind. By the mideighteenth century, the ideas of the real Whigs had so infused colonial thinking that they became an integral part of American revolutionary rhetoric and ideology.

In looking at the developments traced in the following pages, it is important that the themes just outlined be kept in mind. They helped set the stage for the conflict with England in the 1760s and 1770s. Further, they also suggest why, after the war, the new states suffered from factionalism and displayed an almost paranoic fear of a strong central government.

ROYAL GOVERNORS AND COLONIAL ASSEMBLIES

In the eighteenth century the character of colonial politics was influenced by the tightening web of imperial rules and by the growing number of royal officials. Of these the most important was the royal governor.[3] Theoretically, his power in the colony was complete. In practice, it was only as great as the degree of support he received at home. With the continuing intramural argument between Crown and Parliament and among royal officials, that support proved erratic.

In some respects the royal governor's power was greater than the king's. The governor controlled the militia, summoned and dissolved the assembly, had a veto over all legislation, sat along with his council as the highest court of appeal, appointed many lesser officials, nominated members to his own council, enforced the navigation acts, pocketed fees charged for passing papers under the great seal, and by the middle of the eighteenth century, often granted land to his most loyal supporters. Of these powers the greatest and most useful was patronage. With offices to give, the royal governor had little trouble finding colonials willing to give him their loyalty. Many were more than willing to serve on the provincial council, his main advisory group. The council, which usually consisted of twelve men, acted as the upper house in the colonial assembly, as well as the highest judicial court in the land, and as an executive in acting on all decisions made by the governor. It was, indeed, a rich plum.

The royal governors squared off against the lower houses of the colonial assemblies which, in nearly every colony, had important traditions of independent action. As royal governors and other colonial officials tried to satisfy the demands of Crown and Parliament, it was inevitable that the lower houses would fight to protect their rights and prerogatives and even grasp for more power, just as the House of Commons and many of these same assemblies had done a century earlier. In this struggle the lower houses had two important weapons: the right to initiate legislation (though acts were never official until accepted by the Board of Trade) and the power of the purse. The assemblies had the power to raise revenue for the governor and his officials. Why the English would have allowed this oversight, especially remembering the way Commons had used the purse to thwart Charles I, is difficult to understand. Certainly, it was an enigma to royal governors and to English officials like George Dunk, the Earl of Halifax, who sought continuously to establish a permanent revenue for overseas administrators. Actually, Parliament wanted the colonial service to pay for itself, and most members felt that it was perfectly proper for the colonial assemblies to provide monies for their royal officials. What Parliament never seemed to grasp was that those monies were often used to either force concessions from Crown officials or to render them powerless.[4]

The effectiveness of such practices by colonial assemblies was amply demonstrated by the case of Governor Jonathan Belcher of Massachusetts. In 1732 Belcher reported to the Board of Trade that the Massachusetts Assembly refused to pay soldiers and Crown officials in that colony. "The speech I made at the opening of this session [of the Assembly]," he wrote,

> will show your Lordships what a miserable condition the Province is in for want of the Assembly's making the proper & seasonable supplies of money to the publick Treasury, where there has not been a shilling for nineteen months past, altho' there is now upwards of £40,000 due to the officers & soldiers of the King's forts & garrisons, the Judges, the Secretary of the Province, & other people.[5]

But that was not the extent of Belcher's troubles, for the Assembly wanted the Crown to withdraw instructions conveyed to the Assembly by the royal governor at the same session. Belcher went on to describe the legislature's recalcitrance and the humiliation it caused Crown officials in Massachusetts:

> nor am I yet able to judge whether the Assembly will raise any money before they rise; but as they have, My Lords, taken a very extraordinary step upon His Majesty's royal instructions to me (the 16th & 30th) by addressing His Majesty a third time to withdraw them, and in case His Majesty will not hear them, then their agent is instructed to apply to the House of Commons. This, My Lords, is what I take to be very extraordinary—to complain to His Majesty's dutifull & faithfull Commons of the severity of his Majesty's proceedings with his people here. I believe, I say, this is without precedent. Nor have I ever heard that any of the King's plantations have presum'd upon anything of this nature. Nor is there that I can see any occasion for treating His Majesty so indecently & disrespectfully.[6]

Factionalism

The increasing struggle between the lower houses and royal governors should not be interpreted as the first sign of a growing revolutionary temperament. Nothing could be more inaccurate. The men who inhabited the assemblies were motivated mostly by self-interest. During the eighteenth century the assemblies became playgrounds for the colonial elites: the merchants, planters, land speculators, and others with hopes for profit. Often they were simply jealous of those around the royal governor and wanted to supplant them—in other words, to win patronage for themselves. Often, too, they battled as much with the governor's instructions as with the governor. Colonials wanted to move into an area of manufacturing which was banned, or they wanted paper money printed, or they wanted trade restrictions lifted on certain commodities going certain places, or they wanted lands in the West opened for speculation. To put it another way, the colonial assemblies of the eighteenth century, reflecting the maturing societies of which they were a vital part, were composed of political factions encompassing members of the social and economic elite who sought political power for their own purposes or who reflected serious religious, ethnic, or regional divisions in their colonies.

Massachusetts' assembly was dominated by powerful merchant and agrarian factions who bickered endlessly with each other and especially with the royal governors. For example, Joseph Dudley became royal governor in 1702 and, for a time, he ruled fairly effectively. He built a governing coalition using patronage and the support of Boston merchants. By the end of his governorship, however, his support had evaporated, largely because of the Crown's refusal to support land banks (paper currency issued with land as security) and because Dudley, at the Crown's insistence, asked continually that royal officials, including the governor, be paid a fixed salary. Subsequent governors—William Shute, Samuel Burnet, and Jonathan Belcher—had even less success manipulating the Assembly; Belcher was finally forced to accept defeat on the salary question. He agreed in 1730 that the Assembly could pay the royal governor whatever it wanted, thus legitimizing an important weapon used by the Assembly to gain ascendancy over the governor. Some of the failures of Shute, Burnet, Belcher, and Dudley, however, were compensated for by the successes of William Shirley, royal governor from 1741 to 1757. Shirley, a Massachusetts lawyer, led the opposition to Belcher in the 1730s and managed to get himself named as Belcher's successor. Using patronage and the necessities of a period marked by almost continuous war with the French, Shirley controlled the Assembly and the political apparatus of Massachusetts more completely than any royal governor of the colonial period.[7]

New York was perhaps the most factionally ridden colony of all. There, great "families" contended for the royal governor's favor and for control of the political apparatus. Factional strife began in New York in the 1670s. A "popular" party battled an older, "aristocratic" group until Jacob Leisler's "revolution" and subsequent hanging in 1691 changed the factions into supporters and opponents of the fallen Leisler. The Leislerians formed the "popular" party and division between Leislerian and anti-Leislerians continued for two decades until order finally came to New York politics during the regime of Governor Robert Hunter (1710 to 1720). Forming an alliance with the ambitious Lewis Morris, Hunter controlled the New York Assembly using cronyism, family ties, and patronage as his major weapons. After Hunter, the dominance of Lewis Morris and the Morris family continued until a fierce struggle for control of the Indian trade resulted in victory for another prominent New York family, the DeLanceys.

The DeLanceys formed an alliance with Royal Governor William Cosby (1732 to 1736). They were both challenged by the Morrises and other families—a contest which, incidentally, led to one of the most famous court cases in early American history. In 1734 a newspaperman, John Peter Zenger, was jailed for printing libelous statements about Governor Cosby. At Zenger's trial his lawyer, Andrew Hamilton of Philadelphia, made an impassioned plea for freedom of the press and asked (and received) a verdict of acquittal from a jury—the first time such a case had been tried before a jury. The case has since been hailed as a landmark in our tradition of a free press. Perhaps it was, but at the time it was just another episode of "family" politics. Zenger was backed by Lewis Morris, and his victory was interpreted as a victory for the Morrises. Still, the DeLanceys controlled New York politics until the 1750s when they were successfully challenged by a Presbyterian faction led by William Livingston. While the great families maneuvered and fought, the power of the royal governor slipped badly. It began in the 1730s with Cosby, then accelerated in the 1740s with George Clinton. The main issues were control of the court system and the purse strings of the colony. Governor George Clinton pressed the Crown's prerogative so vehemently during the 1740s that the DeLanceys broke with him and sided with the Assembly. The result was that in the 1740s and 1750s the Assembly asserted its control over New York's financial affairs and most other important matters as well.[8]

Factionalism and feuding between governors and assemblies was not limited to royal colonies. Proprietary colonies had their share of turmoil as well. Pennsylvania was a good example. Early in the colony's history the Quaker leaders divided into a "Proprietor's party," composed mainly of Philadelphia merchants, and a "country party," led by David Lloyd and supported, in part, by wealthy landowners outside Philadelphia. The country faction took control of the lower house of the Pennsylvania Assembly and hammered away at the privileges of the proprietary governor and the various designated agents of the Penn family. By 1750 the factions remained but their composition had changed drastically. Ironically, the "Proprietor's party" contained mainly Anglicans and Presbyterians while the "country party" had become a Quaker bastion. Though the power of the Penn family had been drastically reduced over the years—and the power of the proprietary governor as well—the Quaker opposition continued to decry the despotic behavior of the governor and the proprietary faction, charging that it was the Penn family's intention to "seize power by encroaching on the constitutional representation of the people and by establishing a vast system of patronage."[9]

One exception to this pattern of continuous factional squabbling was Virginia, where the economic climate was not nearly so volatile. Virginia did not completely escape factionalism, for immigrant Scotch-Irish "planters"—most of whom were Presbyterians—and born-again Baptist farmers from the Great Awakening attacked both the Anglican establishment and the Tidewater planters' dominance of political institutions in the years before the American Revolution. Nevertheless, Virginia's political system was controlled by a few hundred men and a solid phalanx of rich families (primarily English in origin) between 1720 and 1760. These men and their families formed a self-styled "aristocracy" based on tobacco and slaves. Their control could be found at all levels of government, from the House of Burgesses to the county courts. They lived in harmony with the royal governors primarily because few of the governors tried to press the Crown's prerogative or interfere with local institutions or the activities of the Burgesses. One historian has remarked that an important reason why Virginia produced so many statesmen of the revolutionary and early federal periods was because of the tremendous experience those men received at all levels of government. Like their English aristocratic counterparts, for them politics was nearly a vocation.[10]

Another exception to the endless factionalism typical of most colonies was New Hampshire, where Governor Benning Wentworth (1741 to 1766) overcame early opposition in the legislature and established complete political control over his colony, thus making him the envy of most royal governors in North America. How Wentworth did this is worth retelling. New Hampshire never developed the agricultural base that was typical of other New England colonies. Instead, its wealth grew from fishing, commerce, and especially lumbering. With its great white pine forests, New Hampshire became an important supplier of timber for the British navy and Massachusetts shipbuilders. Begun as an extension of Massachusetts by Bay Colony merchants, New Hampshire became a royal colony in 1679, although it shared a royal governor with Massachusetts until 1741. After 1679, New Hampshire's political and economic life was heavily influenced by competition between English and Bay Colony merchants. Each group wanted to control New Hampshire's resources, especially the timber.

At the same time, New Hampshire developed its own merchant-entrepreneurs who sought to make fortunes and build careers by creating alliances with either Massachusetts or English mercantile interests. The result was bitter political factionalism from 1680 to 1741. In the 1730s the factions shrunk to two great family interest groups, the Waldrons and the Wentworths. The Waldrons and their supporters were Congregationalists and saw New Hampshire as an extension of Massachusetts. They wanted closer ties to the Bay Colony. The Wentworths were Anglicans who found the cultural heritage of Puritan New England somewhat stultifying. They favored England.

In 1741 the Wentworths won the battle when New Hampshire received its own royal governor, thus severing the last important tie to Massachusetts. Benning Wentworth was named royal governor. For several years the Waldrons continued their opposition and they made numerous attempts to discredit Benning Wentworth and have him removed from office. Unfortunately, the Waldron clan collapsed with the death of its leader, Richard Waldron, Jr. But the Waldrons' demise was not the sole explanation for Benning Wentworth's autocratic control over New Hampshire politics. A more important reason was that the Wentworths gained dominance over New Hampshire's most important resources—timber and the timber trade—through an alliance with a powerful English merchant and politician, John Thomlinson. Thomlinson determined many of the contractors for the Royal Navy and he directed contracts for masts and other naval stores to the Wentworths. That favoritism plus the normal patronage of royal governors cemented the power for Benning Wentworth until his death in 1766 and secured the position of the Wentworth family until the American Revolution.[11]

In the face of all the factionalism and self-interest in colonial politics, the voters generally paid little notice, except in times of crisis. Part of this was due to the importance of local institutions in the affairs of eighteenth-century Anglo-Americans. Following seventeenth-century traditions, eighteenth-century colonials continued to look to and jealously guard the local institutions they had created from English models. Freshly settled areas of New England developed around the town, imitating the pattern established in the first settlements a century earlier. Elsewhere the county prevailed in importance. Pennsylvania, for example, with its many Germans and other non-English, borrowed the English county government of the southern colonies. In Virginia the vestry solidified its position as the center of local life. If there was a significant change in the local government of the eighteenth century, it was not because of the impact of the colonial assembly or the colonial governor but because of the increasing importance of the county-court system. Everywhere, including New England, county courts, with their reliance on English common law, assumed significant roles in governing ordinary citizens as other local institutions became overtaxed by burgeoning populations and more complicated problems. There were other English courts (like admiralty courts and equity courts) also established in the colonies in the eighteenth century, but none matched the importance to common people of county courts. Moreover, with the proliferation of various kinds of courts in the eighteenth century, the figure most distrusted by the middling and lower-class English—the lawyer—began to appear in British America and began, also, to gain a certain amount of legitimacy and respect.[12]

Historians of eighteenth-century Anglo-America sometimes underestimate the significance of local institutions for most Anglo-Americans. They may assume that British America was a little like Latin America where *primate cities* (Potosi, Lima, Havana, Puebla, Mexico City, Rio de Janeiro, Buenos Aires, Caracas, Santiago) were the administrative, political, economic, and cultural centers for vast agricultural and/or mining regions. The primate city totally dominated the surrounding rural areas. Political and administrative decisions radiated out from the city to the countryside. The reverse was never true. The economic life of the province or region depended heavily upon the merchants of the cities and their ability to move raw materials out and to bring finished products in. The great landowners of the countryside maintained homes in the cities. It was a mark of their status and importance to be able to do so. If a landowner could not afford two homes he was labeled a provincial and his influence suffered accordingly. The cultural life of the province, like the political life, was the private domain of the urban center.[13]

British North America never developed primate cities like those which dominated colonial Latin America. True, urban areas such as Boston, New York, Philadelphia, Baltimore, and Charleston grew rapidly in wealth, influence, and importance in the last half of the eighteenth century, but they developed because of trade, not because of their imperial administrative functions or their cultural or political importance. Eighteenth-century British America continued to be a land of farms and hamlets with just seven percent of the population living in communities with more than 2500 inhabitants and only five cities (the ones just mentioned) with populations greater than 10,000. In 1790, Philadelphia, the largest Anglo-American city (population 42,000) was about one-third the size of Mexico City (population 112,926), the largest Latin American urban center. Both cities should be compared to London, the leading metropolis of Europe, which had 550,000 inhabitants in 1700 and 900,000 by 1800.[14]

These facts make it easier to understand how the growing administrative or economic or military demands of the British empire or the factional feuding of the colonial assemblies might have failed to have had much impact upon large segments of the colonial population. For example, we know that Concord, Massachusetts, only a few miles from Boston, was little affected by and was only mildly interested in the tumultuous events of the 1760s and early 1770s which marked the disintegration of the British empire in North America and which were centered, to a great extent, in Boston. Only when war appeared imminent and Concord assumed strategic importance in 1774 and 1775 were the *minutemen* dragged from their local concerns and forced to face issues of life and death.[15]

Localism was a dominant feature of eighteenth-century British America and it was an important reason why many ordinary men and women did not pay too much attention to the constant din of political battle emanating from the colonial governments. Equally important, though, was the way the ordinary voters perceived the functioning of the political processes of which they were small parts. Operating from the notion that they should and were electing their "betters," and that society was meant to be both hierarchical and deferential, they believed that their representatives could conduct politics and government as they saw fit, so long as the interests of the people were served in the end. Historians have probably overstated the degree of deference shown by eighteenth-century Anglo-Americans toward their rulers (we have mentioned already a number of obvious exceptions to the pattern), but it is true that most colonials at least paid lip service to the idea of deferential politics. It was simply more true of some colonies than others. Massachusetts citizens, for example, apparently deferred to their rulers much more than did the more contentious inhabitants of the so-called "land of steady habits," neighboring Connecticut. An important part of an Anglo-American's cultural heritage, deferential politics reflected the traditional dominance of the landed aristocracy and England's class society. But it should be remembered, also, that deference was a prime factor in the stability of the ancient Roman republic, and, by the middle of the eighteenth century, many colonials knew about as much about the dynamics of the great cultures of antiquity as they knew about the reality of life in England.

Another reason for the continued acceptance of deference politics came from the fact that eighteenth-century assemblies and assemblymen had greater claims to legitimacy than even their seventeenth-century counterparts because of a constantly expanding franchise. Although different from colony to colony and region to region, the election process was generally more "democratic" and reflective of popular concerns than anywhere in the world. The best estimates suggest that about 70 percent of all white males could vote, although only about half of those eligible did vote. The reason for the expanded suffrage was primarily economic, not ideological. Colonies continued to require the ownership of property as the prerequisite for voting and they did not significantly increase the amount needed. As the standard of living of all colonists grew in the eighteenth century, more and more white males found that they could meet property qualifications.[16]

Two important results came from the factional strife and the battles between royal governors and assemblies. First, in every colony except New Hampshire, Rhode Island, and Connecticut (the latter two had no royal governors), the power of the governors was severely crippled by 1763. This came about largely because of the policy of salutary neglect and the failure of English officialdom at home to respond adequately to cries for help from beleaguered officials across the seas. Thus, by 1763, colonial assemblies had won enormous new power at the expense of the governors—including control of royal officials' salaries, the prerogatives of the upper houses, the process of appointing officials, and the granting of land. It was a stunning blow to imperial control, and it was high on the list of abuses to be rectified by men like Pitt and Halifax.

Second, in conjunction with the factional battles, there emerged a litany of republican arguments about popular government and arbitrary rule. Though sometimes used to mask the opportunism and greed of individuals and factions, these arguments were more than mere rhetoric. In part they reflected traditional beliefs and concerns of Anglo-Americans: abuses of power, the liberties of Englishmen, government by the consent of the governed, the theory of a compact or contract among the people as the basis for society or government, the idea of mixed government, and the supposed link between Catholicism, monarchy, and tyranny. But colonial arguments also revealed the radicalization of traditional notions of government. Some rather novel ideas emerged, ideas borrowed mainly from English political debates of the first half of the eighteenth century.

The Real Whigs

The most popular English political writers among the colonists were representatives of a faction in England known as the real Whigs.[17] The real Whigs applied arguments germane to both the Whig opposition to James II and the old republican themes of the Civil War era. They had many targets but chief among them were the alleged excesses of the Crown's ministers. The real Whigs embellished older republican notions that liberty was perpetually threatened by executive authority and that excessive power in any one individual or office produced tyranny. Although those ideas had formed part of the basis for the traditional Whig opposition to the Stuarts, the real Whigs gradually shaped them into a theory of conspiracy involving the Hanoverian kings, George I and II, the Crown's ministers, leading members of Parliament, and various economic "interests."

During the 1720s and 1730s the attention of the real Whigs focused upon Sir Robert Walpole, England's first "prime" minister. Some of the real Whigs' fear of Walpole reflected their belief that, by the settlement of 1688, Crown and Parliament were entirely separate organs of government and Parliament was above the Crown. Thus, Walpole's legendary success in manipulating the Commons to support the policies of the Hanoverians not only offended the real Whigs, but it suggested a constitutional crisis. Much of the fear of Walpole, however, reflected a dislike for the venality and greed which seemed to characterize his behavior, that of his supporters, and that of many politicians of that time. The alleged corruption and other excesses of the politicians lowered public esteem for all government officials and for Parliament in particular. J. H. Plumb wrote of Walpole that, for all his greatness, "his imperfections were many and glaring. He loved money; he loved power; he enjoyed adulation and hated criticism."[18] Worse, "his whole manner of life bred detestation wherever he went. He paraded his wealth with ever greater ostentation . . . he gloried in his power, spoke roughly if not ungenerously of others, and let the whole world know that he was master." Such a way of life invited "criticism on a personal level."[19]

Walpole's career, then, Plumb asserted, was marred continually by stories of his high living and the corruption and debauchery of himself, his friends, and England's governing class. Plumb summarized the scene as follows:

> All the opposition Press revelled in portraying the grossness of Walpole's life. . . . His friends did little better; the institutions by which he governed worse. The Court was corrupt, his ministers feather-witted, his Treasury a swindle, his Parliament bought, the Church a political trade. . . . Day after day, week after week, month after month, year after year through the two decades of his ministry this twisted and malicious criticism never ceased: and embedded in the heart of the sludge was a grain of truth. . . .[20]

As a result, Plumb concluded, "public life and the institutions of government were thereby brought into disrepute: by 1734 Parliament had lost much of the respect it had enjoyed in the early years of the century."[21]

Thus, for a variety of reasons—each perhaps reflecting a "grain of truth"—the real Whigs declared that the Crown's ministers conspired with members of Parliament and men of wealth to thwart popular will and rob English citizens of their rights. Even further, the real Whigs insisted that too much power, political or economic, *always* led to corruption unless checked. Inevitably, rulers would scheme to increase their power unless prevented by law and institutions of popular control. The greater power they acquired, the less liberty was enjoyed by the people. Absolute power meant tyranny, for its existence meant the people's descent into bondage.

In a way, the real Whigs described the relationship between liberty and authority as a sliding scale. If political or economic power increased, liberty decreased, and vice versa. For the real Whigs, though, an excess of liberty was always preferable to an excess of power. England's traditional balance of authority as reflected in its mixed constitution of laws, popular liberties, parliamentary sovereignty, and royal power represented the ideal system of government.

The best-known English real-Whig theorists in America were John Trenchard and William Gordon. Their essays, *Cato's Letters* and the *Independent Whig,* were published collectively in many editions between 1721 and 1754 (seven English editions for the former, six for the latter, and American editions in 1724 and 1740). Actually, they attacked much more than just the dangers posed by English politicians or interest groups. They characterized standing armies as instruments of oppression by tyrants, attacked the established church, the dangers of Catholic power and the evil designs of the Pope, and, ironically, the dangers of factions and parties. They were immensely popular in all of the mainland American colonies. Historian Richard Beale Davis, an authority on the reading habits of colonial southerners, finds that Trenchard and Gordon's writings appeared in just about every southern gentleman's library and were far more popular than John Locke's treatises, even though the real Whigs endorsed many Lockeian principles.[22] More importantly, colonials borrowed and used real-Whig arguments in their own political discourse. In fact, the ideology of the real Whigs probably had a greater impact upon Anglo-Americans than upon English people of the same period.

The radicalization of colonial political thinking in the first half of the eighteenth century reflected some colonists' realization that, like it or not, they were being drawn closer to England and Europe. The solitude and autonomy their ancestors had enjoyed was slipping away as the English and colonial economies became interdependent. Anglo-Americans enjoyed their prosperity but, salutary neglect notwithstanding, most cared little for the regulations, the enlarged bureaucracy, and the imperial rivalries that came with it. Simply stated, Britain's growing imperial might only made many Anglo-Americans aware of their own inferiority and dependence. Frequent reminders that they lived to serve the purposes of imperial England made them feel powerless and violated their political, religious, and economic traditions as well as their historic sense of why they had come to the New World. True, they learned to live with their changed circumstances, but few liked them.

The royal governors symbolized both English imperial might and colonial weakness, and Anglo-Americans expressed their irritation over the course of events with frequent outbursts against these Crown officials. We have already noted how mainland colonists reduced the power and effectiveness of most royal governors by 1763. The real-Whig analysis provided a rationale for colonial behavior. Royal governors had, at least in theory, absolute power over Anglo-Americans, greater than the Crown had ever enjoyed in England. The only checks on their power were those exerted by their employers. Their subjects had none. That situation angered colonists who had left England or Europe to escape arbitrary power, who had been lured to America with promises of self-rule, economic opportunity, and religious freedom, and who had enjoyed varying degrees of autonomy for generations.

Naturally, many colonists asked how they had arrived at such a state of affairs. The real Whigs provided an answer, and it was one which spoke directly to the colonists' own cherished traditions of political and religious opposition. Colonial polemicists interpreted real Whiggery to mean that royal governors represented a government no longer conforming to the English constitution. Crown and Parliament were now one—or nearly so—and the breakdown of the traditional distance between the two bodies meant that nothing stood in the way of an aggressive monarch's quest for power at popular expense. The results of the Glorious Revolution of 1688 had been undermined and overturned. The real Whigs told colonials weaned on theories of Stuart excess that the Hanoverians had achieved what the Stuarts had not. Therefore, what were royal governors but agents of tyranny? Their arbitrary decisions simply indicated the British government's waning concern for liberty and representative government.

John Peter Zenger turned the logic and the arguments of both the real Whigs and John Locke on the royal governor of New York, William Cosby, and his supporters in the New York Assembly. Reprinting *Cato's Letters,* Zenger also wrote a series of fiery editorials in which he branded Cosby a tyrant and, by implication, an agent of a despotic English government. "They (the people of the city and province of New York) think, as matters now stand," he wrote in 1734, "that their LIBERTIES and PROPERTIES are precarious, and that SLAVERY is like to be entailed on them and their posterity if some past things be not amended."[23] Zenger quoted the remarks of a man who had fled to Pennsylvania to escape Cosby's administration:

> I think the law itself is at an end; We (the people of New York) see Men's deeds destroyed, judges arbitrarily displaced, new courts erected without consent of the legislature, by which it seems to me trials by juries are taken away when a governor pleases; men of known estates denied their votes contrary to the received practice, the best expositor of any law: Who is then in that province (New York) that call anything his own, or enjoy any liberty longer than those in the administration will condescend to let them do it? For which reason I have left it (New York), as I believe more will.[24]

Zenger was tried for libel and acquitted, "upon which," he wrote later, "there were three huzzas in the hall which was crowded with people."[25] His acquittal may have been a victory for one faction over another in New York politics, but it also demonstrated the extent to which republican sympathies pervaded the body politic of the colony.

COLONIAL NEWSPAPERS AND WHIG IDEOLOGY

Far different from modern newspapers, colonial papers were small and usually contained whatever the editor wanted to print. There was, as we have seen, no tradition of a free press or legal guarantees thereof. In addition, editors like Zenger typically used their papers to support their own religious and political biases. No accepted codes of ethical behavior among journalists and no standards of fair and unbiased reporting existed. Editors printed what they thought they could get away with. They borrowed heavily from each other and from English newspapers and they rarely worried about the accuracy of what they printed. Usually, they prefaced a distant story with "we have heard . . . ," or "news has reached us that . . . ," or "it is reported that . . . ." Articles which were signed often bore aliases, usually classical figures like Cato, or pseudoclassical names like Britannicus or Americus. Because newspapers depended upon their subscribers, not advertisers, for support they tried to publish what their subscribers wanted to read and thus, to some extent, reflected popular opinion. It is estimated that, by the time of the American Revolution, at least one in four Anglo-Americans read a newspaper on a regular basis.[26]

The first paper, the *Boston News-Letter,* was founded by John Campbell in 1704. Soon every city had at least one newspaper and, by 1763, twenty-three were circulating in the colonies. They averaged about 500 subscribers per paper, but single issues passed through many hands. All operated within an uncertain framework of legal restrictions. Some papers supported royal government or the administration of a proprietor; others opposed them, at least from time to time. Some were published by bona fide eccentrics—like Andrew Bradford of Philadelphia who published the *American Weekly Mercury.* Others were edited and published by men whose names became symbols of early American greatness, like Benjamin Franklin and John Peter Zenger. Some served as the mouthpieces for factions or families. Others were fiercely independent. All were Protestant, although they reflected a variety of religious persuasions like Anglicanism, Presbyterianism, or Congregationalism. At least one German-language paper was printed.

Ironically, considering the distances between cities, the difficulties of communication, the lack of "journalism schools" to produce editors and standards of craftsmanship, and the variety of political and religious views held by editors, the newspapers published remarkably similar material. The fact that they borrowed from each other or from English papers was only a partial explanation. Apparently their readers had quite similar tastes. The newspapers usually contained one or two pages of opinion, two to four pages of foreign and domestic news, and one page of advertisements. Like Zenger, most editors at one time or another printed *Cato's Letters.* They also published letters for and against the opinions of Trenchard and Gordon, usually written by friends of the editors. Most letters spoke favorably of Cato and lauded his sentiments, among which was a strong argument for a free press. Not all the editors went as far as Zenger in openly using real-Whig arguments to attack a royal official, but usually they did not have to. Their readers knew what was intended.

Andrew Bradford started his paper in Philadelphia about the same time *Cato's Letters* were appearing in England. Bradford was an Anglican and a strong supporter of the Proprietor's party in Pennsylvania. In addition, he had strong ties with the Quaker establishment in Philadelphia. His brother, William Bradford, started a paper in New York City and became a spokesman for the Cosby regime in its later battle with Zenger. Thus, for various reasons, Andrew Bradford was no enemy of imperial government—at least not publicly. And yet, within a year of the first English edition of *Cato's Letters,* Andrew Bradford began printing the letters in his *American Weekly Mercury.* He continued at regular intervals for the next few years, publishing several local responses to Cato as well. Most were favorable. "Americo-Britanus" wrote in May, 1722, that:

> You [Andrew Bradford] have obliged these Western Parts of the World with several letters from Cato, and we have found them worthy of that name, since they give us the true Notions of Liberty, and the Policy of a free Government, both in its Freedom and particular restraints, such a Government as encourages Virtue, depresses Vice, and punishes Tyranny and bad rule in Magistracy. From these Hints we find it easy to symbolize, to our Sorrow, many Characters of men by whom Rome lost her Freedom, and can find a Triumviri ruling in some parts of this English Empire, with as powerful a Nod as ever that mischievous Number did in that once flourishing Empire of the Romans. And since you have thus gratified us with CATO's Notions, I beg You'd oblige us with the Opinion of PLATO too, in the following Letter transcribed verbatum from the Author.[27]

"Plato's" letter was published in the same issue. Both Cato and Plato expressed some traditional concerns of republicans. While Cato warned free people to guard their liberties against the encroachments of tyrants and to watch for corruption and venality among their rulers, Plato cautioned readers of the *American Weekly Mercury* not to defer blindly to leaders just because they appeared wise and held positions of importance. Plato introduced "Lord Plausible" who was assumed to be wise because of his eloquent, "lofty" language, the "sublime" nature of his "Gate" and his "Words," and the "unrelenting Gravity in his Looks." Lord Plausible, Plato went on, grew "important without suffering a Bit in his Character for his natural Shallowness and acquir'd Folly, unseen by the Bulk of his Party, who think him an Oracle . . . ." Following such a man, Plato concluded, led to the ruin of all:

> And this is what Men frequently get by trusting more to the Understanding of others than to their own, though often the better of the two; and therefore we find in many Instances, that Fools mislead and govern Men of Sense. In Things where Men know nothing, they are apt to think that others know more than they, and so blindly trust to bold Pretensions; and here is the great Cause and first Rise of Sharpers and Bubbles of all Denominations, from Demagogues and their Followers down to Mountebanks and their Mobs.[28]

While *Cato's Letters* provided fascinating reading for the subscribers to most early newspapers, the foreign reports were equally interesting and revealing. For the most part, the colonial newspapers—taking material mainly from English papers—chronicled the unending Catholic "conspiracy" against freedom-loving, peace-loving Protestants. The stories were sometimes factual—such as the plight of German Protestants in the Palatinate—and sometimes sensational—such as the discovery of a secret training spot for nuns and priests in some remote part of England and the revelations of what went on inside. They even bordered on the ludicrous, such as the report of a secret memorandum from the Pope to a certain King or Cardinal proving the Pope's involvement in an international conspiracy. Nevertheless, the stories consistently linked Catholicism with absolutism (monarchy) and civil and religious oppression. The Wars for Empire between England, France, Spain, and a host of other European nations were portrayed as essentially religious wars which would determine the fates of both the Protestant religion and free government. Plots against England—from both within and without—were being hatched and uncovered constantly.[29]

With that kind of foreign news, it is easy to understand why *Cato's Letters,* with their explicit link between Catholicism, the institution of monarchy, and abuses of power by rulers would be printed by Anglo-American editors. They fit well with the majority of items listed as foreign news. Taken together, the newspapers of early America charted the progress of free Protestant peoples in a world menaced by Catholicism and its byproduct, absolutism. Aside from the historic revelations of the pro-Catholic feelings of several of the Stuarts, though, the connections between Catholicism, Walpole, tyranny, and English royal governors were never fully explained. Were the Hanoverians tools of the Catholic conspiracy? Was English monarchy doomed because of the assumed relationship between Catholicism and monarchy? Was the deterioration of the English Constitution described by the real Whigs due either directly or indirectly to Catholic subversion? Was a royal governor like Cosby an unknowing agent of the Pope? Would opposition to a Cosby somehow cripple papal designs? If Anglo-American newspaper editors or their readers answered "yes" to any or all of these questions, they never said so in public, at least not before 1763. But it seems obvious, at least from one important source of American opinion, that colonials saw world events through an anti-Catholic prism. Many of them adopted the republican radicalism of the real Whigs not only because of the threat of the royal governors' powers to their heritage of self-rule but, possibly, because it was a Protestant ideology that viewed monarchy and its representatives as tools of Catholicism. Thus, the liberty-versus-tyranny theme (introduced in Chapter five) used by many later generations of American writers—including those of the revolutionary era—to explain the peculiar evolution of British North America was as old as the colonies themselves. As our Bicentennial speaker in Chapter six suggested, Anglo-American political philosophy reflected a thoroughly Protestant people.

10

Toward a Protestant Pattern of Culture: Religion and Society

The preceding chapters have related how eighteenth-century Anglo-America experienced a dramatic shift in its relationship to England, the rapid growth of its economy and population, and the maturation of its political institutions. As we see in this chapter, some equally significant changes occurred in the area of Anglo-American religion and culture as well. During the eighteenth century, the colonies witnessed a resurgence of religiosity and a phenomenal increase in church membership. At the same time, however, the Protestant roots of Anglo-American culture nourished an increasingly secular society. Finally, for really the first time, colonial literary, artistic, and other cultural activities achieved a style and character that looked distinctly American.

Although a great many factors led to these developments, two forces—the Great Awakening and the Enlightenment—exerted perhaps the greatest influences upon the thoughts and attitudes of eighteenth-century Anglo-Americans. In some respects these two movements struck very different chords. The Awakening sparked a revival of spirituality and faith, the Enlightenment a stimulation of human intellect. The Awakening stressed the experiential, the Enlightenment the rational. The Awakening exalted the power of God, the Enlightenment the potential of man. The Awakening thrived most among the lower and lower-middle classes; the Enlightenment stirred the colonial elite and well-to-do. But in other respects, the movements were strangely similar. Both drew their origins and inspiration from Europe. Both sought harmony between people but aroused conflict. Both challenged existing institutions and looked for a better, more ideal society. Both appealed to the individualistic strain within Anglo-American culture. Above all, despite the different ideas and directions they provoked, both the Great Awakening and the Enlightenment fostered notions about God, man, and society that reinforced America's peculiar Protestant view of its past and future. That fact, in and of itself, contributed to the colonial drive toward independence in the 1770s.

THE CRISIS OF THE EIGHTEENTH CENTURY: ANGLO-AMERICAN RELIGION

In the earlier discussion of religion in Anglo-America, it was argued that the strongly "Protestant" heritage of the early settlers formed a central element of Anglo-American culture. Specifically, three strands of Protestant thought were identified: opposition, authority, and conscience. The very nature of Protestantism (that is, its "protest" of certain Catholic practices), coupled with the importance the movement placed upon millenarian ideas, produced a strong sense of being in opposition, of being Christians oppressed and threatened by Antichrist's—that is, Catholic—forces. Second, Protestantism's attack upon the Catholic Church implicitly challenged the established political as well as religious authority of European society. Finally, even as Protestants sought to substitute their own version of a pure church for the Catholic one, their simultaneous exaltation of conscience as the final judge of faith and behavior undermined the concept of the institutional church. Further, it caused the Protestant movement to splinter and led some to a religious justification for political and social revolution. By the end of the seventeenth century, the autonomous tendency inherent in Protestantism became the dominant element within Anglo-American religion. Although the inpulse for religious conformity led to the creation of established churches within the colonies, even in New England they remained weak and only marginally effective in controlling the practices and behavior of church members, let alone the rest of society.

By 1700, many colonial churches felt a deep sense of crisis. They saw that they did not function as their European counterparts, but they did not know precisely what their role should be. As early as the midseventeenth century, laypeople and clergy had become acutely aware of the church's ineffectiveness in maintaining religious orthodoxy. Despite expressed, shared concern over religious purity, colonial churches generally went their own separate ways in matters of church practice and even doctrine. In addition, the churches seemed less and less able to uphold high moral standards throughout the community. Church leaders worried that their people had grown lax and lost the religious zeal and purpose of the early founders. Finally, as much as anything, some colonial churches saw their failure to keep membership abreast of population growth. Once among the greatest powers within the community, their influence had shriveled along with their relative numbers.

Such concerns were particularly keen in New England. From 1660 to 1700 meetinghouses all over New England echoed the sentiments of ministers and magistrates convinced of New England's impending demise. Clergyman Michael Wigglesworth described just that in his poem, *God's Controversy with New England* (1662):

Ah, dear New England; dearest to me;
  Which unto God hath hitherto been dear,
And may be still more dear than formerly,
  If to his voice thou wilt incline thine ear.
Consider well and wisely what the rod,
  Wherewith thou art from year to year chastized,
Instructeth thee, Repent, and turn to God,
  Who will not have his nurture despised . . . .[1]

Other colonials worried that the simple, virtuous life of the early settlers had been lost to later generations seduced by the lure of wealth. In *New England's Crisis* (1676), Benjamin Thompson, another chronicler of decay and decline, mournfully compared the old ways with the new:

Let this dear Lord the sad conclusion be
Of poor New-Englands dismal tragedy:
Let not the glory of thy former work
Blasphemed be by pagan Jew or Turk:
But in its funeral ashes write thy Name
So fair all Nations may expound the same:
Out of her ashes let a Phoenix rise
That may outshine the first and be more wise.[2]

Many clergy and laypeople grew convinced that society was heading quickly toward unbridled individualism and the pursuit of wealth for its own sake. They responded with a litany of condemnation. But even at the beginning of settlement, hard work and financial success had never been condemned in themselves, so long as they were pursued in a proper manner. A society based upon wealth, colonists had always believed, was pleasing to God if that wealth was achieved and used for godly purposes. No less a figure than Boston's famous clergyman, Cotton Mather, sounded the Anglo-American notes of optimism about the compatible relationship between a Christian's spiritual duty and his earthly "calling" in 1701:

There are *Two Callings* to be minded by *all Christians,* Every Christian hath a *General Calling*; Which is to Serve the Lord Jesus Christ, and Save his own Soul . . . . But then, every Christian hath also a *Personal Calling,* or a certain *Particular Employment,* by which his *Usefulness* in his Neighborhood, is distinguished. God hath made man a *Sociable* Creature. *We* expect Ben[e]fits from *Human Society.* It is but equal, that *Human Society* should Receive Benefits From us . . . .

A Christian, at his *Two Callings,* Is a man in a Boat, Rowing for Heaven; the *House* which our Heavenly Father hath intended for us. If he mind but one of his *Callings,* be it which it will, he pulls the *Oar,* but *on one side* of the Boat, and will make but a poor dispatch to the Shoar of Eternal Blessedness. It is not only necessary, that a Christian should follow his *General Calling*; it is of necessity, that he follow his *Personal Calling,* too.[3]

Further, Mather not only recognized the importance of the Christian's daily work activity, but he also encouraged the virtuous Christian to seek material success. "I tell you," he wrote,

> With *Diligence* a man may do marvellous things. *Young* man, *Work hard* while you are *Young*; You'll Reap the Effects of it when you are *Old. Yea,* How can you ordinarily Enjoy any Rest at *Night,* if you have not been well at Work in the *Day*? Let your *Business* Engross the *most* of your Time.[4]

Even though clergymen like Mather endorsed hard work and economic prosperity, once settled in America some Protestants grew ill at ease with even the limited material success they achieved, simply because harmonizing individual and group goals was easier in theory than it was in practice. John Winthrop, Governor of Massachusetts, warned "that the care of the public must over-sway all private respect." Various colonies created laws regulating economic activity. In 1676, for example, Connecticut followed the example of other colonies by passing statutes regulating wages and prices. The Connecticut assembly cautioned "all tradesmen and laborers to consider the religious end of their callings, which is that receiving such moderate profit as may enable them to serve God and their neighbors with their arts and trades comfortably." The Assembly further admonished the colonists not to "enrich themselves suddenly and inordinately (by oppressing prices and wages to the impoverishing of their neighbors and rendering them in great measure incapable of convenient subsistence). . . ."[5] Especially after 1660, numerous clergymen railed against greed and material excess and condemned the "worldliness" of the people and their excessive selfishness. Still, like Cotton Mather, most colonists viewed work as an imperative for a Christian and wealth as its just reward. They too admonished the Christian that "when you follow your business, have your dependence on God for the succeeding of it."[6] In other words, to Mather and his fellow colonists, a Christian's work was acceptable and pleasing to God when it followed certain moral precepts. Further, they believed such work would be rewarded with success. But whether a Christian achieved material success or not, the decision was God's, not his.

That position was repeated in a somewhat different form by Benjamin Franklin. Franklin was no doctrinaire Protestant, but he came from a Calvinist background, and his famous maxims for material success contained in his *Advice to a Young Tradesman, Poor Richard's Almanac,* and *Autobiography* did not differ fundamentally from Mather's. A man was meant to work hard and to succeed. But for Franklin, as well as for Mather, there was a moral—as well as immoral—road to success. "Industry" and "frugality" stood as prominent Franklinian virtues; but so did the welfare of the community. Franklin, too, warned against excessive pride, conspicuous consumption, and hedonism. Above all, like Mather, Franklin cautioned the "young tradesman" that God, not man, would determine his success or failure; and that determination would be based on the tradesman's moral and spiritual rectitude:

> He that gets all he can honestly, and saves all he gets (necessary Expences excepted) will certainly become RICH; If that Being who governs the World, to whom all should look for a Blessing on their honest Endeavours, doth not in His wise Providence otherwise determine.[7]

Cotton Mather and Benjamin Franklin are rarely linked together, but in the area of work and wealth they were much closer than what is generally believed.

Eighteenth-century colonial Protestants, like their seventeenth-century predecessors, never condemned wealth per se, for in so doing they would have condemned their own mission into the American wilderness. Nor did they create an unbridgeable chasm between religious idealism and material success. What they did establish was a moral and immoral way to achieve wealth. The latter formed the heart of a secular, materialistic, "worldly" society: where men sought their own ends with little or no regard for the welfare of the community; where men wallowed in vulgar displays of wealth; where men took pride in their own accomplishments without recognizing their debt to a higher power; where men, in the name of business, cheated for an extra shilling; where men inherited wealth and then wasted it in idle pleasure. That was *corruption* and a debasement of God's charge to follow a general and personal calling. As many Anglo-American Protestants looked around them in the eighteenth century, they saw far more of the immoral than the moral society envisioned by Franklin and Mather.

By the early 1700s several additional developments increased anxiety among the Protestant churches of America. One was the success of the Counter-Reformation in previously Protestant areas of Europe. The resurgence of Catholicism in Europe fired the already strong millenarian sense among colonials that they were living in the last days. Certain of their identity as God's chosen remnant, they felt besieged by the French and Spanish forces around them and they feared a Catholic triumph in Anglo-America. Perhaps, if the religious decline they perceived continued unhalted, the colonies would fail in their mission and succumb to Antichrist.

Finally, Anglo-American churches had to contend with the influx of representatives from just about every Protestant religious persuasion in western Europe and also with religious toleration officially sanctioned by England's Parliament in 1689. Toleration, plus the arrival of thousands of non-English into the colonies, weakened the position of the already-wavering established churches in Anglo-America. The non-English flooded unsettled regions of the seaboard colonies, pushing the line of white settlement farther and farther west into the mountains. Religious and ethnic groups who had once lived in peaceful isolation now had to contend with newcomers in their midst. The Congregationalists of Massachusetts and Connecticut, as well as the Anglicans of Virginia, faced growing numbers of dissenters in their areas. The new arrivals clamored for public recognition, demanded tax revenues for ministerial or building maintenance, and quietly won converts away from the established churches.[8]

Probably more than any other factor, the tremendous influx of non-English immigrants into the colonies during the eighteenth century deepened the sense of crisis among Anglo-America's churches. The wave of immigration had an especially strong negative impact upon Congregationalism—the church system which was probably the most significant legacy of seventeenth century Anglo-American Puritanism. New arrivals, who held religious beliefs different from Congregationalists, were little attracted to their churches. Instead, the newcomers created rival, competing religious institutions that succeeded in drawing members away from the Congregationalists. Still, Congregationalism remained the most populous Protestant group in the colonies during the mideighteenth century, and it even experienced significant growth from natural increase. Understandably, Congregationalists were concentrated almost entirely in New England, with a few churches in South Carolina and New Jersey. Numerically, Congregationalists had formed sixty-two churches by 1650, 465 by 1750, and over 700 by 1775. Although this was seemingly a dramatic increase, their numbers actually declined in comparison with the growth of the colonial population as a whole.

The second largest group of Protestants in the colonies by the time of the American Revolution was the Presbyterians. During the seventeenth century, Presbyterian numbers had remained extremely small. Their growth during the eighteenth century was attributable almost solely to the tremendous influx of Scotch-Irish into North America. In 1660, for example, less than a dozen churches existed. By 1750, their numbers had expanded to 233; by 1775, to 450. The churches were organized primarily in Pennsylvania, New Jersey, New York, and Delaware—the colonies which benefited most from eighteenth-century immigration. Lesser numbers of Presbyterian churches existed in Virginia, Maryland, and South Carolina, with still fewer in Massachusetts, New Hampshire, Connecticut, and Maine.

Another Protestant faith that increased dramatically because of eighteenth-century immigration was the German Lutheran church. German Lutherans settled primarily in Pennsylvania, where in 1748 Henry Muhlenberg organized the first Lutheran synod in America. But Lutherans also migrated in substantial numbers to New York, New Jersey, and to a lesser extent to South Carolina, Virginia, Delaware, and Maryland. From no churches in the seventeenth century, German Lutheranism established 138 churches by 1750, and 225 by 1775.

An equally potent force in Pennsylvania was, of course, Quakerism. A negligible group until after the 1680s (only one church had organized by 1650), Quaker migration during the eighteenth century was so rapid that by 1770 Pennsylvania alone had over sixty meetinghouses, with about 250 in the colonies by 1750. One of the most noted of all Quaker historians, Rufus M. Jones, estimated that the southern colonies had perhaps 11,000 to 13,000 Quakers by the 1770s. All total, probably as many as 40,000 to 50,000 Quakers lived in the colonies by the late eighteenth century.

The last significant elements within colonial Protestantism to increase greatly as a result of European immigration were the reformed churches of Germany and Holland, labeled "reformed" because of their Calvinist roots. No German Reformed churches even existed in Anglo-America until around 1720, when perhaps a half dozen were formed. By 1750, however, there were about ninety, and by 1775 more than 175. The German Reformed church settled predominantly in Pennsylvania, but a few churches were also organized in New York, New Jersey, Maryland, Virginia, and South Carolina. The Dutch Reformed church had an earlier history, arriving in the colonies with the Dutch settlements at New Amsterdam. But in 1659 only three churches could be found. This situation changed considerably in the eighteenth century. By 1700 twenty-six churches had been formed; by 1750 there were seventy-nine, and by 1775 over 100. Not surprisingly, the Dutch heritage in New York induced the new wave of Dutch immigrants to settle there primarily, with a substantial number also in New Jersey, and some in Pennsylvania. Few Dutch Reformed strayed beyond the middle colonies. In passing, the fate of the French Reformed church (the Huguenots) should also be mentioned. Boasting of fifteen churches in 1700, this group declined to less than half that number by 1750. They survived in New York City and Charlestown.[9]

Although the influx of new immigrants produced phenomenal growth of their respective religious persuasions, that development was not the only one to have a significant impact upon the religious life of the colonies. Under the impetus of the Society for the Propagation of the Gospel in Foreign Parts (SPG), Anglicanism witnessed truly spectacular growth during the eighteenth century. From only thirty-one churches in 1650, the English state church organized 289 parishes by 1750. Writing about the impact of the SPG in South Carolina around 1730, David Humphreys observed that "tho' there was scarce any Face of the Church of England in this Province, when this Society was first established, there have been 13 Churches, and 4 Chapels of Ease since built . . . ."[10] Humphrey's comment could well have been applied to many of the other colonies too. By 1760 there were around 300 Anglican churches in the colonies, and by 1775 almost 400. Virginia and Maryland experienced most of the growth; but Anglican numbers also rose in New York, New Jersey, Pennsylvania, Delaware, and South Carolina. Largely due to the missionary activities of the SPG, Anglicanism even made inroads in New England. Connecticut, for example, had no Anglican Church until 1724, but by 1776 it boasted of thirty-seven. By the time of the Revolution, Rhode Island had seven churches, New Hampshire also seven, Maine three, and Massachusetts twenty-two.[11]

Baptists represented another segment of Protestantism that rose from obscurity in the seventeenth century to prominence in the eighteenth century. In 1660 one could find only four Baptist churches in the colonies, all of them in Rhode Island. By 1750 the number had increased to 132, and fifteen years later it had risen to 425. Although Baptists found a welcome reception in Pennsylvania and Rhode Island, they also experienced some success in New Jersey, Connecticut, Massachusetts, and North Carolina.

Although we have stressed the Protestant character of Anglo-America and the strong anti-Catholic bias there, the small but significant growth of the Catholic church should be mentioned. In 1650 six Catholic churches—all in Maryland—had been formed. By 1750 they numbered thirty, and by 1775 about fifty. The increase in Catholic churches was due primarily to the immigration of some Catholic Irish and Germans during the eighteenth century. In part because of their unpopularity, these Catholics settled in Maryland and Pennsylvania, the two most tolerant colonies.[12]

The phenomenal growth of new Protestant groups put the established churches on the defensive, and by the early eighteenth century an atmosphere of hostility and distrust began to develop. From being the sole guarantor of public morality and social stability, the established churches instead became fierce competitors with other religious bodies for social position and membership. An aggressive combativeness began to appear among the churches which had not existed before. This, coupled with secularism and materialism, expanding Catholicism, toleration, and a militant Anglicanism, created a sense of spiritual and social crisis among Anglo-America's Protestant majority that helped spur a movement that would become known as the Great Awakening.

THE GREAT AWAKENING

The Great Awakening was born out of imported evangelical movements that first took root in England and Germany. The term *Great Awakening* aptly described the movement. Ministerially inspired, it sought to counter both materialism and secularism. Moreover, it tried to mitigate the ecclesiastical and doctrinal arguments separating Protestants by returning them to the basic dilemma posed by John Calvin two centuries earlier: the sinful nature of humanity, the awesome majesty of God, and people's inability to save themselves. The movement fostered an "awakening" of the Spirit of God in its participants. To the observer, it was an awakening of men and women reared in the Calvinist tradition to the central truth of that tradition—that individuals must prostrate themselves before an angry God, admit their sinfulness and inadequacy, and hope for the free gift of grace. "O sinner," went the typical refrain of the time,

> Consider the fearful danger you are in: it is a great furnace of wrath, a wide and bottomless pit, full of the fire of wrath, that you are held over in the hand of God, whose wrath is provoked and incensed as much against you, as against many of the damned in hell. You hang by a slender thread, with the flames of divine wrath flashing about it, and ready every moment to singe it, and burn it asunder; and you have no interest in any Mediator, and nothing to lay hold of to save yourself, nothing to keep off the flames of wrath, nothing of your own, nothing that you ever have done, nothing that you can do to induce God to spare you one moment.[13]

Awakeners criticized both the materialism and secularism of contemporary culture. At the same time, they attacked what they considered the "formalism" of many churches and church members—an emphasis upon outward conformity to God's teachings rather than upon spiritual regeneration. They also decried the growing tendency among some Protestants to portray God as a reasonable being who behaved in a way intelligible to people as well as the tendency to describe the path to salvation as smooth and relatively effortless. To such "rationalist" arguments, the Awakener declared that God's will could be understood through the heart and soul alone, not through the mind. Sinners could only prostrate themselves before God, admit their worthlessness, ask for forgiveness, and pray for the "blinding light" of grace.

In an age when men and women—buoyed by the prospect of wealth, status, and a far better life than that enjoyed by any of their ancestors—sought to elevate the worth of man and to extol human accomplishments, the Awakener tried to deflate the bubble of pride which everywhere seemed bent upon destroying and denying the will of God. Many Awakeners were millennially inspired—that is, they believed that the Awakening marked the imminent reign of Christ on earth and the last great struggle between Christ and the Antichristian forces of evil (associated with the Pope). But whatever their sources of inspiration, Awakeners found many willing listeners all over Anglo-America.

Although the Awakening had its greatest impact in the rural areas of New England, Virginia, Pennsylvania, and New York, its message was carried to the cities by famed "evangelists" such as the Englishman, George Whitefield. All in all, tens of thousands of colonists, both English and non-English, were converted or "born again" between 1720 and 1780. The Great Awakening introduced to the American scene the "hell-fire" sermon, the traveling preacher or evangelist, the "revival," and mass conversions. It lacked the camp-meeting atmosphere of later revivals; but because it tended to emphasize the quick conversion, it became associated with all sorts of bizarre and often immoral behavior by those supposedly undergoing a spiritual transformation.

Effects of the Awakening

The Great Awakening had profound effects on both religion and society in Anglo-America. In many areas it revitalized public and private morality and intensified religious zeal when they seemed to be lagging. Reflecting on the course of revivalism in Northampton, Massachusetts, Jonathan Edwards, perhaps the most famous colonial evangelical of all, remarked approvingly in 1743:

> Even since the great Work of God that was wrought here about nine Years ago, there has been a great abiding Alteration in this Town in many Respects. There has been vastly more Religion kept up in the Town, among all Sorts of Persons, in religious Exercises and in common Conversation, than used to be before. There has remained a more general Seriousness and Decency in attending the public Worship. There has been a very great Alteration among the Youth of the Town, with respect to revelling, frolicking, profane and unclean conversation, and lewd Songs: Instances of Fornication have been very rare: There has also been a great Alteration among both old and young with Respect to Tavern-haunting. I suppose the Town has been in no Measure so free of Vice in these Respects, for any long Time together, for this sixty Years, as it has been this nine Years past.[14]

Names such as Edwards (a Congregationalist), Gilbert Tennent of New Jersey (a Presbyterian), Theodore Freylinghuysen of New York (a Dutch Reformed), and Samuel Davies of Virginia (a Presbyterian) became synonymous with evangelicalism and revivalism. These ministers and many like them wrought thousands of conversions among church members and nonmembers alike all over the colonies. In the process they made revivalism and the evangelical spirit permanent and perhaps dominant parts of the Protestant tradition in America. They gave the churches a means to compete with each other for members and influence, and enhanced their roles as leaders against evil and corruption in society.

But the immediate effect of the Awakening was to create divisiveness in both churches and society. Although partly ecumenical in outlook, the movement had an equally strong internal thrust, aimed at reforming the error and corruption within the churches. Its techniques and achievements raised controversy that spread beyond ministers to churches and towns. New Lights or New Sides (supporters of the Awakening) battled Old Lights or Old Sides (opponents) in nearly every colony. The result was a permanent schism in American Protestantism. Henceforth, evangelicals would uphold a religion "of the heart" and reject attempts to maintain doctrinal precision, ceremony in church services, or reason as the guide to God's will. Opponents of the Awakening would define their own positions less from a sense of traditional beliefs and practices and more from a hatred of the Awakening and what they saw as its excesses.

Borrowing from the Enlightenment of the eighteenth century, many opponents of the Awakening argued for reason as a guide to Divine Will and human nature. Charles Chauncey, the minister of Boston's First Congregational Church—the church of John Winthrop and John Cotton—became a bitter opponent of the

Awakening and an outspoken advocate of rationalism. In 1742, Chauncey described the Awakening and its character in the following words:

> For my self, I am among those who are clearly in the Opinion, that there never was such a Spirit as Superstition and Enthusiasm reigning in the Land before; never such gross Disorders and bare-faced Affronts to common Decency; never such scandalous Reproaches on the Blessed Spirit, making Him the author of the greatest Irregularities and Confusions. Yet, I am of the Opinion also, that the Appearances among us (so much out of the ordinary Way, and so unaccountable to persons not acquainted with the History of the World) have been the Means of awakening the Attention of many; and a good Number, I hope, have settled into a truly Christian Temper. Tho' I must add, at the same time, that I am far from thinking, that the Appearance, in general, is any other than the effect of enthusiastick Heat.[15]

For Chauncey and many others, the Spirit of God did not work instantaneous conversions or change lives in a matter of moments. It did not cause moaning, shrieking, writhing, fits, or visions. Conversion was a slow process with discernible steps. God was benevolent and His universe reflected harmony and balance, not whimsy and caprice. To place distance between himself and the Awakeners, Chauncey and his supporters attacked the methods of Edwards, the Tennents, and others. They condemned the "hell-fire" Awakeners preached and the conversions they produced. In the process Chauncey and others of like persuasion began a tradition of rationalism in religion which would lead to the Unitarianism of a century later.

The divisions created between supporters and opponents of the Awakening became so bitter and so fundamental that the future pluralistic character of American religious life was guaranteed. In New England, particularly, a common Calvinist theological tradition was torn to shreds by a continuing debate between rationalists and disciples of Jonathan Edwards known as "New Divinity" men. Other aspects of Protestantism's American establishment crumbled as well. The Awakening produced a bewildering array of "separatist" groups, which together with the influx of non-English Protestants left many colonial churches in shambles. The Awakening forced toleration upon Anglo-Americans in a way that moved against the mainstream of their religious heritage. Furthermore, each of the new separatist groups formed by the Awakening declared its own inherent righteousness, just as it condemned the imperfections of its rivals. That destroyed the integrity and autonomy of many congregations as well as the notion of a collective conscience. From that point onward, conscience became more and more an individualized, uniquely personal set of moral precepts. At the institutional level, those religious groups that survived the Awakening and prospered did so by turning more and more to a hierarchical structure of governance and leadership above the congregation, looking toward the Protestant denominationalism of the nineteenth century. The Protestant groups that continued to stress congregational autonomy—such as the Congregationalists and the Quakers—began to decline in importance in American religious life.

Finally, the Great Awakening contributed to the development of some important and sizable divisions in other areas of Anglo-American society as well. While representing all classes and regions of Anglo-America, the Awakening, nevertheless, tended to win the support of western agricultural areas composed of the middle or lower social and economic groups. Sneered at by the movers and shakers of their time, the Awakened tended to adopt fairly hostile attitudes toward persons in authority. Moreover, the struggles the Awakening fostered not only irreparably fragmented towns and churches, but also divided colonists over political and economic issues as well. Tiny Connecticut's development in the mideighteenth century, for example, was dominated by the furor over the Awakening. In the midst of rapid economic expansion, land speculators tended to coalesce into Old Light and New Light factions and to take their battles into the courts and the colonial assembly. By the 1770s the New Lights had emerged victorious and vanquished their opponents.

In the southern colonies, the struggles over the Awakening proved just as serious and damaging to the social and political fabric. In Virginia, for example, New Light Presbyterians, relying heavily on recent Scotch-Irish immigrants and led by the indefatigible Samuel Davies, attacked the Anglican establishment and won many converts away from the established church during the mideighteenth century. Following the Presbyterians came similar successful forays from evangelical groups such as the Separate Baptists. Moreover, the attacks by evangelicals also reflected economic and political discontent among small tobacco planters, subsistence-level farmers, tradesmen and artisans, and newly arrived non-English immigrants. They resented the planter establishment and its control of Virginia's social, economic, and political life. By assaulting the Anglican church, these elements also attacked the planters who supported it. The Awakening, then, provided the vehicle whereby the "common people" undermined the power and prestige of Virginia's ruling planter elite. Elsewhere the story was not always as dramatic, but more than one historian has suggested that the antiauthoritarian, anticorruption, combative attitudes of the Great Awakening sowed the seeds of revolt against Great Britain.[16]

THE ENLIGHTENMENT

The most significant intellectual force in much of the Western world in the eighteenth century was the Enlightenment. It grew out of the scientific discoveries of earlier figures such as Galileo (1563–1642), Sir Isaac Newton (1642–1727), and Rene Descartes (1590–1650). The findings of those men and others gave birth to modern science by suggesting that the universe was like a great perpetual-motion machine whose workings were governed by knowable, divinely inspired "natural" laws. Although God, the Supreme Creator, watched over His creation, He never intervened. The implications of those theories were revolutionary. Not only did they render obsolete previous speculations, but they drove a sharp wedge between the "new science" and the older traditional explanations of man and the universe offered by organized religions. More important, the new science suggested that individuals had the power, through reason, to unlock the secret laws of the universe and to apply them (as Newton's "laws" of gravity were being applied) for the betterment of all peoples. The application of science put a new word, *progress,* into the English and European vocabularies and suggested that individuals no longer needed to be the victims of natural forces but could be the masters of them. The Enlightenment thus held out the hope that humanity, through science, could forge a better world, a kind of heaven on earth.

Some thinkers carried the notion of progress even farther. They suggested that progress was not only possible but perhaps inevitable. They reasoned that if the natural world was governed by understandable laws, then perhaps the same was true of human society. Could individuals, using reason, apply a scientific "method" to the affairs of men and women and deduce laws governing human behavior which could then be applied to improve the condition of people everywhere? Many philosophers and political theorists answered affirmatively. In writing on government and society Enlightenment thinkers used their "discovery" of natural laws governing the affairs of men and women to give the theory of progress a new and radical dimension. It became possible, they believed, to think not only of material progress through science, but social progress as well.

Between 1680 and 1800 the Enlightenment went through several different stages. During the first stage, which lasted until about 1750, Enlightenment thinkers such as Newton and Locke emphasized the themes of rationality, harmony, balance, order, and above all the regularity of God's universe. Then, in the middle of the eighteenth century, a second group of thinkers—including such French *philosophes* as François Voltaire, Denis Diderot, the Baron de Montesquieu as well as the Scotsman David Hume and the English historian Edward Gibbon—speculated further upon Enlightenment notions and developed the concepts of empiricism and pragmatism. Finally, toward the end of the century, a third stage of thought emerged from the writings of such men as Jean Jacques Rousseau and Thomas Paine. What distinguished them from their intellectual predecessors was their conviction that the Enlightenment signaled the dawn of a new age, an age in which people would abolish the inhibiting "Gothic" relics of the past and would build new societies that would ensure their own well-being and happiness. In addition, these writers expanded the belief in the individual's potential to improve into a doctrine positing the innate goodness of humanity.

Buoyed by such notions, disciples of the Enlightenment looked enthusiastically toward the New World. It appeared to them to be a great laboratory awaiting experimentation by the advocates of the new thinking. Some were eager to examine the flora, fauna, and wildlife of America, since the Old World had no wilderness with similar possibilities. Others wished to study the Indians and learn more of their origins and behavior. Above all, many Enlightenment thinkers looked upon the New World as an uninhabited, unspoiled space awaiting the application of new theories about society. John Locke, for example, had America firmly in mind when he described the progress of humanity from the "state of nature" to the "state of society" and postulated individuals' "natural rights."

The students who attended Anglo-American colleges—the sons of Boston merchants or Virginia planters—absorbed the theories of the Enlightenment and saw as well their implications for America. Some became Deists, believers in a benevolent, rational God, a supreme Creator of the universe whose thoughts and wishes were comprehensible to "rational" people. The Deists and their notion of the power of human reason stood in stark opposition to the apostles of the Great Awakening who emphasized a capricious, all-powerful God. Other Americans, such as John Bartram, sought to unlock the secrets of the natural world and corresponded frequently and eagerly with natural scientists in Europe.

The Enlightenment placed a premium on "useful" knowledge—that is, knowledge that could improve the condition of humanity. That emphasis struck a particularly responsive chord among the educated minority in America, for it corresponded with the traditional American emphasis upon moral virtue and hard work. Benjamin Franklin brought those ideas together in his *Autobiography* when he argued for the "self-made man." Franklin suggested that the American environment, with its opportunity and open-class structure, was an ideal place for the virtuous man to apply himself and seek success. Franklin's book, modeled on a very popular English literary style of the time, was a compendium of "useful knowledge" for the rational, moral man seeking to improve himself. Franklin conducted experiments in electricity, developed the famous Franklin stove, and was influential in the formation of the first lending library in Philadelphia. In various ways throughout his life he promoted the creation and dissemination of "useful knowlege."

The Enlightenment greatly encouraged the practical, work-oriented, success-oriented strain in Anglo-Americans. Those imbued with Enlightenment theories accepted the notion of the powers of human reason and hinted at the unlimited possibilities for human and social progress in America. Franklin's life and writings exemplified how Enlightenment theories could be adapted to the traditional notions of America's uniqueness and its potential for humanity's "salvation." In many ways the Enlightenment served as the impetus for a kind of secular religion in America, a religion which suggested that America might become a "redeemer nation," leading the backward, corrupt societies of Europe to a better world through spiritual and moral progress.

To many the very fact that Anglo-America was created out of the wilderness seemed to lend credence to notions like John Locke's that individuals existed in a state of society which was the opposite of the state of nature. Many theorists in Europe saw the practical applications of the social "contract" in America. Some Anglo-Americans, on the other hand, began to see themselves as participants in a great social experiment. No simple colonists, they were social scientists testing and disproving old assumptions while devising new forms of social and political organization. They found and applied "useful knowledge" to the structure of their own society for the betterment of all people. Thus, they moved easily and swiftly to what historian Henry May calls the "revolutionary" Enlightenment with its emphasis on the creation of a new order of things. These ideas proved heady, impetuous, and even arrogant; but if one reads the documents of the American Revolutionary era carefully, all of the components of an American "Enlightenment" appear: reason, progress, useful knowledge, social and political engineering, and "millennial" expectations concerning the formation of a unique place for America in human history and human affairs. Many supporters of the revolutionary Enlightenment in Europe interpreted the American Revolution in exactly the same fashion. No simple colonial revolt, the American Revolution announced the creation of a new social, political, and moral order. It proclaimed the triumph of reason, progress, and social engineering over a feudal heritage based upon ignorance and superstition. The "Age of Revolution" had begun.[17]

ANGLO-AMERICAN WOMEN

Despite the optimism sparked by the Enlightenment, the movement had little impact on the role or status of women during the eighteenth century. Reflecting the European and English traditions brought with them, Anglo-Americans considered women to be the weaker sex, both physically and morally. The female's naturally inferior position to men made her properly the object of male domination as well as protection. Given her perceived physical and intellectual limitations, her natural role consisted mainly of domestic servitude, marriage, and motherhood. The women who migrated to North America expected to fulfill those roles.

Except for New England, where migration commonly occurred in families, men arrived first in most of the first settlements and the women arrived later. To attract women for the colonial male population, trading-company officials, proprietors, and colonists offered indentured status to women. In early Maryland, men competed fiercely for the affection of women leaving indenture, and most exservants became wives almost immediately. Thus, although the overwhelming majority of women arrived as wives   with expectations of marriage, women shared the male colonial's vision that America would provide them a better life. The female's position of inferiority and economic dependence in Europe made her expectations of an improved situation in the colonies somewhat more modest than the male's, but she had a dream just the same.

In general, the pattern of legal and moral discrimination, of economic dependence, and of male dominance established in Europe and England continued in Anglo-America. Nevertheless, some important changes did take place which slightly improved the position of women in the colonies. For one, Anglo-America fostered the growth of a tradition of female leadership in the churches. Protestantism, with its doctrine of the priesthood of all believers, made women equal with men in the eyes of God. Though lacking education and barred from the ministry, many women played important roles in England's religious turmoil during the seventeenth century. They became lay preachers or led men and women in small devotional study groups. Thus, English nonconformity possessed a tradition of the female spiritual leader which had an even greater impact in the colonies than in the Old World.

Generally, the leadership of colonial churches reacted adversely to women in the powerful mold of Anne Hutchinson. Nevertheless, gradually women, not men, set the spiritual tone and standards of many congregations in New England and elsewhere. They often voted in church matters and participated in congregational discussions. By the end of the seventeenth century, women outnumbered men in the churches by about a three to two margin. Although women were barred from holding church office, their numerical superiority gave them a dominant voice in many churches, much to the chagrin of the clergy.

In the mid- and late seventeenth century, many churches of New England adopted the ministerially contrived category of pseudochurch membership known as the Half-Way Covenant. As explained earlier, the Half-Way Covenant granted a partial membership status to persons of faith who could not meet the spiritual or moral requirements for full membership. The clergy hoped that such persons would achieve full membership by being brought under the care and discipline of the church. As it turned out, men dominated the lists of half-way members in the late seventeenth century; and of these, a large proportion were the husbands of female church members.

In some respects the Great Awakening represented an attempt by some clergymen to remedy the sexual imbalance in their congregations. When the Awakening began in New England during the 1720s and 1730s, those numbered among the awakened included a preponderance of men, many of whom had formerly been half-way members and sons or husbands of women who enjoyed full church membership. However, as the Awakening progressed, women—both church members and nonmembers—comprised the majority of the awakened and set the standard of spiritual experience within the movement. Typical of their religiosity was the following expression of one woman:

> After God had first begun to pour out his Spirit in this our Day and I came to hear the enlivened Ministers preach, I was put under some serious consideration about my soul, and was convinced in some measure of my need of a Saviour to save me from Hell and Damnation; and for two years before I was married, I was under considerable concern and at Length thought I received comfort, but have been convinced since that it was only counterfeit; for ye comfort yt I then received did not humble me, as I find what I have received since does, even the least degree of it, and after this at Times I was under considerable concern and it would wear off again 'till the time of my first Lying in; and then I was in my own apprehension brought to the very brink of eternity; and that night I received comfort.[18]

Not surprisingly, at that point some of the loudest male critics of the Awakening appeared, charging that the movement suffered from excessive religious "enthusiasm." Such attacks stemmed at least in part from the traditional stereotype of the woman as an emotional and irrational creature. But whether labeled saints or deviants, colonial women of the early eighteenth century produced a rich and eloquent heritage of spiritual striving and Christian devotion.

While Anglo-American society emulated the paternalistic patterns of England and Europe, the continuing scarcity of women improved the female's status ever so slightly. In the midseventeenth century, for example, there were six men to every woman in Virginia and three men to every two women in New England. Although the sex ratio gradually evened out, as late as 1763 many areas of Anglo-America still had a shortage of women. As a consequence of this shortage men tended to prize their wives and treat them with more affection and compassion than elsewhere.

More important, however, was that the scarcity of women led to legal concessions. Most of those were related to marriage and reflected a developing Anglo-American family structure. In England, the wife was virtually her husband's property. Unable to own possessions, make contracts, keep her own earnings, sue in court, or obtain a divorce, she was hardly recognized by law. Men could and did "discipline" or abuse their wives with legal sanction. Men committed adultery and received more lenient treatment than wives who did the same. In Anglo-America, the notion of the wife as property was mitigated by certain developments. In early Plymouth Colony, women—single and married—were allowed to enter into some contracts. Moreover, within marriage, the law tended to recognize women's rights. The sale of property by a husband required the consent of his wife. The same was true for "putting out" children into another home for apprenticeship: The decision had to be a joint one by husband and wife. In addition, Plymouth granted widows greater legal consideration than did England. Whereas English common law recognized as customary but not binding a widow's share of one-third her husband's estate, in Plymouth this dower interest became a right. A similar pattern developed in early Maryland. In that colony, wills usually gave widows considerable control over their husbands' estates.

The enhancement of the woman's position in marriage continued in the eighteenth century. New England court records indicate not only that divorce grew almost common (the divorce rate rose faster than the increase of population in the mideighteenth century) but also that women filed for divorce in greater numbers than men. Although a woman's petition was less likely to be granted than a man's, the number of women winning divorce progressively grew.

Despite such legal advances, colonial white women failed to achieve economic independence. Even though some colonies allowed married women to own some property, or at least implied joint ownership by husband and wife, married women were still generally limited to domestic chores and child rearing. In the seventeenth century, when the scarcity of labor demanded it, many married women performed male tasks such as running a gristmill or building furniture. But when labor grew more plentiful, those occupations were closed to women. Few seventeenth-century women lived alone or tried to achieve economic independence. Life was simply too insecure and dangerous. But there were a few exceptions. One was Margaret Brent, who came to Maryland with her sister and some other women in 1638. Brent became a planter and something of a lawyer. In 1647 Governor Leonard Calvert named her the executor of his estate. As such, she assumed a position known as the "Attorneyship of Baltimore" which gave her a seat in the Maryland Assembly. Brent tried to occupy the seat but the Assembly repeatedly prevented her. Despite that failure, Brent operated in a man's world successfully for her time and probably deserves to be considered one of the founders of American feminism.

In the eighteenth century a number of white women attempted to sustain themselves economically, and not simply as widows managing husbands' estates. Some were forced to seek work by the massive exodus of young men to the frontier. Especially in New England, the situation created the "spinster," a woman of marriageable age for whom marriage was highly unlikely. The percentage of such women may have reached proportions as high as 15 percent of the female population in some areas in New England. Other women tried farming or used an inheritance to pursue another occupation. Legally, those women had many of the same rights as men, even to the point of voting in some elections. But in a male-dominated society, their lives were difficult. Often both men and women considered them "strange."

Still, women seeking economic independence appeared in increasing numbers during the eighteenth century. Many played an important role in the growing commercial and business affairs of New England. Others developed successful careers as midwives. In fact, most of the medicine practiced in the colonial era was practiced by women. Many single women supported themselves as domestic servants. Others, with loftier aspirations, managed or owned shops and taverns. Quite a few took up printing, a relatively new colonial occupation. Of the seventy-eight or so newspapers founded during the colonial era, sixteen were edited at one time or another by women. One of the most famous of the female editors was Mary Katherine Goddard. During the mideighteenth century Goddard assumed control of *The Pennsylvania Chronicle* in Philadelphia from her brother. Later she took over another paper her brother had started in Baltimore. That paper achieved tremendous circulation and Goddard's fame as an editor spread. She printed most of the copies of the Declaration of Independence that were circulated in the colonies in 1776. She also served as postmistress of Baltimore for fourteen years.

For most white women, however, the traditional roles of women dominated colonial life: marriage, child rearing, and household chores. The German, Scotch-Irish, and other non-English women entering the colonies in the eighteenth century found their situations little different from what they had left behind. They experienced the same discrimination and second-class status, though under somewhat improved economic circumstances. The following notation from a young farm woman's diary written in 1775 described the experience of most Anglo-American women throughout the colonial era:

> Fix'd Gown for Prude Just to clear my teeth–Mend Mother's Riding hood–Ague in my face–Ellen was spark'd last night–Mother spun short thread–Fix'd two Gowns for Welch's girls–Carded tow–spun linen–worked on Cheese Basket–Hatchel'd Flax with Hannah and we did 51 lb a piece–Pleated and ironed–Read a sermon of Dodridges–Spooled a piece–milked the cows–spun linen and did 50 knots–made a broom of Guinea wheat straw–Spun thread to whiten–Went to Mr. Otis's and made them a swinging visit–Israel said I might ride his jade (horse)–Set a red Dye–Prude stay'd at home and learned Eve's Dream by heart–Had two scholars from Mrs Taylor's–I carded two pounds of whole wool and felt Nationly–Spun harness twine–Scoured the Pewter.[19]

EDUCATION

If the status of women advanced only marginally during the eighteenth century, the story of education proved far better. In particular some important changes occurred in the educational structure and mental outlook of Anglo-Americans. As the social order underwent profound alterations, the old equation of society and education began to break down. The family–the great educational institution of the seventeenth century–became less the child and ward of other institutions and more an isolated unit, unable to meet satisfactorily all of the demands made upon it. The state grew less concerned with the structure and welfare of the family as government came under the influence of economic interests. The church, torn apart by the Great Awakening, saw its community role shrink in the midst of adversity. Anglo-American society responded to these changes by placing a greater reliance upon formal education. Although the majority continued to receive education within the context of the family, grammar schools and colleges appeared in almost every colony. The grammar school continued to place moral education at the core of its curriculum, but it increasingly recognized the practical value of reading and writing. By the mideighteenth century Anglo-America, especially New England, achieved a level of literacy unmatched in Europe.

Colleges sprang up as more families gained sufficient wealth and status to educate their sons in the European fashion. Some of the wealthiest sent their sons to England or France, but most had to be content with William and Mary, Harvard, King's College (Columbia), or Yale. The Great Awakening led to the creation of several colleges. Of those, the founding of the College of New Jersey (Princeton) in 1746 had the greatest impact. Two of the prime movers behind the college were the famous evangelicals, Gilbert Tennent and Samuel Davies, who readily admitted that the basic reason for their college was–like that of Harvard a century earlier–

to provide trained ministers for "the great Number of Christian Societies then lately form'd in various Parts of the Country." But, unlike Harvard, the College of New Jersey had another mission, one reflecting the changed social situation of the eighteenth century and the changed educational attitudes which followed. In a brochure describing the college, Davies and Tennent wrote:

> Nothing has a more direct Tendency to advance the Happiness and Glory of a Community, than the founding of public Schools and Seminaries of Learning, for the Education of Youth, and adorning their Minds with useful Knowledge and Virtue. Hereby the Rude and Ignorant are civiliz'd and render'd humane; Persons, who would otherwise be useless Members of Society, are qualified to sustain with Honour, the Offices they may be invested with, for the public Service; Reverence of the Deity, Filial-Piety, and Obedience to the Laws, are inculcated and promoted.[20]

Not only had the function of a college changed but "adorning their minds with useful knowledge and virtue" reflected the fact that college curricula had changed drastically in the eighteenth century as well. The new curricula followed similar shifts in Europe as the Enlightenment swept the intelligentsia on both sides of the Atlantic.[21]

LITERATURE

Like education, Anglo-American literature acquired a more sophisticated and complex appearance during the eighteenth century. In line with Benjamin Franklin's *Autobiography,* some of the literature in America during the eighteenth century reflected Enlightenment themes. However, much of it did not. As certain writers argued for the value of reason and the wonders of progress, others urged the resurrection of old values. Both religious and secular Anglo-American literature represented a microcosm of a debate consuming the best minds of Europe and England. There, apostles of the Enlightenment did battle with those supporting older notions about man, society, and the universe. The fact that Anglo-Americans argued over the same matters testified to the derivative character of Anglo-American culture. But, just as Anglo-American society incorporated institutions which were both similar and dissimilar to those in England and Europe, so the imaginations of eighteenth-century Anglo-Americans provided some peculiarly native twists to ideas which were clearly English and European in origin.

Essentially, eighteenth-century Anglo-Americans progressively toyed with the question of whether America had a special role to play in human affairs. It was a question first posed at the dawn of European expansion into the New World. Generally, most eighteenth-century Americans answered "yes" but they did so for different reasons. Often, their positions reflected two attitudes prominent in colonial society: one fairly comfortable with the rationalism and materialism of a rapidly developing commercial climate, the other less at ease with materialism, openly hostile to rationalism, and caught up in a great wave of spiritual and moral reform.

Benjamin Franklin wrote for the former. He was prepared to accept the notion that America was a redeemer nation commissioned to lead the Old World out of corruption and degradation after centuries of moral and spiritual blindness. As an Enlightenment figure he could accept, with mild reservations, that America was destined to lead the world into an era of material and spiritual splendor through reason and the ingenuity of moral individuals applying useful knowledge. Jonathan Edwards wrote for the latter, the America of an evangelical, rejuvenated, Calvinistic Protestantism. No believer in the inevitability or even desirability of progress, Edwards argued that America was and continued to be a land of survivors surrounded by enemies. America's special role was to help bring about the millennium through the destruction of Antichrist. For Edwards, the Great Awakening signaled the opening of the final struggle between good and evil. America was no redeemer nation; it was an island of the elect awaiting deliverance from its enemies. While Franklin suggested that Anglo-Americans could produce heaven on earth, Edwards argued for an earthly kingdom of God.

There were other views as well. Robert Beverly and William Byrd each made important contributions to eighteenth-century Anglo-American literature. Both men came from the Virginia "gentry," and both wrote between 1705 and 1750 (Byrd published a diary and Beverly wrote a history of Virginia). Both men lauded the material sufficiency of America, but neither viewed it, necessarily, as a vehicle for human or social progress. Rather, if America had a special significance for either writer it lay in the ability of a wealthy person to live like an aristocrat while avoiding the evils associated with European and English nobilities. Both men, for the most part, applauded the life of the Virginia planter and accepted the slave system that supported it. Both borrowed the language and distinctive styles of genteel English writers of the period. Both admitted that the Virginia gentry's goal was to achieve the material opulence of the English nobility, complete with carriages, servants, great halls, large libraries, fine clothes and furniture, gracious manners, and distrust of the common people. Yet, each was convinced that Virginia planters were morally superior to their English cousins. Virginians worked for what they earned and owned; English aristocrats, they believed, did not work at all. Virginians practiced charity toward inferiors, even if they did not like them; and they worked for the good of society, not just for themselves or their class. It was a pompous, arrogant view to be sure, but it contained many of the elements of the "virtuous worker" then outlined by Cotton Mather in his *A Christian at His Calling* and by Benjamin Franklin in his *Advice to a Young Tradesman.* When obtained by correct means and used for proper ends, wealth was a perfectly natural and laudable goal.

If either man had reservations about Virginia life, it was that natural bounty discouraged really hard work or creative use of the available resources. Wealth came too easily, even to someone of questionable virtue. Beverly dwelt on the alleged failing at considerable length, urging his compatriots to pursue more stringently the steady habits and moral behavior expected of a Christian "gentleman," lest, by implication, they fall into the trap of laziness and lethargy associated with Old World aristocracies. Virginians, he warned:

> depend altogether upon the Liberality of Nature, without endeavoring to improve its gifts by art or industry. They sponge upon the blessings of a warm sun and a fruitful soil and almost grutch [grudge] the pains of gathering in the bounties of the earth. I should be ashamed to publish this slothful indolence of my countrymen but that I hope it will rouse them out of their

> lethargy and excite them to make the most of all those happy advantages which nature has given them. And if it does this I am sure they will have the goodness to forgive me.[22]

Few native writers were very critical of Anglo-America. An exception was a Quaker, John Woolman, who published a journal of his life in America in 1774. In it he rejected the material wealth, ambition, and selfishness that he saw around him. Particularly opposed to slavery, he wrote:

> In visiting people of note in the society [of Friends] who had Slaves and labouring with them in brotherly love on that account, I have seen, and the sight has affected me, that a conformity to some customs distinguishable from pure wisdom has entangled many, and the desire of gain to support these customs greatly opposed the work of truth.[23]

Although Woolman sought spiritual purity and love, he found little of either in the New World. Rather than producing goodness or virtue, the new land seemed to exaggerate very old human traits like greed, envy, and lust. Woolman hated Anglo-America's treatment of blacks, and he was appalled by society's behavior toward Indians. He argued that God loved all people, even the wicked, and that humanity's redemption depended on that love. Such a notion, he concluded, was not American; it was universal.[24]

Popular Literature

In a sense, eighteenth-century Anglo-America had little "popular" literature as we know it—that is, literature written for the masses. Yet, colonial booksellers and publishers did print and/or distribute several forms of literary endeavor that possessed a much broader appeal than any of the writings discussed to this point. These included the almanac, the broadside, and the periodical magazine. The almanac in particular proved to be an especially popular brand of colonial literature. A combination of calendar, folk wisdom, medical advice, agricultural tips, foreign news, and astrological predictions, the almanac provided both information and entertainment for much of the colonial population. Publication estimates show that it rivaled and even exceeded the Bible in sales. A few almanacs, such as Nathanael Low's *Astronomical Diary,* Benjamin Franklin's *Poor Richard's Almanac,* and Nathaniel Ames' *Astronomical Diary or Almanack,* reached circulations in the thousands during the eighteenth century. Although almanacs appearing in Anglo-America were printed largely by colonial publishers, for the most part their contents were pilfered from sixteenth- and seventeenth-century English sources. In that sense, then, almanacs were hardly native "American" products, or even contemporary English ones for that matter. Yet, the colonial almanac appealed strongly to colonial Americans because it reflected many of their religious, scientific, political, and philosophical attitudes and prejudices.

The almanac's popularity among colonials hinged in part upon its astrological content. Like the sixteenth- and seventeenth-century sources from which they borrowed, colonial almanacs were fundamentally astrological timetables or maps from which personal horoscopes could be determined and ill or good fortune predicted.

Although a pseudoscience to the modern world, astrology represented an important, accepted part of the early modern European's and Anglo-American's intellectual framework for understanding the physical world and certain human behavior. Generally, almanacs contained three astrological elements: a list or "almanac" of stellar and planetary occurrences for the year; a calendar of days for each week of the year; and a forecast or "Prognostication"–essentially a compilation of political, agricultural, and meteorological predictions. Armed with a trusty almanac, colonials presumably could not only ascertain what their personal futures held in store, but also the events likely to occur in the world.

Besides its utility as a tool of prognostication, the almanac received wide credence as an authority on personal health. Most almanacs contained an "anatomy," or a coarse sketch of the human body which located the areas susceptible to particular signs of the zodiac. The positions of the stars and planets, it was believed, affected the balance of body "humours"–internal fluids which, according to accepted theory, dictated the personality and health of every individual. The almanac enabled a person to determine what particular medical cure would prove effective for a given infirmity on a particular day of the year. By the eighteenth century, almanacs added medical "recipes" for curing a variety of ailments and also became filled with medical advertisements. Hence, the almanac often substituted as the colonial's medical handbook.[25]

As an example of colonial literature, however, the almanac is perhaps especially significant for its subtle to overt anti-Catholic bias. Throughout the colonial period, almanacs stirred their readers with tales of Catholic atrocities against Protestants in Europe, warnings against supposed Jesuit plots to infiltrate and enslave the colonies, or renditions of the famous Gunpowder Plot of 1604, in which a few Catholic conspirators attempted to blow up the Houses of Parliament. (Known as Guy Fawkes Day after one of the plotters, the event's anniversary was celebrated annually in both England and the colonies.) John Tulley's almanac for the year 1695, for example, contained "An Account of the Cruelty of the Papists; acted upon the Bodies of the Bloody Martyrs." Although purportedly a true occurrence, the story was an ill-disguised plagiarism of John Foxe's widely read sixteenth-century work, *The Book of Martyrs.* J. N. Hutchins' almanac of 1765 reported how Irish Catholics were persecuting their Protestant compatriots. In his almanac for 1775, Nathanael Low predicted that the legalization of Catholicism in Canada (accomplished by the Quebec Act of 1774) would lead to the spread of abominable popery into the thirteen colonies. Certainly, the anti-Catholic overtones which permeated colonial almanacs reinforced ideas and attitudes in a society already noted for its intensely "Protestant" character.[26]

Another genre of popular literature, the colonial broadside, also reflected the anti-Catholic undercurrent in Anglo-American society, though to a much lesser extent than the almanac. In part its brevity and multipurpose nature destined the broadside to serve more mundane and functional uses. A single sheet of often no more than four columns, the broadside was commonly devoted to a particular event or issue, but by its very limitations it offered a medium that touched the Anglo-American populace quickly and inexpensively. During the late seventeenth century the broadside came into more common use, and by the mideighteenth century it became a favorite choice for disseminating information. Most often the broadside served as a vehicle for governmental or religious pronouncements, such as the passage of new legislation, or notice of a religious celebration. But during the eighteenth century, the broadside expanded and even catered to sensational or controversial topics. It proclaimed the succession of British monarchs to the throne, applauded English victories over the French, eulogized deceased colonial notables, reported unusually heinous crimes, and warned of dire catastrophies to follow such events as the passing of Haley's comet. With such a wide scope, local, colony, and imperial issues all found their way into this medium. By the mideighteenth century, then, the broadside not only functioned as an official organ of information, but also served as an important barometer for colonial concerns and interests.[27]

Along with the broadsides, colonial newspapers also began to appear during the eighteenth century. Initially, the newspaper closely resembled the broadside. It extended perhaps three or four sheets and appeared sporadically as occasions might warrant a special notice. In the 1690s two rival Boston printers, Richard Pierce and Samuel Green, Jr., experimented with newspaper-type publications. Although both of their creations were short-lived, within a decade two other Boston printers, Bartholomew Green and John Campbell, together launched the first continuous newspaper in the colonies, the *Boston News-Letter.* The paper published until the Revolutionary War.

In content, early colonial newspapers, not surprisingly, copied the format used in England. They collected foreign and domestic news, and frequently reprinted stories taken directly from their British rivals. Because the early papers derived a large portion of their revenues from printing "official" news, they often became tools of the government to sway public opinion. This use prompted the rise of "opposition" papers, such as Zenger's in New York. In addition to printing political news, the early papers also sought out advertisements. In the first issue of the *Boston News-Letter,* the printers inserted their own advertisement. It read: "This News Letter is to be continued Weekly; and all Persons who have any Houses, Lands, Tenements, Farmes, Ships, Vessels, Goods, Wares or Merchandizes, &c. to be Sold, or Lett; or Servants Run away; or Goods Stoll or Lost, may have the same Inserted at a Reasonable Rate . . ." They added that regular subscriptions were also available to "All Persons in Town and Country . . . upon reasonable tearms."[28]

Finally, during the 1740s a few periodicals began to circulate within the colonies to form a fourth significant type of popular literature. For the most part, magazines suffered severe financial difficulties and usually lasted for only short periods of time. Yet, a few existed long enough to build notable followings. Several magazines adopted the title, *American Magazine and Historical Chronicle.* But equally popular were names such as *The Christian's Magazine, Christian's History,* or the *American Museum.* The titles of periodicals suggested that their intent was to educate the public or provide a permanent record for memorable or historical information. Indeed, particularly during the decades before and after the American Revolution, periodicals discussed war and colonial politics. But in addition, many magazines attempted to tantalize a wide audience. To do so they covered a variety of topics including travel accounts, reports of religious revivals or "awakenings," scholarly articles, and even poetry. This form of popular literature, however, experienced difficulty despite attempts to appeal to a broad audience, and it was not until the beginning of the nineteenth century that periodicals became a flourishing element of American popular culture.[29]

Of Savages and Shipwrecks

Besides the popular literature already discussed, Anglo-Americans also read two rather unique types of writing during the eighteenth century. One was the narrative of white men and women who had been captured by Indians. The other was the account of disaster at sea. Both revealed much about the Protestant imaginations of eighteenth-century Anglo-Americans, and both influenced heavily the creation of a distinct "American" literature in the nineteenth century.

Since war between France and England continued for most of the first six decades of the eighteenth century, settlements on the Anglo-American frontier were attacked repeatedly by Indian allies of the French. As a result, many whites were captured and carried away by the Indians, and suffered ordeals that lasted a few days or many years. Some died during captivity, but others were eventually released, or escaped, and returned to a world eager to learn about life among the Indians. The 500 or so narratives published in the eighteenth century, however, revealed much more about colonial life than about Indian ways. Although the accounts were marked by realism and considerable accurate information about Indian life, few "redeemed" captives could overcome their own prejudices or biases. They filtered their accounts accordingly, reinforcing stereotypes of Indian thought and behavior that have persisted to the present day.

Two diametrically opposed themes dominated the narratives. Both reflected prejudices the Elizabethan English had brought with them to the New World as well as attitudes shaped by newer intellectual forces like the Enlightenment. One portrayed the Indian as subhuman, capable of cruelty and torture undreamed of by placid whites. The Indians were neither the pawns of the French nor the English; they were simply "savages" whose lives and habits reflected men who lived in a state of nature. The Indian was the "natural man." He was the beast residing in everyone. He was what would result when man rejected civilization and Christian morality, and gave freedom to his passions. Indians epitomized barbarism, and the narrative was meant to remind people just how frail and tenuous the bonds of civilized society were and how close the forces of evil and chaos loomed.

One of the most famous narratives was also one of the earliest: a journal kept by Mary Rowlandson (1635–1678) of Lancaster, Massachusetts, about her abduction during King Phillip's War (1675 to 1676). Rowlandson's account was published in 1682. In it she contrasted the Christian civilization of New Englanders with the savagery of the Indians who were the devil's henchmen. Rowlandson credited her faith in Christ and God's "providence" (His plan) for her eventual return to society. However, she also attributed her capture to Providence, saying that it was God's will that she and her society be punished for individual and collective wickedness. Her ordeal, then, became not only a penalty but also a test from which she emerged a stronger person. "But now I see the Lord had his time to scourge and chasten me," she wrote:

> Affliction I wanted, and affliction I had, full measure (I thought) pressed down and running over; yet I see, when God calls a Person to any thing, and through every so many difficulties, yet he is full able to carry them through and make them see, and say they have been gainers thereby. And I hope I can say in some measure, as David did, *It is good for me that I have been afflicted.* The Lord hath shewed me . . . That we must rely on God himself,

> and our whole dependance must be upon him . . . I have learned to look beyond present and smaller troubles, and to be quieted under them as Moses said, Exod. 14.13. *Stand still and see the salvation of the Lord.*[30]

Rowlandson's view was consistent with what most men and women of seventeenth-century Anglo-America believed about society. It also reflected the traditional Christian view of the baseness of human nature.

The other theme treated the Indian as the innocent, simple, virtuous child of nature. Although the captive narratives accepted the Indians' barbaric condition and the cruelty it manifested, at the same time they emphasized that the Indians remained uncorrupted by the evils of human society. They showed no greed or envy; they had no preoccupation with material possessions. They lived in perfect harmony with the wilderness and with nature, and because they did so, the white colonials attributed to them a native intelligence (uncorrupted reason) and virtue that was alien to society. The Indians were completely free. That freedom gave them a set of priorities that mystified and intrigued the whites. The Indians found beauty in nature and nature's creations, and they were little impressed with the creations of people. This, said the narratives, was good. They went on to encourage all readers to imitate the natural, unspoiled life of the "noble savage." Not surprisingly, some of the persons who conceived of captivity in this manner eventually rejected white society entirely and returned to the forests.

This view of the Indians reflected an idea of man's innocence in the state of nature that was as old as the Adam and Eve story. It was a view revived during the Renaissance and accepted by many Elizabethan English. It was endorsed by some Enlightenment thinkers eager to prove that human society was artificial and, therefore, subject to change and improvement, that human nature reflected more good than evil, and that degenerate societies could corrupt men and women. The English, Europeans, and Anglo-Americans who believed in the innocence of natural man were impressed by the Indians' apparent ability to live virtuously and harmoniously with the laws of nature and the mind of God through reason (which in natural man was instinct). What the narratives suggested—at least to minds influenced both by traditional English attitudes and some theories of the Enlightenment—was the need for society to curb the baser instincts of man and to bring out his better rational powers. Moreover, the narratives implied that individuals could and should alter society to bring it in line with nature's laws. This view lauded and accepted the notion of spiritual and moral progress while at the same time it questioned the ideal of materialism which so many Anglo-Americans seemed to embrace.

While the narratives of Indian capture and redemption represented a peculiarly Anglo-American literary form, some of the important themes of those narratives were similar to ones contained in another important kind of literature: stories of shipwrecks and sea disasters. Those stories were *not* American in origin. In the early modern era, their prevalence and popularity grew in direct proportion to Europe's expansion into the new world. As early as the midsixteenth century, they began to appear in anthologies such as Giovanni Ramusio's *Navagationi et Viaggi* (1550) and, slightly later, Richard Hakluyt's *Of Principall Navigations, Voiages, and Discoveries of the English Nation* (1589, 1600). By the eighteenth century, they formed an important kind of popular literature in most of the seafaring nations of the Atlantic world, and appeared as inexpensive pamphlets hawked by street peddlers in countries as diverse as Portugal and England.

As Anglo-America grew increasingly commercialized in the eighteenth century, tales of sea disasters and shipwrecks appeared as pamphlets and also became regular features in all colonial newspapers. Thus, their popularity equaled and probably surpassed that enjoyed by the narratives of Indian capture. The sea-disaster stories which were read by Anglo-Americans dealt mainly with the experiences of colonials at sea and thus formed a distinct subsection of a much larger genre. Their appeal—like that of the Indian tales—had much to do with a general appetite for violence and sensationalism. In that regard, American readers differed little from their English or European counterparts. Anglo-Americans shared with the inhabitants of all the nations surrounding the Atlantic the knowledge that sea travel was dangerous and that no voyage was routine or safe from the forces of nature or the incompetence of humans. Still, in at least one area of experience—their physical isolation—Anglo-Americans differed from other seafaring peoples and that may have given the tales of sea disasters a special importance to them. Sea stories, combined with the captive narratives, reminded colonials that they faced two dangerous frontiers. Indeed, they reminded them that they were surrounded by hostile forces, some to be found in the sea to the east, the southeast, and the northeast, and others in the wilderness to the west, the south, and the north. Sea-disaster tales and Indian captive narratives, taken together, preached to Anglo-Americans that theirs was a frail Protestant, Christian civilization with danger and, perhaps, death waiting no more than a few days' travel in any direction. It was a sobering and, at the same time, an exciting thought—one Anglo-Americans passed on to subsequent generations. Both kinds of stories continued their popularity well into the nineteenth century and heavily influenced such great "American" writers as Herman Melville (*Billy Budd* and *Moby Dick*), Edgar Allan Poe (*The Narrative of Arthur Gordon Pym*), and James Fenimore Cooper (*Leatherstocking Tales*).

Like the narratives of Indian capture and redemption, the Anglo-American tales of shipwrecks and sea disasters fell into two distinct categories. The earliest tales—dating from the beginnings of settlement but continuing throughout the colonial era—closely resembled Mary Rowlandson's account of captivity and deliverance during King Phillip's War. The tales were told accurately and realistically, but the emphasis was on trial, punishment, and the lessons learned. "Providence" was the central explanation for the events that transpired. The victim's fate was decreed by God as punishment for individual and collective sins. Civilization and savagery were sharply depicted. Divorced from the security of society, for example, desperate sailors occasionally turned to cannibalism.

Providence also decreed the narrator's redemption and, just as in Rowlandson's case, the reason involved a "test" which the author recognized and passed. A sea disaster not only brought suffering and death, it also brought courage, strength, and a renewed and revitalized faith in God and His power. Thus, although surviving incredible hardships, the authors of sea-disaster narratives often credited their own survival to a special purpose selected for them by God. Their own faith and character strengthened by what they had been through, they were to "witness" for the benefit of others. In 1660, Benjamin Bartholomew, survivor of the wreck of the *Exchange,* bound from Boston to Barbados, wrote in verse:

Twase God alone that in our state did Move
What for to render doth it us Behove:
O let us tel abrod his wondrous acts
Lets Glorifie his Name for all his facts
Who bringeth loe and raiseth up againe
God surly doth not these great things in vaine
He is expecting from us some Great thing
and lookes more prayes we to his name should bring.[31]

Nearly a century later, Joseph Bailey, a survivor of the wreck of the Brigantine *Alida and Catharine* (New York to Antigua), explained his motive for writing:

> It's not with a View or Design to move any One's Pity or Compassion towards the Unfortunate and Distress'd; neither is it out of vain Ostentation that my name may be recorded, that moves me to write the following Narrative; but it is, as I conceive, My bounden Duty towards the Supreme Being, to declare his wonderful acts of Providence, and tender Mercies towards the most undeserving of Mankind.[32]

Like the Indian-captive narratives, some of the sea-disaster stories seemed to reveal the impact of Enlightenment rationality. But it was a different strain of the Enlightenment from that found in the captive narratives. Instead of describing the noble savage in the state of nature and viewing both as basically benign, these sea stories drew a sharp contrast between the disorder and unpredictability of the state of nature (the sea, a storm, and all the calamities associated with shipwreck and the period before rescue) and the harmony and rationality of society. Instead of telling the reader of the wonderful, unspoiled character of man in a state of nature, such stories extolled the virtues of society based on reason and characterized the state of nature as something to be approached with care and foreboding.

In these tales the God whose providence determined the fates of individuals remained, but the world and universe reflected order and His inherent goodness and rationality (the "moderate" Enlightenment), not His wrath and sense of justice (the Calvinist tradition). The terrors of the sea continued to constitute a test of individual courage and wisdom as well as a call to witness and influence others. For a short time, people experienced the true chaos of the natural state. Then they returned to civilization fortified, enlightened, and better able to appreciate the necessity of the well-ordered society. For example, in 1765, Captain David Harrison survived a disaster aboard his sloop *Peggy* as it headed for New York from the Azores. The ship encountered a severe storm which took its sails and masts and left it to drift helplessly. Famine ensued among the crew. Harrison wrote later:

> The occurrences of my late unfortunate voyage, are of a nature so extraordinary, and my preservation is a circumstance so miraculous, that sensible as I am at present of the Divine goodness, it would look like a want of gratitude to the great disposer of all things, if I neglected to employ a few hours in the recital of some particulars, where his Providence has been singularly manifested, and where he has given an incontestible lesson to all his creatures, to dread the impiety of despair, since his assistance may be nearest at hand when they are least in expectation of relief.[33]

Nathaniel Pierce survived weeks of drifting aboard the wreck of the Brigantine *Portsmouth,* originally bound to Louisbourg, Nova Scotia, from Portsmouth, New Hampshire. While crediting God's mercy for his redemption, he extolled the wonders and amenities of society. After his rescue and subsequent recovery at Oporto, Portugal, Pierce recalled:

> . . . when I was able to take my Passage for England, they [his rescuers] procured a Passage for me, in the *Mary,* Capt. Francis Smith, for London, and laid in all Manner of stores necessary for a Gentleman, and five Moidores [Portuguese coins] in my pocket, all at their own Cost and Charge. Nor must I forget the Kindness of Dr. Bromley, who was so good as to attend me every Day that I was at Oporto . . . . Nor can I omit to mention the Present made me by the Masters of the Ships then at Oporto . . . .
>
> On the 15th day of July, 1753, I arrived at Boston, in New England, an affecting Instance, more especially to my Friends, of the Goodness of that Being, who is the Confidence of the Ends of the Earth; and of them that are afar off upon the Sea.[34]

Although the Enlightenment probably had some impact, on the whole both the Indian captive narratives and the tales of sea disasters more closely reflected the concerns of Jonathan Edwards, the Tennents, Samuel Davies, and the tradition of moral and spiritual reform characteristic of the Great Awakening than any other literary tradition of the eighteenth century. They revealed that Benjamin Franklin's rationalism and genteel materialism, for example, did not necessarily typify most of eighteenth-century colonial thought and culture. The captive narratives and sea-disaster stories demonstrated a brooding, introspective, largely Calvinist side of the Anglo-American character on the eve of the revolt against England. The strongest motif that emerged from the tales of savages and shipwrecks was that of trial and survival. This theme, as we have seen, antedated English expansion into the New World. Moreover, it reflected the Old World experience of the Protestant colonists of Anglo-America—English and non-English. They *were* the persecuted remnant, the survivors of various English and European political, economic, religious, and military dislocations and upheavals.

The tales of savages and shipwrecks provided evidence that, like Edwards, many Anglo-Americans continued to see themselves as survivors and as persecuted, suffering saints. At the same time they were considerably more than a chosen people living on an isolated continent thousands of miles from their old enemies. They faced adversaries all around them: French Catholics to the north and west, Spanish Catholics to the south and southwest, Indians and a dangerous forbidding wilderness to the west, and a cruel sea to the east. Instead of quaking in mortal fear, though, the colonists turned their peril to advantage. They entered the wilderness seeking new lands. They crossed the sea with their domestic products and returned with foreign imports. In the process, a few underwent trials testing their faith and fortitude, just as their Protestant ancestors had been tested in Europe and England. The result was, like the Great Awakening, a strengthening of courage and a rebirth of moral and spiritual zeal.

Like Edwards and other evangelicals, the actors in the sea stories and captive narratives were expected by God to use their own moral and spiritual rebirths to bring about similar experiences in others. Survival thus became a key to collective strength. For many Anglo-Americans, to meet and overcome an adversary unlocked new moral, spiritual, and physical vigor which prepared them, in turn, for the next encounter. They were survivors who faced powerful enemies—both human and supernatural—but they were not losers.

But what was their collective goal or mission? Were they meant, as some evangelicals suggested, to usher in the millennium? Or were they intended, as some rationalists suggested, to lead the world to heaven on earth? The tales of savages and shipwrecks provided no definitive answers. But they did hint that Anglo-Americans, as suffering saints, had no "mission" greater than survival and the maintenance of high standards of morality and spirituality. The tales never prophesied that enemies would be vanquished ultimately. In fact, like the persecuted of any epoch, enemies seemed necessary to Anglo-Americans to guarantee their collective well-being. The tales suggested only that continual struggle with malevolent forces promised moral, spiritual, and physical vitality. Put another way, as an embattled Protestant people doing God's work, Anglo-Americans could hope to emerge a superior people. That hope reflected a New World culture which both affirmed and rejected its Old World heritage.

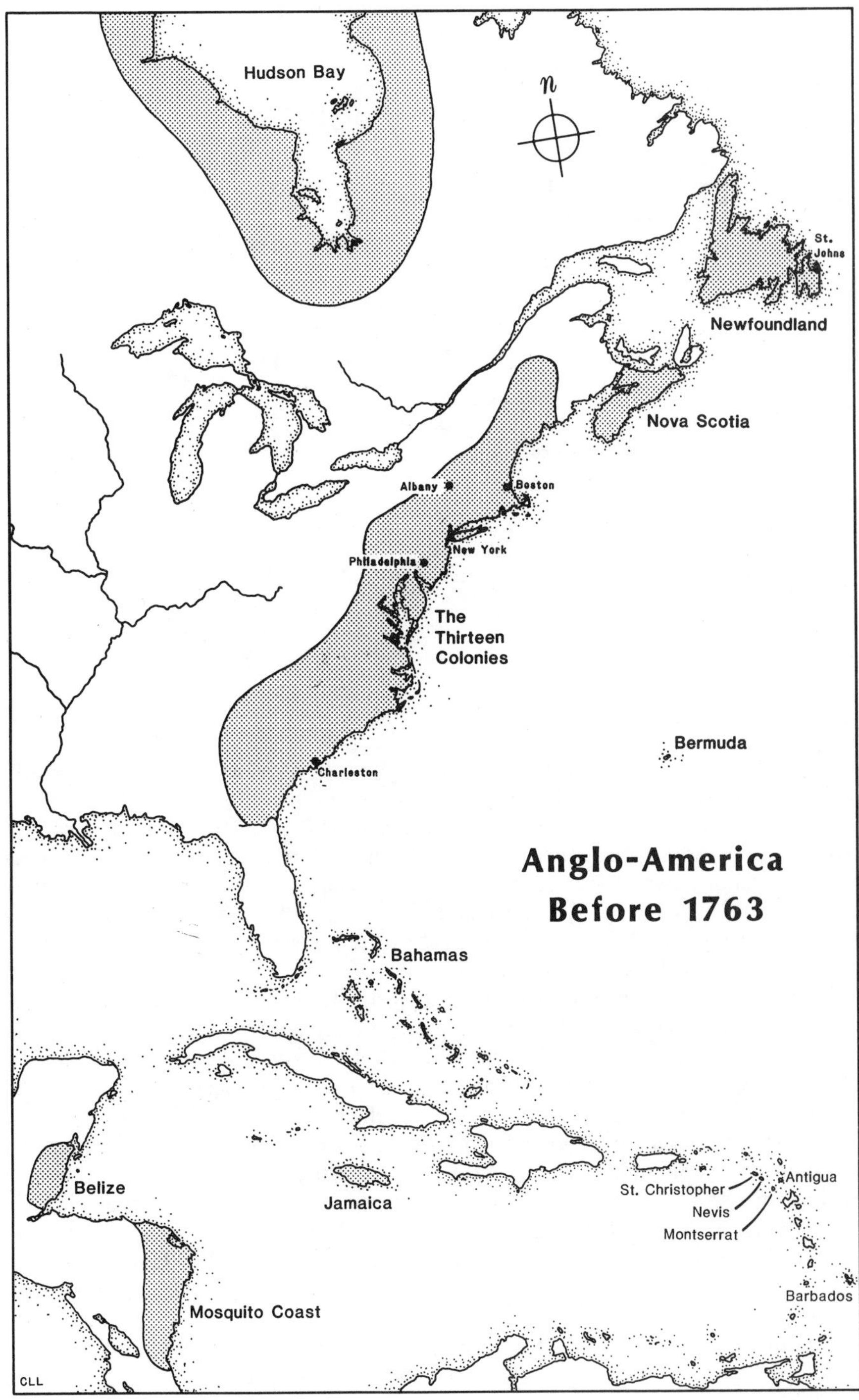
Hudson Bay
n
St. Johns
Newfoundland
Nova Scotia
Albany
Boston
New York
Philadelphia
The Thirteen Colonies
Bermuda
Charleston
Anglo-America Before 1763
Bahamas
Antigua
St. Christopher
Nevis
Montserrat
Belize
Jamaica
Barbados
Mosquito Coast
CLL

11

The Revolutionary Era and Beyond

Throughout the preceding chapters, the American Odyssey has been carefully related. From primitive beginnings the English colonies slowly evolved into the "Thirteen United States of America" that challenged the might of the British Empire and achieved independence from it. This book has attempted to answer some fundamental questions about our past that Americans have always raised: Who were the colonists? What did they believe and value? How did they succeed in building a strong nation from humble settlements? In the process of answering these questions, the continuities as well as the changes in early American history were stressed.

To explain the evolution of British North America, the colonial experience was organized around three major themes: the unique yet derivative quality of American culture; the tremendous importance of the fundamental purposes behind the founding of the colonies; and the significance of ideological as well as material concerns in shaping Anglo-America. The first theme hoped to challenge the either/or character of much current debate about America's early development. Either one accepted the thesis that Anglo-America was, from the beginning, the antithesis of Europe, or one argued that Anglo-America fit the pattern of preindustrial societies everywhere. We have tried to suggest that both arguments are valid, albeit exaggerated. From the beginning Anglo-America reflected English/European ideals and institutions. But the colonists comprised only a small, unrepresentative sample, not a cross section of Europe and England. Further, the colonies lacked central European institutions such as a Crown, an hereditary aristocracy, and a strong established church. Thus, the ideas, experiences, and institutions colonials brought with them ensured the creation of an imperfect imitation of English/European society. Over the years, as the mutant character of the colonial Old World heritage combined with such environmental factors as the abundance of land and the inability of Anglo-American institutions to exert much control over the colonial population, British North America began to express a culture that was both uniquely "American" and yet derivative of Old World values and customs.

The second theme emphasized how the planners and architects of British North America intended to found colonies that would create wealth for England and thus facilitate Britain's rise to world power and glory. This purpose represented a significant departure from both the experience of the Spanish, Portuguese, and French, as well as the original intentions of English imperialists. Before Jamestown, the importance of the New World seemed to lie in fulfilling the fantasy tales of finding exotic, rich civilizations, or in discovering and tapping the abundant stores of precious metals that lay in the New World. Although English imperialists knew it would be difficult to duplicate the Spanish success in North America, they still carried that hope. A series of early colonizing disasters changed English thinking and brought Britain to a new conception of empire. Along with English mercantilists and nationalists, British policy makers came to define New World "treasure" as foreign trade. For the colonies to be useful, they would have to contribute to the growth of British commercial wealth.

The colonial contribution of North America lay in making the land, forests, and seas produce raw materials for English manufacturing and European consumption. That task required labor in numbers not heretofore envisioned by any European or English imperial schemer. The English quickly gave up the idea of enslaving the scattered, belligerent Indian tribes of North America. Instead, they attempted to entice the English, and later on the non-English, to settle in Anglo-America and provide labor. When labor-intensive crops such as rice, indigo, and tobacco increased the demands for a work force, colonists began importing thousands of African slaves for that purpose.

The fundamental shift in English imperial thinking—from the acquisition of precious metals already there, to the creation of wealth through trade—points to the third theme: the importance of ideological as well as material factors in the expansion of British North America. Those who accepted the hazards of life in the wilderness were men and women who either had nothing better in the Old World, or who had strong reasons to leave the comfort and safety of the homeland. Anglo-America was settled by an unusually large number of people whose "radical" political, religious, and economic views prompted them to seek out a new life where they could freely express and practice their beliefs. This characteristic of Anglo-American colonists helps to explain why ideology proved so important to colonial history and why Protestant ideology in particular became such a significant element of colonial culture.

Although the three themes just outlined provide a guide for understanding the broad developments in Anglo-American society prior to the American Revolution, it still remains for us to explain—admittedly all too quickly—why the Anglo-American colonies broke away from the British empire and how the leaders of the revolutionary era succeeded in making independence a success. Let us turn first to the problem of explaining the American Revolution.[1]

When the French and Indian War ended in 1763, the English government faced an enormous security and administrative problem. Up until the defeat of the French, British territory in North America had barely extended 100 or 200 miles beyond the sea coast. With the acquisition of the vast territories of New France, the British government suddenly inherited an area more than double the size of its thirteen existing colonies. Yet, over that extensive territory, Britain employed only a handful of colonial officials supported by a few troops and ships. More troops, ships, and administrators would be needed and that meant additional expenses. Even more serious, England was burdened by a huge public debt. In 1763 the English national debt stood at around £133 million, a staggering figure for that time. British military campaigns between 1757 and 1763 alone had cost £866 million. As a result of war, the national debt had increased by £60 million between 1755 and 1763. The end of the imperial wars, thus, signaled a severe financial as well as administrative crisis for the English government.

To try and resolve the administrative crisis King George III issued the Proclamation of 1763. Some of the territory taken from the French became the colonies of East and West Florida and Canada. In addition, British North America was divided east and west by a line running roughly north and south along the Appalachian mountains. The plan was to keep Anglo-Americans from moving west of the Appalachians, thus saving the region for the Indians. It did not work. Colonists invaded and settled in Indian territory, forcing the English to negotiate with the Indian tribes—especially the Cherokees and the Iroquois—to move the Proclamation line farther west.

In response to the financial crisis ministers of the Crown and leaders of Parliament suggested various ways to retire the debt and pay the costs of protecting and governing an empire. One of the most popular suggestions was to levy taxes directly upon the hitherto untaxed colonials. Since much of the debt had accumulated while protecting the colonies from foreign encroachment, the British reasoned that the colonies ought to be willing to bear a portion of the financial burden of war. Another, more sinister side of the argument to tax the colonies also existed. Anglo-Americans, especially, were perceived as having too much freedom and too little patriotism. Many English officials believed that the Americans were searching for an opportunity to break away from the empire. Indeed, some colonists and colonial governments had behaved poorly during the French and Indian War. Many had continued to trade with the French, and often colonial governments resisted material support for English troops or cooperated only when foreign armies knocked at their doors. English suspicions about Anglo-American intentions prompted Benjamin Franklin to assure the British that the colonists did not want independence and union among the colonies was impossible. But even Franklin's disclaimer ended with a warning:

> When I say such a union is impossible, I mean, without the most grievous tyranny and oppression. People who have property in a country which they may lose, and privileges which they may endanger, are generally disposed to be quiet, and even to bear much, rather than hazard all. While the government is mild and just, while important civil and religious rights are secure, such subjects will be dutiful and obedient.[2]

Franklin's words proved prophetic. The colonists resorted to revolution only after they perceived that they suffered and would continue to suffer "most grievous tyranny and oppression." This is not to say that England intended tyranny and oppression or that even by a reasonable definition of those terms Britain imposed them. What England did in the years between 1763 and 1775 reflected many motives, but none involved malice for its own sake or a desire to reduce Anglo-America to "slavery." First, the English acted from an entirely defensible desire to raise revenue to offset what was to them a staggering tax burden already shouldered by the English (Anglo-Americans paid about 1/20th as much in taxes as did the English). Second—and this motive grew in importance as the years passed and Anglo-Americans became more recalcitrant—certain elements within the Crown, Parliament, and the English ruling class wanted the English government to exert much tighter control over Anglo-America. As we saw in Chapter seven, this was a continuing concern of many Britons throughout the eighteenth century. Their designs, however, had been thwarted by the more compelling demands of nearly constant imperial warfare with France. Walpole and Newcastle practiced the policy of "salutary neglect" to placate the Anglo-Americans and make them happy wartime allies. With the defeat of the French in 1763, however, the rationale for salutary neglect ended, and a more belligerent stance toward Anglo-America became almost a certainty.

A factor which contributed to this belligerency was ignorance of and disdain for Anglo-Americans and Anglo-America. Many upperclass Britons assumed, for example, that because most colonials came from the lower, poorer classes of English and European society, they represented undesirable elements at best, or criminals at worst. On the whole, though, the general English populace, whether of high or low station, probably knew and cared little about Anglo-America. Their concern centered upon keeping the colonies producing and consuming goods in a manner that benefited England's foreign trade and England's domestic prosperity.

Of course, whether the English knew a great deal or very little about the colonies, or whether they considered them saints or sinners, is probably irrelevant. For in the end, the British would probably have treated Anglo-America the same in either case. English leaders believed they needed new sources of revenue, and they believed they needed to assert tighter control over their far-flung empire. This they proceeded to do. In so acting, the harmony and cooperation that characterized England's relationship with the North American colonies slowly dissolved, while friction, anger, and hostility gradually increased.[3]

With England's imperial purposes clear, Parliament proceeded to pass the Revenue Act of 1764. It represented the first act that was directed to raise revenue from the colonies, not regulate trade. It was opposed on that basis. The Revenue Act, also known as the Sugar Act, attempted to stop colonial smuggling and provide moneys to maintain the British army in North America. It confirmed the Sugar Act of 1733, for which enforcement had been lax or nonexistent. In effect, the act told colonials that the British army and navy stationed in American territory and waters would be used to force compliance. During the same year Parliament enacted the Currency Act, which prohibited colonial legislatures from making colonial currency legal tender for the payment of debts. The act was aimed mainly at Virginia. The colonists responded by boycotting English goods.

And so it began. In 1765 one of the most controversial pieces of legislation of the period, the Stamp Act, emerged from Parliament. Also designed to support the British military units in North America, it required colonials to purchase and place an English "stamp" upon all legal documents. Though never put into effect, the

Stamp Act created a wave of colonial protest, especially in Virginia and Massachusetts. At the request of Massachusetts, representatives from all of the colonies met in New York in a Stamp Act Congress. Caesar Rodney, one of the representatives of Delaware, described the grim determination of the delegates in a letter to his brother:

> You and many others are surprised, perhaps, to think we should sit so long, when the business of our meeting seemed only to be the petitioning the king, and remonstrating to both houses of parliament; but when you consider that we are petitioning and addressing that august body, the great legislature of the empire, for redress of grievances,—that, in order to point out those grievances, it was likewise necessary to set forth the liberty we have and ought to enjoy (as free-born Englishmen) according to the British constitution. This we are about to do by way of declaration, in the nature of resolve, as a foundation to the petition and address; and was one of the most difficult tasks I ever yet saw undertaken . . . .[4]

The Congress condemned the Stamp Act and also the Sugar Act of the year earlier. Such strong and vociferous colonial opposition led to the repeal of the Stamp Act and the fall of George Grenville's government. Following this debacle Parliament made a show of reasserting its authority over the North American colonies and its other imperial possessions by passing the Declaratory Act in 1766.

In 1767 another heavy blow fell upon the colonies with the passage of the Townshend Acts, so named after the Chancellor of the Exchequer, Charles Townshend. Townshend intended to raise money for the colonial military establishment, but he hoped also to curb some of the newly won "powers" of colonial legislatures by using tax revenues to secure the financial independence of colonial governors, judges, and various colonial officials. The duties imposed by the Townshend Acts would have taxed nearly all Anglo-American imports. The legislation was drafted under the erroneous presumption that Anglo-Americans would accept an "external" tax on trade but not an "internal" tax such as that represented by the Stamp Act. In addition to its taxing provision, the Townshend Acts reorganized and strengthened the colonial admiralty courts and created a board of customs officials to administer custom laws. The Acts also legitimized *writs of assistance* or warrants that authorized customs officers to search private premises such as warehouses in order to look for smuggled goods.

The Townshend Acts produced a firestorm of colonial protest that stretched over several years. Many colonists agreed to refuse to import British goods. For example, in June, 1769, representatives of the counties of Maryland agreed that:

> . . . we will not, at any time hereafter, directly or indirectly, import or cause to be imported, any manner of goods, merchandise, or manufactures, which are, or shall hereafter be, taxed by act of parliament, for the purpose of raising a revenue in America (except paper not exceeding six shillings per ream, and except such articles only as orders have been already sent for) but, that we will always consider such taxation, in every respect, as an absolute prohibition to the articles that are, or may be taxed.[5]

Eventually, in 1770, Parliament repealed all of the Townshend duties except the one on tea; but repeal did little to repair the damage done to relations between England and the colonies. More than their actual material impact, the Townshend duties created a serious—perhaps, one might argue, an irreparable—breach between Anglo-America and England because they encouraged old colonial fears of oppression and corruption. These fears were rooted in the Protestant heritage of Anglo-America, a heritage which had been expanded and quickened during the eighteenth century by the Great Awakening, the ideas of the real Whigs, and the theories of the Enlightenment. Colonial "patriots" began to detect a conspiracy against their liberty and property; and they reacted as Franklin had warned earlier.

Rather than simply responding to events, colonists began to anticipate British moves and interpret all imperial utterances as evidence of a conspiracy. They came to believe that a coterie of English merchants, private citizens, Crown officials, and members of Parliament were engaged in nefarious activities designed, ultimately, to enslave them. Colonial thinking of this kind, coupled with British suspicions, embarassment, and anger, led to terrible incidents such as the Boston Massacre of 1770 or the more humorous Boston Tea Party of 1773.

The British government missed the humor of the Tea Party. Instead, the first minister, Lord North, presented a series of punitive measures to Parliament—directed mainly at Massachusetts—which became known as the Coercive or Intolerable Acts of 1774. The North ministry told Parliament:

> that nothing could be done by either civil, military, or naval officers, to effectuate the re-establishment of tranquility and order in that province [Massachusetts], without additional parliamentary powers to give efficacy to their proceedings . . . And that it was therefore incumbent on every member, to weigh and consider, with an attention suitable to the great importance of the subject, the purport of the papers before them, and totally laying all prejudices aside, to form his opinion upon the measures most eligible to be pursued, for supporting the supreme legislative authority, the dignity of parliament, and the great interests of the British Empire.[6]

Acting from a deep sense of frustration, anger, and perhaps confusion, Parliament passed the Coercive Acts. Understandably, they were deeply resented by Anglo-Americans. The acts included the Boston Port Act, which closed the port of Boston; the Massachusetts Government Act, which increased the power of the royal governor of that colony at the expense of the legislature; the Quartering Act, which required colonists to provide permanent quarters for British soldiers and sailors; and the Administration of Justice Act, which allowed British officials accused of murder in one colony to have their cases transferred to a different colony. At about the same time Parliament passed the Quebec Act, which legalized French customs, laws, and the Catholic religion in Canada. This piece of legislation made French Canadians happy, but it further intensified the deep-rooted fears of Protestant colonists that Antichrist was mounting an attack on Anglo-America. Colonists considered the Quebec Act to be a central part of the legislative package which they labeled the Intolerable Acts.

In response to these Acts, the Massachusetts legislature called a continental congress. All colonies except Georgia sent representatives. Thomas Jefferson drafted a set of instructions for the Virginia delegates which, though too radical for the convention selecting the delegates, became a classic of American political theory. Published as *A Summary View of the Rights of British America,* the pamphlet questioned Parliament's authority over America. "America was conquered," Jefferson wrote:

> and her settlements made and firmly established, at the expense of individuals, and not of the British public. Their own blood was split in acquiring lands for their settlement, their own fortunes expended in making that settlement effectual. For themselves they fought, for themselves they conquered, and for themselves alone they have right to hold . . . .[7]

"We are willing, on our part," he concluded:

> to sacrifice everything which reason can ask, to the restoration of that tranquility for which we all must wish. On their part, let them be ready to establish union on a generous plan. Let them name their terms, but let them be just. Accept of every commercial preference it is in our power to give, for such things as we can raise for their use, or they make for ours. But let them not think to exclude us from going to other markets to dispose of those commodities which they cannot use, nor to supply those wants which they cannot supply. Still less, let it be proposed, that our properties, within our own territories, shall be taxed or regulated by any power on earth, but our own. The God who gave us life, gave us liberty at the same time; the hand of force may destroy, but cannot disjoin them. This, Sire, is our last, our determined resolution . . . .[8]

The First Continental Congress, as it became known, tried to negotiate with the British for a return to the imperial situation that had existed before 1763. Meanwhile, some colonials prepared for war, as did the British. Massachusetts, considering itself to be in the eye of the storm, told its delegates to the Continental Congress that:

> We must fight, if we can't otherwise rid ourselves of British taxation, all revenues, and the constitution or form of government enacted for us by the British parliament. It is evil against right—utterly intolerable to every man who has any idea or feeling of right or liberty.[9]

Sadly, in 1775 colonial militia and British regulars fought and died in skirmishes at Lexington and Concord, Massachusetts, when British troops attempted to seize hidden caches of weapons. These events led directly to the convening of the Second Continental Congress. Meeting in Philadelphia, this body resolved to put the colonies in a "state of defence." It appointed George Washington as commander-in-chief of the Continental Army and Issued a "Declaration of Causes of Taking Up Arms." Thousands of able-bodied men sought to join the Continental Army. A farmer from Pennsylvania explained his decision to enlist with a stirring appeal to patriotism:

> I have observed that some of you are a little surprised that I, with so many inducements as I have to remain at home, should have resolved to quit my family, and my farm for the fatigues and dangers of war. I mean you should be perfectly satisfied as to my motives. I am an American: and am determined to be free. I was born free: and have never forfeited my birth-right; nor will I ever, like the infatuated son of Isaac, sell it for a mess of pottage. I will part with my life sooner than my liberty, for I prefer an honorable death to the miserable and despicable existence of a slave . . . .[10]

Soon states such as Virginia were dissolving their colonial governments and creating new ones. In July, 1776, the Second Continental Congress adopted the *Declaration of Independence.* It began:

> When in the course of human events, it becomes necessary for one people to dissolve the political bonds which have connected them with another, and to assume among the powers of the earth the separate and equal station to which the laws of nature and of nature's God entitle them, a decent respect to the opinions of mankind requires that they should declare the causes which impel them to the separation.[11]

What started as a quarrel over England's right to tax her colonies became a question of whether the British empire would stay whole or collapse amid the carnage of battle.

Why did the Anglo-American colonies revolt against England? No other portion of the British empire joined the mainland colonies. No other British colony even complained particularly about the revenue measures passed between 1764 and 1775 (we must remember that these acts extended to all of Britain's overseas possessions, not just Anglo-America). In part, as we have suggested, Anglo-America possessed a strong ideological disposition to expect tyranny and oppression. Yet, that alone does not explain the revolt. Another part of the answer lay in British mistakes—mistakes which were rooted in misinformation and ignorance about Anglo-America and Anglo-Americans. Still another reason lay in the fact that many British policy makers were simply indifferent to the colonists. As long as the colonies served the imperial purpose, most of the English were happy. As one historian wrote, "Trade, Shipping, the Navy—not colonization—were the true imperial interests of Englishmen in the hundred years after the Restoration of Charles II."[12] In other words, the British government worried little about who the colonists were or how they lived, so long as they fulfilled their mission to keep British ships—and British cash boxes—full.

A few British leaders went even farther, and suggested that the colonies hampered the British economy and did little to enhance English trade or imperial power, especially considering the degree of freedom the colonists already possessed. Malachy Postlethwayt, for example, was one such figure. An economist and a leading critic of England's conduct of empire before 1763, Postlethwayt called for drastic reforms and tighter control. He declared that the colonies "interfered" with England "in her native produce and in some of her staple manufactures, and these distinct parts of the British Empire do also greatly interfere in their produce and fabrics with each other."[13] In common with many other English mercantilists, he believed that the colonies competed with England more than they complemented and assisted its trade. Although the American colonies found a few champions in Parliament, most of the English felt little sympathy with colonial remonstrances.

However, as colonial protests grew louder and apparently more violent, English leaders increasingly characterized the dispute as a constitutional crisis, one that revolved around Parliament's right to rule the empire. Most Britons could understand and sympathize with this explanation. Their own protracted internal conflict during the seventeenth century, they believed, had resolved the question of Parliament's sovereignty. Parliament could make and enforce any law that did not violate the fundamental rights of English citizens set out in the Magna Carta and common law. Still, if Parliament possessed sovereignty, the question remained: how many rights did the colonial have? There were various opinions on this question, but by and large most English leaders believed that during the pivotal years between 1764 and 1775, colonial rights were considered and protected.

The colonists, however, did not share the English view of the empire or the English explanation for the quarrel between Britain and Anglo-America. In the colonial mind, the empire embraced several territories and peoples who possessed status equal to Britain and all rights as English citizens. Colonists tended to conceive of their own legislatures as having the same authority as the English Parliament, and of themselves as living in a society that essentially was an extension of England, a "greater England." The sense of existing as partners in a common venture had grown steadily over the years, though it was fully articulated only during the 1760s and 1770s.[14] However, this conception of empire was based upon the colonials' belief in a contract between the English architects of colonization and the men and women who trekked to Jamestown, Plymouth, Massachusetts Bay, and elsewhere. As we have seen in the pages of this book, the colonial position had considerable basis in fact. The contract was struck when the English gave up hope of finding precious metals and opted instead for societies of imported colonists who would farm the land, cut the timber, fish the seas, and supply England with needed raw materials. The colonists whom English imperialists attracted to America possessed their own private dreams, and the right to pursue them comprised part of the bargain of settlement. If they risked danger and death in the wilderness to create wealth for England, then they expected Britain to pay the price.

Thousands and thousands of English and non-English flooded the shores of North America seeking the main chance. They came to America because for one reason or another their private dreams could not be pursued in England or Europe. And what were those dreams? They hoped for land, modest amounts of wealth, freedom to act out the drama of the Protestant Reformation, or some measure of control over their own destinies in a political sense. Above all, the colonists asked for and expected autonomy.

For the most part, Anglo-Americans received their requests. The colonists were, as stressed earlier, a peculiar people. They were anything but representative of the common English or European citizen. On the contrary, they were the disaffected and alienated segments of society. They were indeed "vexed and troubled," as Carl Bridenbaugh so accurately labeled them. Fortunately, the private dreams of colonists conformed nicely to the public goals of English expansion. By pursuing individual and imperial goals, Anglo-Americans created wealth, increased English imperial power, and spread English political and religious ideals and institutions. Thus was the bargain struck. In return for doing the hard and dangerous work of creating wealth where none existed, the settlers of early America were promised land, a modicum of self-government, a dissenting Protestant haven, and considerable autonomy.

As we have seen, over the years English planners and mercantilists sought to undo the bargain created in the first years of settlement. Shifting their interests primarily toward trade and then dreaming new dreams of self-sufficiency, English officials exerted greater control over the lives of Anglo-Americans. But their success—especially in regulating trade—occurred largely because the colonials found the arrangements to their liking. Attempts to reorder the political, social, and religious evolution of the colonies, however, proved less successful. Some were even laughable. Although Britain increased the numbers of English officials, troops, and ships in the colonies and intensified the economic demands of empire, the resulting dependency of the colonies—from the colonial viewpoint—worked to their advantage, not disadvantage. Anglo-Americans learned to work within the imperial system, and until 1763 it caused them few problems. When the French and Indian War ended in 1763, Anglo-Americans rejoiced along with the English at the destruction of the French menace. Colonists, like their brethren on the English mainland, reveled in Britain's national greatness.

But from 1763 to 1775, from the colonial perspective, the old contract was broken by England. This did not occur at once, but gradually. Anglo-Americans perceived that ever so slowly English thinking and behavior underwent a profound change. Instead of upholding their end of the contract, the British violated it. After 1768 many colonials suspected a conspiracy against colonial liberties by a cabal of high-placed English leaders. By 1775 they were certain of this, only by then the stakes were higher and the freedoms of liberty-loving peoples everywhere were threatened by a "corrupt English government." By corruption, colonials meant that their place as equal partners in the empire had been denied, their autonomy challenged, their modicum of self-government imperiled, their property threatened, and their Protestantism attacked.

Anglo-Americans assumed that the changes they saw were products of conspiracy and English tyranny because, with a heritage of political, religious, and economic radicalism, they had lived for more than 150 years with notions of conspiracies and tyrants. Colonial identity was in part fueled by a sense of opposition to established orders as well as a sense of being pursued by demons of one sort or another. On the one hand, the radical or even revolutionary tendencies inherent within the colonials' Protestant culture had been checked by the bargain they had struck with English colonizers. On the other hand, many of those very tendencies had developed and matured in the ideology and institutions that composed the cultural baggage of Anglo-Americans of the eighteenth century. Consider the position developed by Thomas Jefferson in his *Summary View,* for example. Though critical of many Protestant beliefs, Jefferson understood the historical relationship between a sense of opposition and Anglo-American identity and he made it the foundation for his argument. He wrote:

> That thus have we hastened thro' the reigns which preceded his majesty's George III, during which the violation of our rights were less alarming, because repeated at more distant intervals, than that rapid and bold succession of injuries which is likely to distinguish the present from all other periods of American story. Scarcely have our minds been able to emerge from the astonishment into which one stroke of parliamentary thunder has involved us, before another more heavy and more alarming is fallen on us. Single acts of tyranny may be ascribed to the accidental opinion of a day; but a series of oppressions, begun at a distinguished period, and pursued unalterably thro' every change of ministers, too plainly prove a deliberate, systematical plan of reducing us to slavery.[15]

Thomas Paine shared Jefferson's ambivalence toward Protestantism. Moreover, Paine had been in the colonies only a short time in 1776. Yet, in *Common Sense,* he appealed bluntly and directly to the same deeply held Anglo-American prejudices that quickened and enlivened Jefferson's argument:

> This New World has been the asylum for the persecuted lovers of civil and religious liberty from every part of Europe. Hither have they fled, not from the tender embraces of the mother, but from the cruelty of the monster; and it is so far true of England that the same tyranny which drove the first emigrants from home pursues their descendants still.[16]

In describing the attempts of colonials to understand the events prior to the Revolutionary War, some writers have noted the development of a conspiracy theory and a shift toward a "republican" ideology. In making this observation, they have labeled Anglo-Americans paranoid—that is, men and women who believed deeply in an ideology that lacked material evidence to support it. Although this book also noted the colonial belief in a conspiracy theory, it found a basis for that belief not simply in new mideighteenth-century thinking, but in long-standing, deep-rooted cultural attitudes—attitudes that grew out of the Protestant heritage of Anglo-America, the mingling of that heritage with the New World environment, and the colonial conception of empire as an arrangement to pursue private as well as imperial goals.

Of course, not all Anglo-Americans followed John Adams, Samuel Adams, Richard Henry Lee, Thomas Jefferson, Thomas Paine, and others toward revolution. But research has shown that neither the Loyalists (British sympathizers), who numbered perhaps as many as a third of the colonists, nor the neutral or uncommitted—who also numbered perhaps another third—differed ideologically from American revolutionaries. Our understanding of why some colonists remained loyal to the Crown differs considerably from Thomas Paine who asked, "What is a Tory?", and answered, "Good God! what is he? . . . Every Tory is a coward; for servile, slavish, self-interested fear is the foundation of Toryism; and a man under such influence, though he may be cruel, never can be brave . . . ."[17] We know that Loyalists, or Tories, possessed stronger feelings of allegiance to the Crown, perhaps a greater sense of class snobbishness, and certainly a fear of the democratic and anarchic tendencies which war would unleash. But they shared with revolutionaries most of the grievances against England. Loyalists as well as revolutionaries understood the contract that had bound English and non-English colonials alike to Great Britain. They too realized that the contract had been broken; but they simply refused to believe that it could not be mended—until it was too late.[18]

These feelings emerged again and again in letters and memoirs written by Loyalists both during and after the war. For example, from exile Peter Van Schaack of New York explained the dilemma of Loyalists in poignant terms:

> . . . I can say with the most sacred regard to truth, I was actuated by no motive unfriendly to my country, nor by any consideration of a personal private nature. Men's hearts are not always known, even to themselves; but, believe me that I spared no pains in examining into all the secret recesses of mine . . . and if America is happier for the revolution, I declare solemnly that I shall rejoice that the side I was on was the unsuccessful one.[19]

A generation later Henry Van Schaack analyzed his father's motives in more detail:

> Mr. Van Schaack was opposed to the measures of the British ministry; he anxiously desired a redress of grievances . . . but, when it was required of him to take up arms, or to give a pledge contemplating measures of force, his conscience and his deliberate views of duty, and of the direful consequences which he apprehended would befall his country, . . . would not permit him to sanction this ultimate step in the progress of the public measures.[20]

Thus, the ferocity of the Revolutionary War proved a great tragedy for Loyalists and fence sitters. They saw their world snatched away forever. At the same time, the radical heritage which had molded Anglo-America was freed to move in whatever directions the winds of change carried it. Let us now consider how the architects of revolution tried to control those winds and build a new nation.

THE NATION AND THE CONSTITUTION

Some historians have suggested that Anglo-America's break from England in 1776 resulted from colonial economic, political, and social maturity. They argue that the colonists had achieved parity with England or had perhaps surpassed the parent country in one or all of these respects.[21] Actually, quite the reverse was the case. By the mideighteenth century the advanced state of England's development along with the associated prosperity of its colonies revealed Anglo-America's *dependence* upon Britain, not its independence. England controlled most colonial resources. Anglo-America produced raw materials for export to England and consumed English manufactured goods in return. Consequently, the colonial economy developed very unevenly. In areas encouraged by Britain, such as agriculture and fishing, Anglo-America achieved high levels of production and considerable economic sophistication. In areas discouraged or completely prohibited by imperial regulations, such as manufacturing, Anglo-America scarcely reached an infant stage. The rapid economic growth experienced in the colonies during the eighteenth century had the effect of increasing colonial dependence upon England. Thus, when Britain prospered, Anglo-America prospered—not the other way around.

Likewise, in a political sense, Anglo-American development remained backward. That might sound surprising, given the great importance Americans have always placed upon the growth of "democracy." But, as noted earlier in the chapters on colonial politics, local government, not colonial or imperial government, remained the most important political arena for colonials. The town or village government exerted the most control and had the greatest impact upon the daily lives of Anglo-Americans. It was largely for that reason that when colony legislatures met, they faced the perpetual problem of contentious factionalism among their members. Those elected to colonial assemblies carried local interests and concerns with them. In the face of war, the colonies marshaled sufficient unity of purpose to organize an army, finance the war, and even defeat the British. But following victory, the now "united" thirteen colonies fell back into old habits and pursued their separate interests.

In that respect, the United States had a colonial "burden" to overcome: localism and economic dependence. Perhaps some Anglo-American ideals and institutions proved suitable to growth and modernization but they alone did not produce the ultimate success of the United States. Some force or forces had to crack the cycle of economic dependency and overcome localism before sustained independent growth was possible. The American Revolution was not such a force. For all that has been written about the "shot heard 'round the world," the fact remains that the Revolution achieved only political independence. It neither fomented a social or cultural revolution nor produced economic independence. The 1770s were momentous years in our collective development, but they were not the key to that development.

Here, generations of commentators have done Americans a disservice by characterizing the Revolution as our single greatest historic event. They have erred by suggesting that all which came before it inexorably led to it, and all which came after it was somehow its product. Actually, in many respects the American Revolution paled as a "revolution" when compared to those elsewhere. Conflict followed an attempt by England to reform and streamline the imperial system. As the French and Indian War drew to a close, England tightened its economic and political dominance over its colonies and also sought ways to shift a portion of the financial burdens of the war with France to Anglo-America. Some Anglo-American colonists, but by no means a majority of them, resisted that abrupt departure from traditional policy, and eventually violence erupted. The events and consequences of this break were momentous, but they hardly foretold or guaranteed future world economic, political, or military leadership.

The driving force behind Anglo-America's independence movement came mainly from the colonial elites who utilized the Revolution to secure their power. Consequently, the Revolution fostered only minimal internal social, economic, or political upheaval. It did not give property to the propertyless or power to the powerless; neither did it end poverty or slavery. It failed to produce better treatment of Indians or improve the position of women. Furthermore, the American Revolution failed to produce a strong central government or strong political union. Rather, it created a weak "confederation" of sovereign states. Even then state governments suffered from internal friction and jealousies. They struggled to maintain unity and consensus among the localities that balked at anything that might challenge their autonomy.

Finally, the American Revolution either partially or completely repudiated some truly revolutionary political principles it first endorsed. At the outbreak of the American Revolution, its leaders drew upon and embellished certain ideas and institutions from the colonial era. Encouraged by important colonial traditions such as Protestant millennialism and anti-Catholicism and social-contract theory, as well as eighteenth-century European imports such as real Whig notions and the Enlightenment theories of Montesquieu, Rousseau, and others, the revolutionary leadership made liberty the symbol of America and tyranny the symbol of England. From simple opposition to parliamentary taxation, trade legislation, and administrative reform evolved the theory of a conspiracy against American liberties and a corresponding revolutionary rhetoric. Anglo-Americans, the patriots declared, could either follow the American route to a new society embracing the rights of man and republican institutions, or the Old World route to monarchical or aristocratic tyranny and slavery.

As hostilities commenced revolutionary rhetoric soared to unforeseen heights. In *Common Sense* (1776) Thomas Paine declared the dawn of a new age and the beginning of a universal struggle for human rights. John Adams portrayed America as the antithesis of Europe and saw a degree of virtue and rationality in Americans that made them superior to all other peoples. Implying that the era of social progress had arrived, writers like Paine argued that the Revolution would lead to a heaven on earth; henceforth, reason would prevail in human affairs. In early 1776 John Adams told George Wythe of Virginia that Americans lived "at a time when the greatest lawgivers of antiquity would have wished to live. How few of the human race," he asked excitedly:

> have ever enjoyed an opportunity of making an election of government, more than of air, soil, or climate, for themselves or their children! When, before the present epocha, had three millions of people full power and a fair opportunity to form and establish the wisest and happiest government that human wisdom can contrive?[22]

Reflecting Protestant assumptions, other writers viewed the Revolution as a struggle with Antichrist which would herald the coming of the millennium. It was the Protestant remnant's opportunity to destroy its enemies and be transformed from suffering saints and persecuted survivors into the architects of God's earthly kingdom. The Revolution became the event toward which all previous trials of faith and fortitude had been directed. Whatever their perspective, apologists for the Revolution agreed that the American people had a divinely sanctioned mission to break with the past and establish a society based on liberty and possibly even equality.[23]

Moreover, as violence continued and rhetoric increased, even the colonial past seemed in jeopardy. Formerly guardians of republican institutions that restrained liberty with authority and inhabitants of a society that assumed the inequality of men, Anglo-Americans edged toward a true internal social, political, and economic upheaval. Abigail Adams wrote to her husband John in March, 1776, reminding him that "in the new code of laws which I suppose it will be necessary for you to make, I desire you would remember the ladies and be more generous and favorable to them than your ancestors. Do not put such unlimited power into the hands of the husbands. Remember, all men would be tyrants if they could."[24] At about the same time, Congregational minister Samuel Hopkins of Rhode Island told the Second Continental Congress to apply American revolutionary ideals and end the institution of slavery:

> But if we obstinately refuse to reform what we have implicitly declared to be wrong, and engaged to put away the holding of Africans in slavery, which is so particularly pointed out by the evil with which we are threatened and is such a glaring contradiction to our professed aversion to slavery and struggle for civil liberty . . . have we not the greatest reason to fear, yea, may we not with great certainty conclude, God will punish us yet seven times more?[25]

Jefferson's *Declaration of Independence* justified a revolution for the natural rights of men and suggested the equality of all people. As Tory opponents fled by the thousands, their lands were confiscated and redistributed. Slaves were promised freedom by both British and Americans if they fought for one side or the other and slavery was abolished in some of the new American states. Everywhere liberty became the watchword and official standard of judgment for all ideas and institutions. The new states disavowed their English allegiance, dissolved colonial governments, called state conventions, and drafted new "constitutions" reflecting their belief that sovereign peoples could destroy old governments and form new ones. The Constitution of Vermont, adopted July 8, 1777, affirmed that "government ought to be instituted and supported, for the security and protection of the community as such, and to enable the individuals who compose it, to enjoy their natural rights . . . ." It declared that "whenever those great ends of government are not obtained, the people have a right, by common consent, to change it, and take such measures as to them may appear necessary to promote their safety and happiness."[26] Although the new creations resembled the old colonial governments, the states added certain distinctly republican features. The rights and liberties of the people were spelled out in the constitutions. Many of them abolished religious qualifications for voting and holding office, and a few ended state support for a single church (such as the Church of England). Legislatures were no longer bound by obnoxious restraints and restrictions, except those imposed by the people; and executives were rendered either powerless or abolished. America declared that it needed neither kings nor governors.

At the same time and while the war progressed, Anglo-Americans created a central government befitting liberty-loving republicans who were moving toward a *Novus Ordo Seclorum,* a new order of the ages, as the Great Seal of the United States proclaimed in the early 1780s. Under the *Articles of Confederation,* an American version of the old British Empire reemerged. The *Articles* created a league of sovereign states loosely connected in a confederation governed by a congress. The powers of Congress were strictly limited to what the states were willing to grant. Proposed in 1777, the *Articles* were not approved by all the states until 1781. Meanwhile the conduct of war was carried on by the Second Continental Congress, which also needed the states' approval to act. Having imbibed the liberty-versus-tyranny rhetoric of the 1770s, colonials broke with their own past and tilted their republican governments toward liberty and away from authority.

Within a short time, however, the patriots began to reverse themselves. France's intervention quieted some of the more extreme proponents of America's purity and Europe's corruption. Republican zeal and millennial hopes dissipated as common people tired of the costly, bloody war and as politicians wrangled over matters bearing little relationship to the public interest. It became difficult to find men willing to fight in the Continental Army. In Concord, Massachusetts, home of the "minutemen," only the poor joined the army after 1777 and they did so because they received a bounty to enlist. Not even the poor, however, went to war readily. One pound sterling enticed a colonial into the army for a month and a half in 1775; by 1780 it commanded about one day's service.[27] George Washington deplored the shallow patriotism of so many of his compatriots. In December, 1778, he wrote that:

> If I was to be called upon to draw A picture of the times, and of Men; from what I have seen, heard, and in part know I should in one word say that idleness, dissipation, and extravagance seems to have laid fast hold of most of them. That Speculation, peculation, and an insatiable thirst for riches seems to have got the better of every other consideration and almost of every order of Men. That party disputes and personal quarrels are the great business of the day, while the momentous concerns of an empire . . . are but secondary considerations . . . I am alarmed and wish to see my Countrymen roused.[28]

To some, republicanism began to seem a synonym for anarchy and legislative inaction. Cooperation among the states lagged as ratification of the *Articles* stalled over a land dispute in Maryland and as the Second Continental Congress made strident pleas for greater support of the war effort. A growing number of people worried that the Revolution had gone too far and that the revolutionary settlement might lead to social cataclysm. Everywhere, Americans argued that the new country needed less liberty and more authority, and slowly the pendulum began to swing back. Most states drafted new constitutions with strong executives. At the same time, and even before the new government of the *Articles* had begun to function, a movement developed to create an even stronger central government.

Other than political independence for thirteen sovereign states, then, the American Revolution accomplished little. The radicalism of 1776 disappeared, and Anglo-America's colonial heritage of political, social, and religious institutions and ideals passed, virtually intact, into the 1780s. So too, did the economic dependence of the former colonies. Almost as soon as hostilities ceased, representatives of English merchants reappeared in America offering credit in return for trade. Thus, after a short period of depression brought on by wartime disruption of trade with England, Europe, and the West Indies, commerce and agricultural production resumed and the American economy righted itself to the same position of dependence upon England it had occupied before the war.[29]

Then, between 1787 and 1791 a virtual second American Revolution occurred. That revolution, involving the creation and ratification of the *Constitution* and the subsequent addition of the *Bill of Rights,* produced some of the most important events in our collective history. It was then that North Americans guaranteed their political independence and moved toward harnessing their colonial heritage by institutionalizing its best parts and discarding or muting its worst. This process, however, proved to be neither simple nor easy. The Philadelphia Convention of 1787 that produced the *Constitution* was a long, rancorous affair and it ended in a series of compromises which left no one completely happy. Then, when the *Constitution* went to the states for ratification, stiff opposition emerged from people called anti-Federalists who feared the power of the proposed central government and who believed that it might trample the liberties of the people and the prerogatives of the states. Supporters of the *Constitution,* called Federalists, defused most of the opposition by promising to add a *Bill of Rights* at the earliest opportunity. This was done during the first session of the new Congress (1789) when Federalist James Madison wrote and submitted ten amendments to the *Constitution.* Congress accepted the amendments and by 1791 they were ratified by the states.[30]

The *Constitution* emerged, not because things were proceeding poorly, but rather because many Americans believed that the first revolutionary settlement would ultimately fail. Those "nationalists" recognized how little the first American Revolution had transformed American life and how much of America's colonial heritage—with all its strengths and weaknesses—remained untouched and unrefined. They argued that some aspects of that heritage needed to be magnified and others destroyed or at least neutralized, if the United States were to succeed. It was not that the nationalists were simply visionaries or dreamers who conjured images of a special messianic mission America would some day perform in world affairs. Rather, they were both dreamers and very practical people who possessed an extraordinary grasp of the character of their own past. They recognized that both materially and ideologically, Americans had much to offer the world, but they saw an enormous colonial burden as well. That burden, they believed had to be lightened or the United States would remain an economic and cultural appendage of England and Europe—or worse, it would lose its political independence. "The Revolution is but half completed,"[31] said poet Joel Barlow in Hartford, Connecticut, on July 4, 1787. Dr. Benjamin Rush of Philadelphia—statesman, physician, and patriot—agreed:

> Patriots of 1774, 1775, 1776—heroes of 1778, 1779, 1780! come forward! your country demands your services! Philosophers and friends to mankind, come forward! your country demands your studies and speculations! Lovers of peace and order, who declined taking part in the late war, come forward! your country forgives your timidity and demands your influence and advice! Hear her proclaiming, in sighs and groans, in her governments, in her finances, in her trade, in her manufactures, in her morals, and in her manners, "The Revolution Is Not Over!"[32]

Specifically, the nationalists who forged the *Constitution* and engineered its ratification saw two fatal flaws in their own colonial past. One was the parochialism (we have called it localism) of America's citizens. Their zeal for autonomy and local control—elements that had brought most of their ancestors to America in the first place—virtually nullified sustained collective action. Parochialism represented the single greatest peril to America's future political independence and security. The second flaw was America's economic dependence upon England and Europe. This economic status, the nationalists believed, had once fueled colonial growth and prosperity, but now it promised only to stunt that growth. As students of history and believers in the dominant geo-political theories of the eighteenth century, nationalists argued vehemently that the United States had to become economically independent and virtually self-sufficient to survive and achieve greatness. To do that Americans needed no colonial empire. Rather, they needed to expand and exploit the land and resources of their own continent while developing a complex economy based on a mixture of agriculture, manufacturing, and commerce. They needed also to generate their own capital and establish a sound financial system.

At the same time nationalists saw in colonial ideals and institutions much vital to America's future. Mainly, they endorsed the elements we have discussed: economic opportunity and the acquisition of property; republican political institutions and beliefs; religious idealism, spiritual and moral strength, and religious pluralism; and finally, a peculiar strain of individualism which stressed the need for the individual to achieve but also postulated the necessity to harmonize individual goals and interests with those of the community and society. In each of these areas nationalists believed that the people had been ill-served by the first American Revolution.

To achieve their goal of securing the future of the American republic the architects of the *Constitution* and *Bill of Rights* had to accomplish some incredible feats. First, they had to tie the past to the present *and* future by institutionalizing what they believed to be the most important features of America's colonial past. In Article I of the *Bill of Rights* and Article VI of the *Constitution* they followed the lead of Thomas Jefferson's famous "Bill for Establishing Religious Freedom" (adopted by the Virginia House of Delegates in 1786) by separating church and state at the national level. To do so they banned Congress from making any law "prohibiting the free exercise" of religious belief or worship (*Bill of Rights*) and they expressly forbade that any "religious Test shall ever be required as a Qualification to any Office or public Trust under the United States" (*Constitution*). They took those steps not because they feared religion but because they recognized its awesome power in early America and its positive contributions to colonial development. They gave approval to religious pluralism and, by implication, to the emerging competitive evangelical spirit of colonial Protestantism. They hoped that competing sects would give future generations of Americans a sound moral and spiritual foundation.

Through another vein in the *Constitution,* the Founding Fathers tried to harness and perpetuate the economic aggressiveness of the colonial heritage and ensure the powerful hope of all immigrants for a better life by making property and its protection an integral part of America's future. They knew that land had played the central role in attracting the English and Europeans to America. They knew also that easy accessibility and wide distribution of property had prevented the establishment of a landed aristocracy or even a solidified class structure. The Founding Fathers sanctified and protected property because they understood that its possession was the private dream of all Americans.

The architects of the *Constitution* and the *Bill of Rights* also codified Anglo-America's republican heritage. In their documents they enshrined popular sovereignty, representative assemblies, civil liberties, and rule of law: all vital components of the colonial past. The drafters of the *Constitution* even developed several novel twists to the traditional republican theories and practices from which they borrowed. One was to have the central government act directly upon individuals and not through the states. A second involved representation in the Congress. In Philadelphia the delegates to the Constitutional Convention resolved this problem in what came to be known as the *Great Compromise.* Large states and small states—each fearing that the other bloc would dominate the new legislature—agreed to a plan whereby the Senate would give each state equal representation while the House would be based on a proportional system determined by population. Senators would be chosen by state legislatures while House members would be elected directly by the people.

James Madison thought that the Great Compromise was the most novel aspect of the *Constitution.* Thomas Jefferson (who was in France during the convention) both criticized and lauded the scheme. "I like the power given the Legislature to levy taxes," he wrote Madison:

> and for that reason solely approve of the greater house being chosen by the people directly. For tho' I think a house chosen by them will be very illy qualified to legislate for the Union . . . Yet this evil does not weigh against the good of preserving inviolate the fundamental principle that the people are not to be taxed but by representatives chosen immediately by themselves. I am captivated by the compromise of the opposite claims of the great and little states, of the latter to equal and the former to proportional influence.[33]

As both republican innovations revealed the Founding Fathers hoped to achieve what appeared to be contradictory goals. On the one hand they hoped to correct some of the presumed "excesses" of the first revolution and to create a proper balance between liberty and authority by giving the central government some real power. That they tried to achieve in many ways, not the least of which was allowing the central government to act directly on citizens. On the other hand they tried to erect an elaborate filtering system—just as the English and Anglo-Americans had always sought to do—to protect the people from their government, and vice versa. That filtering system emerged in the Great Compromise, the separation of powers, the system of checks and balances, and the procedure for electing a president. However, when the *Constitution* was presented to the people, skeptics saw only the awesome power of the central government embodied in its ability to legislate directly upon citizens. That "defect" was remedied by the *Bill of Rights.*

The Founding Fathers had solutions for the more onerous components of their colonial heritage as well. While a strong general government with greater authority than the states provided their answer to localism or parochialism, the concept of federalism was their device to make centralized authority palatable to a fiercely independent citizenry. James Madison described the spirited and lengthy debate over federalism in the Constitutional Convention in these words:

> The due partition of power between the general and local governments was, perhaps of all, the most nice and difficult. A few contended for an entire abolition of the states, some, for indefinite power of legislation in the Congress, with a negative on the laws of the states; some, for such a power without a negative; some, for a limited power of legislation, with such a negative; the majority, finally, for a limited power without the negative. The question with regard to the negative underwent repeated discussions, and was finally rejected by a bare majority.[34]

In a sense, federalism represented another component of the filtering system described earlier; but more importantly, it was a cumbersome, rather peculiar instrument meant to give Americans both localism and "a more perfect Union." It did not try to destroy localism so much as it tried to use it. The Founding Fathers recognized that this phase of the *Constitution* was one of the most experimental and ran a great risk of failure. Nevertheless, they hoped the people would accept the power of the central government, just as they had once accepted the authority of the Crown and Parliament, once they understood that the people retained sovereignty and could amend the *Constitution* at any time. Even then, to secure the

Constitution's approval from the states required enormous effort, concessions (such as the *Bill of Rights*), and much special pleading, such as the powerful and eloquent *Federalist Papers* of Alexander Hamilton, James Madison, and John Jay. Localism, of course, persisted in American life. As the founders feared, it nearly proved the republic's undoing during the Civil War.

The creators of the *Constitution* and *Bill of Rights* attacked the problem of America's economic dependency upon England and Europe with considerable vigor and nearly as much imagination. But they could not legislate economic independence; they could only provide the central government with the tools to promote America's economic development. Protecting private property was one such tool. Others included the powers to regulate foreign commerce, to coin money and control currency, to raise revenue and borrow on the credit of the United States, to make "Duties, Imports, and Excises," to regulate interstate commerce, and to promote technological innovation through patents. Equally important, in Section Ten of Article I, the *Constitution* enumerated those things the states could not do, such as "enter into any Treaty, Alliance, or Confederation; grant Letters of Marque and Reprisal; coin Money; Emit Bills of Credit; make any Thing but gold and silver Coin a Tender in Payment of Debts; pass any Bill of Attainder, ex post facto Law, or Law impairing the Obligation of Contracts . . . ."[35]

The *Constitution* embodied no single economic vision of America's future; perhaps no such vision existed among its creators. But it did devise the apparatus needed to mold a single vision. Most likely that explains why some of the earliest legislation presented to the First United States Congress came from arch-nationalist and new Secretary of the Treasury Alexander Hamilton. Hamilton proposed a national bank, the assumption of state debts, and other aspects of a private dream to base America's economic independence on capital, manufacturing, and an activist central government. Others' dreams would also come forth. In the 1790s the first political parties formed after disagreements between Hamilton and Thomas Jefferson. Jefferson made his own distinctive contributions to America's economic development by becoming a champion of territorial expansion. But that goes beyond our story.

Other aspects of Anglo-America's heritage needed to be overcome, but the founders achieved little success with most of them. As we noted earlier, colonial America represented a distorted version of English and European society. Part of that distortion resulted from the treatment of Indians and from the persistence and growth of black slavery. The *Constitution* resolved neither problem. In fact, many of the founders did not consider either slavery or the continuing struggle with native American peoples to be part of the United States' colonial burden. Thus, in those areas, the *Constitution* left a dubious legacy for Americans of the nineteenth and twentieth centuries. But the genius of the document remained.

The *Constitution* was created by men who believed that they were practitioners of something called the "science" of politics. They believed that they were advancing that science by creating a republican form of government for a very large territory. In doing so, they offered, they believed, a new order for affairs among people and an antidote to the repressive monarchies (Jefferson likened them to wolves governing sheep) which prevailed in so many countries of the era. At the same time, as we have seen, the *Constitution* was intended to be a very practical document tailored to the concerns and welfare of a particular people at a particular time. Also, it offered an important lesson for those who were interested. In many ways it was a lesson about the past. The Founding Fathers had a strong sense of both the burdens and freedoms that the past conveyed upon the present and future. Though good eighteenth-century rationalists, they did not see reason as the key to a heaven on earth nor did they believe in the inevitability of human and social progress. They were too aware of human limitations. Reason, they believed, could influence the future, but only if it was enlightened by the wisdom and experience of the past. In order to have a future, they argued, people could neither revere nor fear their past. Instead, they had to know it and they had to use it. Above all else, they had to act. Alexander Hamilton opened his defense of the *Constitution* in *The Federalist Number One* with precisely that sentiment: "It has been frequently remarked," he wrote,

> that it seems to have been reserved to the people of this country, by their conduct and example, to decide the important question, whether societies of men are really capable or not of establishing good government from reflection and choice, or whether they are forever destined to depend for their political constitutions on accident and force. If there be any truth in the remark, the crisis at which we are arrived may with propriety be regarded as the era in which that decision is to be made; and a wrong election of the part we shall act may, in this view, deserve to be considered as the general misfortune of mankind.[36]

The "decision" to which Hamilton referred was not unlike the decisions faced by the immigrant architects of Anglo-America much earlier. Fortunately, by 1787 Americans had almost two centuries of experience upon which to draw—two centuries filled mainly with dreams fulfilled and goals achieved. Hamilton was hopeful that the American Odyssey had ended in the creation of a ship of state that would sail on forever. Many Americans, however, were skeptical. Fisher Ames—a Federalist like Hamilton—wrote that:

> we may, like a wounded snake, drag our slow length along for twenty years; and time will in that period have more to do in fixing our future destiny than our administration. Events govern us . . . We are in a gulf stream, which has hitherto swept us along with more force than our sails and oars. I think the government will last my time. For that reason, I will fatten my pigs, and prune my trees.[37]

Footnotes

PROLOGUE

[1] As Nathan Glazer and Daniel Patrick Moynihan pointed out in their classic study, *Beyond the Melting Pot: The Negroes, Puerto Ricans, Jews, Italians and Irish of New York City* (Cambridge, Mass.: M.I.T. Press, 1963), the notion of a "melting pot" was as old as the nation itself and dominated public speculation about an "American character" from the 1780s until well into the twentieth century. It was, they wrote, "an idea close to the heart of the American self-image" (p. 288). It faded in the twentieth century but it did not die. It returned in different forms, including Will Herberg's powerful and influential endorsement of a melting pot with three distinct parts in *Protestant-Catholic-Jew* (Garden City, N.Y.: Doubleday, 1956).

[2] Turner presented his ideas to the American Historical Association in 1893 in an essay entitled, "The Significance of the Frontier in American History." The essay was published in the Association's *Report* for 1893 and was reprinted in Turner's *The Frontier in American History* (New York: Holt, Rinehart & Winston, 1920). Arguments for and against Turner's thesis are summarized in George Rogers Taylor, ed., *The Turner Thesis Concerning the Role of the Frontier in American History,* 3rd ed. (Boston: D. C. Heath, 1972).

[3] Vine DeLoria Jr., *We Talk, You Listen: New Tribes, New Turf* (New York: Macmillan, 1971) and DeLoria, *God is Red* (New York: Grosset & Dunlap, 1973); Malcolm X, *The Autobiography of Malcolm X* (New York: Grove Press, 1965); and Armando Rendon, *Chicano Manifesto* (New York: Macmillan, 1971) are examples of minority-group representatives arguing persuasively against the notion of a common American character. Their views are supported by the research and conclusions of many scholars. An early advocate of the existence of cultural pluralism was Horace Kallen. See, for example, his *Culture and Democracy in the United States,* rep. ed. (New York: Arno Press, 1979). More recent works are Glazer and Moynihan, *Beyond the Melting Pot*; John Higham, *Send These to Me: Jews and Other Immigrants in Urban America* (New York: Atheneum Press, 1975); and Michael Novak, *The Rise of the Unmeltable Ethnic* (New York: Macmillan, 1972). Some of the possible hazards of cultural pluralism are outlined by Gordon Daniel Morgan in *America Without Ethnicity* (Port Washington, N.Y.: Kennikat Press, 1981).

[4] J. Hector St. John de Crevecoeur, *Letters from an American Farmer and Sketches of 18th-Century America,* ed. Albert E. Stone (New York: Penguin Books, 1981), 69–70.

[5] Perry Miller, *The New England Mind: The Seventeenth Century* (Cambridge, Mass.: Harvard University Press, 1939); and Miller, *The New England Mind: From Colony to Province* (Cambridge, Mass.: Harvard University Press, 1953); Daniel Boorstin, *The Americans: The Colonial Experience* (New York: Random House, 1958); Louis Hartz, *The Liberal Tradition in America* (New York: Harcourt, Brace, 1955).

[6] Kenneth A. Lockridge, *A New England Town, The First Hundred Years: Dedham, Massachusetts, 1636–1736* (New York: W. W. Norton, 1970); Paul Boyer and Stephen Nissenbaum, *Salem Possessed: The Social Origins of Witchcraft* (Cambridge, Mass.: Harvard University Press, 1974); Bernard Bailyn, *The Ideological Origins of the American Revolution* (Cambridge, Mass.: Harvard University Press, 1967).

[7] Thomas Bender, *Community and Social Change in America* (New Brunswick, N.J.: Rutgers University Press, 1978).

CHAPTER ONE

[1] R. H. Major, trans. and ed., *Select Letters of Christopher Columbus with other Original Documents, Relating to his Four Voyages to the New World* (London: Hakluyt Society, 1847), 1-2, 2-3. See Samuel Eliot Morison, *Admiral of the Ocean Sea: A Life of Christopher Columbus* (Boston: Little, Brown, 1942) for a fine introduction to the life and explorations of Columbus.

[2] The student may consult Hjalmar R. Holand, *Exploration in America before Columbus* (New York: Twayne Publishers, 1956); David B. Quinn, *North America from Earliest Discovery to First Settlements: The Norse Voyages to 1612* (New York: Harper & Row, 1977); and Quinn, *North American Discovery circa 1000–1612* (Columbia, S.C.: University of South Carolina Press, 1971); and Gwyn Jones, *The Norse Atlantic Saga being the Norse Voyages of Discovery and Settlement to Iceland, Greenland, and America* (London: Oxford University Press, 1964); and Jones, *A History of the Vikings* (New York: Oxford University Press, 1968) for further information on Viking explorations of America. Leif Erikson's importance for America is treated in Edward D. Gray, *Leif Eriksson: Discoverer of America A.D. 1003* (London: Oxford University Press, 1930).

[3] Quoted in Gordon Brotherston, *Image of the New World: The American Continent Portrayed in Native Texts* (London: Thames and Hudson, 1979), 156.

[4] The history and culture of the North American Indians are discussed in numerous surveys. Among the most useful are Clark Wissler, *The Indians of the United States: Four Centuries of their History and Culture,* rev. ed. (Garden City, N.Y.: Doubleday, 1966); Harold E. Driver, *Indians of North America,* rev. 2nd ed. (Chicago: University of Chicago Press, 1969); Wilcomb E. Washburn, *The Indian in America* (New York: Harper & Row, 1975); Alvin M. Josephy Jr., *The Indian Heritage of America* (New York: Alfred A. Knopf, 1968); Wendell H. Oswalt, *This Land Was Theirs: A Study of the North American Indian,* 3d ed. (New York: Wiley, 1978); Edward H. Spicer, *A Short History of the Indians of the United States* (New York: Van Nostrand Reinhold, 1969); and *Handbook of North American Indians,* gen. ed. William C. Sturdevant, 15 vols. (Washington, D.C.: Smithsonian Institution, 1978–1981), esp. Vol. XV, *The Northeast,* ed. Bruce G. Trigger.

[5] Cadwallader Colden, *The History of the Five Indian Nations of Canada* originally pub. 1747; rep. 2 vols. (New York: A. S. Barnes and Company, 1904) remains an important primer on the Indian tribes of the Northeast. Donald A. Grinde, *The Iroquois and the Founding of the American Nation* (San Francisco: Indian Historian Press, 1977); and Barbara Graymont, *The Iroquois in the American Revolution* (Syracuse, N.Y.: Syracuse University Press, 1972) trace the impact of the northeastern tribes on European settlement. Differing perspectives on the contact between Indians and whites may be found in Alden T. Vaughan, *New England Frontier: Puritans and Indians, 1620–1675,* rev. ed. (New York: W. W. Norton, 1979); Francis Jennings, *The Invasion of America: Indians, Colonialism and the Cant of Conquest* (Chapel Hill, N.C.: University of North Carolina Press, 1975); Richard Slotkin, *Regeneration through Violence: The Mythology of the American Frontier, 1600–1860* (Middletown, Conn.: Wesleyan University Press, 1973); Bernard W. Sheehan, *Savagism and Civility: Indians and Englishmen in Colonial Virginia* (New York: Cambridge University Press, 1980); and Carl Ortwin Sauer, *Sixteenth Century North America: The Land and the People as Seen by Europeans* (Berkeley, Calif.: University of California Press, 1971).

[6]The history of early modern Europe is summarized and reviewed ably by Sir George Clark, *Early Modern Europe from about 1450 to about 1720* (New York: Oxford University Press, 1966); D. C. Munro, *The Middle Ages, 395–1272* (New York: The Century Co., 1921); N. F. Cantor, *Medieval History: The Life and Death of a Civilization,* 2nd ed. (New York: Macmillan, 1969); and J. Huizinga, *The Waning of the Middle Ages: A Study of the Forms of Life, Thought, and Art in France and the Netherlands in the XIVth and XVth Centuries* (New York: St. Martin's Press, 1967). For an interesting analysis of the medieval European economy and society, see Henri Pirenne, *Economic and Social History of Medieval Europe,* trans. I. E. Clegg (New York: Harcourt, Brace, 1937).

[7]Niccolo Machiavelli, *The Prince,* trans. Christian E. Detmold, ed. with intro. by Lester G. Crocker (New York: Washington Square Press, 1963), 113–114.

[8]Robert R. Ergang, *The Renaissance* (Princeton, N.J.: Van Nostrand, 1967); Wallace K. Ferguson, *Europe in Transition, 1300–1520* (Boston: Houghton-Mifflin, 1962); Ferguson, *Renaissance Studies* (London, Ontario: Humanities Department of the University of Ontario, 1963); and Ferguson, *Renaissance in Historical Thought: Five Centuries of Interpretation* (Boston: Houghton-Mifflin, 1948); S. H. Thomson, *Europe in Renaissance and Reformation* (London: R. Hart Davies, 1963); Myron P. Gilmore, *The World of Humanism, 1453–1517* (New York: Harper & Row, 1962); and J. R. Hale, *Renaissance Europe: Individual and Society, 1480–1520* (London: Wm. Collins Sons, 1971) offer reliable guides to the Renaissance era.

[9]Martin Luther, *Luther's Works,* vols. 1–30 ed. Jaroslav Pelikan (St. Louis: Concordia, 1955–1976); vols. 31–55. ed. Helmut T. Lehman (Philadelphia: Fortress Press, 1955–1976), 32: 112–113.

[10]Owen Chadwick, *The Reformation* (Baltimore: Penguin Books, 1964); and Roland H. Bainton, *The Reformation of the Sixteenth Century* (Boston: Beacon Press, 1963) provide excellent introductions to the history of the Reformation. Norman Sykes, *The Crisis of the Reformation* (London: G. Bles, 1958) examines the theological questions raised by reformers. J. T. McNeill, *The History and Character of Calvinism* (New York: Oxford University Press, 1973) continues to be a standard source for Calvin's teachings; while Roland H. Bainton, *Here I Stand: A Life of Martin Luther* (New York: Abingdon-Cokesbury Press, 1950) explores Luther's life and beliefs. An account of "left-wing" reformers can be found in George H. Williams, *The Radical Reformation* (Philadelphia: Westminster Press, 1962).

[11] For a discussion of the Counter-Reformation, readers should consult B. J. Kidd, *The Counter-Reformation, 1550–1600* (London: Society for Promoting Christian Knowledge, 1933); and Arthur G. Dickens, *The Counter-Reformation* (London: Thames & Hudson, 1968).

[12]The idea of America has been the subject of considerable interest in recent years, and the literature is extensive. Some of the more important studies include Edmundo O'Gorman, *The Invention of America: An Inquiry into the Historical Nature of the New World and the Meaning of its History* (Bloomington, Ind.: Indiana University Press, 1961); Howard Mumford Jones, *O Strange New World: American Culture, The Formative Years* (New York: Viking Press, 1967); Sauer, *Sixteenth Century North America*; David B. Quinn, *England and the Discovery of America, 1481–1620, from the Bristol Voyages of the Fifteenth Century to the Pilgrim Settlement at Plymouth: The Exploration, Exploitation and Trial-and-Error Colonization of North America by the English* (New York: Alfred A. Knopf, 1974); and Hugh Honour, *The New Golden Land: European Images of America from the Discoveries to the Present Time* (New York: Pantheon Books, 1975).

[13]Charles Gibson, ed., *The Black Legend: Anti-Spanish Attitudes in the Old World and the New* (New York: Alfred A. Knopf, 1971), 74–76.

[14] For a solid account of European exploration in general, see Samuel Eliot Morison, *The European Discovery of America: The North American Voyages, A.D. 500–1600* (New York: Oxford University Press, 1971). Spain's activities in America have been studied by numerous historians. In particular J. H. Parry explores the evolution of Spanish imperial notions and practices in his *The Spanish Theory of Empire in the Sixteenth Century* (Cambridge: Cambridge University Press, 1940); and *The Spanish Seaborne Empire,* 2nd ed. (London: Hutchinson, 1966). J. H. Elliott, *Imperial Spain, 1469–1716* (New York: St. Martin's Press, 1964) illuminates aspects of Spain's domestic affairs as they relate to its empire, while Charles Gibson, *Spain in America* (New York: Harper & Row, 1966) examines the development of Spain's colonial system.

[15]France's empire has been the subject of considerable interest among historians. See especially Geoffrey R. R. Treasure, *Seventeenth Century France* (London: Rivingtons, 1966) for a description of the rise of absolutism and the domestic climate that encouraged French overseas expansion. Also, William J. Eccles, *France in America* (New York: Harper & Row, 1972) provides a lively discussion of France's North American empire.

[16] Dutch and Swedish colonizing activities are treated in W. R. Shepherd, *The Story of New Amsterdam,* rep. (Port Washington, N.Y.: Kennikat Press, 1970); Christopher Ward, *The Dutch and the Swedes on the Delaware, 1609–64* (Philadelphia: University of Pennsylvania Press, 1930); and Amandus Johnson, *The Swedish Settlements on the Delaware,* 2 vols. (Philadelphia: Swedish Colonial Society, 1911). It should also be noted that Denmark and Prussia undertook a few expeditions to North America to found colonies. In 1672 the Danish West India Company successfully established a small foothold in the Virgin Islands. Ten years later Prussia also sent out a colonizing force to the West Indies. Since by this time the West Indian islands had already been claimed by other European nations, the Brandenburg African Company, Prussia's representative, attempted to purchase land for a trading settlement. Failing in this, the company did acquire a lease on St. Thomas in the Virgin Islands from the Danes. Within only a few years, however, the Prussians lost even this tenuous presence in North America. The Prussians pursued no further colonizing activities in the New World.

CHAPTER TWO

[1] Ever since the publication of R. H. Tawney's "The Rise of the Gentry," *Economic History Review,* 11, No. 1 (1941), 1–38, scholars of sixteenth- and seventeenth-century England have debated whether social, economic, and politic[illegible]wer shifted from the aristocracy to the gentry and why and how such a shift may have occurred. The literature surrounding this controversy is extensive. Some of the more important contributions to this debate include H. R. Trevor-Roper, "The Gentry, 1540–1640," *Economic History Review Supplement,* No. 1 (London: Cambridge University Press, 1953); Trevor-Roper, "General Crisis of the Seventeenth Century," *Past and Present,* No. 16 (November 1959), 31–62; Eric Hobsbawn, "The Crisis of the Seventeenth Century, Part I," *Past and Present,* No. 5 (May 1954), 33–49; and Hobsbawn, "The Crisis of the Seventeenth Century, Part II," *Past and Present,* No. 6 (November 1954), 44–63; J. H. Hexter, "Storm Over the Gentry," in *Reappraisals in History* (London: Longmans, Green, 1961), 22–34; Hexter, "The English Aristocracy: Its Crises, and the English Revolution, 1558–1660," *Journal of British Studies,* 7, No. 1 (November 1968), 22–78; and Lawrence Stone, *Crisis of the Aristocracy, 1558–1641* (Oxford: Clarendon Press, 1965).

[2] The literature on sixteenth- and seventeenth-century England is voluminous. Some of the more helpful studies include S. T. Bindoff, *Tudor England* (Harmondsworth, Eng.: Penguin Books, 1952); G. R. Elton, *England under the Tudors,* 2nd ed. (London: Methuen, 1974); Roger Lockyer, *Tudor and Stuart Britain, 1471–1714* (New York: St. Martin's Press, 1964); Charles M. Gray, *Renaissance and Reformation England, 1509–1714* (New York: Harcourt Brace Jovanovitch, 1973); John P. Kenyon, *Stuart England* (New York: St. Martin's Press, 1978); and Lacy Baldwin Smith, *This Realme of England, 1399–1688* (Boston: D. C. Heath, 1966).

[3] The importance of the English Reformation is discussed in Arthur G. Dickens, *The English Reformation* (New York: Schocken Books, 1964); Thomas M. Parker, *The English Reformation to 1588,* 2nd ed. (London: Oxford University Press, 1966); David H. Pill, *The English Reformation, 1529–1558* (London: University of London Press, 1973); J. J. Scarsbrick, *Henry VIII* (Berkeley, Calif.: University of California Press, 1968); J. E. Neale, *Queen Elizabeth I* (London: J. Cape, 1934); and Charles H. and Katherine George, *The Protestant Mind of the English Reformation, 1570–1640* (Princeton, N.J.: Princeton University Press, 1961).

[4] The origins of the English Puritan movement are described in George and George, *Protestant Mind;* William Haller, *The Rise of Puritanism; or The Way to the New Jerusalem as Set Forth in Pulpit and Press from Thomas Cartwright to John Lilburne and John Milton, 1570–1643* (New York: Harper & Row, 1957); and Patrick Collinson, *The Elizabethan Puritan Movement* (Berkeley, Calif.: University of California Press, 1967). In *The Puritan Dilemma: The Story of John Winthrop* (Boston: Little, Brown, 1958), Edmund S. Morgan presents an intelligent and lucid account of the differences between separating and nonseparating Congregationalists.

[5] Clement R. Markham, ed., *The Hawkins' Voyages during the Reigns of Henry VIII, Queen Elizabeth, and James I* (London: Hakluyt Society, 1878), 62–63.

[6] A. L. Rowse, *The Expansion of Elizabethan England* (New York: St. Martin's Press, 1955); Carl Bridenbaugh, *Vexed and Troubled Englishmen, 1590–1642* (New York: Oxford University Press, 1968); Wallace Notestein, *The English People on the Eve of Colonization, 1603–1630* (New York: Harper & Row, 1954); A. L. Rowse, *The Elizabethans and America* (London: Alfred Leslie, 1959); David B. Quinn, *England and the Discovery of America, 1481–*

1620 (New York: Alfred A. Knopf, 1974); Quinn, *North America from Earliest Discovery to First Settlements: The Norse Voyages to 1612* (New York: Alfred A. Knopf, 1977); and William P. Cumming, R. A. Skelton, and D. B. Quinn, *The Discovery of North America* (New York: American Heritage Press, 1972) all provide excellent accounts of early English exploration and the climate of opinion that encouraged England's expansion into North America. The best biography of James I is David Harris Willson, *King James VI and I* (New York: Holt, Rinehart & Winston, 1956). Events during the reigns of both James I and Charles I are summarized in Kenyon, *Stuart England.*

[7] Good introductions to the history of Virginia include John E. Pomfret with Floyd M. Shumway, *Founding the American Colonies, 1583-1660* (New York: Harper & Row, 1970), 25-74; Charles M. Andrews, *The Colonial Period of American History,* 4 vols. (New Haven: Yale University Press, 1934-1938), 2: 98-213; Edmund S. Morgan, *American Slavery, American Freedom: The Ordeal of Colonial Virginia* (New York: W. W. Norton, 1975); Richard L. Morton, *Colonial Virginia,* 2 vols. (Chapel Hill, N.C.: University of North Carolina Press, 1960); and Wesley Frank Craven, *The Southern Colonies in the Seventeenth Century, 1607-1689* (Baton Rouge, La.: Louisiana State University Press, 1949).

[8] William Bradford, *Bradford's History of Plymouth Plantation, 1606-1646,* ed. William T. Davis (New York: Barnes & Noble, 1959), 46.

[9] Bradford, *Bradford's History,* 106.

[10] Ibid., 107. Plymouth's history is skillfully treated in George D. Langdon, Jr., *Pilgrim Colony: A History of New Plymouth, 1620-1691* (New Haven: Yale University Press, 1966).

[11] Edward Arber, ed., *Travels and Works of Captain John Smith, President of Virginia and Admiral of New England, 1580-1631,* 2 vols. (Edinburgh: J. Grant, 1910), 1: 212-213.

[12] *Winthrop Papers,* 5 vols. (Boston: Massachusetts Historical Society, 1929-1947), 2: 294-295. There is a wealth of information on the early history of Massachusetts Bay. See, for example, Benjamin Labaree, *Colonial Massachusetts: A History* (Millwood, N.Y.: KTO Press, 1970); Bernard Bailyn, *The New England Merchants in the Seventeenth Century* (Cambridge, Mass.: Harvard University Press, 1955); Darrett B. Rutman, *Winthrop's Boston: Portrait of a Puritan Town, 1630-1649* (Chapel Hill, N.C.: University of North Carolina Press, 1965); Pomfret, *Founding the American Colonies*; and Robert E. Wall, Jr., *Massachusetts Bay: The Crucial Decade, 1640-1650* (New Haven: Yale University Press, 1972).

[13] Gertrude Huehns, *Antinomianism in English History, with Special Reference to the Period, 1640-1660* (London: Cresset Press, 1951) is especially helpful in understanding the antinomian mentality. For the controversy itself, see Charles Francis Adams, "The Antinomian Controversy," in his *Three Episodes in Massachusetts History,* ed. Emery Battis (New York: De Capo Press, 1976); Emery Battis, *Saints and Sectaries: Anne Hutchinson and the Antinomian Controversy in the Massachusetts Bay Colony* (Chapel Hill, N.C.: University of North Carolina Press, 1962); and David Hall, ed., *The Antinomian Controversy, 1636-1638: A Documentary History* (Middletown, Conn.: Wesleyan University Press, 1968).

[14] There are several fine biographies of Roger Williams. In particular see Edmund S. Morgan, *Roger Williams: Church and State* (New York: Harcourt Brace & World, 1967); Cyclone Covey, *The Gentle Radical: A Biography of Roger Williams* (New York: Macmillan, 1966); Perry Miller, *Roger Williams: His Contribution to the American Tradition* (Indianapolis: Bobbs-Merrill, 1953); and John Garrett, *Roger Williams: Witness Beyond Christendom* (New York: Macmillan, 1970). For more information on the history of Rhode Island, see Irving B. Richman, *Rhode Island, Its Making and Its Meaning,* 2 vols. (New York: G. P. Putnam's Sons, 1902); and Sydney V. James, *Colonial Rhode Island: A History* (New York: Charles Scribner's Sons, 1975).

[15] The stories of Connecticut and New Haven are told by Mary Jeanne Anderson Jones, *Congregational Commonwealth: Connecticut, 1636-1662* (Middletown, Conn.: Wesleyan University Press, 1968); Paul R. Lucas, *Valley of Discord: Church and Society along the Connecticut River, 1636-1725* (Hanover, N.H.: University Press of New England, 1976); Robert J. Taylor, *Colonial Connecticut: A History* (Millwood, N.Y.: KTO Press, 1979); and Isabel M. Calder, *The New Haven Colony* (New Haven: Yale University Press, 1934).

[16] Henry S. Burrage, *The Beginnings of Colonial Maine, 1602-1658* (Portland, Maine: Printed for the state, 1914); David E. Van Deventer, *The Emergence of Provincial New Hampshire, 1623-1741* (Baltimore: Johns Hopkins Press, 1976); and Jere R. Daniell, *Colonial New Hampshire: A History* (Millwood, N.Y.: KTO Press, 1981) provide good introductions to the histories of these two colonies.

[17] See Craven, *Southern Colonies*; and Aubrey C. Land, *Colonial Maryland: A History* (Millwood, N.Y.: KTO Press, 1981) for able summaries of colonial Maryland's history.

[18] The Carolinas are treated by Hugh T. Lefler and Albert R. Newsome, *North Carolina:*

The History of a Southern State (Chapel Hill, N.C.: University of North Carolina Press, 1963); Hugh T. Lefler and William S. Powell, *Colonial North Carolina: A History* (New York: Charles Scribner's Sons, 1973); Edward McCrady, *The History of South Carolina under the Proprietary Government, 1670–1719* (New York: Macmillan, 1901); and David D. Wallace, *South Carolina: A Short History, 1520–1948* (Chapel Hill, N.C.: University of North Carolina Press, 1951), a condensation of Wallace's 1934 three-volume history of that state.

[19] The influence of the Dutch in New York is ably discussed in Henry H. Kessler and Eugene Rachlis, *Peter Stuyvesant and his New York* (New York: Random House, 1959); W. R. Shepherd, *The Story of New Amsterdam*, rep. ed. (Port Washington, N.Y.: Kennikat Press, 1970); and Francis W. Halsey, *The Old New York Frontier* (New York: Charles Scribner's Sons, 1901). For further information on British rule of the colony, you may consult David M. Ellis et al., *A History of New York State*, rev. ed. (Ithaca, N.Y.: Cornell University Press, 1967); and Michael Kammen, *Colonial New York: A History* (New York: Charles Scribner's Sons, 1975).

[20] Some of the best treatments of the Jerseys can be found in John E. Pomfret, *The Province of West New Jersey, 1609–1702: A History of the Origins of an American Colony* (Princeton, N.J.: Princeton University Press, 1956); and Pomfret, *The Province of East New Jersey, 1609–1702: The Rebellious Proprietary* (Princeton, N.J.: Princeton University Press, 1962). Also useful are Pomfret's *Colonial New Jersey: A History* (New York: Charles Scribner's Sons, 1973); Wesley Frank Craven, *New Jersey and the English Colonization of North America* (Princeton, N.J.: Van Nostrand, 1964); and Edwin P. Tanner, *The Province of New Jersey, 1664–1738* (New York: Longmans, Green, 1908).

[21] Several older studies of Pennsylvania still provide some of the best introductions to the history of the colony. The importance of the Quakers in the development of Pennsylvania and Delaware is shown in Sydney G. Fisher, *The Quaker Colonies* (New Haven: Yale University Press, 1919); and Rufus M. Jones, *The Quakers in the American Colonies* (New York: Russell & Russell, 1962). Other studies to be consulted include Sydney G. Fisher, *The Making of Pennsylvania* (Philadelphia: J. B. Lippincott, 1932); John A. Munroe, *Colonial Delaware: A History* (Millwood, N.Y.: KTO Press, 1978); and Joseph E. Illick, *Colonial Pennsylvania: A History* (New York: Charles Scribner's Sons, 1976). For the influence of the Swedes in America, see Amandus Johnson, *The Swedish Settlements on the Delaware*, 2 vols. (Philadelphia: Swedish Colonial Society, 1911); and Christopher Ward, *The Dutch and the Swedes on the Delaware, 1609–64* (Philadelphia: University of Pennsylvania Press, 1930).

[22] Amos A. Ettinger, *James Edward Oglethorpe, Imperial Idealist* (Oxford: Clarendon Press, 1936) traces Oglethorpe's activities in the founding of Georgia. More general studies of Georgia include E. M. Coulter, *A Short History of Georgia* (Chapel Hill, N.C.: University of North Carolina Press, 1933); Kenneth Coleman, *Colonial Georgia: A History* (New York: Charles Scribner's Sons, 1976); and Trevor Richard Reese, *Colonial Georgia: A Study in British Imperial Policy in the Eighteenth Century* (Athens, Georgia: University of Georgia Press, 1963).

[23] The standard work on the British West Indies is Sir Alan Burns, *History of the British West Indies*, rev. ed. (London: Allen & Unwin, 1965). Also helpful are Carl and Roberta Bridenbaugh, *No Peace Beyond the Line: The British in the Caribbean 1624–1690* (New York: Oxford University Press, 1972); Richard S. Dunn, *Sugar and Slaves: The Rise of the Planter Class in the English West Indies, 1624–1713* (Chapel Hill, N.C.: University of North Carolina Press 1972); and James A. Williamson, *The Caribbee Islands under the Proprietary Patents* (London: Oxford University Press, 1926).

CHAPTER THREE

[1] There are several fine studies that trace the growth of the British empire and the problems arising from overseas colonies. Charles M. Andrews, *The Colonial Period of American History*, 4 vols. (New Haven: Yale University Press, 1934–1938) is always a reliable beginning. Students should also consult George L. Beer, *The Origins of the British Colonial System, 1578–1660* (New York: Macmillan, 1908); and Beer, *The Old Colonial System, 1660–1754*, 2 vols. (New York: Macmillan, 1912); George D. Ramsay, *English Overseas Trade During the Centuries of Emergence: Studies in Some Modern Origins of the English-Speaking World* (London: Macmillan, 1957); J. A. Williamson, *A Short History of British Expansion, Volume I, The Old Colonial Empire*, 2 vols., 3rd ed. (London: Macmillan, 1958); Stephen S. Webb, *The Governors-General: The English Army and the Definition of the Empire, 1569–1681* (Chapel Hill, N.C.: University of North Carolina Press, 1979); and Carl Ubbelohde, *The American Colonies and the British Empire, 1607–1763* (New York: Thomas Y. Crowell, 1968).

[2] Adam Smith, *An Inquiry into the Nature and Causes of the Wealth of Nations,* gen. ed. R. H. Campbell, tex. ed., A. S. Skinner, 2 vols. (Oxford: Clarendon Press, 1976), 1: 428.

[3] Ibid., 1: 429.

[4] Ibid., 1: 429.

[5] Ibid., 1: 430.

[6] Richard Hakluyt, *A Discourse of Western Planting, Written in the Year 1584,* in *The Original Writings & Correspondence of the Two Richard Hakluyts.,* ser. 2 vols., 76–77, *Hakluyt Society Works,* 2 vols. (London: Hakluyt Society, 1935), 2: 313. Hakluyt spent much of his life compiling, translating, and publishing the stories of English and European exploration and colonization. See, for example, his *Divers Voyages Touching the Discovery of America and the Islands.* This work was first published in 1582. A modern edition was published by the Hakluyt Society in 1850. Hakluyt's most famous work was *The Principall Navigations, Voiages and Discoveries of the English Nation,* published in 1589. A fine modern edition was produced by David B. Quinn and Raleigh A. Shelton as part of the *Hakluyt Society Extra Series,* in 1965.

[7] Hakluyt, *Original Writings,* 2: 314, 319.

[8] Smith, *Wealth of Nations,* 2: 626–627.

[9] *Documents Relative to the Colonial History of the State of New York,* 15 vols. (Albany, N.Y.: Weed, Parsons, 1853–1887), 5: 616. Hereafter cited as *New York Documents.*

[10] Smith, *Wealth of Nations,* 2: 571–572. Eli F. Heckscher, *Mercantilism,* 2 vols., rev. ed. (New York: Macmillan, 1955); and Klaus E. Knorr, *British Colonial Theories, 1570–1850* (Toronto: University of Toronto Press, 1944) discuss the impact of mercantile thought upon British imperial policy. See also Charles H. Wilson, *Mercantilism* (London: Routledge & Kegan Paul, 1958); and Bruno Suviranta, *The Theory of the Balance of Trade in England: A Study in Mercantilism* (Helsingfors, Finland: Printed by Suomal, Kirjall. Seuran Kirjap. O.Y., 1923).

[11] John Winthrop, *Winthrop's Journal, History of New England, 1630–1649,* ed. James Kendall Hosmer, 2 vols. (New York: Charles Scribner's Sons, 1908), 2: 22–23.

[12] Ibid., 1: 316.

[13] Ibid., 1: 316.

[14] Ibid., 1: 316.

[15] Ibid., 1: 317–318.

[16] Bernard Bailyn, ed., *The Apologia of Robert Keayne: The Self-Portrait of a Puritan Merchant* (New York: Harper & Row, 1965), 61.

[17] Mun's book was written in 1630 but was not published until 1663. The best recent edition is that published by the Economic History Society.

[18] Samuel Pepys, *The Diary of Samuel Pepys,* eds. Robert Latham and William Matthews, 9 vols. (Berkeley, Calif.: University of California Press, 1970–1976), 8: 262.

[19] Ibid., 409–410, 411.

[20] William Macdonald, ed., *Select Charters and Other Documents Illustrative of American History, 1606–1775* (New York: Macmillan, 1904), 111. The acts are summarized well in Wesley Frank Craven, *The Colonies in Transition, 1660–1713* (New York: Harper & Row, 1968), 35–38.

[21] Macdonald, *Select Charters,* 111, 114–115.

[22] Ibid., 133–134.

[23] Ibid., 214.

[24] Lawrence Harper, *The English Navigation Laws: A Seventeenth Century Experiment in Social Engineering* (New York: Columbia University Press, 1939), and Oliver M. Dickerson, *The Navigation Acts and the American Revolution* (New York: A. S. Barnes, 1963) provide excellent introductions to British imperial legislation and its impact on the colonies.

[25] "Danforth Papers," in *Collections of the Massachusetts Historical Society,* 2nd ser., 2nd ed. (Boston: Published by The Massachusetts Historical Society, 1826), 8: 100–101, 99–100.

[26] Randolph's activities in New England are ably discussed in Michael G. Hall, *Edward Randolph and the American Colonies, 1676–1703* (Chapel Hill, N.C.: University of North Carolina Press, 1960). See also Craven, *Colonies in Transition,* 166–170.

[27] Thomas Hutchinson, "A Collection of Original Papers Relative to History of the Colony of Massachusetts Bay," in *Hutchinson Papers, Publications of the Prince Society,* vols. 1 and 2, rep. ed., (New York: J. Munsell, 1967), 2: 310–311.

[28] Ibid., 2: 312. For a good treatment of the Glorious Revolution in England, readers may refer to Maurice Ashley, *The Glorious Revolution of 1688* (London: Hodder & Stoughton,

1966); Stuart Prall, *The Bloodless Revolution: England, 1688* (Garden City, N.Y.: Anchor Books, 1972); John R. Western, *Monarchy and Revolution: The English State in the 1680s* (Totowa, N.J.: Rowman & Littlefield, 1972); and George M. Trevelyan, *The English Revolution, 1688-1689* (London: Oxford University Press, 1960).

[29] *New York Documents,* 5: 628, 629–630.

[30] For further discussion of the operation and administration of the colonial system and the formation of colonial policy in the seventeenth century, see in particular Charles M. Andrews, *British Committees, Commissions and Councils of Trade and Plantation, 1622–1675* (Baltimore: Johns Hopkins Press, 1908); Oliver M. Dickerson, *American Colonial Government, 1696–1765: A Study of the British Board of Trade in its Relation to the American Colonies, Political, Industrial, Administrative* (New York: Russell & Russell, 1962); Thomas C. Barrow, *Trade and Empire: The British Customs Service in America, 1660–1775* (Cambridge, Mass.: Harvard University Press, 1967); and Ian K. Steele, *Politics of Colonial Policy: The Board of Trade in Colonial Administration, 1696–1720* (Oxford: Clarendon Press, 1968).

CHAPTER FOUR

[1] John Hammond, *Leah and Rachel, or the Two Fruitful Sisters Virginia and Mary-land; Their Present Condition, Impartially Stated and Related,* in Peter Force, comp., *Tracts and Other Papers Relating Principally to the Origin, Settlement and Progress of the Colonies in North America from the Discovery of the Country to the Year 1776,* 4 vols. (Washington: Printed by P. Force, 1836–1846), 3: No. 14, 7 (all entries are individually paginated). Edmund S. Morgan, among others, has shown that Virginia's reputation was deserved. See his *American Slavery, American Freedom: The Ordeal of Colonial Virginia* (New York: W. W. Norton, 1975), esp. 3–130. In recent years the Chesapeake colonies have attracted considerable scholarly interest. The result has been some important new insights into the early history of this region. Even though opportunities for wealth and success existed in those colonies, many immigrants could not take advantage of them. Working conditions were dismal, the health of colonists was often poor, and death frequently came early. The result was considerable social instability as master-servant relationships, not the family, tended to provide the cement holding the Chesapeake societies together. This situation was far different from what historians have found in the New England colonies during their formative years. The reader should compare the conclusions of John Demos, *A Little Commonwealth: Family Life in Plymouth Colony* (New York: Oxford University Press, 1970) and Philip J. Greven, Jr., *Four Generations: Population, Land and Family in Colonial Andover, Mass.* (Ithaca, N.Y.: Cornell University Press, 1970) with those drawn in Thad W. Tate and David L. Ammerman, eds. *The Chesapeake in the Seventeenth Century: Essays on Anglo-American Society and Politics* (Chapel Hill, N.C.: University of North Carolina Press, 1979).

[2] Force, *Tracts and Other Papers,* 3: No. 14, 20.

[3] John Smith, *A Description of New England: or the Observations and Discoueries of Captain John Smith (Admirall of that Country) in the North America, in the Year of our Lord 1614 . . .* in Force, *Tracts and Other Papers,* 2: No. 1, 9, 11.

[4] Ibid., 11.

[5] Quoted in Kenneth A. Lockridge, *Settlement and Unsettlement in Early America: The Crisis of Political Legitimacy before the Revolution* (New York: Cambridge University Press, 1981), 20.

[6] Don Gleason Hill, et al., eds., *Early Records of the Town of Dedham,* 6 vols. (Dedham Mass.: Dedham Transcript Press, 1886–1936), 3: 2–3.

[7] Edward Johnson, *Johnson's Wonder-working Providence, 1628–1651,* ed. J. Franklin Jameson (New York: Charles Scribner's Sons, 1910), 269–270.

[8] John Winthrop, *Winthrop's Journal, History of New England, 1630–1649,* ed. James Kendall Hosmer, 2 vols. (New York: Charles Scribner's Sons, 1980), 2: 341. The gradual erosion of a communal mentality and some communal goals among early New Englanders is an almost universal theme in modern historiography about seventeenth-century New England. See, for example, Perry Miller, *The New England Mind: The Seventeenth Century* (Cambridge, Mass.: Harvard University Press, 1939) and Miller, *The New England Mind: From Colony to Province* (Cambridge, Mass.: Harvard University Press, 1953); Darrett B. Rutman, *Winthrop's Boston: Portrait of a Puritan Town, 1630–1648* (Chapel Hill, N.C.: University of North Carolina Press, 1965); Richard Bushman, *From Puritan to Yankee: Character and the Social Order in Connecticut, 1690–1765* (Cambridge, Mass.: Harvard University Press, 1967); Edmund S.

Morgan, *The Puritan Family: Religion and Domestic Relations in Seventeenth Century New England* (New York: Harper & Row, 1966); and Kenneth A. Lockridge, *A New England Town, The First Hundred Years: Dedham, Massachusetts, 1636-1736* (New York: W. W. Norton, 1970).

[9] *The Public Records of the Colony of Connecticut, 1636-1776,* 15 vols., vols. 1-3 ed. J. H. Trumbull, vols. 4-15 ed. C. J. Hoadley (Hartford, Conn.: American Publishing, 1850-1890), 3: 294-301.

[10] *Winthrop's Journal,* 2: 249, 248.

[11] Francis D. Pastorius, "A Particular Geographical Description of the Lately Discovered Province of Pennsylvania, Situated on the Frontiers of this Western World, America," in *Old South Leaflets,* 8 vols. (Boston: Directors of the Old South Church, 1883-1904), 4: No. 95, 9 (entries are individually paginated). The reader is also urged to consult Wesley Frank Craven, *The Southern Colonies in the Seventeenth Century* (Baton Rouge, La.: Louisiana State University Press, 1949); Stuart Bruchey, *The Roots of American Economic Growth, 1607-1861: An Essay in Social Causation* (New York: Harper & Row, 1965); and Bernard Bailyn, *The New England Merchants in the Seventeenth Century* (Cambridge, Mass.: Harvard University Press, 1955) for an introduction to colonial economic development. Historians of New England generally argue that their region proceeded from social stability to instability over the course of the seventeenth century. In recent years studies of the Chesapeake region now seem to suggest the opposite view. That is, they stress movement from social instability to relative stability in the Chesapeake by 1700. Still, historians of both New England and the Chesapeake agree that economic opportunity probably declined somewhat in their respective areas as the seventeenth century progressed. They also agree that declining opportunity in the settled coastal regions was offset by the continual opening of new "frontier" areas for settlement and by a gently rising standard of living for colonists everywhere.

[12] A good starting place for learning about English rural society and its people in the sixteenth and seventeenth centuries is Peter Laslett, *The World We Have Lost: England before the Industrial Age* (London: Methuen, 1965). Other books which are helpful for understanding the lives and concerns of ordinary English people are H. L. Gray, *English Field Systems* (Cambridge, Mass.: Harvard University Press, 1959); W. G. Hoskins, *The Midland Peasant: The Economic and Social History of a Leicestershire Village* (London: Macmillan, 1957); Carl Bridenbaugh, *Vexed and Troubled Englishmen, 1590-1642* (New York: Oxford University Press, 1968); and E. A. Wrigley, *Population and History* (New York: McGraw-Hill, 1976).

[13] We have learned much about the lives and behavior of Anglo-American colonists in recent years, a large portion of this information coming from intensive studies of particular localities and communities. Among the best of these are Rutman, *Winthrop's Boston*; Sumner Powell, *Puritan Village: The Formation of a New England Town* (Garden City, N.Y.: Anchor Books, 1965); Greven, *Four Generations*; Lockridge, *New England Town*; Demos, *Little Commonwealth*; James T. Lemon, *The Best Poor Man's Country: A Geographical Study of Early Southeastern Pennsylvania* (Baltimore: Johns Hopkins Press, 1972); Paul Boyer and Stephen Nissenbaum, *Salem Possessed: The Social Origins of Witchcraft* (Cambridge, Mass.: Harvard University Press, 1974); and Carville Earle, *The Evolution of a Tidewater Settlement System: All Hallow's Parish, Maryland, 1650-1783* (Chicago: University of Chicago Press, 1975). See also Tate and Ammerman, *Chesapeake in the Seventeenth Century*; Richard P. Gildrie, *Salem, Massachusetts: A Covenant Community* (Charlottesville: University Press of Virginia, 1975); David Grayson Allen, *In English Ways: The Movement of Societies and Transferal of English Local Law and Custom to Massachusetts Bay in the Seventeenth Century* (Chapel Hill, N.C.: University of North Carolina Press, 1981); Stephanie Grauman Wolf, *Urban Village: Population, Community and Family Structure in Germantown, Pennsylvania, 1683-1800)* (Princeton, N.J.: Princeton University Press, 1976); Michael Zuckerman, *Peaceable Kingdoms: New England Towns in the Eighteenth Century* (New York: Alfred A. Knopf, 1970); Christopher M. Jedrey, *The World of John Cleaveland: Family and Community in Eighteenth Century New England* (New York: W. W. Norton, 1980); Gary M. Nash, *The Urban Crucible: Social Change, Political Consciousness, and the Origins of the American Revolution* (Cambridge, Mass.: Harvard University Press, 1979); Edward M. Cook, Jr., *The Fathers of the Towns: Leadership and Community Structure in Eighteenth Century New England* (Baltimore: Johns Hopkins Press, 1976); and Robert A Gross, *The Minutemen and their World* (New York: Hill & Wang, 1976).

[14] Russell R. Menard, "From Servant to Freeholder," *William and Mary Quarterly,* 3rd ser., 30: No. 1 (January 1973), 32-38. Colonial labor practices are further described in Marcus Wilson Jernegan, *Laboring and Dependent Classes in Colonial America, 1607-1783: Studies of the Economic, Educational, and Social Significance of Slaves, Servants, Apprentices and Poor Folk* (Chicago: University of Chicago Press, 1931); Abbot E. Smith, *Colonists in Bondage: White Servitude and Convict Labor in America: 1607-1776* (Chapel Hill, N.C.: University of North Carolina Press, 1947); and Lois Green Car and Russell R. Menard, "Immigration and

Opportunity: The Freedman in Early Colonial Maryland," in Tate and Ammerman, *Chesapeake in the Seventeenth Century,* 206–242.

[15]Quoted in Lockridge, *Settlement and Unsettlement,* 66. Lockridge wrote that "at its bottom, the Southern society of the seventeenth century culminated in a convict population as dangerous as that of nineteenth-century Australia" (p. 65). Edmund S. Morgan, whose description of indentured labor in seventeenth-century Virginia in *American Slavery, American Freedom* was the principal source for many of my remarks, observed that the "Virginians could be so heavily exploited, legally and illegally, partly because they were selected for that purpose: they were brought to the colony in order to be exploited. From the beginning Englishmen had thought of their New World possessions as a place in which to make use of people who were useless at home" (p. 235). Later in his book Morgan compared Virginia to Elizabethan England: "Virginians of the late seventeenth century," he wrote,

> seemed to be plagued by the same kind of restless, roistering rogues who had wandered through Elizabethan England. England had kept them down by the workhouse, by the gallows, by whipping them back to the parish they came from, by sending them off on military expeditions–and by shipping them to Virginia . . . . Virginians had coped with the problem in several ways: by creating an artificial scarcity of land, which drove freemen back into servitude; by extending terms of service; by inflicting severe penalties for killing the hogs that offered easy food without work. They had also through rents and taxes and fees skimmed off as much as they dared of the small man's small profits for the benefit of burgesses, councillors, and collectors. But the burdens imposed on Virginia's workers placed the colony continually on the brink of rebellion (p. 295).

[16]William W. Hening, ed., *The Statutes at Large; Being a Collection of all Laws of Virginia, from the First Session of the Legislature in the year 1619,* 13 vols. (New York: Printed for the editor by R. & W. & G. Bartow, 1819–1823), 2: 170.

[17]Ibid., 270.

[18]Samuel W. Pennypacker, "The Settlement of Germantown and the Cause which Led to It. An Address Read before the Historical Society of Pennsylvania, Oct. 20, 1879," *The Pennsylvania Magazine of History and Biography,* 4: No. 1 (1880), 28, 29.

[19]The origins and nature of colonial slavery have been the source of considerable controversy among historians. For several different analyses of this topic, see Morgan, *American Slavery, American Freedom;* Richard Sheridan, *Sugar and Slavery: An Economic History of the British West Indies, 1623–1775* (Baltimore: Johns Hopkins Press, 1974); David Brion Davis, *The Problem of Slavery in Western Culture* (Ithaca, N.Y.: Cornell University Press, 1966); Winthrop D. Jordan, *White over Black: American Attitudes toward the Negro, 1550–1812* (New York: W. W. Norton, 1977); Richard S. Dunn, *Sugar and Slaves: The Rise of the Planter Class in the English West Indies, 1624–1713* (Chapel Hill, N.C.: University of North Carolina Press, 1972); Peter Wood, *Black Majority: Negroes in South Carolina from 1670 through the Stono Rebellion* (New York: Alfred A. Knopf, 1974); Wesley Frank Craven, *White, Red, and Black: The Seventeenth Century Virginian* (Charlottesville: University Press of Virginia, 1971); and Oscar and Mary Handlin, "The Origins of the Southern Labor System," *William and Mary Quarterly,* 3rd ser., 7: No. 2 (April 1950), 199–222.

CHAPTER FIVE

[1]The liberty-versus-tyranny argument is forcefully presented in George Bancroft, *History of the United States from the Discovery of the American Continent to the Declaration of Independence,* 7 vols. (Boston: Little, Brown, 1854–1858). A classic critique of this approach is contained in Charles M. Andrews, *The Colonial Period of American History,* 4 vols. (New Haven: Yale University Press, 1934–1938). Daniel J. Boorstin has persuasively argued for the uniqueness of early America in his *The Americans: The Colonial Experience* (New York: Random House, 1958). Older historical views of colonial America are nicely summarized in John Higham, ed., *The Reconstruction of American History* (New York: Humanities Press, 1962), esp. Chapters 1 to 3 and 11. Newer historical perspectives are summarized and synthesized in Michael Kammen, *People of Paradox: An Inquiry Concerning the Origins of American Civilization* (New York: Alfred A. Knopf, 1972).

[2]The term *localism* has been given a variety of definitions by historians of early America. In this book the term connotes characteristics and attitudes that belonged primarily to the premodern Western world, when town, county, or parish institutions held greater importance–even central importance–to the ordinary man and woman than did regional or national institutions. The localism of the early English colonists emerges clearly in the community studies

which have appeared with frequency during the past few years. Some of the best are also some of the oldest. See, for example, Sumner Powell, *Puritan Village: The Formation of a New England Town* (Middletown, Conn.: Wesleyan University Press, 1963); Darrett B. Rutman, *Winthrop's Boston: Portrait of a Puritan Town, 1630–1649* (Chapel Hill, N.C.: University of North Carolina Press, 1965); and Kenneth A. Lockridge, *A New England Town, The First Hundred Years: Dedham, Massachusetts, 1636–1736* (New York: W. W. Norton, 1970). Localism is discussed in a seminal essay by Timothy H. Breen, "Persistent Localism: English Social Change and the Shaping of New England Institutions," reprinted in Breen's *Puritans and Adventurers: Change and Persistence in Early America* (New York: Oxford University Press, 1980). Localism is also one of the themes developed by Michael Kammen in *People of Paradox,* and in a different fashion by Kenneth A. Lockridge in *Settlement and Unsettlement in Early America: The Crisis of Political Legitimacy before the Revolution* (Cambridge, Eng.: Cambridge University Press, 1981).

[3] English political practice from the late Middle Ages to the eve of colonization is discussed and described in J. R. Lander, *Government and Community: England, 1450–1509* (Cambridge, Mass.: Harvard University Press, 1980); R. B. Smith, *Land and Politics in the England of Henry VIII: The West Riding of Yorkshire, 1530–46* (Oxford: Clarendon Press, 1970); Witney R. D. Jones, *The Tudor Commonwealth, 1529–1559: A Study of the Impact of the Social and Economic Developments of Mid-Tudor England upon Contemporary Concepts of the Nature and Duties of the Commonwealth* (London: Athlone Press, 1970); Peter Clark, *English Provincial Society from the Reformation to the Revolution: Religion, Politics, and Society in Kent, 1500–1640* (Hassocks, Sussex, Eng.: Harvester Press, 1977); and Conrad Russell, *Parliaments and English Politics, 1621–1629* (Oxford: Clarendon Press, 1979). Beginning students should also consult "classic" studies of English local government such as Sidney and Beatrice Webb, *English Local Government from the Revolution to the Municipal Corporations Acts,* 11 vols. (London: Longmans, Green, 1903–1929); and Wallace Notestein, *The English People on the Eve of Colonization, 1603–1630* (New York: Harper & Row, 1954).

[4] Carl Bridenbaugh, *Vexed and Troubled Englishmen, 1590–1642* (New York: Oxford University Press, 1972).

[5] J. E. Christopher Hill provides a fine analysis of England's political and constitutional strife during the seventeenth century in *The Century of Revolution, 1603–1714* (Edinburgh: T. Nelson, 1961). See also G. E. Aylmer, *The Struggle for the Constitution, England in the Seventeenth Century* (London: Blandford Press, 1963).

[6] A useful guide to the theory of mixed government and the form of evolution of the English constitution is Corinne C. Weston, *English Constitutional Theory and the House of Lords, 1556–1832* (London: Routledge & Kegan Paul, 1965). See also J. G. A. Pocock, *The Ancient Constitution and the Feudal Law: A Study of English Historical Thought in the Seventeenth Century* (Cambridge, Eng.: Cambridge University Press, 1957).

[7] John Winthrop, *Winthrop's Journal, History of New England, 1630–1649,* ed. James Kendall Hosmer, 2 vols. (New York: Charles Scribner's Sons, 1980), 2: 237–239.

[8] Differing perspectives on these debates may be seen in Perez Zagorin, *A History of Political Thought in the English Revolution* (London: Routledge & Kegan Paul, 1954); Margaret Judson, *Crisis of the Constitution: An Essay in the Constitutional and Political Thought in England, 1603–1645* (New York: Octagon Books, 1964); and Michael Walzer, *The Revolution of the Saints: A Study in the Origins of Radical Politics* (New York: Atheneum Publishers, 1968).

[9] Coke's *Reports* appeared in eleven volumes between 1600 and 1618. Two additional volumes were published after his death in 1634. His *Institutes of the Lawes of England* appeared in four volumes. Volume 1 was published in 1628. It is the most famous of the four and is usually identified as a *Commentary on Littleton.* The three subsequent volumes were published posthumously between 1642 and 1644. Both the *Institutes* and the *Reports* have been published in many editions over the years. Coke's influence in Anglo-America may be seen in William Hamilton Bryson, *Census of Law Books in Colonial Virginia* (Charlottesville: University Press of Virginia, 1978); Herbert A. Johnson, *Imported Eighteenth Century Law Treatises in American Libraries, 1700–1799* (Knoxville: University of Tennessee Press, 1978); and Richard Beale Davis, *A Colonial Southern Bookshelf: Reading in the Eighteenth Century* (Athens, Ga.: University of Georgia Press, 1979).

[10] For the evolution of English legal theory and the court systems during this period, see Godfrey Davies, *The Early Stuarts, 1603–1660* (Oxford: Clarendon Press, 1937); W. H. Greenleaf, *Order, Empiricism, and Politics: Two Traditions of English Political Thought, 1500–1700* (London: Oxford University Press, 1964); Clayton Roberts, *The Growth of Responsible Government in Stuart England* (Cambridge: Cambridge University Press, 1966); Harold Potter, *Historical Introduction to English Law and Its Institutions,* 4th ed. (London: Sweet & Maxwell,

1958); Theodore F. T. Plucknett, *A Concise History of the Common Law,* 5th ed. (Boston: Little, Brown, 1956); and E. S. Corwin, *The "Higher Law" Background of American Constitutional Law* (Indianapolis: Bobbs-Merrill, 1928).

[11] Compare Powell, *Puritan Village* with David Grayson Allen, *In English Ways: The Movement of Societies and Transferal of English Local Law and Custom to Massachusetts Bay in the Seventeenth Century* (Chapel Hill, N.C.: University of North Carolina Press, 1981).

[12] Timothy Breen, *The Character of the Good Ruler: A Study of Puritan Political Ideas in New England, 1630–1730* (New Haven: Yale University Press, 1970); and Michael Kammen, ed., *Deputyes and Libertyes: The Origins of Representative Government in America* (New York: Alfred A. Knopf, 1969) both touch upon colonial theories of liberty and authority. The ambivalence of many early colonists toward the institution of monarchy has never been analyzed in detail, but it is a theme, nonetheless, which is relevant to much of what historians have said about early America. From Perry Miller's *New England Mind: The Seventeenth Century* (Cambridge, Mass.: Harvard University Press, 1939) to Lockridge's *New England Town,* to Edmund Morgan's brilliant *American Slavery, American Freedom: The Ordeal of Colonial Virginia* (New York: W. W. Norton, 1975), the antimonarchical tendencies and sentiments of the first settlers have been suggested or implied. Readers interested in learning more can obtain valuable insights from Edmund Morgan *Roger Williams: The Church and the State* (New York: Harcourt Brace & World, 1967), esp. Chapter 3; Morgan's introduction to *Puritan Political Ideas* (Indianapolis: Bobbs-Merrill, 1965); Breen, "Persistent Localism"; and James F. McClear, "New England and the Fifth Monarchy: The Quest for the Millennium in Early American Puritanism," *William and Mary Quarterly,* 3rd ser., 32, No. 2 (April 1975), 223–260.

[13] For an introduction into English republican ideology in the seventeenth century, see Zera Fink, *The Classical Republicans: An Essay in the Recovery of a Pattern of Thought in Seventeenth Century England* (Evanston, Ill.: Northwestern University Press, 1945); Felix Raab, *The English Face of Machiavelli: Changing Interpretations, 1500–1700* (London: Routledge & Kegan Paul, 1964); and Caroline Robbins, *The Eighteenth-Century Commonwealthman: Studies in the Transmission, Development and Circumstance of English Liberal Thought from the Restoration of Charles II Until the War with the Thirteen Colonies* (Cambridge, Mass.: Harvard University Press, 1959).

[14] Numerous works discuss the early government of Virginia. In particular see Richard L. Morton, *Colonial Virginia, I: The Tidewater Period, 1607–1710* (Chapel Hill, N.C.: University of North Carolina Press, 1960); Bernard Bailyn, "Politics and Social Structure in Virginia," in James Morton Smith, ed., *Seventeenth Century America* (Chapel Hill, N.C.: University of North Carolina Press, 1959); and Warren Billings, "The Growth of Political Institutions in Virginia, 1634 to 1676," *William and Mary Quarterly,* 3rd ser., 31, No. 2 (April 1974), 225–242.

[15] The Proceedings of the First Assembly of Virginia, July, 1619," *Collections of the New York Historical Society,* 2nd ser. (New York: Printed for the New York Historical Society, 1857), 3: 343.

[16] See, for example, James Truslow Adams, *The Founding of New England* (Boston: Little, Brown, 1921); and Thomas Jefferson Wertenbaker, *Puritan Oligarchy: The Founding of American Civilization* (New York: Charles Scribner's Sons, 1947).

[17] John Winthrop, *Winthrop Papers,* 5 vols. (Boston: Massachusetts Historical Society, 1929–1947), 4: 382. For Winthrop's full story of the sow case see *Winthrop's Journal,* 2: 64–66, 116–121.

[18] Texts and comments on these two documents can be found in *Collections of the Massachusetts Historical Society,* 3rd ser., vol. 8 (Boston: Massachusetts Historical Society, 1843), 191–237; Max Farrand, ed., *The Laws and Liberties of Massachusetts* (Cambridge, Mass.: Harvard University Press, 1929); *Winthrop's Journal,* 2: 48–49; and Robert E. Wall, Jr., *Massachusetts Bay: The Crucial Decade, 1640–1650* (New Haven: Yale University Press, 1972).

[19] Town government is discussed in John Sly, *Town Government in Massachusetts, 1620–1930* (Cambridge, Mass.: Harvard University Press, 1930); Ola E. Winslow, *Meetinghouse Hill* (New York: Macmillan, 1957); George Lee Haskins, *Law and Authority in Early Massachusetts* (New York: Macmillan, 1960); and Kenneth A. Lockridge and Alan Kreider, "The Evolution of Massachusetts Town Government, 1640–1740," *William and Mary Quarterly,* 3rd ser. 23, No. 4 (October 1966), 549–574.

[20] William Bradford, *Bradford's History of Plymouth Plantation, 1606–1646,* ed. William T. Davis (New York: Barnes & Noble, 1959), 107.

[21] See in particular Bernard Bailyn, *The Origins of American Politics* (New York: Vintage Books, 1970). Except for some concern for the political ideas of the Puritans, historians of the past fifty years or so have explained Anglo-American politics and government in the seventeenth century with little reference to any ideological context. It is argued generally that al-

though the early colonists sought to legitimize and protect their political institutions, they did so because of a collective desire for survival, not because of an ideological allegiance. By and large, historians have tended to view seventeenth-century Anglo-Americans politically as self-interested, practical, and unsophisticated, despite recognizing the depth of colonial religious idealism.

[22] The standard work on Bacon's Rebellion remains Wilcomb Washburn, *The Governor and the Rebel: A History of Bacon's Rebellion in Virginia* (Chapel Hill, N.C.: University of North Carolina Press, 1957), although Edmund Morgan provides a provocative reappraisal in *American Slavery, American Freedom.* Shortly after the rebellion in Virginia ended, Albemarle County in neighboring Carolina was wracked by a rebellion of tobacco planters against interim Governor Thomas Miller. One of the participants in the ill-fated venture was apparently a former follower of Nathaniel Bacon named John Culpeper. Culpeper was not the leader of the rebellion, but he was nonetheless subsequently tried for treason.

[23] *The Colonial Laws of New York from the Year 1664 to the Revolution,* 5 vols. (Albany: James B. Lyon, 1894-1896), 1: 111-116; David S. Lovejoy, "Equality and Empire: The New York Charter of Libertyes, 1683," *William and Mary Quarterly,* 3rd ser., 21, No. 4 (October 1964), 493-515.

[24] See Michael G. Hall, et al., eds., *The Glorious Revolution in America: Documents on the Colonial Crisis of 1689* (Chapel Hill, N.C.: University of North Carolina Press, 1964); and David S. Lovejoy, *The Glorious Revolution in America* (New York: Harper & Row, 1972).

[25] John Locke, *Two Treatises of Government,* ed. Peter Laslett (New York: New American Library, 1965), 106-135, 309-318, 361-400.

[26] Locke's first treatise was introduced as a refutation of Filmer (Locke, *Two Treatises,* 80-105). Robert Filmer wrote several tracts in defense of a patriarchical monarchy. These include *Patriarcha: A Defence of the Natural Power of Kings against the Unnatural Liberty of the People* (1680); *The Freeholder's Grand Inquest Touching Our Soveraigne Lord the King and His Parliament* (1648); *Observations Upon Aristotle's Politiques Touching Forms of Government Together with Directions for Obedience to Governours in dangerous or doubtfull Times* (1652); *Observations Concerning the Originall of Government, Upon Mr. Hobs Leviathan, Mr. Milton against Salmasius, H. Grotius De Jure Belli* (1652); *The Anarchy of a Limited or Mixed Monarchy* (1648); and *The Necessity of The Absolute Power of all Kings: And in particular of the King of England by John Bodin* (1648). The best collection of Filmer's works is *Patriarcha and Other Political Works of Sir Robert Filmer,* ed. with an intro. by Peter Laslett (Oxford: B. Blackwell, 1949).

[27] Samuel Willard, *The Character of A Good Ruler . . .* (Boston: Printed by B. Harris for M. Perry, 1694), 2-3, 7, 9, 13, 15-18, 20-21.

[28] Gurdon Saltonstall, *A Sermon Preached Before the General Assembly of the Colony of Connecticut . . . May 13, 1697* (Boston: Printed by B. Green and J. Allen, 1697), 41. The views of both Saltonstall and Willard should be compared to the sentiments expressed by a former Connecticut minister, Gershom Bulkeley, in a pamphlet published after the Connecticut Assembly refused to allow the royal Governor of Massachusetts, Sir William Phips, to take control of the Connecticut militia. See Gershom Bulkeley, *Some Seasonable Considerations for the Good People of Connecticut* (New York: Printed by William Bradford, 1694), 1-15.

[29] John Wise, *A Vindication of the Government of New England* (Boston: Printed by J. Allen for N. Boone, 1717), 44-46.

CHAPTER SIX

[1] In *Reason, Ridicule and Religion: The Age of Enlightenment in England, 1660-1750* (Cambridge, Mass.: Harvard University Press, 1976), John Redwood wrote that

> Seventeenth-century thought was God'ridden. Whenever a man took up his pen and attempted to write about the weather, the seasons, the structure of the earth, the constitution of the heavens, the nature of political society, the organization of the Church, social morality or ethics he was by definition taking up his pen to write about God (p. 9).

Though seventeenth- and eighteenth-century Anglo-Americans wrote less than their English counterparts, their world view was the same as the one described by Redwood.

The literature discussing the impact of Protestantism on Anglo-American culture and society is very extensive. Interested readers can begin with Perry Miller, *The New England Mind: The Seventeenth Century* (New York: Macmillan, 1939); and Miller, *The New England Mind: From Colony to Province* (Cambridge, Mass.: Harvard University Press, 1953); H. Richard Niebuhr, *The Kingdom of God in America* (New York: Harper & Brothers, 1937); Sydney E. Ahlstrom, *A Religious History of the American People* (New Haven: Yale University Press, 1972); Alan Heimert, *Religion and the American Mind from the Great Awakening to the Revolution* (Cambridge, Mass.: Harvard University Press, 1966); Philip Greven, *The Protestant Temperament* (New York: Alfred A. Knopf, 1977); Winthrop Hudson, *Religion in America* (New York: Charles Scribner's Sons, 1965); Sacvan Bercovitch, *The Puritan Origins of the American Self* (New Haven: Yale University Press, 1975); Ernest Lee Tuveson, *Redeemer Nation: The Idea of America's Millennial Role* (Chicago: University of Chicago Press, 1968); Winton U. Solberg, *Redeem the Time: The Puritan Sabbath in Early America* (Cambridge, Mass.: Harvard University Press, 1977); Nelson R. Burr, *A Critical Bibliography of Religion in America*, 2 vols. (Princeton N.J.: Princeton University Press, 1961); and Burr, *Religion in American Life* (New York: Goldentree Bibliographies in American History, 1971); and Cushing Strout, *The New Heaven and New Earth: Political Religion in America* (New York: Harper and Row, 1974).

Many of the books just listed consider the terms *Puritan* and *Protestant* to be nearly synonymous in early American history and tend to restrict the definition of *Puritan* to those Congregationalists who settled New England. I take a somewhat broader view in the pages of this book. I suggest that the Protestant mentality of early America reflected attitudes and assumptions common to many or most European and English Protestants, not just one segment of English nonconformity.

[2]Readers interested in seventeenth-century English nonconformity should begin with John F. H. New, *Anglican and Puritan: The Basis of their Opposition, 1558-1640* (Stanford, Calif.: Stanford University Press, 1964); J. E. Christopher Hill, *Puritanism and Revolution* (London: Secker & Warburg, 1958); Hill, *The World Turned Upside Down: Radical Ideas During the English Revolution* (New York: Viking Press, 1972); and Hill, *Society and Puritanism in Pre-Revolutionary England* (New York: Schocken Books, 1967); Michael Walzer, *The Revolution of the Saints: A Study in the Origins of Radical Politics* (Cambridge, Mass.: Harvard University Press, 1965); William Haller, *Liberty and Reformation in the Puritan Revolution* (New York: Columbia University Press, 1955); and David Little, *Religion, Order and Law: A Study in Pre-Revolutionary England* (New York: Harper & Row, 1969).

The Calvinist and Anabaptist influences on English nonconformity may be approached through John T. McNeill, *The History and Character of Calvinism* (New York: Oxford University Press, 1954); Francois Wendell, *Calvin: The Origins and Development of His Religious Thought* (New York: Harper & Row, 1963); Franklin H. Littell, *The Origins of Sectarian Protestantism: The Anabaptist View of the Church* (New York: Macmillan, 1960); and George H. Williams, *The Radical Reformation* (Philadelphia: Westminster Press, 1962).

The relationship between religious ideology and England's expansion into North America is considered by Louis B. Wright, *Religion and Empire: The Alliance Between Piety and Commerce in English Expansion, 1558-1625* (Chapel Hill, N.C.: University of North Carolina Press, 1943); Carl Bridenbaugh, *Vexed and Troubled Englishmen, 1590-1642* (New York: Oxford University Press, 1968); Francis Jennings, *The Invasion of America: Indians, Colonialism and the Cant of Conquest* (Chapel Hill, N.C.: University of North Carolina Press, 1975); David B. Quinn, *England and the Discovery of America, 1481-1620* (New York: Alfred A. Knopf, 1974); and A. L. Rowse, *The Expansion of Elizabethan England* (New York: St. Martin's Press, 1955).

For a discussion of the differences separating Congregationalists and Presbyterians, see especially Geoffrey F. Nuttall, *Visible Saints: The Congregational Way, 1640-1660* (Oxford: Basil Blackwell, 1957); Alan Simpson, *Puritanism in Old and New England* (Chicago: University of Chicago Press, 1955); Larzer Ziff, *Puritanism in America: New Culture in a New World* (New York: Viking Press, 1973); C. G. Bolam et al., *The English Presbyterians from Elizabethan Puritanism to Modern Unitarianism* (London: Allen & Unwin, 1968); and Paul R. Lucas, *Valley of Discord: Church and Society along the Connecticut River, 1636-1725* (Hanover, N.H.: University Press of New England, 1976).

[3]W. T. Whitley, *A History of British Baptists* (London: Charles Griffen, 1923); and A. C. Underwood, *A History of the English Baptists* (London: Baptist Union Publishing Department, 1947) provide fine introductions to General and Particular Baptists.

[4]For a treatment of separating Congregationalists (known in England as Brownists after Robert Browne), see Patrick Collinson, *The Elizabethan Puritan Movement* (Berkeley, Calif.: University of California Press, 1967); Charles and Katherine George, *The Protestant Mind of the English Reformation, 1570-1640* (Princeton, N.J.: Princeton University Press, 1961); and Leonard J. Trinterud, ed., *Elizabethan Puritanism* (New York: Oxford University Press, 1971). See also Norman A. Baxter, *History of the Freewill Baptists: A Study in New England Separatism* (Rochester, N.Y.: American Baptist Historical Society, 1957).

[5]Although many historians do not consider Quakerism within the spectrum of Puritanism, it was one of several radical outgrowths of the English Puritan movement, and indeed the early Quakers drew many of their converts from Congregational and Presbyterian ranks. See

Hugh Barbour, *The Quakers in Puritan England* (New Haven: Yale University Press, 1964); William C. Braithwaite, *The Beginnings of Quakerism* (London: Macmillan, 1912); and Rufus M. Jones, *Spiritual Reformers in the Sixteenth and Seventeenth Centuries* (New York: Macmillan, 1914).

[6] In recent years historians have begun to recognize the importance of millennial beliefs in colonial American religion. See especially Tuveson, *Redeemer Nation*; Aletha Joy Bourne Gilsdorf, "The Puritan Apocalypse: New England Eschatology in the Seventeenth Century" (Unpublished Ph.D. dissertation, Yale University, 1965); J. A. DeJong, *As the Waters Cover the Sea: Millennial Expectations in the Rise of Anglo-American Missions, 1640-1810* (Kampen, Netherlands: J. K. Kok, 1970); Ernest Lee Tuveson, *Millennium and Utopia, A Study in the Background of the Idea of Progress* (Berkeley, Calif.: University of California Press, 1949); James F. Maclear, "New England and the Fifth Monarchy: The Quest for the Millennium in Early American Puritanism," *William and Mary Quarterly*, 3rd ser., 32, No. 2 (April 1975), 223-260; Robert Middlekauff, *The Mathers: Three Generations of Puritan Intellectuals, 1596-1728* (New York: Oxford University Press, 1971); and James West Davidson, *The Logic of Millennial Thought: Eighteenth Century New England* (New Haven: Yale University Press, 1977).

[7] Thomas Hooker, *A Survey of the Summe of Church-Discipline* (London: By A. M. for John Bellamy, 1648), preface (n.p.).

[8] For information on the religious history of colonial America, the reader is urged to consult Ahlstrom, *Religious History of the American People*; Hudson, *Religion in America;* Edwin S. Gaustad, *A Religious History of America* (New York: Harper & Row, 1966); and Gaustad, *Historical Atlas of Religion in America* (New York: Harper & Row, 1962); William Warren Sweet, *Religion in Colonial America* (New York: Charles Scribner's Sons, 1942); Jerald C. Brauer, *Protestantism in America: A Narrative History* rev. ed. (Philadelphia: Westminster Press, 1965); Sidney E. Mead, *The Lively Experiment: The Shaping of Christianity in America* (New York: Harper & Row, 1963); and the denominational histories contained in Philip Schaff et al., gen. eds., *The American Church History Series,* 13 vols. (New York: Christian Literature, 1893-1897).

[9] William Macdonald, ed., *Select Charters and Other Documents Illustrative of American History, 1606-1775* (New York: Macmillan, 1904), 128.

[10] For additional information on the Cambridge Platform see Williston Walker, ed., *The Creeds and Platforms of Congregationalism* 2nd ed. (Boston: The Pilgrim Press, 1960); Joseph B. Felt, *The Ecclesiastical History of New England; Comprising not only Religious, but also Moral and Other Relations,* 2 vols. (Boston: Congregational Library Association, 1855-1862); Robert Emmet Wall Jr., *Massachusetts Bay: The Crucial Decade, 1640-1650* (New Haven: Yale University Press, 1972); and Francis J. Bremer, *The Puritan Experiment: New England Society from Bradford to Edwards* (New York: St. Martin's Press, 1976).

The literature on New England Puritanism is voluminous. Some of the more perceptive studies are Miller, *New England Mind*; David D. Hall, *The Faithful Shepherd: A History of the New England Ministry in the Seventeenth Century* (Chapel Hill, N.C.: University of North Carolina Press, 1972); Edmund S. Morgan, *Visible Saints: The History of a Puritan Idea* (New York: New York University Press, 1963); Ziff, *Puritanism in America*; and Darrett B. Rutman, *American Puritanism: Faith and Practice* (Philadelphia: J. B. Lippincott, 1970). Another approach to the operation of the New England Way is through the many fine community studies that have appeared in recent years. See Chapter Four, footnote 13.

[11] For decades after the publication of Miller's *New England Mind,* especially Volume two, scholars viewed the Half-Way Covenant as evidence of spiritual decline, as Miller had suggested. In the last two decades, however, that interpretation has been challenged and amended. See especially Morgan, *Visible Saints*; Hall, *Faithful Shepherd*; Robert G. Pope, *The Half-Way Covenant: Church Membership in Puritan New England* (Princeton, N.J.: Princeton University Press, 1969); Lucas, *Valley of Discord*; Solberg, *Redeem the Time*; Bercovitch, *Puritan Origins of the American Self*; and Middlekauff, *The Mathers.* The problems of spiritual decline, or *declension,* was compounded by the New England ministerial literature of the late seventeenth century, which implied that New England was awash in sin, corruption, and ungodliness. While there is some evidence that late seventeenth-century New Englanders may not have been as pious as the founders of the region, it is also possible that the New England clergy—like good provincials—were simply echoing the sentiments of most Protestants in the English-speaking world. In *Reason, Ridicule and Religion,* Redwood shows that English clerics and other writers on religious themes in the late seventeenth and early eighteenth centuries were convinced that England was being overwhelmed by materialism, secularism, and godlessness.

[12] William W. Hening, ed., *The Statutes at Large; Being a Collection of all Laws of Virginia, from the first Session of the Legislature in the year 1619,* 13 vols. (New York: Printed for the editor by R. & W. & G. Bartow, 1819-1823), 1: 123.

[13] R. G.?, "Virginia's Cure: Or an Advisive Narrative Concerning Virginia; Discovering the

True Ground of that Churches Unhappiness, and the Only True Remedy," in Peter Force, comp., *Tracts and Other Papers Relating Principally to the Origin, Settlement and Progress of the Colonies in North America from the Discovery of the Country to the Year 1776,* 4 vols. (Washington: Peter Force, 1836–1846); 3: No. 15, 4 (tracts have individual pagination).

[14] David Humphreys, *An Historical Account of the Incorporated Society for the Propagation of the Gospel in Foreign Parts . . . ,* 1730 facsimile rep. ed. (New York: Arno Press and *The New York Times,* 1969), 41–42.

[15] Hening, *Statutes at Large,* 1: 277.

[16] Hening, *Statutes at Large,* 2: 165, 181–182. While studies of New England Puritanism abound, scholarly studies of religion in the southern colonies in the seventeenth century are virtually nonexistent. The reader is directed to George M. Brydon, *Virginia's Mother Church and its Political Conditions Under Which It Grew . . . 1607–1814,* 2 vols. (Richmond, Va.: Virginia Historical Society, 1947–1952); Elizabeth H. Davidson, *The Establishment of the English Church in the Continental American Colonies* (Durham, N.C.: Duke University Press, 1936); William Wilson Manross, *A History of the American Episcopal Church* 2nd ed., rev. and enlg. (New York: Morehouse-Gorham, 1950); and Raymond W. Albright, *A History of the Protestant Episcopal Church* (New York: Macmillan, 1964). The Quaker presence in Virginia during the midseventeenth century is discussed by Rufus M. Jones, *The Quakers in the American Colonies* (New York: Russell & Russell, 1962), 265–280.

[17] Humphreys, *Historical Account,* 25.

[18] The religious history of the Carolinas is discussed in Manross, *History of the American Episcopal Church*; Albright, *History of the Protestant Episcopal Church*; Davidson, *Establishment of the English Church*; and Stephen B. Weeks, *The Religious Development in the Province of North Carolina* (Baltimore: Johns Hopkins Press, 1892); Ernest T. Thompson, *Presbyterians in the South* (Richmond: John Knox Press, 1963); and Jones, *Quakers in the American Colonies,* 265–353.

[19] Quoted in Lawrence C. Wroth, "The First Sixty Years of the Church of England in Maryland, 1632 to 1692," *Maryland Historical Magazine,* 11, No. 1 (March 1916), 22.

[20] Catholicism in Maryland is discussed by John Tracy Ellis, *Catholics in Colonial America* (Baltimore: Helicon Press, 1965); and John Gilmary Shea, *The Catholic Church in Colonial Days,* 2 vols. (New York, John G. Shea, 1886).

[21] Humphreys, *Historical Account,* 201. See also Edward Tanjore Corwin, "The Ecclesiastical Condition of New York at the Opening of the Eighteenth Century," *Papers of the American Society of Church History,* 2nd ser., 3 (1912), 81–115; and Hugh Hastings, ed., *Ecclesiastical Records. State of New York,* 7 vols. (Albany: J. B. Lyon, State Printer, 1901–1916).

[22] For a treatment of religion in the middle colonies during the seventeenth century, see especially Albert C. Myers, ed., *Narratives of Early Pennsylvania, West New Jersey and Delaware 1630–1707* (New York: Charles Scribner's Sons, 1912); Jones, *Quakers in the American Colonies,* 357–508; Margaret Hope Bacon, *The Story of the Quakers in America* (New York: Basic Books, 1969); and Amandus Johnson, *The Swedish Settlements on the Delaware,* 2 vols. (Philadelphia: University of Pennsylvania Press, 1911).

[23] Nathaniel B. Shurtleff, ed., *Records of the Governor and Company of the Massachusetts Bay in New England,* 5 vols. in 6 (Boston: From the Press of William W. White, 1853–1854); 2: 6–7.

[24] Shurtleff, *Records,* 2: 203.

[25] For a thorough introduction to colonial education see in particular Bernard Bailyn, *Education in the Forming of American Society* (Chapel Hill, N.C.: University of North Carolina Press, 1960); Lawrence A. Cremin, *American Education: The Colonial Experience, 1607–1783* (New York: Harper & Row, 1970); and James Axtell, *The School Upon a Hill: Education and Society in Colonial New England* (New Haven: Yale University Press, 1974).

[26] Edward Johnson, *Johnson's Wonder-Working Providence, 1628–1651,* ed. J. Franklin Jameson (New York: Charles Scribner's Sons, 1910), 145–146.

[27] See Middlekauff, *The Mathers,* and David Levin, *Cotton Mather: The Young Life of the Lord's Remembrancer, 1663–1703* (Cambridge, Mass.: Harvard University Press, 1978) for a more detailed discussion of Cotton Mather's literary activities. There are several excellent surveys and sourcebooks on early American literature. See in particular Moses Coit Tyler, *A History of American Literature, 1607–1765* (Ithaca, N.Y.: Cornell University Press, 1961); Vernon L. Parrington, *Main Currents in American Thought. Volume One, 1620–1800: The Colonial Mind* (New York: Harcourt Brace Jovanovich, 1954); John C. Miller, ed., *The Colonial Image: Origins of American Culture* (New York: George Braziller, 1962); Roy Harvey Pearce, ed., *Colonial American Writings,* 2nd ed. (New York: Holt, Rinehart & Winston, 1969); Perry

Miller and Thomas H. Johnson, ed., *The Puritans: A Sourcebook of their Writings* (New York: American Book Company, 1938). See also Kenneth A. Lockridge, *Literacy in Colonial New England; An Enquiry into the Social Context of Literacy in the Early Modern West* (New York: W. W. Norton, 1974); Louis B. Wright, *The Cultural Life of the American Colonies, 1607-1763* (New York: Harper & Row, 1957); Richard Beale Davis, *Intellectual Life in the Colonial South, 1588-1763,* 2 vols. (Knoxville, Tenn.: University of Tennessee, 1979); Samuel E. Morison, *The Intellectual Life of Colonial New England,* 2nd ed. (New York: New York University Press, 1956); and Morison, *The Founding of Harvard College* (Cambridge, Mass.: Harvard University Press, 1935).

CHAPTER SEVEN

[1] The best introduction to the English colonial administration in Anglo-America continues to be Leonard W. Labaree, *Royal Government in America; A Study of the British Colonial System before 1783* (New Haven: Yale University Press, 1930). See also Oliver M. Dickerson, *American Colonial Government, 1696-1765: A Study of the British Board of Trade in its Relation to the American Colonies, Political, Industrial, Administrative* (Cleveland: Arthur H. Clark, 1912). For an exhaustive and probably definitive account of the evolution of the British empire before the American Revolution, consult Lawrence H. Gipson, *The British Empire before the American Revolution,* rev. ed., 14 vols. (New York: Alfred A. Knopf, 1939-1969). See also sources cited in Chapter Three.

[2] For a discussion of the role of colonial agents and the impact of interest politics on imperial policy, see especially Michael Kammen, *A Rope of Sand: The Colonial Agents, British Politics, and the American Revolution* (Ithaca, N.Y.: Cornell University Press, 1968); and Kammen, *Empire and Interest: The American Colonies and the Politics of Mercantilism* (Philadelphia: J. B. Lippincott, 1970); and James Henretta, *"Salutary Neglect": Colonial Administration under the Duke of Newcastle* (Princeton, N.J.: Princeton University Press, 1972). The importance of interests in the operation of English politics during the eighteenth century has been argued most effectively by Sir Lewis Namier and his followers. See in particular Sir Lewis Namier, *England in the Age of the American Revolution,* 2nd ed. (London: Macmillan, 1961); Namier, *The History of Parliament: The House of Commons, 1754-1790,* 3 vols. (New York: Oxford University Press, 1964); and Namier, *The Structure of Politics at the Accession of George III,* 2nd ed. (London: Macmillan, 1957).

[3] William Wood, *Survey of Trade in Four Parts . . .* (London: W. Hinchlieffe, 1718). For further discussion of this tract, see Kammen, *Empire and Interest,* 45-47.

[4] The impact of imperial legislation on the colonial iron industry is discussed in Arthur C. Bining, *British Regulation of the Colonial Iron Industry* (Philadelphia: University of Pennsylvania Press, 1933). For an abbreviated version of the Iron Act of 1750, see Jack P. Greene, ed., *Great Britain and the American Colonies, 1607-1763* (New York: Harper & Row, 1970), 272-274.

[5] William Macdonald, ed., *Select Charters and Other Documents Illustrative of American History, 1606-1775* (London: Macmillan, 1904), 249.

[6] The currency problem in the colonies as well as the currency acts of 1751 and 1764 are ably treated in Lesley V. Brock, *The Currency of the American Colonies, 1700-1764: A Study in Colonial Finance and Imperial Relations* (New York: Arno Press, 1975); Curtis P. Nettels, *The Money Supply in the American Colonies before 1720* (Madison, Wis.: University of Wisconsin Press, 1934); Eric P. Newman, *The Early Paper Money of America* (Racine, Wis.: Whitman Publishing, 1967); Jack P. Greene and Richard M. Jellison, "The Currency Act of 1764 and Imperial-Colonial Relations, 1764-1776," *William and Mary Quarterly,* 3rd ser., 18, No. 4 (October 1961), 485-518; and Joseph A. Ernst, "Genesis of the Currency Act of 1764: Virginia Paper Money and the Protection of British Investments," *William and Mary Quarterly,* 3rd ser., 22, No. 1 (January 1965), 33-74. An abbreviated version of the Currency Act of 1750 can be found in Greene, *Great Britain and the American Colonies,* 279-282.

[7] The standard biography of Walpole is J. H. Plumb, *Sir Robert Walpole,* 2 vols. (London: Cresset Press, 1961).

[8] The story of the South Sea Bubble has been told by J. Carswell in *The South Sea Bubble* (London: Cresset Press, 1960).

[9] Plumb, *Sir Robert Walpole,* 2: 330.

[10] Dorothy Marshall, *Eighteenth Century England* (New York: D. McKay, 1962), 184. The English political and constitutional matrix which produced people such as Walpole and influenced their thinking and behavior is introduced in Robert Walcott, *English Politics in the*

Early Eighteenth Century (Cambridge, Mass.: Harvard University Press, 1956); and J. H. Plumb, *The Growth of Political Stability in England, 1675–1725* (Baltimore: Johns Hopkins Press, 1969). See also E. N. Williams, ed., *The Eighteenth Century Constitution* (Cambridge, Eng.: Cambridge University Press, 1960).

[11] There has yet to be written a modern biography of George Montague Dunk, Second Earl of Halifax. For some insights into his role as imperial policy maker, students may consult Dickerson, *American Colonial Government*; and Labaree, *Royal Government.*

[12] Leonard Labaree, ed., *Royal Instructions to British Governors, 1670–1776,* 2 vols. (New York: D. Appleton-Century, 1935), 1: 190–191. The activities of the Board of Trade are discussed in detail in I. K. Steele, *Politics of Colonial Policy: The Board of Trade in Colonial Administration: 1696–1720* (Oxford: Clarendon Press, 1968); Arthur H. Basye, *The Lords Commissioners of Trade and Plantation* (New Haven: Yale University Press, 1925); and Dickerson, *American Colonial Government.*

[13] Alexander Johnston and James Albert Woodburn, eds., *American Orations: Studies in American Political History,* 4 vols. (New York: G. P. Putnam's Sons, 1896–1897), 1: 11–12.

[14] Quoted in W. J. Eccles, *France in America* (New York: Harper & Row, 1972), 40.

[15] George Washington, *The Writings of George Washington,* ed. John C. Fitzpatrick, 39 vols. (Washington, D.C.: U.S. Government Printing Office, 1931–1944), 1: 151.

[16] The most reliable guides to the colonial theater of the wars for empire are Howard H. Peckham, *The Colonial Wars, 1689–1762* (Chicago: University of Chicago Press, 1964); Douglas Edward Leach, *The Northern Colonial Frontier, 1607–1762* (New York: Holt, Rinehart & Winston, 1966); and Leach, *Arms for Empire: A Military History of the British Colonies in North America, 1607–1763* (New York: Macmillan, 1973). W. L. Dorn, *Competition for Empire, 1740–1763* (New York: Harper & Brothers, 1940) offers a solid introduction to the French and Indian War. Julian S. Corbett, *England in the Seven Years' War,* 2 vols. (London: Longmans, Green, 1907) traces the war from England's perspective, while the French viewpoint and the growth of the French Empire are analyzed in Eccles, *France in America.*

[17] Benjamin Franklin, *The Papers of Benjamin Franklin,* 22 vols. to date, vols. 1–14 ed. Leonard W. Labaree, assoc. ed. Whitefield J. Bell, Jr., vols. 15–22 ed. W. B. Willcox (New Haven: Yale University Press, 1959–) 9: 90–91.

CHAPTER EIGHT

[1] Though historians are still trying to understand fully the intricacies of Atlantic commerce in the colonial era, readers wanting information on the growth of Anglo-American trade and the rise of colonial merchants can find it in Bernard Bailyn, *The New England Merchants in the Seventeenth Century* (Cambridge, Mass.: Harvard University Press, 1955); Ralph Davis, *The Rise of the Atlantic Economies* (Ithaca, N.Y.: Cornell University Press, 1973); and Davis, *A Commercial Revolution: English Overseas Trade in the Seventeenth and Eighteenth Centuries* (London: Historical Association, 1967); W. E. Minchinton, ed., *The Growth of English Overseas Trade in the Seventeenth and Eighteenth Centuries* (London: Methuen, 1969); James F. Shepherd and Gary M. Walton, *Shipping, Maritime Trade, and the Economic Development of Colonial North America* (Cambridge, Eng.: Cambridge University Press, 1972); Paul G. E. Clemens, *The Atlantic Economy and Colonial Maryland's Eastern Shore: From Tobacco to Grain* (Ithaca, N.Y.: Cornell University Press, 1980); James F. Shepherd and Gary M. Walton, *The Economic Rise of Early America* (Cambridge, Eng.: Cambridge University Press, 1979); and Edwin J. Perkins, *The Economy of Colonial America* (New York: Columbia University Press, 1980). My estimates of English trade come from information contained in articles by F. J. Fisher and Ralph Davis in Minchinton, *Growth of English Overseas Trade.*

[2] Peter Kalm, *Travels into North America . . . ,* trans. John Reinhold Forster, in John Pinkerton [ed.], *A General Collection of the Best and Most Interesting Voyages and Travels in all Parts of the World; Many of Which are Now First Translated into English,* 17 vols. (London: Longman, Hurst, Rees, & Orme, 1808–1814), 13: 458.

[3] Pinkerton, *General Collection,* 13: 449.

[4] Students may consult Evarts B. Greene and Virginia D. Harrington, *American Population before the Federal Census of 1790* (New York: Columbia University Press, 1932); J. Potter, "The Growth of Population in America, 1700–1860," in D. V. Glass and D. E. C. Eversley, eds., *Population in History* (Chicago: Aldine, 1965); Stella H. Sutherland, *Population Distribution in Colonial America* (New York: Columbia University Press, 1936); Robert V. Wells, *The Population of the British Colonies in America before 1776: A Survey of Census Data* (Princeton, N.J.:

Princeton University Press, 1975); and United States Bureau of Census, *Statistical History of the United States from Colonial Times to the Present,* (New York: Basic Books, 1976) for more detailed information about colonial population. My estimates of Anglo-America's economic growth are based upon conclusions drawn from Marc Egnal, "The Economic Development of the Thirteen Continental Colonies, 1720–1775," *William and Mary Quarterly,* 3rd ser., 32, No. 2 (April 1975), 191–222. See also Raymond W. Goldsmith, "Long Period Growth in Income and Product," in Ralph Andreano, ed., *New Views on American Economic Development* (Cambridge, Mass.: Schenkman, 1965); and Robert E. Gallman, "The Pace and Pattern of American Economic Growth," in Lance E. Davis, et al., *American Economic Growth: An Economist's History of the United States* (New York: Harper & Row, 1972).

[5] See Shepherd and Walton, *Economic Rise of Early America,* esp. Chapters 4, 5, and 6, for trade statistics cited in text. These chapters summarize many of the conclusions of their *Shipping, Maritime Trade and the Economic Development of Colonial America.* See also Richard Pares, *Yankees and Creoles: The Trade between North America and the West Indies before the American Revolution* (Cambridge, Mass.: Harvard University Press, 1956).

[6] For an amplification of the regional characteristics of the colonial economy outlined in the preceding discussion, the reader should consult Egnal, "Economic Development of the Thirteen Continental Colonies"; James A. Henretta, *The Evolution of American Society, 1700–1815: An Interdisciplinary Analysis* (Lexington, Mass.: D. C. Heath, 1973); Charles S. Sydnor, *Gentlemen Freeholders: Political Practices in Washington's Virginia* (Chapel Hill, N.C.: University of North Carolina Press, 1952); Daniel B. Smith, *Inside the Great House: Planter Family Life in Eighteenth Century Chesapeake Society* (Ithaca, N.Y.: Cornell University Press, 1980); James T. Lemon, *The Best Poor Man's Country: A Geographical Study of Early Southeastern Pennsylvania* (Baltimore: Johns Hopkins Press, 1972); Stephanie Grauman Wolf, *Urban Village: Population, Community, and Family Structure in Germantown, Pennsylvania* (Princeton, N.J.: Princeton University Press, 1977); Carville Earle, *The Evolution of a Tidewater Settlement System: All Hallow's Parish, Maryland, 1650–1783* (Chicago: University of Chicago Press, 1975); Clemens, *Atlantic Economy*; Carl Bridenbaugh, *Cities in the Wilderness: The First Century of Urban Life in America, 1625–1742* (New York: Alfred A. Knopf, 1955); and Bridenbaugh, *Cities in Revolt: Urban Life in America, 1743–1776* (New York: Alfred A. Knopf, 1955); Gary B. Nash, *The Urban Crucible: Social Change, Political Consciousness, and the Origins of the American Revolution* (Cambridge, Mass.: Harvard University Press, 1979); Stuart Bruchey, *The Roots of American Economic Growth, 1607–1861: An Essay in Social Causation* (New York: Harper & Row, 1965); Percy Wells Bidwell and John I. Falconer, *History of Agriculture in the Northern United States, 1620–1860* (Washington, D.C.: The Carnegie Institution of Washington, 1925); and Lewis Cecil Gray, *History of Agriculture in the Southern United States to 1860* (Washington, D.C.: Carnegie Institute, 1933).

[7] Benjamin Franklin, *The Papers of Benjamin Franklin,* 22 vols. to date, vols. 1–14 ed. Leonard W. Labaree, assoc. ed. Whitefield J. Bell, Jr., vols. 15–22 ed. W. B. Willcox (New Haven: Yale University Press, 1959–), 3: 306.

[8] *Virginia Magazine of History and Biography,* 11, No. 1 (July 1903), 2. The relationship between the colonial monetary system and Anglo-American economic growth is explored in Curtis P. Nettels, *The Money Supply of the American Colonies before 1720* (Madison, Wis.: University of Wisconsin Press, 1934); Leslie V. Brock, *The Currency of the American Colonies, 1700–1764: A Study in Colonial Finance and Imperial Relations* (New York: Arno Press, 1975); Joseph A. Ernst, *Money and Politics in America, 1755–1775: A Study of the Currency Act of 1764 and the Political Economy of Revolution* (Chapel Hill, N.C.: University of North Carolina Press, 1973); and John J. McCusker, *Money and Exchange in Europe and America, 1600–1775: A Handbook* (Chapel Hill, N.C.: University of North Carolina Press, 1978).

[9] The statistics on the immigration and distribution of slaves are drawn from Ira Berlin, "Time, Space and the Evolution of Afro-American Society on British Mainland North America," *American Historical Review,* 85, No. 1 (February 1980), 44–78; and from Wells, *Population of the British Colonies.*

[10] The statistics on slave population and sugar production in the West Indies have been gleaned from Richard Sheridan, *Sugar and Slavery: An Economic History of the British West Indies, 1623–1775* (Baltimore: Johns Hopkins Press, 1974); Richard S. Dunn, *Sugar and Slaves: The Rise of the Planter Class in the English West Indies, 1624–1717* (Chapel Hill, N.C.: University of North Carolina Press, 1972); Carl and Robert Bridenbaugh, *No Peace Beyond the Line: The British in the Caribbean, 1624–1690* (New York: Oxford University Press, 1972); and Philip Curtin, *The Atlantic Slave Trade: A Census* (Madison, Wis.: University of Wisconsin Press, 1969). The slave trade is also the subject of Herbert S. Klein, *The Middle Passage: Comparative Studies in the Atlantic Slave Trade* (Princeton, N.J.: Princeton University Press, 1978); and Henry A. Gemery and Jan S. Hogendorn, eds., *The Uncommon Market: Essays in the Economic History of the Atlantic Slave Trade* (New York: Academic Press, 1979). For an

analysis of the racial composition of the British island colonies and its implications, see Wells, *Population of the British Colonies,* 172–258.

[11] The best account of slavery in colonial South Carolina is Peter H. Wood, *Black Majority: Negroes in Colonial South Carolina from 1670 through the Stono Rebellion* (New York: Alfred A. Knopf, 1974). See also Verner W. Crane, *The Southern Frontier, 1670–1732* (Durham, N.C.: Duke University Press, 1928); Converse D. Clowse, *Economic Beginnings of Colonial South Carolina, 1670–1730* (Columbia: University of South Carolina Press, 1971); and M. Eugene Sirmans, "The Legal Status of the Slave in South Carolina, 1640–1740," *Journal of Southern History,* 28 (November 1962), 462–473.

[12] Ann Maury, ed., *Memoirs of a Huguenot Family* (New York: G. P. Putnam, 1853), 351–352.

[13] Ibid., 351–352. For an analysis of slavery in colonial Virginia, see Edmund S. Morgan, *American Slavery, American Freedom: The Ordeal of Colonial Virginia* (New York: W. W. Norton, 1975); Gerald W. Mullin, *Flight and Rebellion: Slave Resistance in Eighteenth Century Virginia* (New York: Oxford University Press, 1972); Thad W. Tate Jr., *The Negro in Eighteenth Century Williamsburg* (Charlottesville: University Press of Virginia, 1965). See also U. B. Phillips, *Life and Labor in the Old South* (Boston: Little, Brown, 1929); Allan Kulikoff, "The Origins of Afro-American Society in Tidewater Maryland and Virginia, 1700–1790," *William and Mary Quarterly,* 3rd ser., 35, No. 2 (April 1978), 226–259; Russell Menard, "The Maryland Slave Population, 1658–1730: A Demographic Profile of Blacks in Four Counties," *William and Mary Quarterly,* 3rd ser., 32, No. 1 (January 1975), 29–54; and Darold D. Wax, "Preferences for Slaves in Colonial America," *Journal of Negro History,* 58, No. 4 (October 1973), 371–401.

[14] Niel Caplan, ed., "Some Unpublished Letters of Benjamin Colman, 1717–1725," *Massachusetts Historical Society Proceedings, January–December 1965,* vol. 77 (Boston: Massachusetts Historical Society, 1966), 131. There are several fine studies of northern slavery. See in particular Edgar J. McManus, *Black Bondage in the North* (Syracuse, N.Y.: Syracuse University Press, 1973); and McManus, *A History of Negro Slavery in New York* (Syracuse, N.Y.: Syracuse University Press, 1966); and Lorenzo J. Greene, *The Negro in Colonial New England, 1620–1776* (New York: Columbia University Press, 1942).

[15] On the whole my conclusions follow the arguments of McManus, *Black Bondage*; Berlin, "Time, Space and the Evolution of Afro-American Society"; Gary B. Nash, " Slaves and Slaveowners in Colonial Philadelphia," *William and Mary Quarterly,* 3rd ser., 30, No. 2 (April 1973), 223–256; James G. Lydon, "New York and the Slave Trade, 1700–1774," *William and Mary Quarterly,* 3rd ser., 35, No. 2 (April 1978), 375–394; and Jerome H. Wood, "The Negro in Early Pennsylvania: The Lancaster Experience, 1730–1790," in Elinor Miller and Eugene Genovese, eds., *Plantation, Town and County: Essays on the Local History of American Slave Societies* (Urbana, Ill.: University of Illinois Press, 1974). See also Herbert G. Gutman, *The Black Family in Slavery and Freedom, 1750–1925* (New York: Pantheon Books, 1976); Lester B. Scherer, *Slavery and the Churches in Early America, 1618–1819* (Grand Rapids, Mich.: Wm. B. Eerdmans, 1975); and William D. Pierson, "Afro-American Culture in Eighteenth-Century New England" (Ph.D. dissertation, Indiana University, 1975).

[16] My description of Georgian society is brief, but the interested reader will find additional information in Dorothy Marshall, *Eighteenth Century England* (New York: D. MacKay, 1962); and Marshall, *The English People in the Eighteenth Century* (London: Longmans, Green, 1956); Robert Walcott, *English Politics in the Early Eighteenth Century* (Cambridge, Mass.: Harvard University Press, 1956); G. E. Mingay, *English Landed Society in the Eighteenth Century* (London: Routledge & Kegan Paul, 1963); J. H. Plumb, *Men and Centuries* (Boston: Houghton-Mifflin, 1963); A. S. Tuberville, *House of Lords in the Eighteenth Century* (Oxford: Oxford University Press, 1927); E. N. Williams, *Life in Georgian England* (New York: G. P. Putnam's Sons, 1962); and the comprehensive W. E. H. Lecky, *England in the Eighteenth Century,* 8 vols. (London: Longmans, Green, 1829–1890).

[17] Jackson Turner Main, *The Social Structure of Revolutionary America* (Princeton, N.J.: Princeton University Press, 1965); Charles S. Grant, *Democracy in the Connecticut Frontier Town of Kent* (New York: Columbia University Press, 1961). See also Gloria L. Main, "Inequality in Early America: The Evidence of Probate Records from Massachusetts and Maryland," *Journal of Interdisciplinary History,* 7, No. 4 (Spring 1977), 559–581; and Alice Hanson Jones, *Wealth of a Nation to Be: The American Colonies on the Eve of the Revolution* (New York: Columbia University Press, 1980).

[18] Aubrey Land, "Economic Base and Social Structure: The Northern Chesapeake in the Eighteenth Century," *Journal of Economic History,* 25, No. 4 (December 1965), 639–654.

[19] Historians are divided over just how egalitarian and economically democratic early America was. They disagree also over the amount of economic opportunity that was available to the enterprising colonial. Much of the recent scholarship has emphasized the growing in-

equality of wealth among eighteenth-century Anglo-Americans. Those same studies have suggested declining opportunity as well. However, even the most pessimistic appraisals of wealth distribution and availability of opportunity in early America seem to agree that British America offered more political and economic opportunity than either Europe or England. They also agree that economic opportunity, social mobility, and the acquisition and concentration of wealth varied considerably from place to place and over time. Historians interested in the colonial family have offered considerable support for the latter view by showing the complex and diverse nature of colonial families and how wealth and family size were related. See Wells, *Population of the British Colonies,* 297–333.

In addition to the books and articles already mentioned, the student may examine the various perspectives on wealth, opportunity, and mobility in early America through Robert E. Brown, *Middle-Class Democracy and the Revolution in Massachusetts, 1691–1780* (Ithaca, N.Y.: Cornell University Press, 1955); Robert E. Brown and B. Katherine Brown, *Virginia, 1705–1786: Democracy or Aristocracy* (East Lansing: Michigan State University Press, 1964); G. B. Warden, *Boston, 1689–1776* (Boston: Little, Brown, 1970); and Warden, "Inequality and Instability in Eighteenth Century Boston, A Reappraisal," *Journal of Interdisciplinary History,* 6, No. 4 (Spring 1976), 585–620; Richard Bushman, *Puritan to Yankee: Character and the Social Order in Colonial Connecticut, 1690–1765* (Cambridge, Mass.: Harvard University Press, 1967); Gary B. Nash, "Urban Wealth and Poverty in Pre-Revolutionary America," *Journal of Interdisciplinary History,* 6, No. 4 (Spring 1976), 545–584; James A. Henretta, "Economic Development and Social Structure in Colonial Boston," *William and Mary Quarterly,* 3rd ser., 22, No. 1 (January 1965), 75–92; Abbot E. Smith, *Colonists in Bondage: White Servitude and Convict Labor in America, 1607–1776* (Chapel Hill, N.C.: University of North Carolina Press, 1947); Kenneth A. Lockridge, "Social Change and the Meaning of the American Revolution," *Journal of Social History,* 6, No. 4 (Summer 1973), 403–439; Peter J. Coleman, *Debtors and Creditors in America: Insolvency, Imprisonment for Debt, and Bankruptcy, 1607–1900* (Madison, Wis.: University of Wisconsin Press, 1974); Richard D. Brown, *Modernization: The Transformation of American Life, 1600–1865* (New York: Hill & Wang, 1976); Randolph Shipley Klein, *Portrait of an Early American Family: The Shippens of Pennsylvania across Five Generations* (Philadelphia: University of Pennsylvania Press, 1975); Sung Bok Kim, *Landlord and Tenant in Colonial New York: Manorial Society, 1664–1775* (Chapel Hill, N.C.: University of North Carolina Press, 1978); James T. Lemon and Gary B. Nash, "The Distribution of Wealth in Eighteenth Century America: A Century of Changes in Chester County, Pennsylvania, 1689–1802," *Journal of Social History,* 2, No. 1 (Fall 1968), 1–29; Allan Kulikoff, "The Progress of Inequality in Revolutionary Boston," *William and Mary Quarterly,* 3rd ser., 28, No. 3 (July 1971), 375–412; and Morgan, *American Slavery, American Freedom.*

[20] T[homas] M[athew], *The Beginning, Progess and Conclusion of Bacon's Rebellion in Virginia, In the Years 1675 and 1676,* in Peter Force, comp., *Tracts and Other Papers Relating Principally to the Origin, Settlement and Progress of the Colonies in North America from the Discovery of the Country to the Year 1776,* 4 vols. (Washington: Peter Force, 1836–1846), 1: No. 8, 20, 24 (tracts are individually paginated). The reader should consult Thomas Jefferson Wertenbaker, *Torchbearer of the Revolution: The Story of Bacon's Rebellion and Its Leader* (Princeton, N.J.: Princeton University Press, 1940); Wilcomb E. Washburn, *The Governor and the Rebel: A History of Bacon's Rebellion in Virginia* (Chapel Hill, N.C.: University of North Carolina Press, 1957); and Jane Carson, *Bacon's Rebellion, 1676–1976* (Jamestown, Va.: Jamestown Foundation, 1976) for contrasting views on the significance of Bacon's Rebellion.

[21] *Pennsylvania Colonial Records or Minutes of the Provincial Council of Pennsylvania,* 16 vols. (Harrisburg: Published by the State, 1851–1853) 9: 141, 138. (Vols. 1–10 contain the minutes of the provincial council; vols. 11–16 contain the minutes of the Supreme Executive Council of Pennsylvania.) The story of the Paxton Boys is told in Brook Hindle, "The March of the Paxton Boys," *William and Mary Quarterly,* 3rd ser., 3, No. 4 (October 1946), 461–486; and the introduction to John R. Dunbar, ed., *The Paxton Papers* (The Hague: Martinus Nijhoff, 1957). See also Charles H. Lincoln, *The Revolutionary Movement in Pennsylvania,* rep. ed. (Cos Cob, Conn.: J. E. Edwards, 1968); Joseph E. Illick, *Colonial Pennsylvania: A History* (New York: Charles Scribner's Sons, 1978); and James Kirby Martin, "The Return of the Paxton Boys and the Historical State of the Pennsylvania Frontier, 1764–1774," *Pennsylvania History,* 38, No. 2 (April 1971), 117–133.

[22] Richard J. Hooker, ed., *The Carolina Back-Country on the Eve of the Revolution: The Journal and Other Writings of Charles Woodmason, Anglican Itinerant* (Chapel Hill, N.C.: University of North Carolina Press, 1953), 213–214. Marcus Lee Hansen, *The Atlantic Migration, 1607–1860: A History of the Continuing Settlement of the United States* (Cambridge, Mass.: Harvard University Press, 1940) describes both English and non-English immigration into North America during the colonial era. See Richard M. Brown, *The South Carolina Regulators* (Cambridge, Mass.: Belknap Press of Harvard University Press, 1963); Rachel M. Klein, "Ordering the

Backcountry: The South Carolina Regulation," *William and Mary Quarterly,* 3rd ser., 38, No. 4 (October 1981), 661–680; and James M. Wittenburg, "Planters, Merchants, and Lawyers: Social Change and the Origins of the North Carolina Regulation," *William and Mary Quarterly,* 3rd ser., 34, No. 2 (April 1977), 215–238 for further discussion of the Regulator movement in the Carolinas.

[23] Ibid., 221.

[24] Ibid., 215.

[25] Jerome A. Reich, *Leisler's Rebellion: A Study of Democracy in New York, 1664–1720* (Chicago: University of Chicago Press, 1953); David S. Lovejoy, *The Glorious Revolution in America* (New York: Harper & Row, 1972); Bernard Mason, "Aspects of the New York Revolt of 1689," *New York History,* 30, No. 2 (April 1949), 165–180; and Thomas J. Archdeacon, *New York City, 1664–1710: Conquest and Change* (Ithaca, N.Y.: Cornell University Press, 1975) all discuss Leisler's Rebellion. Of these studies Archdeacon's offers the most comprehensive explanation for the rebellion. However, Archdeacon considers it more of an example of conflict between ethnic groups than a struggle over political or constitutional principles. James Henretta outlines some of the social and sectional conflict in Anglo-America in *Evolution of American Society,* Chapter 4. See also Richard Maxwell Brown, *Strain of Violence: Historical Studies of American Violence and Vigilantism* (New York: Oxford University Press, 1975); and Sally Smith Booth, *Seeds of Anger: Revolts in America, 1607–1771* (New York: Hastings House, 1977).

CHAPTER NINE

[1] The charters may be found in Francis N. Thorpe, comp. and ed., *The Federal and State Constitutions, Colonial Charters, and other Organic Laws of the States, Territories, and Colonies Now or Heretofore Forming the United States of America,* 7 vols. (Washington, D.C.: U.S. Government Printing Office, 1909); and in William Macdonald, ed., *Select Charters and Other Documents Illustrative of American History, 1606–1775* (New York: Macmillan, 1904), 128.

[2] Macdonald, *Select Charters,* 122.

[3] The role of the royal governor is discussed in many books, but the two standard introductions are Leonard W. Labaree, *Royal Government in America: A Study of the British Colonial System before 1783* (New Haven: Yale University Press, 1930); and Volume 4 of Charles M. Andrews, *The Colonial Period of American History,* 4 vols. (New Haven: Yale University Press, 1934–1938). Also important are Everts B. Greene, *The Provincial Governor in the English Colonies of North America* (New York: Longmans, Green, 1898); and Stephen S. Webb, *The Governors-General: The English Army and the Definition of Empire, 1569–1681* (Chapel Hill, N.C.: University of North Carolina Press, 1979). Webb's book does not cover the eighteenth century, but his argument is pertinent. Another way to study the role of the colonial governor is through biography. Some helpful works are John A. Schutz, *Thomas Pownall, British Defender of American Liberty: A Study of Anglo-American Relations in the Eighteenth Century* (Glendale, Calif.: Arthur H. Clark, 1951); and Schutz, *William Shirley: King's Governor of Massachusetts* (Chapel Hill, N.C.: University of North Carolina Press, 1961); Bernard Bailyn, *The Ordeal of Thomas Hutchinson* (Cambridge, Mass.: Harvard University Press, 1974); and a collective biography, W. W. Abbot, *The Royal Governors of Georgia 1754–1775* (Chapel Hill, N.C.: University of North Carolina Press, 1959).

[4] Jack P. Greene, *The Quest for Power: The Lower Houses of Assembly in the Southern Royal Colonies, 1689–1776* (Chapel Hill, N.C.: University of North Carolina Press, 1963), 3–18. See also Mary P. Clarke, *Parliamentary Privilege in the American Colonies* (New Haven: Yale University Press, 1943); and John F. Burns, *Controversies between Royal Governors and their Assemblies in the Northern American Colonies* (Boston: The Wright and Potter Printer Co., 1923).

[5] *Collections of the Massachusetts Historical Society,* 6th ser., 6 (Boston: Massachusetts Historical Society, 1893), 226.

[6] Ibid.

[7] See Benjamin Labaree, *Colonial Massachusetts: A History* (Millwood, N.Y.: KTO Press, 1979); Schutz, *William Shirley*; and Robert Zemsky, *Merchants, Farmers, and River Gods: An Essay on Eighteenth Century American Politics* (Boston: Gambit Press, 1971).

[8] Stanley N. Katz, *Newcastle's New York: Anglo-American Politics, 1732–1753* (Cambridge, Mass.: Harvard University Press, 1968); Patricia U. Bonomi, *A Factious People: Politics*

and Society in Colonial New York (New York: Columbia University Press, 1971); and Michael Kammen, *Colonial New York: A History* (New York: Charles Scribner's Sons, 1979). For the Zenger affair see Leonard W. Levy, *Legacy of Suppression: Freedom of Speech and Press in Early American History* (Cambridge, Mass.: Harvard University Press, 1960); and Stanley Katz's introduction to James Alexander, *A Brief Narrative of the Case and Trial of John Peter Zenger, Printer of the New York Weekly Journal,* 2nd ed. (Cambridge, Mass.: Belknap Press of Harvard University Press, 1972).

[9] Quoted in Bernard Bailyn, *The Origins of American Politics* (New York: Vintage Books, 1967), 118. See also Gary B. Nash, *Quakers and Politics: Pennsylvania, 1681–1726* (Princeton, N.J.: Princeton University Press, 1968); and Joseph Illick, *Colonial Pennsylvania: A History* (New York: Charles Scribner's Sons, 1976).

[10] Charles Sydnor, *Gentlemen Freeholders: Political Practices in Washington's Virginia* (Chapel Hill, N.C.: University of North Carolina Press, 1952); Edmund S. Morgan, *American Slavery, American Freedom: The Ordeal of Colonial Virginia* (New York: W. W. Norton, 1975); Rhys Isaac, "Evangelical Revolt: The Nature of the Baptists' Challenge to the Traditional Order in Virginia, 1765 to 1775," *William and Mary Quarterly,* 3rd ser., 31, No. 3 (July 1974), 345–368; and Isaac, "Religion and Authority: Problems of the Anglican Establishment in Virginia in the Era of the Great Awakening and the Parsons' Cause," *William and Mary Quarterly,* 3rd ser., 30, No. 4 (October 1973), 13–36.

[11] David E. Van Deventer, *The Emergence of Provincial New Hampshire, 1623–1741* (Baltimore: Johns Hopkins Press, 1976), 149, 221–225; Jere Daniell, *Experiment in Republicanism: New Hampshire Politics and the American Revolution, 1741–1794* (Cambridge, Mass.: Harvard University Press, 1970).

[12] The persistence of localism in the eighteenth century is a conclusion shared by many historians. See, for example, Michael Zuckerman, *Peaceable Kingdoms: New England Towns in the Eighteenth Century* (New York: Alfred A. Knopf, 1970); Edward M. Cook, Jr., *The Fathers of the Towns: Leadership and Community Structure in Eighteenth Century New England* (Baltimore: Johns Hopkins Press, 1976); Robert A. Gross, *The Minutemen and their World* (New York: Hill & Wang, 1976); Thomas Bender, *Community and Social Change in America* (New Brunswick, N.J.: Rutgers University Press, 1978); Christopher M. Jedrey, *The World of John Cleaveland: Family and Community in Eighteenth Century New England* (New York: W. W. Norton, 1979); Carville Earle, *The Evolution of a Tidewater Settlement System: All Hallow's Parish, Maryland, 1650–1783* (Chicago: University of Chicago Press, 1975); James T. Lemon, *The Best Poor Man's Country: A Geographical Study of Early Southeastern Pennsylvania* (Baltimore: Johns Hopkins Press, 1972); and Stephanie Grauman Wolf, *Urban Village: Population, Community, and Family Structure in Germantown, Pennsylvania, 1683–1800* (Princeton, N.J.: Princeton University Press, 1976). For the county court see Sydnor, *Gentlemen Freeholders*; David Koenig, *Law and Society in Puritan Massachusetts, Essex County, 1629–1692* (Chapel Hill, N.C.: University of North Carolina Press, 1979); and Paul M. McCain, *The County Court in North Carolina before 1750* (Durham, N.C.: Duke University Press, 1954). See also William E. Nelson, *Dispute and Conflict Resolution in Plymouth County, Mass., 1725–1825* (Chapel Hill, N.C.: University of North Carolina Press, 1981); and Nelson's superb study, *The Americanization of the Common Law* (Cambridge, Mass.: Harvard University Press, 1975).

[13] The character of a primate city is discussed in Jorge Hardoy and R. P. Schaedel, *The Urbanization Process in America from its Origin to the Present* Buenos Aires: Editorial del Instituto, 1969) and is demonstrated in James R. Scobie, *Argentina: A City and a Nation,* 2nd ed. (New York: Oxford University Press, 1971). The role of the city in colonial Latin America is described in various sections of Charles Gibson, *Spain in America* (New York: Harper & Row, 1966).

[14] See Carl Bridenbaugh, *Cities in the Wilderness: The First Century of Urban Life in America, 1625–1742* (New York: Alfred A. Knopf, 1955); and Bridenbaugh, *Cities in Revolt: Urban Life in America, 1743–1776* (New York: Alfred A. Knopf, 1955). See also Gary B. Nash, *The Urban Crucible: Social Change, Political Consciousness, and the Origins of the American Revolution* (Cambridge, Mass.: Harvard University Press, 1979). Population statistics are drawn from E. A. Wrigley, *Population and History* (New York: World University Library, 1971), 148; Richard D. Brown, *Modernization: The Transformation of American Life, 1600–1865* (New York: Hill & Wang, 1976), 107; James A. Henretta, *The Evolution of American Society, 1700–1815; An Interdisciplinary Analysis* (Lexington, Mass.: D. C. Heath, 1973), 80; and Nicolas Sanchez-Albornoz, *The Population of Latin America: A History* (Berkeley, Calif.: University of California Press, 1974), 128–129.

[15] Gross, *Minutemen and their World,* 10–29.

[16] Robert J. Dinkin, *Voting in Provincial America: A Study of Elections in the Thirteen*

Colonies, 1689–1776 (Westport, Conn.: Greenwood Press, 1977), 54–58, 208–210; J. R. Pole, *Political Representation in England and the Origins of the American Republic* (Berkeley, Calif.: University of California Press, 1971), 172–189, 205–214, Part V. See also Chilton Williamson, *American Suffrage from Property to Democracy, 1760–1860* (Princeton, N.J.: Princeton University Press, 1960). For decades historians have debated whether political democracy existed in eighteenth-century Anglo-America. The debate has failed to provide an acceptable answer. Most scholars believe that although British North America was far more "democratic" than England or Europe at the time, its political system was radically different from our modern one. The main arguments for and against democracy in early America are brought together in Michael G. Kammen, ed., *Politics and Society in Colonial America* (Hinsdale, Ill.: Dryden Press, 1973). See especially the essays by Michael Zuckerman, Robert Zemsky, Richard Buel, and Robert E. and B. Katherine Brown.

[17]The real Whigs are analyzed and discussed by Caroline Robbins in *The Eighteenth-Century Commonwealthman: Studies in the Transmission, Development and Circumstances of English Liberal Thought from the Restoration of Charles II until the War with the Thirteen Colonies* (Cambridge, Mass.: Harvard University Press, 1959). The discussion of the real Whigs which follows owes much to Robbins and to Bernard Bailyn, *The Ideological Origins of the American Revolution* (Cambridge, Mass.: Harvard University Press, 1967); Bailyn, *The Origins of American Politics* (New York: Alfred A. Knopf, 1968); and J. G. A. Pocock, *The Machiavellian Moment: Florentine Political Thought and the Atlantic Republican Tradition* (Princeton, N.J.: Princeton University Press, 1975). The extent to which recent historians have embraced the argument that the revolutionaries of 1776 were the heirs of the real-Whig tradition is evident in J. R. Pole's comment in Pole, *Political Representation.* The evolution of Anglo-American history in the seventeenth and eighteenth centuries, he writes, culminated in an "inner revolution" in 1776 which

> was nothing less than the American fulfillment of the great Whig tradition, which had once, not inappropriately, been known as "the good old cause" (this was the name given to a republican ideology espoused by many opponents of Oliver Cromwell, the Lord Protector of England, in the 1650s). The American Whigs of the revolutionary era and their British contemporaries were fellow-citizens of a Whig Republic (p. 503).

[18]J. H. Plumb, *Sir Robert Walpole,* 2 vols. (London: Cresset Press, 1961), 1: xiii.

[19]Plumb, *Walpole,* 2: 331–332.

[20]Plumb, *Walpole,* 2: 332.

[21]Ibid., 2: 332.

[22]Richard Beale Davis, *A Colonial Southern Bookshelf: Reading in the Eighteenth Century* (Athens, Ga.: University of Georgia Press, 1979), 55–56.

[23]Katz, *Brief Narrative of the Case of Zenger,* 133.

[24]Katz, *Brief Narrative of the Case of Zenger,* 136.

[25]Katz, *Brief Narrative of the Case of Zenger,* 101.

[26]The standard introductions to the colonial newspaper are through Sidney Kobre, *The Development of the Colonial Newspaper* (Pittsburgh: Colonial Press, 1944); and Frank L. Mott, *American Journalism: A History of Newspapers in the United States through 260 Years: 1690 to 1950,* rev. ed. (New York: Macmillan, 1950). In a perceptive essay Lawrence Leder analyzes the contributions of the colonial press to Anglo-American political thinking in *Liberty and Authority: Early American Political Ideology, 1689–1763* (New York: W. W. Norton, 1976), 19–36.

[27]*American Weekly Mercury,* No. 129, May 24–May 31, 1722.

[28]*American Weekly Mercury,* No. 129.

[29]Examples of this kind of "foreign news" are legion and may be gleaned from any issue of any colonial newspaper at almost any time. For example, the February 10, 1734, issue of the *New York Weekly Journal* devoted seven of its eight columns of foreign news to the activities of Catholics. On December 20, 1736, the same paper gave six and one-half of eight columns of foreign news to Catholic machinations. To cite another example, the *South Carolina Gazette* covered Catholic affairs in six of twelve columns of foreign news in its May 14, 1744, issue and nine of twelve columns of foreign news in its December 3, 1744, issue. The best analysis of Protestant British America's fear of Catholicism remains Sister Mary Augustina Ray, *American Opinion of Roman Catholicism in the Eighteenth Century* (New York: Columbia University Press, 1936). Although Ray devotes only a few pages to anti-Catholic articles and essays in colonial newspapers, she notes that "To cite the colonial newspapers which printed anti-Catholic items would be to call the roll of the colonial press. In this as in so many other respects of provincial society, British precedent served as a model" (p. 182).

CHAPTER TEN

[1] Michael Wigglesworth, *God's Controversy with New England,* in John C. Miller, ed., *The Colonial Image: Origins of American Culture* (New York: George Braziller, 1962), 358.

[2] Benjamin Thompson, *New England's Crisis,* in Perry Miller and Thomas H. Johnson, eds., *The Puritans: A Sourcebook of their Writings,* rev. ed., 2 vols. (New York: Harper & Row, 1963), 2: 640.

[3] Cotton Mather, *A Christian at His Calling: Two Brief Discourses, One Directing a Christian to his General Calling; Another Directing Him to his Personal* (Boston: B. Green & J. Allen, 1701), 36-37, 37-38.

[4] Ibid., 48.

[5] *The Public Records of the Colony of Connecticut, 1636-1776,* 15 vols., vols. 1-3 ed. J. H. Trumbull, vols. 4-15 ed. C. J. Hoadley (Hartford, Conn.: Press of the Case, Lockwood & Brainard Co., 1850-1890), 5: iv-v.

[6] Mather, *Christian at His Calling,* 48. As was discussed briefly in footnote 11 of Chapter Six, historians of early America have emphasized the themes of decline and declension, especially as they pertain to late seventeenth-century New England. Some scholars, such as Perry Miller in *The New England Mind: From Colony to Province* (Cambridge, Mass.: Harvard University Press, 1953), have argued that the rhetoric of declension was Puritan New England's response to the return of monarchy and Anglicanism to England in 1660, as well as a lament over declining piety and religiosity among New England's inhabitants. Others, such as Sacvan Bercovitch in *The Puritan Origins of the American Self* (New Haven: Yale University Press, 1975), and *The American Jeremiad* (Madison, Wis.: University of Wisconsin Press, 1978), find the origins for a distinctively "American" identity in the declension literature. Some historians —myself included—have linked declension arguments to institutional and ideological problems within and among the Anglo-American churches. Still other scholars have suggested that the notion of declension reflected important social and economic changes within colonial society. See, for example, Kenneth A. Lockridge, *A New England Town, The First Hundred Years: Dedham, Massachusetts, 1636-1736* (New York: W. W. Norton, 1970); and Emory Elliott, *Power and the Pulpit in Puritan New England* (Princeton, N.J.: Princeton University Press, 1975). All of these arguments have merit, but as John Redwood points out in *Reason, Ridicule and Religion: The Age of Enlightenment in England, 1660-1750* (Cambridge, Mass.: Harvard University Press, 1976), the themes of decay and decline were commonly held by most English-speaking Protestants during those years. Evidence questioning the reality of religious decline in New England is summarized in Gerald F. Moran and Maris Vinovskis, "The Puritan Family and Religion: A Critical Reappraisal," *William and Mary Quarterly,* 3rd ser., 39, No. 1 (January 1982), 29-63.

[7] Benjamin Franklin, *The Papers of Benjamin Franklin,* 22 vols. to date, vols. 1-14 ed. Leonard W. Labaree, assoc. ed. Whitefield J. Bell, Jr., vols. 15-22 ed. W. B. Willcox (New Haven: Yale University Press, 1959-), 3: 308.

[8] For a greater understanding of the impact that the influx of new religious groups had upon colonial religion, the student may begin with the denominational studies contained in Philip Schaff, et al., gen. eds., *The American Church History Series,* 13 vols. (New York: Christian Literature Company, 1893-1897); John Tracy Ellis, *American Catholicism,* rev. 2nd ed. (Chicago: University of Chicago Press, 1969); and Ellis, *Catholics in Colonial America* (Baltimore: Helicon Press, 1965); Arthur J. Lewis, *Zinzendorf, The Ecumenical Pioneer: A Study in the Moravian Contribution to Christian Mission and Unity* (London: SCM Press, 1962); Carl E. Schneider, *The German Church on the American Frontier* (St. Louis: Eden Publishing House, 1939); Julius F. Sachse, *The German Pietists of Provincial Pennsylvania, 1694-1708* (Philadelphia: Printed for the author, 1895); Charles W. Baird, *History of the Huguenot Emigration to America,* 2 vols. (New York: Dodd, Mead, 1885); James R. Tanis, *Dutch Calvinistic Pietism in the Middle Colonies: A Study in the Life of Theodore Jacobus Frelinghuysen* (The Hague: Martinus Nijhof, 1967); and Jon M. Butler, *Power, Authority and the Origins of American Denominational Order: The English Churches in the Delaware Valley, 1680-1730* (Philadelphia: American Philosophical Society, 1978).

[9] Statistics on the growth of various religious denominations have been drawn largely from Edwin Scott Gaustad, *Historical Atlas of Religion in America* (New York: Harper & Row, 1962); and Sydney E. Ahlstrom, *A Religious History of the American People* (New Haven: Yale University Press, 1972). Information on the Quakers may be gleaned from Rufus M. Jones, *Quakers in the American Colonies,* rep. ed. (New York: Russell & Russell, 1962). Patricia U. Bonomi and Peter R. Eisenstadt have found that the number of Anglo-Americans who were affiliated with a church in the eighteenth century far exceeded those who were not. See their

article, "Church Adherence in the Eighteenth Century British American Colonies," *William and Mary Quarterly,* 3rd ser., 39, No. 2 (April 1982), 245–286.

[10] David Humphreys, *An Historical Account of the Incorporated Society for the Propagation of the Gospel in Foreign Parts,* 1730 facsimile rep. ed. (New York: Arno Press and *The New York Times,* 1969), 127.

[11] For statistical information see Gaustad, *Historical Atlas,* 6–10. The dramatic growth of Anglicanism during the eighteenth century has been described in Carl Bridenbaugh, *Mitre and Sceptre: Transatlantic Faiths, Ideas, Personalities, and Politics, 1689–1775* (New York: Oxford University Press, 1962); Henry P. Thompson, *Into All Lands: The History of the Society for the Propagation of the Gospel in Foreign Parts, 1701–1950* (London: Society for the Promoting of Christian Knowledge, 1951); Arthur L. Cross, *The Anglican Episcopate and the American Colonies* (New York: Longmans, Green, 1902); and Bruce M. Steiner, *Samuel Seabury, 1729–1796: A Study in the High Church Tradition* (Athens, Ohio: Ohio University Press, 1971).

[12] Gaustad, *Historical Atlas,* 29–36; Ellis, *Catholics in Colonial America*; John Gilmary Shea, *The Catholic Church in Colonial Days,* 2 vols. (New York: John G. Shea, 1886); William W. Sweet, ed., *Religion on the American Frontier, Volume 1, The Baptists* (New York: Henry Holt, 1931); and Robert G. Torbet, *A History of the Baptists* (Philadelphia: Judson Press, 1950).

[13] Jonathan Edwards, *The Works of President Edwards,* 8th ed., 4 vols. (New York: Leavitt, 1849), 4: 318.

[14] "Jonathan Edwards to Reverend Thomas Prince, December 12, 1743," in *The Christian History, Containing Accounts of the Revival and Propagation of Religion in Great Britain and America for the Year 1743* (Boston: S. Knesland and T. Green for T. Prince, Jr., 1744), January 14, 1844, 367. There are several fine biographies of Edwards. See especially Ola E. Winslow, *Jonathan Edwards* (New York: Macmillan, 1940); Edward H. Davidson, *Jonathan Edwards: The Narrative of a Puritan Mind* (Boston: Houghton-Mifflin, 1966); Perry Miller, *Jonathan Edwards* (New York: W. Sloane Associates, 1949); Patricia Tracy, *Jonathan Edwards, Pastor: Religion and Society in Eighteenth Century Northampton* (New York: Hill & Wang, 1980). See also Jonathan Edwards, *Apocalyptic Writings,* ed. by Stephen J. Stein (New Haven: Yale University Press, 1977), and Norman Fiering, *Jonathan Edward's Moral Thought and its British Context* (Chapel Hill, N.C.: University of North Carolina Press, 1981).

[15] [Charles Chauncey], "A Letter From a Gentleman in Boston, To Mr. George Wishart, One of the Ministers of Edinburgh, Concerning the State of Religion in New England," in *The Clarendon Historical Society's Reprints* (1st ser.) *1882–1884* (Edinburgh: Privately printed for the Clarendon Historical Society, 1883), No. 7, 80–81. (Volumes are not numbered.)

[16] Historians are divided on the significance of the Great Awakening. Edwin Scott Gaustad explains the theological context of the Great Awakening in *The Great Awakening in New England* (New York: Harper & Row, 1957), while Richard Bushman offers a provocative glimpse into its social and political context in *From Puritan to Yankee: Character and the Social Order in Connecticut 1690–1765* (Cambridge, Mass.: Harvard University Press, 1967). Alan Heimert provides a broad interpretation of the ideological impact of the Awakening in *Religion and the American Mind, from the Great Awakening to the Revolution* (Cambridge, Mass.: Harvard University Press, 1966). Other recommended studies include Wesley M. Gewehr, *The Great Awakening in Virginia, 1740–1790* (Durham, N.C.: Duke University Press, 1930); Charles H. Maxson, *The Great Awakening in the Middle Colonies* (Chicago: University of Chicago Press, 1920); Clarence C. Goen, *Revivalism and Separatism in New England: Strict Congregationalists and Separate Baptists in the Great Awakening* (New Haven: Yale University Press, 1962); Cedric Cowing, *The Great Awakening and the American Revolution* (Chicago: Rand McNally, 1971); Stuart C. Henry, *George Whitefield: Wayfaring Witness* (New York: Abingdom Press, 1957); Tanis, *Dutch Calvinistic Pietism*; Gary Nash, *The Urban Crucible: Social Change, Political Consciousness, and the Origins of the American Revolution* (Cambridge, Mass.: Harvard University Press, 1979); William G. McLoughlin, *Isaac Backus and the American Pietistic Tradition* (Boston: Little, Brown, 1967); Rhys Isaac, *The Transformation of Virginia, 1740–1790* (Chapel Hill, N.C.: University of North Carolina Press, 1982). For a critical reappraisal of the literature and conclusions about the Great Awakening, see Jon M. Butler, "Enthusiasm Described and Decried: The Great Awakening as Interpretive Fiction," *Journal of American History,* 69, No. 2 (September 1982), 305–325.

[17] One of the best books on the Enlightenment in the colonial era is Henry F. May, *The Enlightenment in America* (New York: Oxford University Press, 1976). Other useful books include Donald G. Meyer, *The Democratic Enlightenment* (New York: Capricorn Books, 1976); Brooke Hindle, *The Pursuit of Science in Revolutionary America* (Chapel Hill, N.C.: University of North Carolina Press, 1956); Daniel J. Boorstin, *The Lost World of Thomas Jefferson* (New York: Henry Holt, 1948); Owen Aldridge, *Benjamin Franklin and Nature's God* (Durham, N.C.:

Duke University Press, 1967); Gustav A. Koch, *Republican Religion: The American Revolution and the Cult of Reason* (New York: Henry Holt, 1933); Herbert M. Morais, *Deism in Eighteenth-Century America* (New York: Columbia University Press, 1934); and Ernst Cassirer, *The Philosophy of the Enlightenment* (Princeton, N.J.: Princeton University Press, 1951).

[18] Quoted in Thomas Henry Billings, "The Great Awakening," *Historical Collections of the Essex Institute,* 65, No. 1 (January 1929), 94–95.

[19] Sydney George Fisher, *Men, Women & Manners in Colonial Times,* 2nd ed., 2 vols. (Philadelphia: J. P. Lippincott, 1898), 1: 275. The story of women in the colonial era is just beginning to be told. Useful introductions, both old and new, are Mary Sumner Benson, *Women in Eighteenth Century America: A Study of Opinion and Social Usage* (New York: Columbia University Press, 1935); Carl Holliday, *Woman's Life in Colonial Days* (Boston: Cornhill, 1922); Elizabeth Anthony Dexter, *Colonial Women of Affairs: Women in Business and the Professions in America before 1776,* rev. 2nd ed. (Boston: Houghton Mifflin, 1931); Mary Beard, *America through Women's Eyes* (New York: Macmillan, 1933); Julia Cherry Spruill, *Women's Life and Work in the Southern Colonies* (New York: W. W. Norton, 1972); Eugenie Andruss Leonard, Sophie Hutchinson Drinker, and Miriam Young Holden, *The American Woman in Colonial and Revolutionary Times, 1565–1800* (Philadelphia: University of Pennsylvania Press, 1962); Carol R. Berkin, *Within the Conjurer's Circle: Women in Colonial America* (Morristown, N.J.: General Learning Press, 1974); Page Smith, *Daughters of the Promised Land: Women in American History* (Boston: Little, Brown, 1970); Aileen Kraditor, ed., *Up from the Pedestal: Writings in the History of Feminism* (Chicago: Quadrangle Books, 1968); Laurel Thatcher Ulrich, *Good Wives: Image and Reality in the Lives of Women in Northern New England, 1650–1750* (New York: Alfred A. Knopf, 1982); Nancy F. Cott, "Divorce and the Changing Status of Women in Eighteenth-Century Massachusetts," *William and Mary Quarterly,* 3rd ser., 33, No. 4 (October 1976), 586–614; Louis Green Carr and Lorna S. Walsh, "The Planter's Wife: The Experiences of White Women in Seventeenth-Century Maryland," *William and Mary Quarterly,* 3rd ser., 34, No. 4 (October 1977), 542–571; Lyle Koehler, *A Search for Power, The "Weaker Sex" in Seventeenth Century New England* (Urbana, Ill.: University of Illinois Press, 1980); Mary Beth Norton, *Liberty's Daughters: The Revolutionary Experience of American Women, 1750–1800* (Boston: Little, Brown, 1980); and Joan R. Gunderson and Gwen Victor Gampel, "Married Women's Legal Status in Eighteenth Century New York and Virginia," *William and Mary Quarterly,* 3rd ser., 34, No. 1 (January 1982), 114–134.

[20] Gilbert Tennent and Samuel Davies, *A General Account of the Rise and State of the College, Lately Established in the Province of New-Jersey,* In *America: And of the End and Design of its Institution* (London: Henry Stevens Sons & Stiles, 1754), 3–4.

[21] Colonial education is discussed in exhaustive detail in Lawrence Cremin, *American Education, The Colonial Experience, 1607–1783* (New York: Harper & Row, 1970). See also Bernard Bailyn, *Education in the Forming of American Society* (Chapel Hill, N.C.: University of North Carolina Press, 1960); Paul H. Buck, et al., *The Role of Education in American History* (New York: Fund for the Advancement of Education, 1957); James Axtell, *The School upon a Hill: Education and Society in Colonial New England* (New Haven: Yale University Press, 1974); Robert Middlekauff, *Ancients and Axioms: Secondary Education in Eighteenth-Century New England* (New Haven: Yale University Press, 1962); and John Eadie, ed., *The Classical Tradition in America* (Ann Arbor: University of Michigan Press, 1972).

[22] Robert Beverly, *The History and Present State of Virginia, A Selection* (Indianapolis: Bobbs-Merrill, 1975), 171. Beverly's history was first published in 1705.

[23] John Woolman, *The Journal and Major Essays of John Woolman,* ed. Phillips P. Moulton (New York: Oxford University Press, 1971), 119.

[24] Students interested in early American literature should begin with the old but valuable Moses Coit Tyler, *History of American Literature during the Colonial Period, 1607–1765,* 2 vols. (New York: G. P. Putnam, 1879). Also see Everett Emerson, ed., *Major Writers of Early American Literature* (Madison, Wis.: University of Wisconsin Press, 1972); Richard Beale Davis, *Intellectual Life in the Colonial South, 1588–1763,* 3 vols. (Knoxville: University of Tennessee Press, 1979); Richard M. Gummere, *The American Colonial Mind and the Classical Tradition: Essays in Comparative Culture* (Cambridge, Mass.: Harvard University Press, 1963). See also Max Savelle, *Seeds of Liberty* (Seattle: University of Washington Press, 1967); Louis B. Wright, *The Cultural Life of the American Colonies, 1607–1763* (New York: Harper & Row, 1957), and works cited in Chapter Six previously.

[25] The almanac as a form of popular literature is treated in George L. Kittredge, *The Old Farmer and his Almanack* (Boston: W. Ware, 1904); and Marion B. Stowell, *Early American Almanacs: The Colonial Weekday Bible* (New York: B. Franklin, 1977). See also Victor H. Palsits, *The Almanacs of Roger Sherman* (Worcester, Mass.: American Antiquarian Society, 1977); Jon Butler, "Magic, Astrology, and the Early American Religious Heritage, 1600–1760," *American*

Historical Review, 84, No. 2 (April 1979), 317–346; and Herbert Leventhall, *In the Shadow of the Enlightenment: Occultism and Renaissance Science in Eighteenth Century America* (New York: New York University Press, 1976).

[26] John Tulley, *An Almanack for the Year of our Lord 1695* (Boston: Printed by Samuel Green, 1695); *Hutchins' Improved Family Almanac . . . 1765* (New York: Printed by H. Gaine, 1765); Nathanael Low, *An Astronomical Diary, or Almanack . . . 1775* (Boston: Printed and sold by John Kneeland, [1774]); Matthew A. Stickney, "Almanacs and Their Authors," *Historical Collections of the Essex Institute,* 8, No. 1 (March 1866), 28–32. John Foxe's work was published initially as *Actes and Monuments of these latter and perillous dayes, touching matters of the church, wherein are comprehended and described the great persecution and horrible troubles, that haue bene wrought and practised by the Romishe prelates, speciallye in this realme of England and Scotlande, from the yeare of Our Lorde a thousande, vnto the tyme now present. Gathered and collected . . . by John Foxe.* Understandably the work soon became known as Foxe's *Book of Martyrs.* The anti-Catholic bias evident in much of colonial popular literature is emphasized and discussed by Sister Mary Augustina Ray in *American Opinion of Roman Catholicism in the Eighteenth Century* (New York: Columbia University Press, 1936), esp. 165–211.

[27] See Ola S. Winslow, ed., *American Broadside Verse; From Imprints of the Seventeenth and Eighteenth Centuries* (New Haven: Yale University Press, 1930); and Worthington C. Ford, ed. and comp., *Broadsides, Ballads, etc., printed in Massachusetts, 1639–1800* (Boston: Massachusetts Historical Society, 1922).

[28] *Boston News-Letter,* April 24, 1704, as quoted in Douglas C. McMurtrie, *The Beginnings of the American Newspaper* (Chicago: The Black Cat Press, 1935), 12–13.

[29] Colonial newspapers and periodicals are discussed in George E. Littlefield, *The Early Massachusetts Press, 1638–1711,* 2 vols. (Boston: The Club of Odd Volumes, 1907); William Nelson, *American Newspapers in the Eighteenth Century as Sources of History* (Washington, D.C.: U.S. Government Printing Office, 1910); Sidney Kobre, *The Development of the Colonial Newspaper* (Pittsburgh: Columbia Press, 1944); Lyon N. Richardson, *A History of Early American Magazines, 1741–1789,* 1930 rep. ed. (New York: Octagon Books, 1966); F. L. Mott, *A History of American Magazines, 1741–1850* (New York: Appleton-Century-Crofts, 1930); Lawrence C. Wroth, *An American Bookshelf, 1755* (Philadelphia: University of Pennsylvania Press, 1934); and Wroth, *The Colonial Printer,* enlg. & rev. 2nd ed. (Charlottesville, Va.: Dominion Books, 1964); James C. Austin and Donald A. Koch, eds., *Popular Literature in America: A Symposium in Honor of Lyon N. Richardson* (Bowling Green, Ohio: Bowling Green University Popular Press, 1972); and Bernard Bailyn and John B. Hench, eds., *The Press & the American Revolution* (Worcester, Mass.: American Antiquarian Society, 1980).

[30] Charles H. Lincoln, ed., *Narratives of the Indian Wars 1675–1699* (New York: Charles Scribner's Sons, 1913), 167. After being published in 1682 under the title *The Sovereignty and Goodness of God, togethere with the Faithfulness of His Promises Displayed,* Rowlandson's account of captivity underwent thirty editions. Rowlandson was the wife of Reverend Joseph Rowlandson, minister of a church in Lancaster, Massachusetts. The extensiveness of this genre of literature is amply demonstrated in *The Garland Library of Narratives of North American Indian Captivities,* 111 vols. still under publication (New York: Garland Publishing, 1975–), which are facsimile reprints of Indian captivity narratives from the colonial period through the nineteenth century.

[31] Donald P. Wharton, ed., *In the Trough of the Sea: Selected Deliverance Narratives, 1610–1766* (Westport, Conn.: Greenwood Press, 1979), 123. See also Keith Huntress, *A Checklist of Narratives of Shipwrecks and Disasters at Sea to 1860, with Summaries, Notes and Comments* (Ames, Iowa: Iowa State University Press, 1979).

[32] Wharton, *In the Trough of the Sea,* 12.

[33] Wharton, *In the Trough of the Sea,* 260. See also Huntress, *Narratives,* 47–50.

[34] Wharton, *In the Trough of the Sea,* 250.

CHAPTER ELEVEN

[1] There are several very readable short histories of the revolutionary era which also contain excellent bibliographies. Among them are Edmund S. Morgan, *The Birth of the Republic* (Chicago: University of Chicago Press, 1956); Ian R. Christie, *Crisis of Empire: Great Britain and the American Colonies, 1754–1783* (New York: W. W. Norton, 1966); Robert C. Calhoon, *Revolutionary America: An Interpretative Overview* (New York: Harcourt Brace Jovanovich,

1976); James Kirby Martin, *In The Course of Human Events* (Arlington Heights, Ill.: AHM Publishing, 1979); and John R. Howe, *From the Revolution through the Age of Jackson: Innocence and Empire in the Young Republic* (Englewood Cliffs, N.J.: Prentice-Hall, 1973). For a classic appraisal of the American Revolution's significance for the Western world, see Robert R. Palmer, *The Age of Democratic Revolution: A Political History of Europe and America 1760–1800,* 2 vols. (Princeton, N.J.: Princeton University Press, 1959–1964). Something less than Palmer's magisterial work, but still very stimulating is Stephen G. Kurtz and James H. Hutson, eds., *Essays on the American Revolution* (Chapel Hill, N.C.: University of North Carolina Press, 1973).

[2] Benjamin Franklin, *The Papers of Benjamin Franklin,* 22 vols. to date, vols. 1–14 ed. Leonard W. Labaree, assoc. ed. Whitefield J. Bell, Jr., vols. 15–22 ed. W. B. Willcox (New Haven: Yale University Press, 1959–), 9: 90–91.

[3] The literature on the coming of the Revolution is staggering in both quantity and quality. I do no more here than offer a place to begin. For English politics and its implications for colonial America, consult Sir Lewis Namier's two classics, *The Structure of Politics at the Accession of George III* (London: Macmillan, 1957); and *England in the Age of the American Revolution* (London: Macmillan, 1930). See also P. D. G. Thomas, *British Politics and the Stamp Act Crisis: The First Phase of the American Revolution, 1763–1767* (Oxford: Clarendon Press, 1975); Charles R. Richeson, *British Politics and the American Revolution* (Norman, Okla.: University of Oklahoma Press, 1954); and John Derry, *English Politics and the American Revolution* (London: J. B. Dent, 1976). For colonial policy and the Anglo-American response, see Lawrence Henry Gipson, *The Coming of the Revolution, 1763–1775* (New York: Harper & Row, 1954); Merrill Jenson, *The Founding of a Nation: A History of the American Revolution, 1763–1776* (New York: Oxford University Press, 1968); Bernard Bailyn, *The Ideological Origins of the American Revolution* (Cambridge, Mass.: Harvard University Press, 1967); and Robert A. Gross, *The Minutemen and their World* (New York: Hill & Wang, 1976).

[4] Alden T. Vaughan, ed., *Chronicles of the American Revolution* (New York: Grossett & Dunlap, 1965), 20–21. This volume is a condensed version of Hezekiah Niles' edition of documents of the revolutionary era which appeared as *Principles and Acts of the Revolution in America: or, an Attempt to Collect and Preserve some of the Speeches, Orations, and Proceedings with Sketches and Remarks on Men and Things . . . in 1822.* A second edition was edited and published by Samuel Niles in 1876.

[5] Vaughan, *Chronicles,* 27.

[6] David H. Murdoch, ed., *Rebellion in America: A Contemporary British Viewpoint, 1765–1783* (Santa Barbara, Calif.: Clio Books, 1979), 131. This volume is a compilation of material relevant to the dispute and war between England and Anglo-America which appeared in the eighteenth-century English periodical, the *Annual Register.* The *Register* was produced by parliamentary opponents of Lord North and British policy in America (who were known as Rockingham Whigs). It is a unique source because it chronicles the unfolding drama of the American Revolution on a year-by-year basis, and gives a British perspective on events in America as well as careful, if somewhat biased, reports on the debates in Parliament. Later historians of the Revolution, including William Gordon and David Ramsay, relied heavily on the *Register.*

[7] Merrill D. Peterson, ed., *The Portable Thomas Jefferson* (New York: Viking Press, 1975), 4–5.

[8] Peterson, *Portable Jefferson,* 21.

[9] Vaughan, *Chronicles,* 154.

[10] Vaughan, *Chronicles,* 235.

[11] The *Declaration of Independence* is available in many anthologies and documentary collections. See, for example, Henry Steele Commager, ed., *Documents of American History,* 9th ed., 2 vols. (Englewood Cliffs, N.J.: Prentice-Hall, 1974). See also Peterson, *Portable Jefferson,* 235–241.

[12] C. E. Carrington, *The British Overseas: Exploits of a Nation of Shopkeepers* (Cambridge, Eng.: Cambridge University Press, 1950), 68.

[13] Malachy Postlethwayt, *Britain's Commercial Interest Explained and Improved; In a Series of Dissertations on Several Important Branches of her Trade and Police . . . ,* 1757 facsimile rep. ed., 2 vols. (New York: Augustus M. Kelley, 1968), 1: 56.

[14] See especially Bailyn, *Ideological Origins,* 160–229.

[15] Peterson, *Portable Jefferson,* 9.

[16] Thomas Paine, *Common Sense and Other Political Writings,* ed. with intro. by Nelson F. Adkins (Indianapolis: Bobbs-Merrill, 1953), 21.

[17] Paine, *Common Sense,* 58.

[18] There are many fine books which probe the motives of the Loyalists or which analyze their experience in North America or in exile. See, for example, William H. Nelson, *The American Tory* (New York: Oxford University Press, 1961); William A. Benton, *Whig-Loyalism: An Aspect of Political Ideology in the American Revolutionary Era* (Rutherford, N.J.: Fairleigh Dickinson University Press, 1969); Paul H. Smith, *Loyalists and Redcoats: A Study in British Revolutionary Policy* (Chapel Hill, N.C.: The University of North Carolina Press, 1964); two volumes by Wallace Brown: *The King's Friends: The Composition and Motives of the American Loyalist Claimants* (Providence, R.I.: Brown University Press, 1965); and *The Good Americans: Loyalists in the American Revolution* (New York: William Morrow, 1969); Leonard W. Labaree, *Conservatism in Early American History* (New York: New York University Press, 1948); Robert M. Calhoon, *The Loyalists in Revolutionary America* (New York: Harcourt Brace Jovanovich, 1973); and Mary Beth Norton, *The British Americans: The Loyalist Exiles in England, 1774-1789* (Boston: Little, Brown, 1972). Useful biographies of loyalists are Aubrey C. Land, *The Dulanys of Maryland* (Baltimore: Maryland Historical Society, 1955); L. F. S. Upton, *The Loyal Whig: William Smith of New York and Quebec* (Toronto: University of Toronto Press, 1969); and Bernard Bailyn, *The Ordeal of Thomas Hutchinson* (Cambridge, Mass.: Harvard University Press, 1974).

[19] Morton Borden and Penn Borden, eds., *The American Tory* (Englewood Cliffs, N.J.: Prentice-Hall, 1972), 2.

[20] Borden and Borden, *American Tory,* 110–111.

[21] The notion of colonial "maturity" is important to the arguments of many historians. It has special significance to two groups or "schools" of scholars: the "imperial" group, so named because of its attempt to view the history of the colonies and the Revolution as part of the evolution of the British empire, and the "conservative" group, identified as such because it argues that Anglo-Americans shared common convictions, engaged in no significant internal social or economic conflict as classes or groups, and fought to "conserve" their existing way of life. Among the imperial historians are George Louis Beer, *The Old Colonial System* (New York: Macmillan, 1912); Charles M. Andrews, *The Colonial Period of American History,* 4 vols. (New Haven: Yale University Press, 1934–1938); Herbert L. Osgood, *The American Colonies in the Eighteenth Century,* 4 vols. (New York: Columbia University Press, 1924–1925); and Lawrence H. Gipson, *The British Empire before the Revolution,* 15 vols. (New York: Alfred A. Knopf, 1936–1970). The conservative or "consensus" argument developed in the decades immediately after World War II. Some of the earliest conservative or consensus writers were among the strongest proponents of the theory that the colonies reached social, political, and economic maturity by the time of the Revolution. They include Clinton Rossiter, *Seedtime of the Republic* (New York: Harcourt, Brace, 1953); Daniel Boorstin, *The Americans: The Colonial Experience* (New York: Vintage Books, 1958); and Boorstin, *The Genius of American Politics* (Chicago: University of Chicago Press, 1953); Robert E. Brown, *Middle-Class Democracy and the Revolution in Massachusetts, 1691–1780* (Ithaca, N.Y.: Cornell University Press, 1955); Louis B. Hartz, *The Liberal Tradition in America* (New York: Harcourt, Brace, 1955); and Morgan, *Birth of the Republic.* The conservative impulse is still very strong among scholars of the Revolutionary era. Not all of them believe, however, that Anglo-America represented a mature society.

[22] John Adams, *The Works of John Adams, Second President of the U.S. with a Life of the Author,* ed. C. F. Adams, 10 vols. (Boston: Little, Brown, 1850–1856), 4: 193.

[23] Bernard Bailyn follows the radicalization of revolutionary ideology and rhetoric in his *Ideological Origins.* Chapters 3 to 4 describe the conspiracy theory which led the colonists to believe that they were being victimized by powerful English leaders both inside and outside of government. Chapter 5 analyzes the character of the political ideology colonials employed against the British, while Chapter 7 explains how that ideology led to some important changes in the institutional order of the former colonies. The most important changes were political. Gordon S. Wood, *The Creation of the American Republic, 1776–1787* (Chapel Hill, N.C.: University of North Carolina, 1969) brilliantly outlines and discusses the component parts of the "republican experiment." There are also many fine state and local studies which chart its progress. Two of the better ones are Jere Daniell, *Experiment in Republicanism: New Hampshire Politics and the American Revolution, 1741–1794* (Cambridge, Mass.: Harvard University Press, 1970); and Gross, *Minutemen and their World.*

As John Adams told Hezekiah Niles in 1818, the revolution was to a great extent "in the minds and hearts of the people." Part of the rhetoric of rebellion involved a growing sense of America's uniqueness in human history, a belief in America's moral and cultural superiority vis-à-vis Europe, and an increasing perception that America had a special role to play in fulfilling Christian millennial expectations. The literature on these topics is extensive and provocative. Daniel J. Boorstin, *The Lost World of Thomas Jefferson* (New York: Henry Holt, 1948); Hartz, *Liberal Tradition*; and H. Richard Niebuhr, *The Kingdom of God in America* (New York:

Harper & Brothers, 1937) are good primers. Also important are Ernst Lee Tuveson, *Redeemer Nation: The Idea of America's Millennial Role* (Chicago: University of Chicago Press, 1968); Nathan O. Hatch, *The Sacred Cause of Liberty: Republican Thought and the Millennium in Revolutionary New England* (New Haven: Yale University Press, 1977); Catherine Albanese, *Sons of the Fathers: The Civil Religion of the American Revolution* (Philadelphia: Temple University Press, 1976); Wood, *Creation of the American Republic*; James West Davidson, *The Logic of Millennial Thought: Eighteenth-Century New England* (New Haven: Yale University Press, 1977); Charles Royster, *A Revolutionary People at War: The Continental Army and American Character, 1775-1783* (Chapel Hill, N.C.: University of North Carolina Press, 1974); Cushing Strout, *The New Heavens and New Earth: Political Religion in America* (New York: Harper & Row, 1974); John F. Berens, *Providence and Patriotism in Early America, 1640-1815* (Charlottesville: University Press of Virginia, 1978); Sacvan Bercovitch, *The Puritan Origins of the American Self* (New Haven: Yale University Press, 1975); Alan Heimert, *Religion and the American Mind, from the Great Awakening to the Revolution* (Cambridge, Mass.: Harvard University Press, 1966); Sydney E. Ahlstrom, *A Religious History of the American People* (New Haven: Yale University Press, 1972); Richard Slotkin, *Regeneration through Violence: The Mythology of the American Frontier, 1600-1860* (Middletown, Conn.: Wesleyan University Press, 1973); John F. Wilson, *Public Religion in American Culture* (Philadelphia: Temple University Press, 1979); Conrad Cherry, ed., *God's New Israel* (Englewood Cliffs, N.J.: Prentice-Hall, 1971); Edmund S. Morgan, "The Puritan Ethic and the American Revolution," *William and Mary Quarterly*, 3rd ser., 24, No. 1 (January 1967), 3-43; Thomas More Brown, "The Image of the Beast: Anti-Papal Rhetoric in Colonial America," in Richard Curry and Thomas More Brown, eds., *Conspiracy: The Fear of Subversion in American History* (New York: Holt, Rinehart & Winston, 1972); Philip Greven, *The Protestant Temperament* (New York: Alfred A. Knopf, 1977); and Sacvan Bercovitch, *The American Jeremiad* (Madison, Wis.: University of Wisconsin Press, 1979).

[24] Charles F. Adams, *Familiar Letters of John Adams and his wife, Abigail Adams, during the Revolution, with a memoir of Mrs. Adams* (New York: Hurd & Houghton, 1876), 149.

[25] Samuel Hopkins, *A Dialogue Concerning the Slavery of the Africans,* in *The Antislavery Crusade in America,* advisory eds. James M. McPherson and William Loren Katz, facsimile rep. ed. (New York: Arno Press and *The New York Times,* 1969), 60.

[26] "The Constitution of Vermont, 1777," in Ben Purley Poore, comp., *The Federal and State Constitutions, Colonial Charters, and Other Organic Laws of the United States,* 2nd ed., 2 vols. (Washington, D.C.: U.S. Government Printing Office, 1878), 2: 1857.

[27] Gross, *Minutemen and their World,* 152.

[28] George Washington, *The Writings of George Washington,* ed. John C. Fitzpatrick, 39 vols. (Washington, D.C.: U.S. Government Printing Office, 1931-1944), 13: 466-467.

[29] It seems clear from the evidence compiled by several generations of historians studying the late eighteenth and early nineteenth centuries that the American Revolution had little in common with the French Revolution and was not the harbinger of the social and economic upheavals which have transformed the world in the twentieth century. Rather, our revolution can be more favorably compared to the independence movements in Latin America in the early nineteenth century. First, revolution on both American continents followed attempts by Spain and England to reform and streamline their respective imperial systems. Second, in British and Latin America revolution coincided with the emergence of very radical political ideologies which were later repudiated in part. Third, in both areas, revolution failed to produce a strong central government or a strong political union of sovereign states. Finally, on both American continents revolution resulted from the leadership of powerful indigenous political and economic groups. Those groups survived years of war and greeted independence with their power and position virtually intact.

Put another way, the American Revolution broke our political and constitutional ties to England but it did not substantially reconstruct the matrix of institutions, traditions, and beliefs inherited from the colonial era. Historians of Latin America argue the same for their area. Revolutions against Spain (and Brazil's bloodless separation from Portugal) achieved only political independence. The new nations of nineteenth-century Latin America—although heavily influenced by the ideals of the European Enlightenment and the republican ideology of the United States—nonetheless failed to achieve either economic independence from foreign powers (Britain replaced Spain and Portugal as the economic master of Latin America) or cultural independence from a colonial heritage of repressive and regressive social, economic, and political institutions. As a result Latin American resources in the nineteenth and twentieth centuries continued to be siphoned off by foreign nations, just as they were in the colonial era. Attempts to industrialize and modernize were thwarted by archaic class structures and ancient political and religious institutions and traditions, a heritage that allowed the self-interest of small elites of landowners and businessmen to take precedence over national welfare. Those elites, in the caudillo tradition of the past, controlled the political systems (periodic coups usually replaced one strong man with another) and used them mainly as instruments of repression. The result was a situation in which a few lived in splendor, while the majority lived in poverty and ignorance. (See, for example, E. Bradford Burns, *Latin America: A Concise Interpretive History*, 2nd ed. [Englewood Cliffs, N.J.: Prentice-Hall, 1977].)

If both the United States and the young republics of Latin America had to contend with colonial "burdens" relatively untouched by their respective independence movements, why then were the subsequent histories of the two regions so different? Historians of both continents point to the countries responsible for colonization as one possible answer. Historians Stanley and Barbara Stein, for example, argue that "modernizing" forces were sweeping England and large areas of northern Europe during the sixteenth, seventeenth, and eighteenth centuries. These forces drastically altered the political, social, and economic characters of the countries they touched. As a result, many of these "modern" characteristics were transferred to the infant societies of British America (the slave-dominated, cash-crop societies of the colonial South and the British West Indies notwithstanding).

At the same time England and northern Europe came to dominate Spain and Portugal, siphoning off their New World wealth. That occurred because "modernization" did not visit the Iberian penninsula. Both Spain and Portugal remained late-medieval, precapitalistic states which—even at their imperial heights—refused to bend to the winds of change. Spain and Portugal, therefore, transferred to Latin America a semifeudal heritage, much of which remains intact today. (See Stanley Stein and Barbara Stein, *The Colonial Heritage of Latin America* [New York: Oxford University Press, 1970], 4–26, 188–198.)

This is an argument which is shared by many students of Latin America, though by no means all. Also, it is consistent with the views of many scholars of British America. It fits those like Louis Hartz, who see Anglo-America as possessing liberal institutions inherited from an England which was slowly shedding its own medieval heritage. It coincides with the ideas of those who experiment with "modernization" theory (such as Richard M. Brown, *Modernization: The Transformation of American Life, 1600–1876* [New York: Hill & Wang, 1976]). It is also compatible with those who argue that British America developed a "mature" society which had to break with England in order to survive and prosper.

It is beyond the scope of this book to determine whether the theory of a modernized England and a backward Iberian peninsula explains the character of either colonial Latin America or colonial British America. It is also beyond the scope of this book to try to prove or disprove the widely held notion that the colonial experience significantly affected the post-independence development of both the United States and Latin America. It is sufficient to acknowledge that both the United States and the republics of Latin America had colonial burdens with which to contend and to hypothesize that our Founding Fathers tried to manipulate their colonial heritage through the creation of a central government in the *Constitution.* (Simon Bolivar and other Latin American leaders sought a similar centralization of power and federated union of states but failed to achieve them.)

[30] The literature on the Confederation Period (1781 to 1789) and the drafting and ratification of the *Constitution* and *Bill of Rights* (1787 to 1791) is too rich and varied to be fully covered here. My suggestions are meant only to introduce students and other interested readers to some of the many fine books on this era. Those interested in the military campaigns of the Revolutionary War should start with John R. Alden, *The American Revolution, 1775-1783* (New York: Harper & Row, 1954); and Howard H. Peckham, *The War for Independence: A Military History* (Chicago: University of Chicago Press, 1958). Three books offer excellent though vastly different interpretations of the Confederation Period. Wood's *Creation of the American Republic* provides an imaginative reappraisal of the shifting ideological concerns of the 1780s, while Forest McDonald, *E Pluribus Unum: The Formation of the American Republic, 1776–1790* (Boston: Houghton-Mifflin, 1965) is very good on economic matters. Merrill Jensen, in *The New Nation: A History of the United States during the Confederation, 1781–1789* (New York: Alfred A. Knopf, 1950), argues that the *Articles of Confederation* reflected the aims of the Revolution and that in general the country fared well under the government of the Confederation. Clinton Rossiter offers a fascinating account of the Constitutional Convention in *1787: The Grand Convention* (New York: Crowell-Collier & Macmillan, 1966); while Robert A. Rutland surveys the events after the Convention in *The Ordeal of the Constitution: The Antifederalists and the Ratification Struggle of 1787–1788* (Chapel Hill, N.C.: University of North Carolina Press, 1961). No student should conclude his or her reading without pondering the conclusions of Charles A. Beard in *An Economic Interpretation of the Constitution of the United States* (New York: Crowell-Collier & Macmillan, 1935).

Biography is one of the best ways to approach the events of the 1780s. There are several outstanding one-volume biographies available. See, for example, Peter Shaw, *The Character of John Adams* (Chapel Hill, N.C.: University of North Carolina Press, 1976); and Merrill D. Peterson, *Thomas Jefferson and the New Nation: A Biography* (New York: Oxford University Press,

1970). Real history buffs may wish to try some fine multivolume works, such as James T. Flexner, *George Washington,* 4 vols. (Boston: Little, Brown, 1965–1972); Broadus Mitchell, *Alexander Hamilton,* 3 vols. (New York: Macmillan, 1957–1970); or Dumas Malone, *Jefferson and his Time,* 6 vols. (Boston: Little, Brown, 1948–1981).

Charles Beard's *Economic Interpretation* ended more than a century of filio-pietistic worship of the architects of the *Constitution* by suggesting that the document they created was not sympathetic to the main ends of the Revolution. As a result, for decades a debate has raged over whether the *Constitution* was meant to fulfill the Revolution or frustrate it. Until very recently, the majority of writers argued for the former. I have tried to suggest that the *Constitution* was both the logical conclusion of the Revolution and an antidote for some of the Revolution's failings. In making this argument I feel that I have followed, in principle, the best recent scholarship, especially Wood, *Creation of the American Republic.* I have, however, also been influenced by the perceptive reappraisal of Beard and his critics offered by John P. Diggins in "Power and Authority in American History: The Case of Charles A. Beard and his Critics," *American Historical Review,* 86: No. 4 (October 1981), 701–730.

[31] Vaughan, *Chronicles,* 338.

[32] Vaughan, *Chronicles,* 337–338.

[33] Peterson, *Portable Jefferson,* 429.

[34] James Madison, *Letters and other Writings of James Madison, Fourth President of the United States,* 4 vols. (New York: Published for Congress by R. Worthington, 1884), 1: 346.

[35] The text of the *Constitution* can be found in Commager, ed., *Documents of American History,* I.

[36] Jacob E. Cooke, *The Federalist* (Cleveland: World Publishing, 1961), 3.

[37] Fisher Ames, *Works of Fisher Ames. With a Selection From His Speeches and Correspondence,* ed. Seth Ames, 2 vols. (Boston: Little, Brown, 1854), 1: 336.

Chronology of Development: Colonial and Revolutionary America, 1607-1789

1607	Settlement of Jamestown by the London Company.
1609	Pilgrims leave England for Holland.
1612	Thomas Dale and Thomas Gates enforce Dale's Laws in Virginia.
1618	Beginning of the headright system in Virginia.
1619	Creation of the House of Burgesses in Virginia. First Africans arrive in Jamestown.
1620	Pilgrims settle at Plymouth and create the *Mayflower Compact.*
1622	Opechancanough leads Virginia Indians against the English and kills 347 white settlers.
1624	Virginia becomes a royal colony.
1625	Charles I ascends the English throne upon the death of his father James I (1603–1625).
1626	Dutch establish colony on Manhattan Island.
1627	English settle Barbados in the West Indies, sponsored by the Courteen Associates, a joint-stock company.
1630	Massachusetts Bay Colony is founded by English Puritans.
1630–1640	The *Great Migration* of English Puritans to New England.
1634	George Calvert founds Maryland as a haven for English Catholics.
1635	Roger Williams is banished from Massachusetts and founds the colony of Rhode Island. Connecticut is settled by Massachusetts Puritans led by Reverend Thomas Hooker.
1635–1636	The Antinomian Controversy breaks out in Massachusetts. Anne Hutchinson is banished.

1635–1637	The Pequot War in New England. Expansion of the English into the Connecticut River Valley sparks an attack by the Pequot Indians, who are eventually defeated.
1636	Harvard College is created by the Massachusetts Court to train ministers.
1638	New Haven Colony is founded by Massachusetts Puritans under Reverend John Davenport.
1639	Connecticut inhabitants create a civil government based on the *Fundamental Orders.*
1641	Massachusetts' *Body of Liberties* brings English common-law tradition to New England.
1641–1648	The English Civil Wars.
1643	Massachusetts, Connecticut, Plymouth, and New Haven form the Confederation of New England to solve common problems. Massachusetts assumes jurisdiction over settlements in New Hampshire.
1644	Deputies and Magistrates vote to sit separately in Massachusetts, creating a bicameral legislature.
1647	Massachusetts orders all towns with fifty families or more to organize schools for their children.
1648	The *Cambridge Platform of Church Discipline,* created by New England Churches, spells out the character of Congregationalism.
1649	Charles I is executed by a victorious Parliament. Maryland Assembly passes a Toleration Act guaranteeing religious liberty to all Christians.
1651	The First Navigation Act is passed by Parliament. It attempts to stop the Dutch from trading with the English or English colonies.
1652	Massachusetts takes control of settlements in Maine.
1652–1654	The First Anglo-Dutch War.
1653–1658	The rule of Oliver Cromwell, Lord Protector, in England.
1655	The English capture Jamaica from the Spanish.
1660	The Restoration of Charles II as King of England.
1660–1715	The rule of France by the Sun King, Louis XIV.
1660	The Navigation Act of 1660 is directed against the Dutch. It creates the category of *enumerated* articles, which may be shipped only from Anglo-America to England or another English colony.
1662	New Haven Colony is absorbed by Massachusetts Bay. New England churches create the *Half-Way Covenant,* which allows the baptized children (nonmembers) of church members to have their own children baptized. Michael Wiggesworth of Massachusetts writes his poem, *Day of Doom.*
1663	Parliament passes a Navigation Act ordering that European goods bound for Anglo-America must pass through an English port. Charles II grants a charter to eight nobles to establish a colony in the Carolinas.
1664–1667	The Second Anglo-Dutch War.
1664	New Netherlands is captured by the English and becomes the colony of New York. James, Duke of York and Charles II's brother, is made the proprietor.
1669	The Earl of Shaftesbury, one of Carolina's proprietors, commissions John Locke to write a constitution for Carolina. Locke creates the *Fundamental Constitutions,* which are never put into effect.
1670	Settlers found Charlestown.
1672	The English Royal African Company is formed to bring black slaves to the West Indies.
1672–1674	The Third Anglo-Dutch War.

1673	Parliament passes the Plantation Duty Act, which places a tax on all enumerated goods bound from one English colony to another. Barbados becomes a royal colony.
1675	The Lords of Trade and Plantations is created to oversee colonial affairs.
1675–1676	King Phillip's War breaks out in New England. Reacting to English westward expansion, several tribes unite under Metacomet or King Phillip and attack English border settlements in Connecticut and Massachusetts before being defeated.
1676	New Jersey is divided into an east and west part. West Jersey comes under the control of William Penn while East Jersey becomes the property of George Carteret, one of the Carolina proprietors. Nathaniel Bacon leads an uprising of frontier planters against Governor Berkeley of Virginia. Bacon's Rebellion protests the failures of the Governor and the Burgesses to provide protection for frontier settlements against Indian raids.
1677	Culpepper's Rebellion in North Carolina against proprietary rule. John Culpepper is an exiled follower of Nathaniel Bacon.
1679	New Hampshire becomes a royal colony.
1681	William Penn obtains a charter for Pennsylvania. His colony is to be a haven for Quakers in the New World.
1682	Penn obtains Delaware from the Duke of York. Publication of Mary Rowlandson's account of her capture by Indians during King Phillip's War.
1683	The New York Assembly, meeting for the first time, creates a *Charter of Libertyes* which is subsequently disallowed by British officials.
1685–1688	Reign of King James II.
1685	Creation of the Dominion of New England uniting all of the New England colonies plus New York and New Jersey under a single royal governor, Edmund Andros.
1688	The *Glorious Revolution* in England deposes James II. He is replaced by his daughter, Mary, and her husband, William of Orange, a Dutchman. William is also James II's nephew.
1689	Edmund Andros, unpopular royal governor of the Dominion of New England, is overthrown and jailed. Andros' lieutenant governor, Captain Francis Nicholson, is overthrown in New York by rebels led by Jacob Leisler. Leisler rules New York for a year. A force of 250 Protestants led by John Coode overthrows Maryland's governor, William Joseph. Coode's men represent the Protestant Association. Coode rules until 1692. Parliament passes the Toleration Act granting all Protestants freedom of worship.
1689–1697	War of the League of Augsburg (King William's War in America). First of the great imperial wars between France and England and their allies. The French and their Indian allies raid colonial frontier settlements while an Anglo-American army captures Port Royal, Acadia. Port Royal is recaptured by French troops under Count Frontenac.
1690	Publication of John Locke's *Second Treatise on Government*.
1691	Plymouth is absorbed by Massachusetts Bay. Maryland becomes a royal colony.
1692–1693	Twenty persons are executed for witchcraft in Salem, Massachusetts.
1693	College of William and Mary is founded in Virginia.
1696	King William creates the Board of Trade to oversee colonial affairs. Parliament passes the Navigation Act of 1696. The Act creates a colonial customs service and extends the English vice-admiralty court system to America.

	It defines, also, an "English" ship as one whose crew is 75 percent English or Anglo-American.
1698	The monopoly of the Royal African Company in the slave trade is successfully challenged by independent English and Anglo-American merchants.
1699	Parliament passes the Woolen Act forbidding the exportation of wool or wool products from the colonies.
1701	The Society for the Propagation of the Gospel in Foreign Parts (S.P.G.) is founded. Yale College receives a charter from the Connecticut Assembly.
1702	Cotton Mather publishes his *Magnalia Christi Americana, or the Ecclesiastical History of New England.* West and East Jerseys become a single royal colony.
1702–1714	Rule of England by Queen Anne, sister of Queen Mary.
1702–1713	War of Spanish Succession (Queen Anne's War in America). England and France fight over whether a Bourbon (the French royal family) will assume the throne of Spain. French and Indians raid colonial frontier settlements and a combined English/Anglo-American force tries to invade Canada. Treaty of Utrecht (1713) cedes Acadia and Newfoundland to England.
1704	James Campbell creates the first American newspaper, the *Boston Newsletter.*
1707	Union of Scotland and England.
1708	The Saybrook Platform of church government is created by Connecticut clergy and is endorsed by the Connecticut General Assembly.
1711, 1722	Parliament passes the White Pines Acts prohibiting colonials from cutting down white pines without a license from a royal official.
1713–1763	Due to deteriorating economic, political, and religious conditions in various parts of Europe and the British Isles, thousands of non-English immigrants settle in Anglo-America.
1714–1727	Rule of England by George I, first of the German Hanoverians.
1717	John Wise publishes his *Vindication of the Government of New England Churches.*
1719–1780	Anglo-America experiences a series of religious revivals known as the *Great Awakening.*
1719–1726	Theodore Frelinghuysen arrives in the colonies and starts a religious revival among the Dutch Reformed Churches in New Jersey, signaling the beginning of the Great Awakening.
1721	Boston is hit by a smallpox epidemic. South Carolina becomes a royal colony.
1721–1742	Robert Walpole serves as First Lord of the Treasury, Chancellor of the Exchequer, and the King's chief advisor.
1721–1754	The essays of English real-Whig writers John Trenchard and William Gordon (*Cato's Letters* and the *Independent Whig*) appear in numerous editions in England and Anglo-America.
1727–1760	Rule of England by George II.
1729	North Carolina becomes a royal colony. Gilbert Tennent, a Presbyterian minister, begins a religious revival in his congregation in New Jersey. South Carolina becomes a royal colony.
1731	The Library Company of Philadelphia, one of the first subscription libraries in the colonies, is established.
1732	Parliament passes the Hat and Felt Act preventing colonists from selling felt hats outside the colony where they are made.

	George Oglethorpe receives a charter to establish the colony of Georgia. The colony is intended to be settled by "debtors" and to provide England with some relief from overpopulation.
1733	Parliament passes the Sugar Act or Molasses Act, placing a duty of 6 pence per gallon (in Anglo-America) on foreign molasses. The Act is aimed at French molasses from the West Indies.
1734	John Peter Zenger, editor of the *New York Weekly Journal,* is tried and acquitted of libeling the royal governor of New York, William Cosby.
1734–1735	Jonathan Edwards, Congregationalist minister, sparks a religious revival in Northampton, Massachusetts.
1735–1736	The Great Awakening spreads throughout New England.
1738	New Jersey becomes a royal colony.
1739	The *Stono Rebellion* of black slaves in South Carolina. George Whitefield, an English minister and friend of the founders of Methodism, John and Charles Wesley, arrives in Philadelphia and begins one of several preaching tours of the colonies. His preaching becomes an important force in the Great Awakening.
1739–1742	War of Jenkin's Ear between England and Spain. England attacks Spanish possessions in the Caribbean.
1740	The first nondenominational college, the College of Philadelphia (later the University of Pennsylvania), is founded.
1740–1741	Land Bank is created in Massachusetts. It is banned by Parliament.
1743–1748	The War of Austrian Succession (King George's War in America). The French and English and their allies struggle over who will assume the throne of Austria. In North America, an Anglo-American force captures Fort Louisbourg. The Treaty of Aix-la-Chapelle returns all captured territory to prewar owners.
1746	The College of New Jersey, now Princeton, is established by Presbyterians.
1748	The most famous of several colonial land companies dealing in land speculation, the Ohio Company of Virginia, receives a grant of 200,000 acres on the upper Ohio River. The Earl of Halifax becomes President of the Board of Trade.
1750	Parliament passes the Iron Act limiting colonial iron production.
1751	Parliament passes the Currency Act forbidding the colonists to print paper money.
1752	Georgia becomes a royal colony.
1754	The Albany Congress and the Albany Plan of Union. Instructed by Britain, colonial governors call together an intercolonial congress at Albany, New York, to unify colonial defenses against the French. The Congress endorses the Albany Plan of Union, a proposal by Benjamin Franklin to form a colonial federation. The plan is rejected by the colonies.
1756	William Pitt becomes Prime Minister in England.
1756–1763	The Seven Years' War (French and Indian War in America). The English and French struggle for control of North America. The Treaty of Paris (1763) cedes New France to England.
1760	Beginning of the rule of England by George III. Boston merchants test the legality of the Writs of Assistance. James Otis represents them.
1763	The *Paxton Boys,* a group of Scotch-Irish immigrants in western Pennsylvania, use vigilante tactics to protest the Pennsylvania legislature's failure to protect them from Indian attacks. The Proclamation of 1763 establishes the governments for the territories acquired from the French and Indian War and temporarily closes the land west of the Appalachians to further settlement. Pontiac's Rebellion in the Ohio Valley.

1764 Brown (University) is organized by the Baptists and receives a charter.
Parliament passes the revenue Act of 1764 (the Sugar Act). It is the first piece of legislation concerning the colonies which is specifically designed to raise revenue rather than regulate commerce or manufacturing. The Act is designed also to help maintain the British army in North America and to stop colonial smuggling. It reduces the tax on foreign molasses from 6 pence per gallon to 3 pence per gallon, thus legitimizing New England's ancient trade with French West Indian sugar planters.
Parliament passes the Currency Act of 1764 which prohibits colonial legislatures from making colonial currency legal tender for paying debts. This worsens the already scarce currency situation in America. Colonials protest by boycotting many English goods.

1765 Parliament passes the Stamp Act, another piece of legislation aimed at raising revenue to pay for the British military establishment in North America. It requires a stamp on all legal documents. The Virginia legislature officially protests the Stamp Act through the Virginia Resolves. The Resolves declare that the Stamp Act violates the rights of English citizens. The first representative assembly of all the colonies, the Stamp Act Congress, meets at the invitation of the Massachusetts General Court to condemn both the Sugar and Stamp Acts. Colonial protest leads to the repeal of the Stamp Act and the fall of George Grenville.

1766 When the Stamp Act is repealed Parliament passes the Declaratory Act affirming its right to legislate for the colonies.
Queen's College, now Rutgers University, is founded by the Dutch Reformed Church to educate ministers.

1767 The South Carolina and North Carolina *Regulators* are formed.
Parliament passes the Townshend Acts to raise revenue for the British army in America and to tighten British control over the colonies. The Townshend Acts authorize writs of assistance and create a board of customs commissioners to administer customs laws. They also reorganize the vice-admiralty courts in America.

1768 Authorized by the Earl of Shelburne, Sir William Johnson signs a treaty with the Indians, the Treaty of Fort Stanwix, which establishes a permanent boundary line between Indian and white settlements.
British troops dispatched to Boston.

1770 The *Boston Massacre* takes place as four colonials are killed in an altercation between Bostonians and British sentries at a customs house.
Lord North ministry begins.
All Townshend duties are repealed by Parliament except the tax on tea.

1772 The *Gaspee*, a British revenue patrol ship, is burned by Rhode Islanders who resent British attempts to enforce the Navigation Acts.
Committee of Correspondence formed in Boston.

1773 Parliament tries to save the British East India Company by passing the Tea Act. The Act allows the Company to sell its tea directly to Anglo-Americans without using an intermediary. This places the Company in direct competition with Anglo-American merchants.
To protest the Tea Act, Bostonians board several ships in Boston harbor and dump their cargoes of tea overboard. This becomes known as the Boston Tea Party.

1774 The Intolerable or Coercive Acts are passed by Parliament to stem colonial opposition. They are deeply resented by Anglo-Americans.
The Boston Port Act closes the port of Boston.
The Massachusetts Government Act increases the power of the Massachusetts royal governor. The Quartering Act requires the colonists to provide permanent quarters for British troops.
The Administration of Justice Act allows British officials accused of murder to have their cases transferred to a different colony.

1774 Parliament passes the Quebec Act, confirming the French customs and laws and the Catholic religion of Canada and establishing a government by council and a governor. The Act pacifies French Canadians but angers Anglo-Americans.

Called by the Massachusetts House of Representatives, the First Continental Congress meets. Every colony but Georgia is represented.

1775 Skirmishes between British troops and colonial *minutemen* occur at Lexington and Concord, Massachusetts, after General Gage attempts to arrest Sam Adams and John Hancock and to seize the ammunition stores at Concord.

A new assembly of colonial representatives, the Second Continental Congress, meets in Philadelphia. It resolves to put the colonies "into a state of defence" by appointing George Washington the commander-in-chief of the newly formed Continental Army and by issuing a "Declaration of Causes of Taking up Arms." This body governs the colonies throughout the Revolutionary War.

George III declares the colonists to be in rebellion.

1776 Publication of Adam Smith's *Wealth of Nations.*

A state convention of delegates in Virginia adopts a state constitution creating a new state government with a bicameral legislature, a governor, and separate legislative, executive, and judicial functions. The constitution severely limits the governor's powers.

The Second Continental Congress issues *The Declaration of Independence,* a document drafted by Thomas Jefferson.

The British occupy New York City.

1777 American troops under Horatio Gates and Benedict Arnold defeat General John Burgoyne's Redcoats at the Battle of Saratoga (New York). The battle marks the turning point of the war in the rebels' favor.

The *Articles of Confederation* are passed by the Second Continental Congress.

1778 The United States signs a military alliance with France and receives assistance from the French.

The British leave Philadelphia.

1780 Massachusetts drafts and adopts a constitution to govern the state. The Constitution, strongly reminiscent of the Charter of 1691, creates a *bill of rights* and gives more power to the governor than any other state constitution.

The Americans win at King's Mountain, South Carolina, but lose at Camden and Charleston, South Carolina.

1781 General Cornwallis and the British army are defeated at the Battle of Yorktown (Virginia), thus ending hostilities in America.

The *Articles of Confederation,* America's first constitution, is finally ratified by all of the states.

1782 North ministry falls.

1783 The Treaty of Paris between Britain and the United States recognizes American independence, gives up British territory west to the Mississippi River, and guarantees "perpetual peace" between the two countries.

1785 Land Ordinance for Northwest Territory is created by Congress.

1786 Economic discontent leads farmers of western Massachusetts, led by ex-Revolutionary War Captain Daniel Shays, to take up arms. They are suppressed.

John Jay negotiates with the Spanish minister Diego Gardoqui to establish a commercial treaty with Spain and to settle the boundary of Florida. Jay fails to get the support of the Confederation Congress and negotiations are stalled.

1787 Congress passes the Ordinance of 1787 (The Northwest Ordinance), one of the most important pieces of legislation of the Confederation period. The Ordinance provides for the surveying of the Northwest territory and the

	admission of its sections into the Union as new states. The Ordinance also excludes slavery from the territory.
	A new constitutional convention, representing twelve states, meets in Philadelphia to amend the *Articles of Confederation* and concludes by drafting a new *Constitution* (Rhode Island abstains from the proceedings).
1788	During the struggle over ratification of the *Constitution* in New York, Alexander Hamilton, John Jay, and James Madison write a series of newspaper articles which become known as the *Federalist Papers.*
1788	The Constitution is finally ratified after a long struggle between Federalist and Anti-Federalist forces. North Carolina and Rhode Island reject the *Constitution.*
1789–1791	In order to aid ratification of the *Constitution* James Madison drafts the *Bill of Rights* which becomes incorporated into the *Constitution* as the first ten amendments in 1791.

A Select Bibliography

Every historian plans to write a book of this kind at some point in his or her career. Most never do. Often, the reason is that specialized research interests cause the historian to lose command of the books and articles published in areas other than his or her specialty. Books like *American Odyssey* do not get written because, for example, specialists in religious history discover that they really do not know very much about the latest research in economic history, and vice versa. This is a sad admission to make, but it is easy to understand. If you consult the list of books which follows you will see ample evidence of the knowledge explosion which has reshaped our thinking about early American history in recent decades. Few scholars have the time to read and digest all the books and articles which appear each year. If the scholar has trouble keeping up, what hope is there for the general reader?

I have tried to aid both the specialist and the general reader through discursive chapter notes and the bibliography which follows. Even though many important books and articles are cited in the chapter notes, they represent only a fraction of what is available. The bibliography which follows is more representative of the activity in the field, but it, too, is limited. I have listed many of the books which have influenced my own thinking. At the same time I have tried to give the student, the general reader, and the history buff a useful bibliography of good books. I do not pretend that it is definitive.

I have not included journal articles in this bibliography because there are simply too many good and important articles. To list all of them would require a separate volume. It is enough to say that students of early American history should become familiar with the journals which publish articles in their field. These include: the *William and Mary Quarterly*, the *Journal of American History*, the *American Historical Review*, *American Heritage*, *American History Illustrated*, *American Quarterly*, *American Studies*, *Journal of Economic History*, *Journal of Negro History*, *Journal of American Folklore*, *The Historian*, *Canadian Review of American Studies*, *The American Journal of Legal History*, *Historical Methods*, *Church History*, *The Journal of Social History*, *Proceedings of the American Antiquarian Society*, *The New England Quarterly*, *The New England Historical and Genealogical Register*, *Early American Literature*, *Eighteenth Century Studies*, and *Reviews in American History*. There are also many fine journals dealing with state (colony) and local history—for example, the *Essex Institute Historical Collections*, *The Virginia Magazine of History and Biography*, and *The Pennsylvania Magazine of History and Biography*.

GENERAL WORKS

ABBOT, W. W., *The Colonial Origins of the United States, 1607-1763.* New York: Wiley, 1975.

AHLSTROM, SYDNEY E., *A Religious History of the American People.* New Haven: Yale University Press, 1972.

ANDREWS, CHARLES M., *The Colonial Period of American History,* 4 vols. New Haven: Yale University Press, 1934–1938.

ARENDT, HANNAH, *On Revolution.* New York: Viking Press, 1963.

AUSTIN, JAMES C., and DONALD A. KOCH, eds., *Popular Literature in America: A Symposium in Honor of Lyon N. Richardson.* Bowling Green, Ohio: Bowling Green University Popular Press, 1972.

BANCROFT, GEORGE, *History of the United States from the Discovery of the American Continent to the Declaration of Independence,* 7 vols. Boston: Little, Brown, 1854–1858.

BILLINGTON, RAY A., *America's Frontier Heritage.* New York: Holt, Rinehart & Winston, 1966.

BOORSTIN, DANIEL, *The Americans: The Colonial Experience.* New York: Random House, 1958.

BRAUER, JERALD C., *Protestantism in America: A Narrative History* (rev. ed.). Philadelphia: Westminster Press, 1965.

BURNS, ALAN, *History of the British West Indies* (rev. ed.). London: Allen & Unwin, 1965.

BURNS, E. BRADFORD, *Latin America: A Concise Interpretative History* (2nd ed.). Englewood Cliffs, N.J.: Prentice-Hall, 1977.

CATTON, BRUCE, and WILLIAM B. CATTON, *The Bold and Magnificent Dream: America's Founding Years, 1492–1815.* Garden City, N.Y.: Doubleday, 1978.

CHITWOOD, OLIVER PERRY, *A History of Colonial America* (2nd ed.). New York: Harper, 1948.

COLEMAN, KENNETH, *Colonial Georgia: A History.* New York: Charles Scribner's Sons, 1976.

COULTER, E. M., *A Short History of Georgia.* Chapel Hill, N.C.: University of North Carolina Press, 1933.

CRUDEN, ROBERT, *Many and One: A Social History of the United States.* Englewood Cliffs, N.J.: Prentice-Hall, 1980.

DANIELL, JERE R., *Colonial New Hampshire: A History.* Millwood, N.Y.: KTO Press, 1981.

DAVIS, RICHARD BEALE, *Intellectual Life in the Colonial South, 1588-1763,* 3 vols. Knoxville, Tenn.: University of Tennessee Press, 1979.

DEGLER, CARL, *Out of Our Past: The Forces that Shaped Modern America* (rev. ed.). New York: Harper & Row, 1970.

DRIVER, HAROLD, *Indians of North America* (rev. 2nd ed.). Chicago: Chicago University Press, 1969.

ECCLES, W. J., *France in America.* New York: Harper & Row, 1972.

ELLIS, DAVID M., et al., *A History of New York State* (rev. ed.). Ithaca, N.Y.: Cornell University Press, 1967.

EMERSON, EVERETT, ed., *Major Writers of Early American Literature.* Madison, Wis.: University of Wisconsin Press, 1972.

FISHER, SYDNEY G., *The Making of Pennsylvania.* Philadelphia: J. B. Lippincott, 1932.

_____, *The Quaker Colonies.* New Haven: Yale University Press, 1919.

FONER, PHILLIP, *The History of Black Americans: From Africa to the Emergence of the Cotton Kingdom.* Westport, Conn.: Greenwood Press, 1975.

FRANKLIN, JOHN HOPE, *From Slavery to Freedom: A History of Negro Americans* (4th ed.). New York: Alfred A. Knopf, 1974.

GAUSTAD, EDWIN S., *Historical Atlas of Religion in America.* New York: Harper & Row, 1962.

_____, *A Religious History of America.* New York: Harper & Row, 1966.

GREENE, JACK P., ed., *Great Britain and the American Colonies, 1607–1763.* New York: Harper & Row, 1970.

HALSEY, FRANCIS W., *The Old New York Frontier.* New York: Charles Scribner's Sons, 1901.

HAWKE, DAVID, *The Colonial Experience.* Indianapolis: Bobbs-Merrill, 1966.

HENRETTA, JAMES S., *The Evolution of American Society, 1700–1815: An Interdisciplinary Analysis.* Lexington, Mass.: Heath, 1973.

HIGHAM, JOHN, ed., *The Reconstruction of American History.* New York: Humanities Press, 1962.

HUDSON, WINTHROP, *Religion in America.* New York: Charles Scribner's Sons, 1965.

ILLICK, JOSEPH E., *Colonial Pennsylvania: A History.* New York: Charles Scribner's Sons, 1976.

JAMES, SYDNEY V., *Colonial Rhode Island: A History.* New York: Charles Scribner's Sons, 1975.

JONES, HOWARD MUMFORD, *O Strange New World: American Culture, The Formative Years.* New York: Viking Press, 1967.

KAMMEN, MICHAEL, *Colonial New York: A History.* New York: Charles Scribner's Sons, 1979.

——, *People of Paradox: An Inquiry Concerning the Origins of American Civilization.* New York: Alfred A. Knopf, 1972.

KATZ, STANLEY N. and JOHN M. MURRIN, eds., *Colonial America: Essays in Politics and Social Development* (3rd ed.). New York: Alfred A. Knopf, 1983.

LABAREE, BENJAMIN, *America's Nation Time, 1607-1789.* New York: W. W. Norton, 1976.

——, *Colonial Massachusetts: A History.* Millwood, N.Y.: Kraus International Publications, 1979.

LAND, AUBREY C., *Colonial Maryland: A History.* Millwood, N.Y.: KTO Press, 1981.

LEACH, DOUGLAS, *The Northern Colonial Frontier, 1607-1763.* New York: Holt, Rinehart & Winston, 1966.

LEDER, LAWRENCE, *America, 1603-1789: Prelude to a Nation.* Minneapolis: Burgess Publishing, 1972.

LEFLER, HUGH T., and ALBERT R. NEWSOME, *North Carolina: The History of a Southern State.* Chapel Hill, N.C.: University of North Carolina Press, 1963.

LEFLER, HUGH T., and WILLIAM S. POWELL, *Colonial North Carolina: A History.* New York: Charles Scribner's Sons, 1973.

LIPSET, SEYMOUR, *The First New Nation: The United States in Historical and Comparative Perspective.* New York: W. W. Norton, 1979.

MEAD, SIDNEY E., *The Lively Experiment: The Shaping of Christianity in America.* New York: Harper, 1963.

MILLER, JOHN C., ed., *The Colonial Image: Origins of American Culture.* New York: George Braziller, 1962.

MORRIS, RICHARD B., *The Emerging Nations and the American Revolution.* New York: Harper, 1970.

MORTON, RICHARD L., *Colonial Virginia,* 2 vols. Chapel Hill, N.C.: University of North Carolina Press, 1960.

MUNROE, JOHN A., *Colonial Delaware: A History.* Millwood, N.Y.: KTO Press, 1978.

NETTELS, CURTIS PUTNAM, *The Roots of American Civilization: A History of American Colonial Life* (2nd ed.). New York: Appleton-Century-Crofts, 1963.

O'GORMAN, EDMUNDO, *The Invention of America: An Inquiry into the Historical Nature of the New World and the Meaning of Its History.* Bloomington, Ind.: Indiana University Press, 1961.

PARRINGTON, VERNON L., *Main Currents in American Thought. Volume One, 1620-1800: The Colonial Mind.* New York: Harcourt, Brace, 1954.

PEARCE, ROY HARVEY, ed., *Colonial American Writings.* New York: Holt, Rinehart & Winston, 1950.

POMFRET, JOHN E., *Colonial New Jersey: A History.* New York: Charles Scribner's Sons, 1973.

RICHMAN, IRVING B., *Rhode Island: Its Making and Its Meaning,* 2 vols. New York: G. Putnam's Sons, 1902.

ROSSITER, CLINTON, *Seedtime of the Republic.* New York: Harcourt, Brace, 1953.

RUTMAN, DARRETT B., *The Morning of America, 1603-1789.* Boston: Houghton-Mifflin, 1971.

SAVELLE, MAX, *Seeds of Liberty.* Seattle: University of Washington Press, 1967.

SAVELLE, MAX, and DAROLD D. WAX, *A History of Colonial America* (3rd ed.). Hinsdale, Ill.: Dryden Press, 1973.

SCHAFF, PHILIP, et al., gen. eds., *The American Church History Series,* 13 vols. New York: Christian Literature Co., 1893-1897.

SIMMONS, RICHARD C., *The American Colonies from Settlement to Independence.* New York: W. W. Norton, 1980.

STEIN, STANLEY, and BARBARA STEIN, *The Colonial Heritage of Latin America.* New York: Oxford University Press, 1970.

STURDEVANT, WILLIAM C., gen. ed., *Handbook of North American Indians,* 15 vols. Washington, D.C.: Smithsonian Institution, U.S. Government Printing Office, 1978-1981.

SWEET, WILLIAM WARREN, *Religion in Colonial America.* New York: Charles Scribner's Sons, 1942.

TAYLOR, ROBERT J., *Colonial Connecticut: A History.* Millwood, N.Y.: KTO Press, 1979.

TYLER, MOSES COIT, *History of American Literature during the Colonial Period, 1607-1765,* 2 vols. New York: G. P. Putnam, 1897.

VER STEEG, CLARENCE L., *The Formative Years, 1607-1763.* New York: Hill & Wang, 1964.
WALLACE, DAVID D., *South Carolina: A Short History, 1520-1948.* Chapel Hill, N.C.: University of North Carolina Press, 1951.
WRIGHT, LOUIS B., *The Cultural Life of the American Colonies, 1607-1763.* New York: Harper & Row, 1957.
WRIGLEY, E. A., *Population and History.* New York: McGraw-Hill, 1969.

INTERPRETIVE AND OTHER SPECIALIZED STUDIES

ALBRIGHT, RAYMOND W., *A History of the Protestant Episcopal Church.* New York: Macmillan, 1964.
AXTELL, JAMES, *The School upon a Hill: Education and Society in Colonial New England.* New Haven: Yale University Press, 1974.
BACON, MARGARET HOPE, *The Story of the Quakers in America.* New York: Basic Books, 1969.
BAILYN, BERNARD, *Education in the Forming of American Society.* Chapel Hill, N.C.: University of North Carolina Press, 1960.
BAIRD, CHARLES W., *History of the Huguenot Emigration to America,* 2 vols. New York: Dodd, Mead, 1885.
BEARD, MARY, *America Through Women's Eyes.* New York: Macmillan, 1933.
BENDER, THOMAS, *Community and Social Change in America.* New Brunswick, N.J.: Rutgers University Press, 1978.
BERCOVITCH, SACVAN, *The American Jeremiad.* Madison, Wis.: University of Wisconsin Press, 1978.
BERENS, JOHN F., *Providence and Patriotism in Early America, 1640-1815.* Charlottesville, Va.: University Press of Virginia, 1978.
BERKIN, CAROL R., *Within the Conjurer's Circle: Women in Colonial America.* Morristown, N.J.: General Learning Press, 1974.
BERTHOFF, ROWLAND, *An Unsettled People: Social Order and Disorder in American History.* New York: Harper & Row, 1971.
BIDWELL, P. W., and JOHN I. FALCONER, *History of Agriculture in the Northern United States, 1620-1860.* Washington, D.C.: Carnegie Institute Publications (No. 358), 1925.
BOORSTIN, DANIEL J., *The Genius of American Politics.* Chicago: University of Chicago Press, 1953.
BOOTH, SALLY SMITH, *Seeds of Anger: Revolts in America, 1607-1771.* New York: Hastings House, 1977.
BRAUNTHAL, ALFRED, *Salvation and the Perfect Society: The Eternal Quest.* Amherst, Mass.: University of Massachusetts Press, 1979.
BRIDENBAUGH, CARL, *The Colonial Craftsman.* New York: New York University Press, 1950.
_____, *Myths and Realities: Societies of the Colonial South.* Baton Rouge, La.: Louisiana State University Press, 1952.
BRINTON, CRANE, *The Anatomy of a Revolution* (rev. ed.). Englewood Cliffs, N.J.: Prentice-Hall, 1952.
BROWN, RICHARD D., *Modernization: The Transformation of American Life, 1600-1865.* New York: Hill & Wang, 1976.
BROWN, RICHARD MAXWELL, *Strain of Violence: Historical Studies of American Violence and Vigilantism.* New York: Oxford University Press, 1975.
BRUCHEY, STUART, *The Roots of American Economic Growth, 1607-1861: An Essay in Social Causation.* New York: Harper & Row, 1965.
BUCK, PAUL H., et al., *The Role of Education in American History.* New York: Fund for the Advancement of Education, 1957.
CARRINGTON, C. E., *The British Overseas: Exploits of a Nation of Shopkeepers.* Cambridge, Eng.: Cambridge University Press, 1950.
CLARKE, MARY P., *Parliamentary Privilege in the American Colonies.* New Haven: Yale University Press, 1943.
COLEMAN, PETER J., *Debtors and Creditors in America: Insolvency, Imprisonment for Debt, and Bankruptcy, 1607-1900.* Madison, Wis.: University of Wisconsin Press, 1974.
CONKIN, PAUL KEITH, *Self-Evident Truths: Being a Discourse on the Origins and Development of the First Principles of American Government . . . .* Bloomington, Ind.: Indiana University Press, 1974.

COUSINS, PETER H., *Hog Plow and Stith: Cultural Aspects of Early Agricultural Technology.* Dearborn, Mich.: Greenfield Village and Henry Ford Museum, 1973.
CREMIN, LAWRENCE, *American Education: The Colonial Experience, 1607-1783.* New York: Harper & Row, 1970.
DANIELS, BRUCE C., *The Connecticut Town: Growth and Development, 1635-1790.* Middletown, Conn.: Wesleyan University Press, 1979.
DAVIDSON, ELIZABETH H., *The Establishment of the English Church in the Continental American Colonies.* Durham, N.C.: Duke University Press, 1936.
DAVIS, DAVID BRION, *The Problem of Slavery in the Age of Revolution, 1770-1823.* Ithaca, N.Y.: Cornell University Press, 1975.
——, *The Problem of Slavery in Western Culture.* Ithaca, N.Y.: Cornell University Press, 1966.
DEXTER, ELIZABETH ANTHONY, *Colonial Women of Affairs: Women in Business and the Professions in America before 1776* (2nd ed. rev.). Boston: Houghton-Mifflin, 1931.
EADIE, JOHN, ed., *The Classical Tradition in America.* Ann Arbor, Mich.: University of Michigan Press, 1972.
ELLIS, JOHN TRACY, *Catholics in Colonial America.* Baltimore: Helicon Press, 1965.
FERLING, JOHN E., *A Wilderness of Miseries: War and Warriors in Early America.* Westport, Conn.: Greenwood Press, 1980.
FISHER, SYDNEY GEORGE, *Men, Women and Manners in Colonial Times,* 2 vols. (2nd ed.). Philadelphia: J. P. Lippincott, 1898.
FRANKLIN, WAYNE, *Discoverers, Explorers, Settlers: The Diligent Writers of Early America.* Chicago: University of Chicago Press, 1979.
GALENSON, DAVID W., *White Servitude in Colonial America: An Economic Analysis.* Cambridge, Eng.: Cambridge University Press, 1981.
GENOVESE, EUGENE, *The Political Economy of Slavery: Studies in the Economy and Society of the Slave South.* New York: Random House, 1967.
——, *From Rebellion to Revolution.* Baton Rouge, La.: Louisiana State University Press, 1979.
——, *Roll, Jordan Roll: The World the Slaves Made.* New York: Pantheon Books, 1974.
GRAY, LEWIS, *History of Agriculture in the Southern United States to 1860.* Washington, D.C.: Carnegie Institute Publications (No. 430), 1933.
GREENE, EVARTS B., and VIRGINIA D. HARRINGTON, *American Population before the Federal Census of 1790.* New York: Columbia University Press, 1932.
GREENE, LORENZO J., *The Negro in Colonial New England, 1620-1776.* New York: Columbia University Press, 1942.
GREVEN, PHILIP, *The Protestant Temperament.* New York: Alfred A. Knopf, 1977.
GRINDE, DONALD A., *The Iroquois and the Founding of the American Nation.* San Franciso: Indian Heritage Press, 1977.
GUMMERE, RICHARD M., *The American Colonial Mind and the Classical Tradition: Essays in Comparative Culture.* Cambridge, Mass.: Harvard University Press, 1963.
GUTMAN, HERBERT G., *The Black Family in Slavery and Freedom, 1750-1925.* New York: Pantheon Books, 1976.
HANSEN, MARCUS LEE, *The Atlantic Migration, 1607-1860: A History of the Continuing Settlement of the United States.* Cambridge, Mass.: Harvard University Press, 1940.
HARDOY, JORGE, and R. P. SCHAEDEL, *The Urbanization Process in America from Its Origin to the Present.* Buenos Aires: Editorial del Instituto, 1969.
HARTZ, LOUIS, *The Liberal Tradition in America.* New York: Harcourt, Brace, 1955.
HENNESEY, JAMES, *American Catholics: A History of the Roman Catholic Community in the United States.* New York: Oxford University Press, 1981.
HINE, ROBERT V., *Community on the American Frontier: Separate But Not Alone.* Norman, Okla.: University of Oklahoma Press, 1980.
HOFSTADTER, RICHARD, *The American Political Tradition and the Men Who Made It.* New York: Alfred A. Knopf, 1948.
HOLLIDAY, CARL, *Woman's Life in Colonial Days.* Boston: Cornhill Publishing, 1922.
HONOUR, HUGH, *The New Golden Land: European Images of America from the Discoveries to the Present Time.* New York: Pantheon Books, 1975.
HORNBERGER, THEODORE, *Scientific Thought in the American Colleges, 1638-1800.* Austin: University of Texas Press, 1945.
HUGGINS, NATHAN I., *Black Odyssey: The Afro-American Ordeal in Slavery.* New York: Pantheon Books, 1977.
HUGHES, J. R. T., *Social Control in the Colonial Economy.* Charlottesville: University of Virginia Press, 1976.
JENNINGS, FRANCIS, *The Invasion of America: Indians, Colonialism, and the Cant of Conquest.* Chapel Hill, N.C.: University of North Carolina Press, 1975.
JERNEGAN, MARCUS WILSON, *Laboring and Dependent Classes in Colonial America,*

1607-1783: Studies of the Economic, Educational, and Social Significance of Slaves, Servants, Apprentices, and Poor Folk. Chicago: Chicago University Press, 1931.
JOHNSON, AMANDUS, *The Swedish Settlements on the Delaware,* 2 vols. Philadelphia: Swedish Colonial Society, 1911.
JONES, RUFUS M., *The Quakers in the American Colonies.* New York: Russell & Russell, 1962.
JONG, J. A. de, *As the Waters Cover the Sea: Millennial Expectations in the Rise of Anglo-American Missions, 1640-1810.* Kampen, Netherlands: J. K. Kok, 1970.
JORDAN, WINTHROP D., *White Over Black: American Attitudes Toward the Negro, 1550-1812.* New York: W. W. Norton, 1977.
JOSEPHY, ALVIN M., *The Indian Heritage of America.* New York: Alfred A Knopf, 1968.
KAMMEN, MICHAEL, ed., *Deputyes and Libertyes: The Origins of Representative Government in America.* New York: Alfred A. Knopf, 1969.
KITTREDGE, GEORGE L., *The Old Farmer and his Almanack.* Boston: W. Ware, 1904.
KLEIN, HERBERT S., *The Middle Passage: Comparative Studies in the Atlantic Slave Trade.* Princeton, N.J.: Princeton University Press, 1978.
KOBRE, SIDNEY, *The Development of the Colonial Newspaper.* Pittsburgh: Colonial Press, 1944.
LABAREE, LEONARD W., *Conservatism in Early American History.* New York: New York University Press, 1948.
LAND, AUBREY C., LOIS GREEN CARR, and EDWARD C. PAPENFUSE, eds., *Law, Society, and Politics in Early Maryland.* Baltimore: Johns Hopkins University Press, 1977.
LEACH, DOUGLAS E., *Arms for Empire: A Military History of the British Colonies in North America, 1607-1763.* New York: Macmillan, 1973.
LEONARD, EUGENIE ANDRUSS, SOPHIE HUTCHINSON DRINKER, and MIRIAM YOUNG HOLDEN, *The American Woman in Colonial and Revolutionary Times, 1565-1800.* Philadelphia: University of Pennsylvania Press, 1962.
LEVY, LEONARD W., *Legacy of Suppression: Freedom of Speech and Press in Early American History.* Cambridge, Mass.: Harvard University Press, 1960.
LOCKRIDGE, KENNETH A., *Literacy in Colonial New England: An Enquiry into the Social Context of Literacy in the Early Modern West.* New York: W. W. Norton, 1974.
_____, *Settlement and Unsettlement in Early America: The Crisis of Political Legitimacy before the Revolution.* New York: Cambridge University Press, 1981.
MANROSS, WILLIAM WILSON, *A History of the American Episcopal Church* (2nd ed. rev. and enlg.). New York: Morehouse-Gorham, 1950.
McCUSKER, JOHN J., *Money and Exchange in Europe and America, 1600-1775: A Handbook.* Chapel Hill, N.C.: University of North Carolina Press, 1978.
McLOUGHLIN, WILLIAM G., *New England Dissent 1630-1833: The Baptists and the Separation of Church and State.* Cambridge, Mass.: Harvard University Press, 1971.
MORGAN, EDMUND S., *American Slavery, American Freedom: The Ordeal of Colonial Virginia.* New York: W. W. Norton, 1975.
_____, *Virginians at Home.* New York: Holt, Rinehart & Winston, 1952.
MORRIS, RICHARD BRANDON, *Government and Labor in Early America.* New York: Octagon Books, 1965.
MOTT, FRANK L., *American Journalism: A History of Newspapers in the United States through 260 Years, 1690-1950* (rev. ed.). New York: Macmillan, 1950.
_____, *A History of American Magazines, 1741-1850.* New York: Appleton-Century-Crofts, 1930.
MULHOLLAND, JAMES A., *A History of Metals in Colonial America.* University, Alabama: University of Alabama Press, 1981.
NASH, GARY, B., *Red, White, and Black: The Peoples of Early America.* Englewood Cliffs, N.J.: Prentice-Hall, 1974.
_____, *The Urban Crucible: Social Change, Political Consciousness, and the Origins of the American Revolution.* Cambridge, Mass.: Harvard University Press, 1979.
NEWMAN, ERIC P., *The Early Paper Money of America.* Racine, Wis.: Whitman Publishing, 1967.
NIEBUHR, H. RICHARD, *The Kingdom of God in America.* New York: Harper & Brothers, 1937.
OLSON, ALISON GILBERT, *Anglo-American Politics, 1660-1775: The Relationship between Parties in England and Colonial America.* New York: Oxford University Press, 1973.
OSWALT, WENDELL H., *This Land Was Theirs: A Study of the North American Indian.* New York: Wiley, 1966.
PARES, RICHARD, *Yankees and Creoles: The Trade between North America and the West Indies Before the American Revolution.* Cambridge, Mass.: Harvard University Press, 1956.

PERKINS, EDWIN J., *The Economy of Colonial America.* New York: Cambridge University Press, 1980.

PERRY, RALPH BARTON, *Puritanism and Democracy.* New York: Vanguard Press, 1944.

PIEPKORN, ARTHUR CARL, *Profiles in Belief: The Religious Bodies of the United States and Canada. Volume I: Roman Catholic, Old Catholic Eastern Orthodox.* New York: Harper & Row, 1977.

———, *Profiles in Belief: The Religious Bodies of the United States and Canada. Volume II: Protestant Denominations.* New York: Harper & Row, 1978.

SANCHEZ-ALBORNOZ, NICOLAS, *The Population of Latin America: A History,* trans. by W. A. R. Richardson. Berkeley, Calif.: University of California Press, 1974.

SCHERER, LESTER B., *Slavery and the Churches in Early America, 1618-1819.* Grand Rapids, Mich.: Eerdmans, 1975.

SCHNEIDER, CARL E., *The German Church on the American Frontier.* St. Louis: Eden Publishing, 1939.

SHEA, JOHN DAWSON GILMARY, *The Catholic Church in Colonial Days,* 2 vols. New York: John G. Shea, 1886.

SHEPHERD, JAMES F., and GARY M. WALTON, *Shipping, Maritime Trade and the Economic Development of Colonial North America.* Cambridge, Eng.: Cambridge University Press, 1972.

SHERIDAN, RICHARD, *Sugar and Slavery: An Economic History of the British West Indies, 1623-1775.* Baltimore: Johns Hopkins Press, 1974.

SIMPSON, LEWIS P., *The Dispossessed Garden: Pastoral and History in Southern Literature.* Athens, Ga.: University of Georgia Press, 1975.

SLOTKIN, RICHARD, *Regeneration Through Violence: The Mythology of the American Frontier, 1600-1860.* Middletown, Conn.: Wesleyan University Press, 1973.

SLY, JOHN, *Town Government in Massachusetts, 1620-1930.* Cambridge, Mass.: Harvard University Press, 1930.

SMITH, ABBOT E., *Colonists in Bondage: White Servitude and Convict Labor in America, 1607-1776.* Chapel Hill, N.C.: University of North Carolina Press, 1947.

SMITH, PAGE, *Daughters of the Promised Land: Women in American History.* Boston: Little, Brown, 1970.

SOLBERG, WINTON U., *Redeem the Time: The Puritan Sabbath in Early America.* Cambridge, Mass.: Harvard University Press, 1977.

SPICER, EDWARD H., *A Short History of the Indians of the United States.* New York: Van Nostrand Reinhold, 1969.

SPRUILL, JULIA CHERRY, *Women's Life and Work in the Southern Colonies.* New York: W. W. Norton, 1972.

STROUT, CUSHING, *The New Heaven and Earth: Political Religion in America.* New York: Harper & Row, 1974.

SUTHERLAND, STELLA H., *Population Distribution in Colonial America.* New York: Columbia University Press, 1936.

THOMPSON, ERNEST T., *Presbyterians in the South.* Richmond: John Knox Press, 1963.

THOMPSON, HENRY F., *Into All Lands: The History of the Society for the Propagation of the Gospel in Foreign Parts, 1701-1950.* London: SPCK, 1951.

TORBET, ROBERT G., *A History of the Baptists.* Philadelphia: Judson Press, 1950.

TURNER, FREDERICK JACKSON, *The Frontier in American History.* New York: Holt, Rinehart & Winston, 1920.

TUVESON, ERNEST LEE, *Millennium and Utopia: A Study in the Background of the Idea of Progress.* Berkeley, Calif.: University of California Press, 1949.

———, *Redeemer Nation: The Idea of America's Millennial Role.* Chicago: University of Chicago Press, 1968.

UBBELOHDE, CARL, *The American Colonies and the British Empire, 1607-1763.* New York: Crowell, 1968.

WASHBURN, WILCOMB E., *The Indian in North America.* New York: Harper & Row, 1975.

WELLS, ROBERT V., *The Population of the British Colonies in America before 1776: A Survey of Census Data.* Princeton, N.J.: Princeton University Press, 1975.

WHARTON, DONALD P., ed., *In the Trough of the Sea: Selected Deliverance Narratives, 1610-1766.* Westport, Conn.: Greenwood Press, 1979.

WILSON, JOHN F., *Public Religion in American Culture.* Philadelphia: Temple University Press, 1979.

WINSLOW, OLA E., *Meetinghouse Hill.* New York: Macmillan, 1957.

WISSLER, CLARK, *The Indians of the United States: Four Centuries of their History and Culture* (rev. ed.). Garden City, N.Y.: Doubleday, 1966.

WORRALL, ARTHUR J., *Quakers in the Colonial Northeast.* Hanover, N.H.: University Press of New England, 1980.

WROTH, LAWRENCE C., *The Colonial Printer* (2nd ed., enlg. & rev.). Charlottesville, Va.: Dominion Books, 1964.

ENGLISH AND EUROPEAN BACKGROUND

ASHLEY, MAURICE, *The Glorious Revolution of 1688.* London: Hodder & Stoughton, 1966.

AYLMER, G. E., *The Struggle for the Constitution: England in the Seventeenth Century.* London: Blandford Press, 1963.

BAINTON, ROLAND, *Here I Stand: A Life of Martin Luther.* Knoxville, Tenn.: Abingdon Press, 1950.

_____, *The Reformation of the Sixteenth Century.* Boston: Beacon Press, 1963.

BINDOFF, S. T., *Tudor England.* Harmondsworth, Eng.: Penguin Books, 1952.

BOLAM, C. G., et al., *The English Presbyterians from Elizabethan Puritanism to Modern Unitarianism.* London: Allen and Unwin, 1968.

BRAITHWAITE, WILLIAM C., *The Beginnings of Quakerism.* London: Macmillan, 1912.

CANTOR, N. F., *Medieval History: The Life and Death of a Civilization* (2nd ed.). New York: Macmillan, 1969.

CHADWICK, OWEN, *The Reformation.* Baltimore: Penguin Books, 1964.

CLARK, GEORGE, *Early Modern Europe from about 1450 to about 1720.* New York: Oxford University Press, 1966.

CLARK, PETER, *English Provincial Society from the Reformation to the Revolution: Religion, Politics, and Society in Kent, 1500–1640.* Hassocks, Eng.: Harvester Press, 1977.

COLLINSON, PATRICK, *The Elizabethan Puritan Movement.* Berkeley, Calif.: University of California Press, 1967.

CORBETT, JULIAN S., *England in the Seven Years' War,* 2 vols. London: Longman's, Green, 1907.

CUMMING, WILLIAM P., R. A. SKELTON, and DAVID B. QUINN, *The Discovery of North America.* New York: American Heritage Press, 1972.

DAVIES, GODFREY, *The Early Stuarts, 1603–1660.* Oxford, Eng.: Clarendon Press, 1937.

DAVIS, K. G., *The North Atlantic World in the Seventeenth Century.* Minneapolis: University of Minnesota Press, 1974.

DAVIS, RALPH, *A Commercial Revolution: English Overseas Trade in the Seventeenth and Eighteenth Centuries.* London: Historical Association, 1967.

_____, *The Rise of the Atlantic Economies.* Ithaca, N.Y.: Cornell University Press, 1973.

DERRY, JOHN, *English Politics and the American Revolution.* London: Dent, 1976.

DICKENS, ARTHUR G., *The Counter-Reformation.* London: Thames & Hudson, 1968.

_____, *The English Reformation.* New York: Schocken, 1964.

ELLIOTT, J. H., *Imperial Spain, 1469–1716.* New York: St. Martin's Press, 1964.

ELTON, G. R., *England under the Tudors* (2nd ed.). London: Methuen, 1974.

ERGANG, ROBERT R., *The Renaissance.* Princeton, N.J.: Van Nostrand, 1967.

FERGUSON, WALLACE K., *Europe in Transition, 1300–1520.* Boston: Houghton-Mifflin, 1962.

_____, *The Renaissance in Historical Thought: Five Centuries of Interpretation.* Boston: Houghton-Mifflin, 1948.

_____, *Renaissance Studies.* London, Ont.: Humanities Department of the University of Ontario, 1963.

FILMER, ROBERT, *Filmer,* ed. with an intro. by Peter Laslett. Oxford: Oxford University Press, 1949.

FINK, ZERA, *The Classical Republicans: An Essay in the Recovery of a Pattern of Thought in Seventeenth Century England.* Evanston, Ill.: Northwestern University Press, 1945.

GEMERY, HENRY A., and JAN S. HOGENDORN, eds., *The Uncommon Market: Essays in the Economic History of the Atlantic Slave Trade.* New York: Academic Press, 1979.

GEORGE, CHARLES, and KATHERINE GEORGE, *The Protestant Mind of the English Reformation, 1570–1640.* Princeton, N.J.: Princeton University Press, 1961.

GIBSON, CHARLES, ed., *The Black Legend: Anti-Spanish Attitudes in the Old World and the New.* New York: Alfred A. Knopf, 1971.

_____, *Spain in America.* New York: Harper & Row, 1966.

GIPSON, LAWRENCE H., *The British Empire before the Revolution,* 15 vols. New York: Alfred A. Knopf, 1936–1970.

GRAY, CHARLES M., *Renaissance and Reformation England, 1509–1714.* New York: Harcourt Brace Jovanovich, 1973.

GRAY, EDWARD D., *Leif Erikson: Discoverer of America A.D. 1003.* London: Oxford University Press, 1930.

GRAY, H. L., *English Field Systems.* Cambridge, Mass.: Harvard University Press, 1959.

GREENLEAF, W. H., *Order, Empiricism, and Politics: Two Traditions of English Political Thought, 1500–1700.* London: Oxford University Press, 1964.

HALE, J. R., *Renaissance Europe: Individual and Society, 1480–1520.* London: Collins, 1971.

HALLER, WILLIAM, *Liberty and Reformation in the Puritan Revolution.* New York: Columbia University Press, 1955.

——, *The Rise of Puritanism; or the Way to the New Jerusalem as Set Forth in Pulpit and Press from Thomas Cartwright to John Lilburne and John Milton, 1570–1643.* New York: Harper & Row, 1957.

HARRISON, JOHN F. C., *The Second Coming: Popular Millenarianism, 1780–1850.* New Brunswick, N.J.: Rutgers University Press, 1979.

HECKSCHER, ELI F., *Mercantilism,* 2 vols. (rev. ed.). New York: Macmillan, 1955.

HILL, J. E. CHRISTOPHER, *The Century of Revolution, 1603–1714.* Edinburgh: T. Nelson, 1961.

——, *Intellectual Origins of the English Revolution.* Oxford: Clarendon Press, 1965.

——, *Puritanism and Revolution: Studies in Interpretation of the English Revolution of the Seventeenth Century.* London: Secker & Warburg, 1958.

——, *Society and Puritanism in Pre-Revolutionary England.* New York: Schocken Books, 1967.

——, *The World Turned Upside Down: Radical Ideas during the English Revolution.* New York: Viking Press, 1972.

HOLAND, HJALMAR, R., *Exploration in America before Columbus.* New York: Twayne, 1956.

HOSKINS, W. G., *The Midland Peasant: The Economic and Social History of a Leicestershire Village.* London: Macmillan, 1957.

HUEHNS, GERTRUDE, *Antinomianism in English History, with Special Reference to the Period, 1640–1660.* London: Cresset Press, 1951.

HUIZINGA, JOHAN, *The Waning of the Middle Ages: A Study of the Forms of Life, Thought, and Art in France and the Netherlands in the XIVth and XVth Centuries.* London: Edward Arnold, 1967.

HURSTFIELD, JOEL, *Elizabeth I and the Unity of England.* New York: Harper & Row, 1960.

JONES, GWYN, *A History of the Vikings.* New York: Oxford University Press, 1968.

——, *The North Atlantic Saga Being the Norse Voyages of Discovery and Settlement to Iceland, Greenland, and America.* London: Oxford University Press, 1964.

JONES, RUFUS, *Spiritual Reformers in the Sixteenth and Seventeenth Centuries.* New York: Macmillan, 1914.

JONES, WITNEY R.D., *The Tudor Commonwealth, 1529–1559: A Study of the Impact of the Social and Economic Developments of Mid-Tudor England upon Contemporary Concepts of the Nature and Duties of the Commonwealth.* London: Athlone Press, 1970.

JUDSON, MARGARET, *Crisis of the Constitution: An Essay in the Constitutional and Political Thought in England, 1603–1645.* New York: Octagon Books, 1964.

KENYON, JOHN P., *Stuart England.* New York: St. Martin's Press, 1978.

KIDD, B. J., *The Counter-Reformation, 1550–1600.* London: S.P.C.K., 1933.

KNORR, KLAUS E., *British Colonial Theories, 1570–1850.* Toronto: University of Toronto Press, 1944.

LANDER, J. R., *Government and Community: England 1450–1509.* Cambridge, Mass.: Harvard University Press, 1980.

LASLETT, PETER, *The World We Have Lost: England before the Industrial Age.* London: Methuen, 1965.

LECKY, W. E. H., *England in the Eighteenth Century,* 8 vols. London: Longmans, Green, 1879–1890.

LITTELL, FRANKLIN H., *The Origins of Sectarian Protestantism: The Anabaptist View of the Church.* New York: Macmillan, 1960.

LITTLE, DAVID, *Religion, Order and Law: A Study in Pre-Revolutionary England.* New York: Harper & Row, 1969.

LOCKE, JOHN, *Two Treatises of Government,* ed. Peter Laslett. New York: New American Library, 1965.

LOCKYER, ROGER, *Tudor and Stuart Britain, 1471–1714.* New York: St. Martin's Press, 1964.

MARCUS, C. J., *The Conquest of the North Atlantic.* New York: Oxford University Press, 1981.

MARSHALL, DOROTHY, *Eighteenth Century England.* New York: D. McKay, 1962.
_____, *The English People in the Eighteenth Century.* London: Longmans, Green, 1956.
McNEILL, J. T., *The History and Character of Calvinism.* New York: Oxford University Press, 1973 (1954, 1962).
McNEILL, WILLIAM H., *The Rise of the West: A History of the Human Community.* Chicago: University of Chicago Press, 1963.
MINCHINTON, W. E., ed., *The Growth of English Overseas Trade in the Seventeenth and Eighteenth Centuries.* London: Methuen, 1969.
MINGAY, G. E., *English Landed Society in the Eighteenth Century.* London: Routledge & Kegan Paul, 1963.
MORISON, SAMUEL E., *Admiral of the Ocean Sea: A Life of Christopher Columbus.* Boston: Little, Brown, 1942.
_____, *The European Discovery of America: The North American Voyages, A.D. 500-1600.* New York: Oxford University Press, 1971.
MUNRO, D. C., *The Middle Ages, 395-1272.* New York: Century, 1921.
NAMIER, LEWIS, *England in the Age of the American Revolution* (2nd ed.). London: Macmillan, 1961.
_____, *The History of Parliament: The House of Commons, 1754-1790.* New York: Oxford University Press, 1964.
_____, *The Structure of Politics at the Accession of George III* (2nd ed.). London: Macmillan, 1957.
NEALE, J. E., *Queen Elizabeth I.* London: J. Cape, 1934.
NEW, JOHN F. H., *Anglican and Puritan: The Basis of their Opposition, 1558-1640.* Stanford, Calif.: Stanford University Press, 1964.
NOTESTEIN, WALLACE, *The English People on the Eve of Colonization, 1603-1630.* New York: Harper, 1954.
NUTTALL, GEOFFREY F., *Visible Saints: The Congregational Way, 1640-1660.* Oxford: Basil Blackwell, 1957.
PALMER, ROBERT R., *The Age of Democratic Revolution: A Political History of Europe and America 1760-1800,* 2 vols. Princeton, N.J.: Princeton University Press, 1959-1964.
PARKER, THOMAS M., *The English Reformation to 1588* (2nd ed.). London: Oxford University Press, 1966.
PARRY, J. H., *The Spanish Seaborne Empire* (2nd ed.). London: Hutchinson, 1966.
_____, *The Spanish Theory of Empire in the Sixteenth Century.* Cambridge, Eng.: Cambridge University Press, 1940.
PATTEN, JOHN, *English Towns, 1500-1700.* Hamden, Conn.: Archon Books, 1978.
PILL, DAVID H., *The English Reformation, 1529-1558.* London: University of London Press, 1973.
PIRENNE, HENRI, *Economic and Social History of Medieval Europe,* trans. I. E. Clegg. New York: Harcourt, Brace, 1937.
PLUCKNETT, THEODORE F. T., *A Concise History of the Common Law* (5th ed.). Boston: Little, Brown, 1956.
PLUMB, J. H., *The Growth of Political Stability in England, 1675-1725.* Baltimore: Johns Hopkins University Press, 1969.
_____, *Men and Centuries.* Boston: Houghton-Mifflin, 1963.
_____, *Sir Robert Walpole,* 2 vols. Boston: Houghton-Mifflin, 1961.
POCOCK, J. G. A., *The Ancient Constitution and the Feudal Law: A Study of English Historical Thought in the Seventeenth Century.* Cambridge, Eng.: Cambridge University Press, 1957.
_____, *The Machiavellian Moment: Florentine Political Thought and the Atlantic Republican Tradition.* Princeton, N.J.: Princeton University Press, 1975.
POLE, J. R., *Political Representation in England and the Origins of the American Republic.* Berkeley, Calif.: University of California Press, 1971.
POTTER, HAROLD, *Historical Introduction to English Law and Its Institutions* (4th ed.). London: Sweet & Maxwell, 1958.
PRALL, STUART, *The Bloodless Revolution: England 1688.* Garden City, N.Y.: Anchor Books, 1972.
QUINN, DAVID B., *England and the Discovery of America, 1481-1620, from the Bristol Voyages of the Fifteenth Century to the Pilgrim Settlement at Plymouth: The Exploration, Exploitation and Trial-and-Error Colonization of North America by the English.* New York: Alfred A. Knopf, 1974.
_____, *North America from Earliest Discovery to First Settlements: The Norse Voyages to 1612.* New York: Harper & Row, 1977.
_____, *North American Discovery circa 1000-1612.* Columbia, S.C.: University of South Carolina Press, 1971.

RAAB, FELIX, *The English Face of Machiavelli: Changing Interpretations, 1500–1700.* London: Routledge & Kegan Paul, 1964.

RAMSEY, GEORGE D., *English Overseas Trade during the Centuries of Emergence: Studies in Some Modern Origins of the English-Speaking World.* London: Macmillan, 1957.

REDWOOD, JOHN, *Reason, Ridicule and Religion: The Age of the Enlightenment in England, 1660–1750.* Cambridge, Mass.: Harvard University Press, 1976.

RICHESON, CHARLES R., *British Politics and the American Revolution.* Norman: University of Oklahoma Press, 1954.

ROBBINS, CAROLINE, *The Eighteenth Century Commonwealthman: Studies in the Transmission, Development and Circumstance of English Liberal Thought from the Restoration of Charles II until the War with the Thirteen Colonies.* Cambridge, Mass.: Harvard University Press, 1959.

ROBERTS, CLAYTON, *The Growth of Responsible Government in Stuart England.* Cambridge, Eng.: Cambridge University Press, 1966.

ROWSE, A. L., *The Expansion of Elizabethan England.* London: Alfred Leslie, 1955.

——, *The Elizabethans and America.* London: Alfred Leslie, 1959.

RUSSELL, CONRAD, *Parliaments and English Politics, 1621–1629.* Oxford: Clarendon Press, 1979.

SAUER, CARL ORTWIN, *Sixteenth Century North America: The Land and the People as Seen by the Europeans.* Berkeley, Calif.: University of California Press, 1971.

SCARSBRICK, J. J., *Henry VIII.* Berkeley, Calif.: University of California Press, 1968.

SCHOCHET, GORDON J., *Patriarchalism in Political Thought: The Authoritarian Family and Political Speculation and Attitudes Especially in Seventeenth-Century England.* Oxford: Blackwell, 1975.

SCHWOERER, LOIS G., *No Standing Armies: The Antiarmy Ideology in Seventeenth Century England.* Baltimore: Johns Hopkins University Press, 1975.

SMITH, LACY BALDWIN, *This Realm of England, 1399–1688.* Boston: D. C. Heath, 1966.

SMITH, R. B., *Land and Politics in the England of Henry VIII: The West Riding of Yorkshire, 1530–46.* Oxford: Clarendon Press, 1970.

SOLT, LEO F., *Saints in Arms: Puritanism and Democracy in Cromwell's Army.* Stanford, Calif., Stanford University Press, 1959.

STIEG, MARGARET, *Laud's Laboratory: The Diocese of Bath and Wells in the Early Seventeenth Century.* Lewisburg, Pa.: Bucknell University Press, 1982.

STRAUSS, GERALD, *Luther's House of Learning: Indoctrination of the Young in the German Reformation.* Baltimore: Johns Hopkins University Press, 1978.

STONE, LAWRENCE, *Crisis of the Aristocracy, 1558–1641.* Oxford: Clarendon Press, 1965.

SUVIRANTA, BRUNO, *The Theory of the Balance of Trade in England: A Study in Mercantilism.* Helsingfors, Finland: Suomal Kirjall,. Sueran Kirjap, O.Y., 1923.

SYKES, NORMAN, *The Crisis of the Reformation.* London: G. Bles, 1938.

TAWNEY, R. H., *Religion and the Rise of Capitalism.* New York: Harcourt Brace, 1926.

THOMAS, KEITH VIVIAN, *Religion and the Decline of Magic: Studies in Popular Beliefs in Sixteenth and Seventeenth Century England.* London: Weidenfeld and Nicolson, 1971.

THOMAS, P. D. G., *British Politics and the Stamp Act Crisis: The First Phase of the American Revolution, 1763–1767.* Oxford: Clarendon Press, 1975.

THOMPSON, ROGER, *Women in Stuart England and America.* London: Routledge & Kegan Paul, 1974.

THOMSON, S. H., *Europe in Renaissance and Reformation.* London: R. Hart Davis, 1963.

TREASURE, GEOFFREY, R. R., *Seventeenth Century France.* London: Rivington, 1966.

TREVELYAN, GEORGE M., *The English Revolution, 1688–1689.* London: Oxford University Press, 1960.

TRINTERUD, LEONARD J., ed., *Elizabethan Puritanism.* New York: Oxford University Press, 1971.

TUBERVILLE, A. S., *House of Lords in the Eighteenth Century.* Oxford: Oxford University Press, 1927.

UNDERWOOD, A. C., *A History of the English Baptists.* London: Baptist Union Publication Dept., 1947.

WALCOTT, ROBERT, *English Politics in the Early Eighteenth Century.* Cambridge, Mass.: Harvard University Press, 1956.

WALZER, MICHAEL, *The Revolution of the Saints: A Study in the Origins of Radical Politics.* New York: Atheneum, 1968.

WEBB, SIDNEY, and BEATRICE WEBB, *English Local Government from the Revolution to the Municipal Corporation Acts,* 11 vols. London: Longmans, Green, 1903–1929.

WEDGWOOD, C. V., *The King's Peace, 1637–1641.* New York: Macmillan, 1955.

——, *The King's War, 1641–1647.* New York: Macmillan, 1955.

WENDELL, FRANÇOIS, *Calvin: The Origins and Development of His Religious Thought.* New York: Harper & Row, 1963.

WESTERN, JOHN R., *Monarchy and Revolution: The English State in the 1680s.* Totowa, N.J.: Rowman and Littlefield, 1972.
WESTON, CORINNE C., *English Constitutional Theory and the House of Lords, 1556–1832.* London: Routledge and Kegan Paul, 1965.
WHITLEY, W. T., *A History of British Baptists.* London: Charles Griffen, 1923.
WILLIAMS, E. N., ed., *The Eighteenth Century Constitution.* Cambridge, Eng.: Cambridge University Press, 1960.
____, *Life in Georgian England.* New York: G. P. Putnam's, 1962.
WILLIAMS, GEORGE H., *The Radical Reformation.* Philadelphia: Westminster Press, 1962.
WILLIAMSON, J. A., *A Short History of British Expansion. Volume I of The Old Colonial Empire,* 2 vols. (3rd ed.). London: Macmillan, 1958.
WILLSON, DAVID HARRIS, *King James VI and I.* New York: Holt, 1956.
WILSON, CHARLES, *England's Apprenticeship, 1603–1763.* New York: St. Martin's Press, 1965.
____, *Mercantilism.* London: Routledge & Kegan Paul, 1958.
WINCH, DONALD, *Adam Smith's Politics: An Essay In Historiographic Revision.* London: Cambridge University Press, 1978.
WOLF, JOHN B., *The Emergence of the Great Powers, 1685–1715.* New York: Harper, 1951.
WRIGHT, LOUIS B., *Religion and Empire: The Alliance between Piety and Commerce in English Expansion, 1558–1625.* Chapel Hill, N.C.: University of North Carolina Press, 1943.
WRIGHTSON, KEITH, *English Society, 1580–1680.* New Brunswick, N.J.: Rutgers University Press, 1982.
ZAGORIN, PEREZ, *A History of Political Thought in the English Revolution.* London: Routledge & Kegan Paul, 1954.

ANGLO-AMERICA: THE SEVENTEENTH CENTURY

ADAMS, BROOKS, *The Emancipation of Massachusetts: The Dream and the Reality.* Boston: Houghton-Mifflin, 1887.
ADAMS, CHARLES FRANCIS, "The Antinomian Controversy," in *Three Episodes in Massachusetts History,* ed. Emery Battis. New York: DaCapo Press, 1976.
ADAMS, JAMES TRUSLOW, *The Founding of New England.* Boston: Little, Brown, 1921.
ALLEN, DAVID GRAYSON, *In English Ways: The Movement of Societies and Transferal of English Local Law and Custom to Massachusetts Bay in the Seventeenth Century.* Chapel Hill, N.C.: University of North Carolina Press, 1981.
ANDERSON, TERRY LEE, *The Economic Growth of Seventeenth Century New England.* New York: Arno Press, 1975.
ANDREWS, CHARLES M., *British Committees, Commissions, and Councils of Trade and Plantations, 1622–1675.* Baltimore: John Hopkins Press, 1908.
ARCHDEACON, THOMAS J., *New York City, 1664–1710: Conquest and Change.* Ithaca, N.Y.: Cornell University Press, 1975.
BAILYN, BERNARD, *The New England Merchants in the Seventeenth Century.* Cambridge, Mass.: Harvard University Press, 1955.
BARBOUR, HUGH, *The Quakers in Puritan England.* New Haven: Yale University Press, 1964.
BATTIS, EMERY, *Saints and Sectaries: Anne Hutchinson and the Antinomian Controversy in the Massachusetts Bay Colony.* Chapel Hill, N.C.: University of North Carolina Press, 1962.
BAYSE, ARTHUR H., *The Lords Commissioners of Trade and Plantation.* New Haven: Yale University Press, 1925.
BEER, GEORGE L., *The Origins of the British Colonial System, 1578–1660.* New York: Macmillan, 1908.
BERCOVITCH, SACVAN, *The Puritan Origins of the American Self.* New Haven: Yale University Press, 1975.
BOYER, PAUL, and STEPHEN NISSENBAUM, *Salem Possessed: The Social Origins of Witchcraft.* Cambridge, Mass.: Harvard University Press, 1974.
BREEN, TIMOTHY H., *The Character of the Good Ruler: A Study of Puritan Political Ideas in New England, 1630–1730.* New Haven: Yale University Press, 1970.
____, *Puritans and Adventurers: Change and Persistence in Early America.* New York: Oxford University Press, 1980.
BREEN, TIMOTHY H., and STEPHEN INNES, *"Myne Owne Ground": Race and Freedom on Virginia's Eastern Shore, 1640–1676.* New York: Oxford University Press, 1980.
BREMER, FRANCIS J., *The Puritan Experiment: New England Society from Bradford to Edwards.* New York: St. Martin's Press, 1976.

BRIDENBAUGH, CARL, *Cities in the Wilderness: The First Century of Urban Life in America, 1625–1742.* New York: Alfred A. Knopf, 1955.

——, *Vexed and Troubled Englishmen, 1590–1642.* New York: Oxford University Press, 1968.

——, *Fat Mutton and Liberty of Conscience: Society in Rhode Island, 1636–1690.* Providence, R.I.: Brown University Press, 1974.

——, *Jamestown, 1544–1699.* New York: Oxford University Press, 1980.

BRIDENBAUGH, CARL, and ROBERTA BRIDENBAUGH, *No Peace Beyond the Line: The British in the Caribbean, 1624–1690.* New York: Oxford University Press, 1972.

BRYDON, GEORGE M., *Virginia's Mother Church and Its Political Conditions Under Which It Grew . . . 1607–1814,* 2 vols. Richmond: Virginia Historical Society, 1947–1952.

BURG, B. RICHARD, *Richard Mather of Dorchester.* Lexington, Ky.: University of Kentucky Press, 1976.

BURRAGE, HENRY S. *The Beginnings of Colonial Maine, 1602–1658.* Portland, Me.: Printed for the State, 1914.

CALDER, ISABEL M., *The New Haven Colony.* New Haven: Yale University Press, 1934.

CARROLL, CHARLES F., *The Timber Economy of Puritan New England.* Providence, R.I.: Brown University Press, 1974.

CARSON, JANE, *Bacon's Rebellion, 1676–1976.* Jamestown, Va.: Jamestown Foundation, 1976.

CLOWSE, CONVERSE D., *Economic Beginnings of Colonial South Carolina, 1670–1730.* Columbia: University of South Carolina Press, 1971.

COVEY, CYCLONE, *The Gentle Radical: A Biography of Roger Williams.* New York: Macmillan, 1966.

CRANE, WERNER W., *The Southern Frontier, 1670–1732.* Durham, N.C.: Duke University Press, 1928.

CRAVEN, WESLEY FRANK, *The Southern Colonies in the Seventeenth Century, 1607–1689.* Baton Rouge, La.: Louisiana State University Press, 1949.

——, *New Jersey and the English Colonization of North America.* Princeton, N.J.: Van Nostrand, 1964.

——, *The Colonies in Transition, 1660–1713.* New York: Harper & Row, 1968.

——, *White, Red, and Black: The Seventeenth Century Virginian.* Charlottesville: University Press of Virginia, 1971.

DEMOS, JOHN, *A Little Commonwealth: Family Life in Plymouth Colony.* New York: Oxford University Press, 1970.

DUNN, RICHARD S., *Puritans and Yankees: The Winthrop Dynasty of New England, 1630–1717.* Princeton, N.J.: Princeton University Press, 1962.

——, *Sugar and Slaves: The Rise of the Planter Class in the English West Indies, 1624–1713.* Chapel Hill, N.C.: University of North Carolina Press, 1972.

ELLIOTT, EMORY, *Power and the Pulpit in Puritan New England.* Princeton, N.J.: Princeton University Press, 1975.

ERIKSON, KAI T., *Wayward Puritans: A Study in the Sociology of Deviance.* New York: Wiley, 1966.

FIERING, NORMAN, *Moral Philosophy at Seventeenth Century Harvard: A Discipline in Transition.* Chapel Hill, N.C.: University of North Carolina Press, 1981.

GARRETT, JOHN, *Roger Williams: Witness Beyond Christendom.* New York: Macmillan, 1970.

GILDRIE, RICHARD P., *Salem Massachusetts: A Covenant Community.* Charlottesville: University Press of Virginia, 1975.

GILPIN, W. CLARK, *The Millenarian Piety of Roger Williams.* Chicago: University of Chicago Press, 1979.

GREVEN, PHILIP J., *Four Generations: Population, Land and Family in Colonial Andover, Massachusetts.* Ithaca, N.Y.: Cornell University Press, 1970.

HAFFENDEN, PHILLIP, *New England in the English Nation, 1689–1713.* New York: Oxford University Press, 1974.

HALL, DAVID, ed., *The Antinomian Controversy, 1636–1638: A Documentary History.* Middletown, Conn.: Wesleyan University Press, 1968.

——, *The Faithful Shepherd: A History of the New England Ministry in the Seventeenth Century.* Chapel Hill, N.C.: University of North Carolina Press, 1972.

HALL, MICHAEL G., *Edward Randolph and the American Colonies, 1676–1703.* Chapel Hill, N.C.: University of North Carolina Press, 1960.

HALL, MICHAEL G., *et al,* eds., *The Glorious Revolution in America: Documents on the Colonial Crisis of 1689.* Chapel Hill, N.C.: University of North Carolina Press, 1964.

HARPER, LAWRENCE, *The English Navigation Laws: A Seventeenth Century Experiment in Social Engineering.* New York: Columbia University Press, 1939.

HASKINS, GEORGE LEE, *Law and Authority in Early Massachusetts.* New York: Macmillan, 1960.

HOLIFIELD, E. BROOKS, *The Covenant Sealed: The Development of Puritan Sacramental Theology in Old and New England, 1570–1720.* New Haven: Yale University Press, 1974.

JOHNSON, EDGAR AUGUSTUS JEROME, *American Economic Thought in the Seventeenth Century.* New York: Russell & Russell, 1961.
JOHNSON, RICHARD R., *Adjustment to Empire: The New England Colonies, 1675-1715.* New Brunswick, N.J.: Rutgers University Press, 1981.
JONES, MARY JEANNE ANDERSON, *Congregational Commonwealth: Connecticut, 1636-1662.* Middletown, Conn.: Wesleyan University Press, 1968.
KESSLER, HENRY H., and EUGENE RACHLIS, *Peter Stuyvesant and his New York.* New York: Random House, 1959.
KOEHLER, LYLE, *A Search for Power: The "Weaker Sex" in Seventeenth Century New England.* Urbana, Ill.: University of Illinois Press, 1980.
KONIG, DAVID, *Law and Society in Puritan Massachusetts, Essex County, 1629-1692.* Chapel Hill, N.C.: University of North Carolina Press, 1979.
KUPPERMAN, KAREN ORDAHL, *Settling with the Indians: The Meeting of English and Indian Cultures in America, 1580-1640.* Totowa, N.J.: Rowman and Littlefield, 1980.
LANGDON, GEORGE D., JR., *Pilgrim Colony: A History of New Plymouth, 1620-1691.* New Haven: Yale University Press, 1966.
LEDER, LAWRENCE H., *Robert Livingston, 1654-1728, and the Politics of Colonial New York.* Chapel Hill, N.C.: University of North Carolina Press, 1961.
LEVIN, DAVID, *Cotton Mather: The Young Life of the Lord's Remembrancer, 1663-1703.* Cambridge, Mass.: Harvard University Press, 1978.
LITTLEFIELD, GEORGE E., *The Early Massachusetts Press, 1638-1711,* 2 vols. Boston: Club of Odd Volumes, 1907.
LOCKRIDGE, KENNETH, *A New England Town: The First Hundred Years.* New York: W. W. Norton, 1970.
LOVEJOY, DAVID S., *The Glorious Revolution in America.* New York: Harper & Row, 1972.
LOWANCE, MASON I., *The Language of Canaan: Metaphor and Symbol in New England from the Puritans to the Transcendentalists.* Cambridge, Mass.: Harvard University Press, 1980.
LUCAS, PAUL R., *Valley of Discord: Church and Society along the Connecticut River, 1636-1725.* Hanover, N.H.: University Press of New England, 1976.
McCRADY, EDWARD, *The History of South Carolina under the Proprietary Government, 1670-1719.* New York: Macmillan, 1901.
MIDDLEKAUFF, ROBERT, *The Mathers: Three Generations of Puritan Intellectuals, 1596-1728.* New York: Oxford University Press, 1971.
MILLER, PERRY, *Orthodoxy in Massachusetts.* Boston: Beacon Press, 1933.
_____, *The New England Mind: The Seventeenth Century.* Cambridge, Mass.: Harvard University Press, 1939.
_____, *The New England Mind: From Colony to Province.* Cambridge, Mass.: Harvard University Press, 1953. (a)
_____, *Roger Williams: His Contribution to the American Tradition.* Indianapolis: Bobbs-Merrill, 1953. (b)
_____, *Errand Into the Wilderness.* Cambridge, Mass.: Belknap Press, 1956.
MORGAN, EDMUND S., *The Puritan Dilemma: The Story of John Winthrop.* Boston: Little, Brown, 1958.
_____, *Visible Saints: The History of a Puritan Idea.* New York: New York University Press, 1963.
_____, *Roger Williams: The Church and the State.* New York: Harcourt, Brace, & World, 1967.
MORISON, SAMUEL E., *The Founding of Harvard College.* Cambridge, Mass.: Harvard University Press, 1935.
_____, *The Intellectual Life of Colonial New England* (2nd ed.). New York: New York University Press, 1956.
NETTLES, CURTIS P., *The Money Supply in the American Colonies before 1720.* Madison, Wis.: University of Wisconsin Press, 1934.
PETTIT, NORMAN, *The Heart Prepared: Grace and Conversion in Puritan Spiritual Life.* New Haven: Yale University Press, 1966.
POMFRET, JOHN E., *The Province of East New Jersey, 1609-1702: The Rebellious Proprietary.* Princeton, N.J.: Princeton University Press, 1962.
_____, *The Province of West New Jersey, 1609-1702: A History of the Origins of an American Colony.* Princeton, N.J.: Princeton University Press, 1956.
POMFRET, JOHN H., and FLOYD M. SHUMWAY, *Founding the American Colonies, 1583-1660.* New York: Harper & Row, 1970.
POPE, ROBERT G., *The Half-Way Convenant: Church Membership in Puritan New England.* Princeton, N.J.: Princeton University Press, 1969.
POWELL, SUMNER C., *Puritan Village: The Formation of a New England Town.* Garden City, N.Y.: Anchor Books, 1965.
REICH, JEROME A., *Leisler's Rebellion: A Study of Democracy in New York, 1664-1720.* Chicago: University of Chicago Press, 1953.

REID, JOHN G., *Acadia, Maine, and New Scotland: Marginal Colonies in the Seventeenth Century.* Toronto: University of Toronto Press, 1981.
RUSSELL, HOWARD S., *Indian New England before the Mayflower.* Hanover, N.H.: University Press of New England, 1980.
RUTMAN, DARRETT B., *American Puritanism: Faith and Practice.* Philadelphia: J. B. Lippincott, 1970.
____ , *Winthrop's Boston: Portrait of a Puritan Town, 1630–1649.* Chapel Hill, N.C.: University of North Carolina Press, 1965.
SACHSE, JULIUS F., *The German Pietists of Provincial Pennsylvania, 1694–1708.* Philadelphia: Printed for the author, 1895.
SALISBURY, NEAL, *Manitou and Providence: Indians, Europeans, and the Making of New England, 1500–1643.* New York: Oxford University Press, 1982.
SHEEHAN, BERNARD W., *Savagism and Civility: Indians and Englishmen in Colonial Virginia.* New York: Cambridge University Press, 1980.
SHEPHERD, W. R., *The Story of New Amsterdam* (rep.). Port Washington, N.Y.: Kennikat Press, 1970.
SIMPSON, ALAN, *Puritanism in Old and New England.* Chicago: University of Chicago Press, 1955.
SMITH, JAMES MORTON, ed., *Seventeenth Century America: Essays in Colonial History.* Chapel Hill, N.C.: University of North Carolina Press, 1959.
SOSIN, JACK M., *English America and the Restoration Monarchy of Charles II: Transatlantic Politics, Commerce, and Kinship.* Lincoln, Neb.: University of Nebraska Press, 1980.
STOEVER, WILLIAM K. B., *A Faire and Easie Way to Heaven: Covenant Theology and Antinomianism in Early Massachusetts.* Middletown, Conn.: Wesleyan University Press, 1978.
TANNER, EDWIN P., *The Province of New Jersey, 1664–1738.* New York: Longmans, Green, 1908.
TATE, THAD W., and DAVID L. AMMERMAN, eds., *The Chesapeake in the Seventeenth Century: Essays on Anglo-American Society and Politics.* Chapel Hill, N.C.: University of North Carolina Press, 1979.
ULRICH, LAUREL THATCHER, *Good Wives: Image and Reality in the Lives of Women in Northern New England, 1650–1750.* New York: Alfred A. Knopf, 1982.
VAN DEVENTER, DAVID E., *The Emergence of Provincial New Hampshire, 1623–1741.* Baltimore: Johns Hopkins University Press, 1976.
VAUGHAN, ALDEN T. and FRANCIS J. BREMER, eds., *Puritan New England: Essays on Religion, Society, and Culture.* New York: St. Martin's Press, 1977.
VAUGHAN, ALDEN T., *New England Frontier: Puritans and Indians, 1620–1675* (rev. ed.). New York: W. W. Norton, 1979.
WALL, ROBERT E., JR., *Massachusetts Bay: The Crucial Decade, 1640–1650.* New Haven: Yale University Press, 1972.
WARD, CHRISTOPHER, *The Dutch and the Swedes on the Delaware, 1609–64.* Philadelphia: University of Pennsylvania Press, 1930.
WASHBURN, WILCOMB, *The Governor and the Rebel: A History of Bacon's Rebellion in Virginia.* Chapel Hill, N.C.: University of North Carolina Press, 1957.
WEBB, STEPHEN S., *The Governors-General: The English Army and the Definition of Empire, 1569–1681.* Chapel Hill, N.C.: University of North Carolina Press, 1979.
WERTENBAKER, THOMAS JEFFERSON, *Puritan Oligarchy: The Founding of American Civilization.* New York: Charles Scribner's Sons, 1947.
____ , *Torchbearer of the Revolution: The Story of Bacon's Rebellion and Its Leader.* Princeton, N.J.: Princeton University Press, 1940.
____ , *Virginia under the Stuarts, 1607–1688.* Princeton, N.J.: Princeton University Press, 1914.
WILLIAMSON, JAMES A., *The Caribbee Islands under the Proprietary Patents.* London: Oxford University Press, 1926.
ZIFF, LARZER, *Puritanism in America: New Culture in a New World.* New York: Viking Press, 1973.

ANGLO-AMERICA: THE EIGHTEENTH CENTURY

ABBOT, W. W., *The Royal Governors of Georgia, 1754–1775.* Chapel Hill, N.C.: University of North Carolina Press, 1959.
ADAMS, JAMES T., *Revolutionary New England, 1691–1776.* Boston: Atlantic Monthly Press, 1923.

ALDRIGDE, OWEN, *Benjamin Franklin and Nature's God.* Durham, N.C.: Duke University Press, 1967.

AMMERMAN, DAVID, *In the Common Cause: American Response to the Coercive Acts of 1774.* Charlottesville, Va.: University of Virginia Press, 1974.

BAILYN, BERNARD, *The Origins of American Politics.* New York: Vintage, 1970.

BARROW, THOMAS C., *Trade and Empire: The British Customs Service in America, 1660–1775.* Cambridge, Mass.: Harvard University Press, 1967.

BAXTER, NORMAN A., *History of the Freewill Baptists: A Study in New England Separatism.* Rochester, N.Y.: American Baptist Historical Society, 1957.

BEER, GEORGE L., *The Old Colonial System, 1660–1754,* 2 vols. New York: Macmillan, 1912.

BENSON, MARY SUMNER, *Women in Eighteenth Century America: A Study of Opinion and Social Usage.* New York: Columbia University Press, 1935.

BINING, ARTHUR C., *British Regulation of the Colonial Iron Industry.* Philadelphia: University of Pennsylvania Press, 1933.

BONOMI, PATRICIA U., *A Factious People: Politics and Society in Colonial New York.* New York: Columbia University Press, 1971.

BOORSTIN, DANIEL J., *The Lost World of Thomas Jefferson.* New York: Henry Holt, 1948.

BRIDENBAUGH, CARL, *Rebels and Gentlemen: Philadelphia in the Age of Franklin.* New York: Reynal and Hitchcock, 1942.

_____, *Cities in Revolt: Urban Life in America, 1743–1776.* New York: Alfred A. Knopf, 1955.

_____, *Mitre and Sceptre: Transatlantic Faiths, Ideas, Personalities, and Politics, 1689–1775.* New York: Oxford University Press, 1962.

BROCK, LESLEY V., *The Currency of the American Colonies, 1700–1764: A Study in Colonial Finance and Imperial Relations.* New York: Arno Press, 1975.

BROWN, ROBERT E., *Middle-Class Democracy and the Revolution in Massachusetts, 1691–1780.* Ithaca, N.Y.: Cornell University Press, 1955.

BROWN, ROBERT E., and B. KATHERINE BROWN, *Virginia, 1705–1786: Democracy or Aristocracy.* East Lansing: Michigan State University Press, 1964.

BUSHMAN, RICHARD, *From Puritan to Yankee: Character and the Social Order in Connecticut, 1690–1765.* Cambridge, Mass.: Harvard University Press, 1967.

BUTLER, JON M., *Power, Authority and the Origins of American Denominational Order: The English Churches in the Delaware Valley, 1680–1730.* Philadelphia: American Philosophical Society, 1978.

CARROLL, PETER N., *The Other Samuel Johnson: A Psychohistory of Early New England.* Rutherford, N.J.: Fairleigh Dickinson University Press, 1978.

CARSWELL, J., *The South Sea Bubble.* London: Cresset Press, 1960.

CASSIRER, ERNST, *The Philosophy of the Enlightenment.* Princeton, N.J.: Princeton University Press, 1951.

CHERRY, CONRAD, *The Theology of Jonathan Edwards.* Gloucester: Peter Smith, 1974.

CLEMENS, PAUL G. E., *The Atlantic Economy and Colonial Maryland's Eastern Shore: From Tobacco to Grain.* Ithaca, N.Y.: Cornell University Press, 1980.

CONFORTI, JOSEPH A., *Samuel Hopkins and the New Divinity Movement: Calvinism, the Congregational Ministry, and Reform in New England between the Great Awakenings.* Grand Rapids, Mich.: Christian University Press, 1981.

COOK, EDWARD M., *The Fathers of the Towns: Leadership and Community Structure in Eighteenth Century New England.* Baltimore: Johns Hopkins Press, 1976.

COWING, CEDRIC, *The Great Awakening and the American Revolution.* Chicago: Rand McNally, 1971.

CRANE, VERNER WINSLOW, *Benjamin Franklin and a Rising People.* Boston: Little, Brown, 1954.

CROSS, ARTHUR L., *The Anglican Episcopate and the American Colonies.* New York: Longmans, Green, 1902.

CROWLEY, J. E., *This Sheba, Self: The Conceptualization of Economic Life in Eighteenth Century America.* Baltimore: Johns Hopkins University Press, 1974.

DALLIMORE, ARNOLD, *George Whitefield,* 2 vols. London: Banner of Truth Trust, 1970, 1980.

DAVIDSON, EDWARD H., *Jonathan Edwards: The Narrative of a Puritan Mind.* Boston: Houghton-Mifflin, 1966.

DAVIDSON, JAMES WEST, *The Logic of Millennial Thought: Eighteenth Century New England.* New Haven: Yale University Press, 1977.

DICKERSON, OLIVER M., *American Colonial Government, 1696–1765: A Study of the British Board of Trade in its Relation to the American Colonies, Political, Industrial, Administrative.* New York: Russell & Russell, 1962.

DINKIN, ROBERT J., *Voting in Provincial America: A Study of Elections in the Thirteen Colonies, 1689–1776.* Westport, Conn.: Greenwood Press, 1977.

DORN, WALTER L., *Competition for Empire, 1740–1763.* New York: Harper & Row, 1940.
EARLE, CARVILLE, *The Evolution of a Tidewater Settlement System: All Hallow's Parish, Maryland, 1650–1783.* Chicago: University of Chicago Press, 1975.
EKIRCH, A. ROGER, *"Poor Carolina": Politics and Society in Colonial North Carolina, 1729–1776.* Chapel Hill, N.C.: University of North Carolina Press, 1981.
ETTINGER, AMOS A., *James Edward Oglethorpe, Imperial Idealist.* Oxford: Clarendon Press, 1936.
FIERING, NORMAN, *Jonathan Edward's Moral Thought and Its British Context.* Chapel Hill, N.C.: University of North Carolina Press, 1981.
GAUSTAD, EDWIN SCOTT, *The Great Awakening in New England.* New York: Harper & Row, 1957.
GEWEHR, WESLEY M., *The Great Awakening in Virginia, 1740–1790.* Durham, N.C.: Duke University Press, 1930.
GOEN, CLARENCE C., *Revivalism and Separatism in New England: Strict Congregationalists and Separate Baptists in the Great Awakening.* New Haven: Yale University Press, 1962.
GRANT, CHARLES S., *Democracy in the Connecticut Frontier Town of Kent.* New York: Columbia University Press, 1961.
GREENE, EVARTS B., *The Provincial Governor in the English Colonies of North America.* New York: Longmans, Green, 1898.
GREENE, JACK P., *The Quest for Power: The Lower Houses of Assembly in the Southern Royal Colonies, 1689–1776.* Chapel Hill, N.C.: University of North Carolina Press, 1963.
HENRETTA, JAMES, *"Salutary Neglect": Colonial Administration under the Duke of Newcastle.* Princeton, N.J.: Princeton University Press, 1972.
HENRY, STUART C., *George Whitefield: Wayfaring Witness.* New York: Abingdon Press, 1957.
HOFSTADTER, RICHARD, *America at 1750: A Social Portrait.* New York: Vintage Books, 1973.
JEDREY, CHRISTOPHER M., *The World of John Cleaveland: Family and Community in Eighteenth Century New England.* New York: W. W. Norton, 1980.
JONES, ALICE HANSON, *Wealth of a Nation to Be: The American Colonies on the Eve of the Revolution.* New York: Columbia University Press, 1980.
JONES, DOUGLAS LAMAR, *Village and Seaport: Migration and Society in Eighteenth-Century Massachusetts.* Hanover, N.H.: University Press of New England, 1981.
KAMMEN, MICHAEL, *Empire and Interest: The American Colonies and the Politics of Mercantilism.* New York: J. B. Lippincott, 1970.
KATZ, STANLEY N., *Newcastle's New York: Anglo-American Politics, 1732–1753.* Cambridge, Mass.: Harvard University Press, 1968.
KELLEY, JOSEPH J., JR., *Pennsylvania: The Colonial Years, 1681–1776.* Garden City, N.J.: Doubleday, 1980.
KIM, SUNG BOK, *Landlord and Tenant in Colonial New York: Manorial Society, 1664–1775.* Chapel Hill, N.C.: University of North Carolina Press, 1978.
KLEIN, RANDOLPH SHIPLEY, *Portrait of an Early American Family: The Shippens of Pennsylvania across Five Generations.* Philadelphia: University of Pennsylvania Press, 1975.
LABAREE, LEONARD W., *Royal Government in America: A Study of the British Colonial System before 1783.* New Haven: Yale University Press, 1930.
LAND, AUBREY C., *The Dulanys of Maryland.* Baltimore: Maryland Historical Society, 1955.
LEDER, LAWRENCE, *Liberty and Authority: Early American Political Ideology, 1689–1763.* New York: W. W. Norton, 1976.
LEMAY, J. A. LEO, and P. M. ZALL, eds., *The Autobiography of Benjamin Franklin.* Knoxville, Tenn.: University of Tennessee Press, 1981.
LEMON, JAMES T., *The Best Poor Man's Country: A Geographical Study of Early Southeastern Pennsylvania.* Baltimore: Johns Hopkins University Press, 1972.
LEVENTHALL, HERBERT, *In the Shadow of the Enlightenment: Occultism and Renaissance Science in Eighteenth Century America.* New York: New York University Press, 1976.
LEWIS, ARTHUR J., *Zinzendorf, the Ecumenical Pioneer: A Study in the Moravian Contribution to Christian Mission and Unity.* London: SCM Press, 1962.
LITTLEFIELD, DANIEL C., *Rice and Slaves: Ethnicity and the Slave Trade in Colonial South Carolina.* Baton Rouge, La.: Louisiana State University Press, 1981.
MAXSON, CHARLES H., *The Great Awakening in the Middle Colonies.* Chicago: University of Chicago Press, 1920.
MAY, HENRY F., *The Enlightenment in America.* New York: Oxford University Press, 1976.
McCAIN, PAUL M., *The County Court in North Carolina before 1750.* Durham, N.C.: Duke University Press, 1954.

McLOUGHLIN, WILLIAM G., *Isaac Backus and the American Pietistic Tradition.* Boston: Little, Brown, 1967.

McMANUS, EDGAR, J., *Black Bondage in the North.* Syracuse, N.Y.: Syracuse University Press, 1966.

MEYER, DONALD G., *The Democratic Enlightenment.* New York: Capricorn Books, 1976.

MIDDLEKAUFF, ROBERT, *Ancients and Axioms: Secondary Education in Eighteenth Century New England.* New Haven: Yale University Press, 1963.

MILLER, PERRY, *Jonathan Edwards.* New York: Macmillan, 1949.

MILLS, FREDERICK V., SR., *Bishops by Ballot: An Eighteenth-Century Ecclesiastical Revolution.* New York: Oxford University Press, 1978.

MORAIS, HERBERT M., *Deism in Eighteenth-Century America.* New York: Columbia University Press, 1934.

MULLIN, GERALD W., *Flight and Rebellion: Slave Resistance in Eighteenth Century Virginia.* New York: Oxford University Press, 1972.

NASH, GARY B., *Quakers and Politics: Pennsylvania, 1681-1726.* Princeton, N.J.: Princeton University Press, 1968.

NELSON, WILLIAM, *American Newspapers in the Eighteenth Century as Sources of History.* Washington, D.C.: U.S. Government Printing Office, 1910.

NELSON, WILLIAM E., *Dispute and Conflict Resolution in Plymouth County, Massachusetts, 1725-1825.* Chapel Hill, N.C.: University of North Carolina Press, 1981.

PALSITS, VICTOR H., *The Almanacs of Roger Sherman.* Worcester, Mass.: American Antiquarian Society, 1907.

PECKHAM, HOWARD H., *The Colonial Wars, 1689-1762.* Chicago: University of Chicago Press, 1964.

RAY, SISTER MARY AUGUSTINA, *American Opinion of Roman Catholicism in the Eighteenth Century.* New York: Columbia University Press, 1936.

REESE, TREVOR RICHARD, *Colonial Georgia: A Study in British Imperial Policy in the Eighteenth Century.* Athens, Ga.: University of Georgia Press, 1963.

RICHARDSON, LYON N., *A History of Early American Magazines, 1741-1789.* New York: Octagon Books, 1930.

ROEBER, A. G., *Faithful Magistrates and Republican Lawyers: Creators of Virginia Legal Culture, 1680-1810.* Chapel Hill, N.C.: University of North Carolina Press, 1981.

ROTHERMUND, DIETMAR, *The Layman's Progress: Religious and Political Experience in Colonial Pennsylvania, 1740-1770.* Philadelphia: University of Pennsylvania Press, 1961.

SCHUTZ, JOHN A., *Thomas Pownall, British Defender of American Liberty: A Study of Anglo-American Relations in the Eighteenth Century.* Glendale, Calif.: Arthur H. Clark, 1951.

_____, *William Shirley: King's Governor of Massachusetts.* Chapel Hill, N.C.: University of North Carolina Press, 1961.

SMITH, DANIEL B., *Inside the Great House: Planter Family Life in Eighteenth Century Chesapeake Society.* Ithaca, N.Y.: Cornell University Press, 1980.

STEELE, IAN K., *Politics of Colonial Policy: The Board of Trade in Colonial Administration, 1696-1720.* Oxford: Clarendon Press, 1968.

STEINER, BRUCE M., *Samuel Seabury, 1729-1796: A Study in the High Church Tradition.* Athens, Ohio: Ohio University Press, 1971.

STOWELL, MARION B., *Early American Almanacs: The Colonial Weekday Bible.* New York: B. Franklin, 1977.

SYDNOR, CHARLES S., *Gentlemen Freeholders: Political Practices in Washington's Virginia.* Chapel Hill, N.C.: University of North Carolina Press, 1952.

TANIS, JAMES R., *Dutch Calvinistic Pietism in the Middle Colonies: A Study in the Life of Theodore Jacobus Frelinghuysen.* The Hague: Martinus Nijhof, 1967.

TATE, THAD W., *The Negro in Eighteenth Century Williamsburg.* Charlottesville, Va.: University Press of Virginia, 1965.

TOLLES, FREDERICK, *Meetinghouse and Countinghouse: The Quaker Merchants of Colonial Philadelphia, 1682-1763.* Chapel Hill, N.C.: University of North Carolina Press, 1948.

TRACY, PATRICIA, *Jonathan Edwards, Pastor: Religion and Society in Eighteenth Century Northampton.* New York: Hill & Wang, 1980.

WALLER, GEORGE MACGREGOR, *Samuel Veatch, Colonial Enterpriser.* Chapel Hill, N.C.: University of North Carolina Press, 1960.

WARD, HARRY M., *"Unite or Die": Intercolony Relations, 1690-1763.* Port Washington, N.Y.: Kennikat Press, 1971.

WARDEN, G. B., *Boston, 1689-1776.* Boston: Little, Brown, 1970.

WEEKS, STEPHAN B., *The Religious Development in the Province of North Carolina.* Baltimore: Johns Hopkins University Press, 1892.

WINSLOW, OLA E., *Jonathan Edwards.* New York: Macmillan, 1940.

WOLF, STEPHANIE GRAUMAN, *Urban Village: Population, Community, and Family Structure in Germantown, Pennsylvania, 1683–1800.* Princeton, N.J.: Princeton University Press, 1976.

WOOD, JEROME H., JR., *Conestoga Crossroads: Lancaster, Pennsylvania, 1730–1790.* Harrisburg: Pennsylvania Historical and Museum Commission, 1979.

WOOD, PETER, *Black Majority: Negroes in South Carolina from 1670 through the Stono Rebellion.* New York: Alfred A. Knopf, 1974.

YOUNGS, J. WILLIAM T., JR., *God's Messengers: Religious Leadership in Colonial New England, 1700–1750.* Baltimore: Johns Hopkins University Press, 1976.

ZEMSKY, ROBERT, *Merchants, Farmers, and River Gods: An Essay on Eighteenth Century American Politics.* Boston: Gambit, 1971.

ZUCKERMAN, MICHAEL, *Peaceable Kingdoms: New England Towns in the Eighteenth Century.* New York: Alfred A. Knopf, 1970.

REVOLUTIONARY AMERICA

ADAMS, WILLI PAUL, *The First American Constitutions: Republican Ideology and the Making of the State Constitutions in the Revolutionary Era,* trans. Rita Kimber and Robert Kimber. Chapel Hill, N.C.: University of North Carolina Press, 1980.

ALBANESE, CATHERINE, *Sons of the Fathers: The Civil Religion of the American Revolution.* Phladelphia: Temple University Press, 1976.

ALDEN, JOHN R., *The American Revolution, 1775–1783.* New York: Harper & Row, 1954.

BAILYN, BERNARD, *The Ideological Origins of the American Revolution.* Cambridge, Mass.: Harvard University Press, 1967.

——, *The Ordeal of Thomas Hutchinson.* Cambridge, Mass.: Harvard University Press, 1974.

BAILYN, BERNARD, and JOHN B. HENCH, eds., *The Press and the American Revolution.* Worcester, Mass.: American Antiquarian Society, 1980.

BEARD, CHARLES A., *An Economic Interpretation of the Constitution of the United States.* New York: Crowell-Collier & Macmillan, 1935.

BECKER, ROBERT A., *Revolution, Reform, and the Politics of American Taxation, 1763–1783.* Baton Rouge, La.: Louisiana State University Press, 1980.

BEEMAN, RICHARD R., *Patrick Henry: A Biography.* New York: McGraw-Hill, 1974.

BENTON, WILLIAM A., *Whig-Loyalism: An Aspect of Political Ideology in the American Revolutionary Era.* Rutherford, N.J.: Fairleigh Dickinson University Press, 1969.

BERKIN, CAROL, *Jonathan Sewall: Odyssey of an American Loyalist.* New York: Columbia University Press, 1974.

BROWN, RICHARD D., *Revolutionary Politics in Massachusetts: The Boston Committee of Correspondence and the Towns, 1772–1774.* Cambridge, Mass.: Harvard University Press, 1970.

BROWN, RICHARD M., *The South Carolina Regulators.* Cambridge, Mass.: Belknap Press of Harvard University Press, 1963.

BROWN, WALLACE, *The King's Friends: The Composition and Motives of the American Loyalist Claimants.* Providence, R.I.: Brown University Press, 1965.

——, *The Good Americans: Loyalists in the American Revolution.* New York: William Morrow, 1969.

BUCKLEY, THOMAS E., *Church and State in Revolutionary Virginia, 1776–1787.* Charlottesville, Va.: University Press of Virginia, 1977.

BUEL, RICHARD, JR., *Securing the Revolution: Ideology in American Politics, 1789–1815.* Ithaca, N.Y.: Cornell University Press, 1972.

CALHOON, ROBERT M., *The Loyalists in Revolutionary America.* New York: Harcourt Brace Jovanovich, 1973.

——, *Revolutionary America: An Interpretative Overview.* New York: Harcourt Brace Jovanovich, 1976.

CHRISTIE, IAN R., *Crisis of Empire: Great Britain and the American Colonies, 1754–1783.* New York: W. W. Norton, 1966.

COHEN, LESTER H., *The Revolutionary Histories: Contemporary Narratives of the American Revolution.* Ithaca, N.Y.: Cornell University Press, 1980.

COLBOURN, H. TREVOR, *The Lamp of Experience: Whig History and the Intellectual Origins of the American Revolution.* Chapel Hill, N.C.: University of North Carolina Press, 1965.

COLLIER, CHRISTOPHER, *Roger Sherman's Connecticut: Yankee Politics and the American Revolution.* Middletown, Conn.: Wesleyan University Press, 1971.

COOKE, JACOB E., *Alexander Hamilton.* New York: Charles Scribner's Sons, 1982.

COUNTRYMAN, EDWARD, *A People in Revolution: The American Revolution and Political Society in New York: 1760-1790.* Baltimore: Johns Hopkins University Press, 1981.

CUNNINGHAM, NOBLE E., JR., *The Jeffersonian Republicans: The Formation of Party Organization, 1789-1801.* Chapel Hill, N.C.: University of North Carolina Press, 1957.

DICKERSON, OLIVER M., *The Navigation Acts and the American Revolution.* New York: A. S. Barnes, 1963.

DOUGLASS, ELISHA P., *Rebels and Democrats: The Struggle for Equal Political Rights and Majority Rule During the American Revolution.* Chapel Hill, N.C.: University of North Carolina Press, 1955.

ERNST, JOSEPH A., *Money and Politics in America, 1755-1775: A Study in the Currency Act of 1764 and the Political Economy of Revolution.* Chapel Hill, N.C.: University of North Carolina Press, 1973.

FERGUSON, E. JAMES, *The Power of the Purse: A History of American Public Finance, 1776-1790.* Chapel Hill, N.C.: University of North Carolina Press, 1961.

FLEXNER, JAMES T., *George Washington,* 4 vols. Boston: Little, Brown, 1965-1972.

_____, *Washington, The Indispensable Man.* Boston: Little, Brown, 1973.

FONER, ERIC, *Tom Paine and Revolutionary America.* New York: Oxford University Press, 1976.

FREEMAN, DOUGLAS SOUTHALL, *George Washington: A Biography,* 7 vols. New York: Charles Scribner's Sons, 1948-1957. (Volume 7 was written in collaboration with J. A. Carroll and M. W. Ashworth.)

GERLACH, LARRY, *Revolution or Independence? New Jersey, 1760-1776.* New Brunswick, N.J.: Rutgers University Press, 1976.

GILBERT, FELIX, *To the Farewell Address: Ideas of Early American Foreign Policy.* Princeton, N.J.: Princeton University Press, 1961.

GIPSON, LAWRENCE HENRY, *The Coming of the Revolution, 1763-1775.* New York: Harper & Row, 1954.

GRAYMONT, BARBARA, *The Iroquois in the American Revolution.* Syracuse, N.Y.: Syracuse University Press, 1972.

GROSS, ROBERT A., *The Minutemen and their World.* New York: Hill & Wang, 1976.

HATCH, NATHAN O., *The Sacred Cause of Liberty: Republican Thought and the Millennium in Revolutionary New England.* New Haven: Yale University Press, 1977.

HEIMERT, ALAN, *Religion and the American Mind, from the Great Awakening to the Revolution.* Cambridge, Mass.: Harvard University Press, 1966.

HENDERSON, H. JAMES, *Party Politics in the Continental Congress.* New York: McGraw-Hill, 1974.

HIGGINBOTHAM, DON, *The American War for Independence: Military Attitudes, Policies and Practice, 1763-1789.* New York: Macmillan, 1971.

HINDLE, BROOK, *The Pursuit of Science in Revolutionary America.* Chapel Hill, N.C.: University of North Carolina Press, 1956.

HOFFMAN, RONALD, *A Spirit of Dissension: Economics, Politics, and the Revolution in Maryland.* Baltimore: Johns Hopkins University Press, 1974.

HOOK, ANDREW, *Scotland and America: A Study of Cultural Relations, 1750-1835.* Glasgow: Blackie, 1975.

HOWE, JOHN R., *From the Revolution through the Age of Jackson: Innocence and Empire in the Young Republic.* Englewood Cliffs, N.J.: Prentice-Hall, 1973.

HUTSON, JAMES H., *John Adams and the Diplomacy of the American Revolution.* Lexington, Ky.: University Press of Kentucky, 1980.

ISAAC, RHYS, *The Transformation of Virginia, 1740-1790.* Chapel Hill, N.C.: University of North Carolina Press, 1982.

JENSEN, MERRILL, *The Articles of Confederation: An Interpretation of the Social-Constitutional History of the American Revolution, 1774-1781.* Madison, Wis.: University of Wisconsin Press, 1940.

_____, *The New Nation: A History of the United States during the Confederation, 1781-1789.* New York: Alfred A. Knopf, 1950.

_____, *The Founding of a Nation: A History of the American Revolution, 1763-1776.* New York: Oxford University Press, 1968.

KAMMEN, MICHAEL, *A Rope of Sand: The Colonial Agents, British Politics, and the American Revolution.* Ithaca, N.Y.: Cornell University Press, 1968.

_____, *A Season of Youth: The American Revolution and the Historical Imagination.* New York: Alfred A. Knopf, 1978.

KERBER, LINDA, *Women of the Republic: Intellect and Ideology in Revolutionary America.* Chapel Hill, N.C.: University of North Carolina Press, 1980.

KETCHAM, RALPH, *From Colony to Country: The Revolution in American Thought, 1750-1820.* New York: Macmillan, 1975.

KNOLLENBERG, BERNHARD, *The Origins of the American Revolution, 1759–1766* (rev. ed.). New York: Collier Books, 1961.

KOCH, GUSTAV A., *Republican Religion: The American Revolution and the Cult of Reason.* New York: Henry Holt, 1933.

KURTZ, STEPHEN G., and JAMES H. HUTSON, eds., *Essays on the American Revolution.* Chapel Hill, N.C.: University of North Carolina Press, 1973.

LABAREE, BENJAMIN W., *The Boston Tea Party.* New York: Oxford University Press, 1965.

LAUNITZ-SCHÜRER, LEOPOLD S., JR., *Loyal Whigs and Revolutionaries: The Making of the Revolution in New York: 1765–1776.* New York: New York University Press, 1980.

LINCOLN, CHARLES H., *The Revolutionary Movement in Pennsylvania* (rep. ed.). Cos Cob, Conn.: J. E. Edwards, 1968.

MACKESY, PIERS, *The War for America, 1775–1783.* London: Longmans, Green, 1964.

MAIER, PAULINE, *From Resistance to Revolution: Colonial Radicals and the Development of American Opposition to Britain, 1765–1776.* New York: Alfred A. Knopf, 1972.

———, *The Old Revolutionaries: Political Lives in the Age of Samuel Adams.* New York: Alfred A. Knopf, 1980.

MAIN, JACKSON TURNER, *The Anti-Federalists: Critics of the Constitution, 1781–1788.* Chapel Hill, N.C.: University of North Carolina Press, 1961.

———, *The Social Structure of Revolutionary America.* Princeton, N.J.: Princeton University Press, 1965.

———, *Political Parties before the Constitution.* Chapel Hill, N.C.: University of North Carolina Press, 1972.

MALONE, DUMAS, *Jefferson and his Time,* 6 vols. Boston: Little, Brown, 1948–1981.

MARTIN, JAMES KIRBY, *Men in Rebellion: Higher Government Leaders and the Coming of the American Revolution.* New Brunswick, N.J.: Rutgers University Press, 1973.

———, *In the Course of Human Events.* Arlington Heights, Ill.: AHM Publishing, 1979.

McCAUGHEY, ELIZABETH P., *From Loyalist to Founding Father: The Political Odyssey of William Samuel Johnson.* New York: Columbia University Press, 1980.

McCOY, DREW R., *The Elusive Republic: Political Economy in Jeffersonian America.* Chapel Hill, N.C.: University of North Carolina Press, 1980.

McDONALD, FORREST, *We, the People: The Economic Origins of the Constitution.* Chicago: University of Chicago Press, 1958.

———, *Alexander Hamilton: A Biography.* New York: W. W. Norton, 1979.

———, *E Pluribus Unum: The Formation of the American Republic, 1776–1790.* Boston: Houghton-Mifflin, 1965.

McLEOD, DUNCAN, *Slavery, Race and the American Revolution.* Cambridge, Eng.: Cambridge University Press, 1974.

MITCHELL, BROADUS, *Alexander Hamilton,* 3 vols. New York: Macmillan, 1957–1970.

MORGAN, EDMUND S., *The Birth of the Republic.* Chicago: University of Chicago Press, 1956.

MORGAN, EDMUND S., and HELEN MORGAN, *The Stamp Act Crisis: Prologue to Revolution.* Chapel Hill, N.C.: University of North Carolina Press, 1953.

NELSON, WILLIAM E., *The Americanization of the Common Law.* Cambridge, Mass.: Harvard University Press, 1975.

NELSON, WILLIAM H., *The American Tory.* New York: Oxford University Press, 1961.

NORTON, MARY BETH, *The British Americans: The Loyalist Exiles in England, 1774–1789.* Boston: Little, Brown, 1972.

———, *Liberty's Daughters: The Revolutionary Experience of American Women, 1750–1800.* Boston: Little, Brown, 1980.

PAPENFUSE, EDWARD C., *In Pursuit of Profit: The Annapolis Merchants in the Era of the American Revolution, 1763–1805.* Baltimore: Johns Hopkins University Press, 1975.

PECKHAM, HOWARD H., *The War for Independence: A Military History.* Chicago: University of Chicago Press, 1958.

PENCAK, WILLIAM, *War, Politics and Revolution in Provincial Massachusetts.* Boston: Northeastern University Press, 1981.

PETERSON, MERRILL D., *Thomas Jefferson and the New Nation: A Biography.* New York: Oxford University Press, 1970.

QUARLES, BENJAMIN, *The Negro in the American Revolution.* Chapel Hill, N.C.: University of North Carolina Press, 1961.

RAKOVE, JACK N., *The Beginnings of National Politics: An Interpretive History of the Continental Congress.* Baltimore: Johns Hopkins University Press, 1979.

REID, JOHN PHILLIP, *In a Defiant Stance: The Conditions of Law in Massachusetts Bay, the Irish Comparison, and the Coming of the American Revolution.* University Park: Pennsylvania State University Press, 1977.

RISJORD, NORMAN K., *Chesapeake Politics, 1781-1800.* New York: Columbia University Press, 1978.

ROSSITER, CLINTON, *1787: The Grand Convention.* New York: Crowell-Collier & Macmillan, 1966.

ROYSTER, CHARLES, *A Revolutionary People at War: The Continental Army and American Character, 1775-1783.* Chapel Hill, N.C.: University of North Carolina Press, 1979.

RUTLAND, ROBERT A., *The Ordeal of the Constitution: The Antifederalists and the Ratification Struggle of 1787-1788.* Chapel Hill, N.C.: University of North Carolina Press, 1961.

SHAW, PETER, *The Character of John Adams.* Chapel Hill, N.C.: University of North Carolina Press, 1976.

SHEEHAN, BERNARD W., *Seeds of Extinction: Jeffersonian Philanthropy and the American Indian.* Chapel Hill, N.C.: University of North Carolina Press, 1973.

SHY, JOHN, *Toward Lexington: The Role of the British Army in the Coming of the American Revolution.* Princeton, N.J.: Princeton University Press, 1965.

_____, *A People Numerous and Armed: Reflections on the Military Struggle for American Independence.* London: Oxford University Press, 1976.

SKAGGS, DAVID CURTIS, *The Roots of Maryland Democracy, 1753-1776.* Westport, Conn.: Greenwood Press, 1973.

SMITH, PAUL H., *Loyalists and Redcoats: A Study of British Revolutionary Policy.* Chapel Hill, N.C.: University of North Carolina Press, 1964.

STOUT, NEIL R., *The Perfect Crisis: The Beginning of the Revolutionary War.* New York: New York University Press, 1976.

SZATMARY, DAVID P., *Shays' Rebellion: The Making of an Agrarian Insurrection.* Amherst: University of Massachusetts Press, 1980.

TAYLOR, ROBERT J., *Western Massachusetts in the Revolution.* Providence, R.I.: Brown University Press, 1954.

UPTON, L. F. S., *The Loyal Whig: William Smith of New York and Quebec.* Toronto: University of Toronto Press, 1969.

WILLIAMSON, CHILTON, *American Suffrage from Property to Democracy, 1760-1860.* Princeton, N.J.: Princeton University Press, 1960.

WILLS, GARRY, *Explaining America: The Federalist.* Garden City, N.Y.: Doubleday, 1981.

_____, *Inventing America: Jefferson's Declaration of Independence.* Garden City, N.Y.: Doubleday, 1978.

WOOD, GORDON S., *The Creation of the American Republic, 1776-1787.* Chapel Hill, N.C.: University of North Carolina Press, 1969.

YOUNG, ALFRED F., *The Democratic Republicans of New York: The Origins, 1763-1797.* Chapel Hill, N.C.: University of North Carolina Press, 1967.

_____, *The American Revolution: Explanations in the History of American Radicalism.* Dekalb, Ill.: Northern Illinois University Press, 1976.

ZOBEL, HILLER B., *The Boston Massacre.* New York: W. W. Norton, 1970.

ZILVERSMIT, ARTHUR, *The First Emancipation: The Abolition of Slavery in the North.* Chicago: University of Chicago Press, 1967.

Index